RHETORICS OF WHITENESS

RHETORICS OF WHITENESS

POSTRACIAL HAUNTINGS IN POPULAR CULTURE, SOCIAL MEDIA, AND EDUCATION

Edited by
TAMMIE M. KENNEDY
JOYCE IRENE MIDDLETON
KRISTA RATCLIFFE

With a Foreword by LILIA D. MONZÓ and PETER MCLAREN

Southern Illinois University Press
Carbondale

Southern Illinois University Press
www.siupress.com

20 19 18 17   4 3 2 1

Publication has been partially funded by a grant from the CLA-EVPRP subvention
support fund at Purdue University.

Library of Congress Cataloging-in-Publication Data
Names: Kennedy, Tammie M. | Middleton, Joyce Irene. | Ratcliffe, Krista, 1958–
Title: Rhetorics of Whiteness : Postracial Hauntings in Popular Culture, Social
    Media, and Education / edited by Tammie M. Kennedy, Joyce Irene Middleton,
    and Krista Ratcliffe ; with a foreword by Lilia D. Monzó and Peter McLaren.
Description: Carbondale : Southern Illinois University Press, [2017] | Includes
    bibliographical references and index.
Identifiers: LCCN 2016022984 | ISBN 9780809335466 (pbk. : alk. paper) | ISBN
    9780809335473 (e-book)
Subjects: LCSH: Racism in popular culture—United States. | Racism in mass media—
    United States. | Social media—United States. | Racism in education—United States.
    | Whites—Race identity—United States. | African Americans—Race identity. |
    United States—Race relations. | Post-racialism—United States. | Rhetoric—Social
    aspects—United States. | Rhetoric—Political aspects—United States.
Classification: LCC E184.A1 R464 2017 | DDC 305.800973—dc23
LC record available at https://lccn.loc.gov/2016022984

To all the cultural critics and activists who have identified and challenged the functions of whiteness since its inception as an identity and structural category in the early seventeenth century

In this country American means white. Everybody else has to hyphenate.   —Toni Morrison

CONTENTS

FOREWORD: UNLEASHED—WHITENESS AS PREDATORY CULTURE

Lilia D. Monzó and Peter McLaren

THESE ARE FRIGHTENING and dangerous times in the United States. Amid the growing precarious economic conditions for the working poor, endless wars, and the threat of ISIS (Islamic State of Iraq and al-Sham) around the world, fear among the working classes and the unchecked arrogance of the capitalist class have shredded away the fine layers of "tolerance" that marked the era of political correctness (and that served as the ideological correlative to redistributive Keynesianism), revealing centuries-old disdain for, and rejection and exclusion of, those who conspicuously fail to meet the narrow standards of Anglo-American whiteness, such as people of color, LGBTQIA (lesbian, gay, bisexual, transexual, queer, intersex, and asexual), and the Muslim community. Today, even as conservatives and liberals alike nail their whiteness to the mast of multiculturalism and trumpet the United States as a "postracial" nation, we increasingly evidence an unchecked and unabashed display of white supremacy reminiscent of pre–civil rights times, in which the Other is *openly* dehumanized and violently targeted. Consider the numerous unarmed black men who have been killed at the hands of trigger-happy police officers and the lack of remorse they displayed upon realizing that the deaths of these young men (Tamir Rice was just a boy) were probably avoidable (Monzó and McLaren, 2014). The failure to indict these officers seems to have further spurred the white arrogance (what McLaren calls the white supremacist capitalist id) that can be heard from (at the time of this writing) Republican presidential candidate Donald Trump, who has taken an unmitigated, politically motivated, hate-inducing, and scapegoating stance toward nondominant communities, publically accusing Mexicans in the United States of being "rapists" and, in the wake of the terrorist attack on Paris and the mass shooting in San Bernardino, California, calling for a "total and complete shutdown of Muslims entering the U.S." (Capehart; Cruz). It is as if, once unleashed, the predatory monster of white supremacy has gained strength and momentum.

While these examples of visible racism abound, even more insidious are the examples of invisible racism that seem to pervade so much of our everyday reality. Consider the recent occupation of a federal wildlife refuge in Oregon by an armed militia group, Citizens for Constitutional Freedom, seeking rights to manage public lands whose federal management has hurt ranchers. Local sheriffs *talked* with the leaders to persuade them to leave and offered to escort them out of state for their protection. Can we imagine what the police and political response to this armed invasion would have been had this been a predominantly black or Muslim armed group? In instances such as these, it becomes clear that white supremacy is far from a discredited metanarrative or part of an outdated binary cast into the dustbin of obsolete concepts that have been bracketed into oblivion inside university seminar rooms. It continues to function as a major antagonism that is heavily inscribed with class interests and fatal consequences. Here we see how the public subscribes to the continued dominance of the widely shared social logic, articulated in the media in a number of diverse and even conflicting ways, that whites are primarily nonviolent, reasonable, and can be trusted, and if they choose to participate in an armed occupation, then it should be considered a forgivable deviation from their constitutional right to bear arms and demonstrate against the government. Indeed, it is clearer than ever to us that the notion of a postracial era is mere fiction caught in the contradictions of political necessity.

Rhetorics of Whiteness is an extraordinary collection of essays revealing how whiteness is invisibly entrenched across all our institutions, from film and social media to schooling, the law, and politics. It is also a much-needed theoretical and practical contribution to our understanding of one of the most insidious problems in history. As the editors astutely point out and the authors so acutely demonstrate, racism cannot be fully apprehended without recognizing its direct relationship to a system of white supremacy that is held up by a host of both material conditions and ideological assumptions that position the "white race" and its normalized values and practices as "naturally" superior. The authors skillfully deconstruct this "common sense" reality to reveal the hidden meanings that serve both to deploy and protect whiteness. *Rhetorics of Whiteness* bring us numerous key theoretical concepts, including "oxymoronic whiteness" (Kennedy, Middleton, and Ratcliffe "Introduction"), "the spectacle of black suffering," (Jay chapter 1), the "disciplining of racial rhetoric" (McDuffie chapter 4), and "white innocence and black abstraction" (Beech chapter 7), that illuminate how whiteness remains at the helm, directing our perceptions of the world—sometimes strategically and at other times even as we attempt to be inclusive and equitable. Indeed, inclusion can be conceived as bringing the Other into compliance—coopting or sanitizing our ability to see the world differently and destroying our ability to make whiteness visible and to create structures that decenter it.

While whiteness studies as an academic field came into prominence in the 1990s, whiteness understood as a way of being and seeing the world from a position of dominance that seeks to maintain its dominance can be found in the writings of Franz Fanon. For Fanon, whiteness was found among the European colonizers and sought after among the colonized black Antilleans. Fanon states,

> To speak means being able to use a language . . . but it means above all assuming a culture and bearing the weight of civilization. . . . [T]he more the Black Antillean assimilates the French language, the whiter he gets—i.e., the closer he comes to becoming a human being. (2)

Here Fanon points out that within the colonial world where the European was dominant, it is whiteness that defines one as human. Whiteness is the adoption of the way of life of the colonizer—his ideologies, his values, his desires and ambitions. Thus to be an Other is to be less than human. Moreover, whiteness is seen as unable to coexist with the languages of the Other. Whiteness is, thus, imbued with the negation of the black man and by extension the negation of all those whose otherness is made such by its distinction to whiteness. Importantly too often whiteness studies have neglected to theorize the gendered nature of whiteness and how whiteness haunts the hyperexploitation and violence endured among women of color. Indeed it is our contention that all antagonisms must be examined in their gendered distinctions. This is not, however, to suggest that difference and singularity of experience are such that they preclude all possibilities of knowing and uniting based on shared experiences of oppression and interests. This emphasis on deconstruction brought about by the postmodern age has problematically rendered us unable to engage a praxis of social transformation.

This requires that we populate the language of the Oppressor with the words, ideologies, and perspectives of the Other—to essentially negate the negation of the other, such that whiteness (what counts in dominant spheres and is normalized) ceases to be defined by its distinction from the Other. To eradicate whiteness is not to eradicate those who claim identities as whites but rather their position of dominance in the world and the prescription of their ways of being and knowing as normal, civilized, moral—in short, human. The negation of whiteness is thus the negation of the negation of the Other.

Importantly, while Fanon focuses on the internalization of whiteness and the psychological trauma that the colonized black man and woman endure, he is clear that the economic—the material—is the first order of this colonial assault, and it is therefore necessary to establish new material relations that will allow us to challenge whiteness. And here we are not referring to the materialism-as-language (textuality) theory but to capitalist social relations of production. As Marxist humanists, we see whiteness and capitalism as dialectically (internally) related. Each is an aspect of the other. That is, whiteness encompasses the values and goals of capitalism—unfettered competition, development as continuous growth and accumulation, private property as an inalienable right. White supremacy is both established through capitalism and supports its maintenance as a transnational capitalist class. The negation of white supremacy thus also requires the negation of capitalism. We cannot hope to end whiteness without understanding the relations of exploitation that undergird how people produce their means of subsistence under capitalism. We must go further than challenging the "obvious" cultural meanings that support racist social relations. White supremacy is no longer a term that can be reserved for white men in buzzcuts wearing blue uniforms and carrying guns. We need to move beyond challenging dominant racialized epistemes simply by performing whiteness differently or resignifying or redescribing its various instantiations that have collected like barnacles on the hull of history. White supremacy is, after all, more than a self-legitimating ideological regime of aleatory power that mediates everyday consciousness; it also consists of relations of signification (cultural, representational, political, and juridical) that are inextricably entangled within everyday capitalist relations of exploitation. New relations of production—which we choose to call socialist—are necessary to allow all persons the right to be recognized as human.

Rhetorics of Whiteness is a book that warrants serious study and engagement, a book that has arrived at a new crossroads in race relations in the United States.

Works Cited

Capehart, Jonathan. "Donald Trump's 'Mexican Rapists' Rhetoric Will Keep the Republican Party Out of the White House." *Washington Post*, 17 June 2015. Web. 21 Dec. 2015.

Cruz, Caitlin. "Trump Camp Contradicts Itself on Whether Muslim Ban Covers US Citizens." *TPM*, 8 Dec. 2015. Web. 21 Dec. 2015.

Fanon, Franz. *Black Skins, White Masks*. 1952. New York: Grove P, 2008. Print.

McLaren, Peter. *Pedagogy of Insurrection: From Resurrection to Revolution*. New York: Peter Lang, 2015. Print.

Monzó, Lilia D., and Peter McLaren. "Red Love: Toward Racial, Economic and Social Justice." *Truthout*, 18 Dec. 2014. Web. 21 Dec. 2015.

RHETORICS OF WHITENESS

INTRODUCTION:
OXYMORONIC WHITENESS—FROM THE WHITE HOUSE TO FERGUSON

Tammie M. Kennedy, Joyce Irene Middleton, and Krista Ratcliffe

THIS COLLECTION ESPOUSES a rhetorical lens for employing theories and methods of whiteness studies to analyze twenty-first-century texts and contexts; as such, it argues for the continued relevancy of whiteness studies in the twenty-first century. In particular, this collection identifies new sites for analyses of racialized whiteness, such as digitized representations of whiteness on the web and implicit representations of racialized whiteness in educational policies and politics. In the process, this collection exposes how seemingly progressive gains made in representing nonwhites in various cultural sites often reify a normative, racialized whiteness.

Our attempt to revivify whiteness studies from its demise during the first decade of the twenty-first century is necessary because, in the words of one anonymous reviewer of this manuscript, whiteness studies had become "exhausted. Stagnant. Its momentum stalled in the wake of post-racial self-congratulations. Tedious . . . Critical Race Theory in whiteface. Insular and self-congratulatory. Mattering mostly only in the academy with little impact on or a relationship to social policy or to those outside of the academy." To counter such a demise, our collection offers broadly engaging analyses that inform academic readers interested in rhetoric, social media, whiteness studies, cultural studies, critical ethnic studies, communication studies, and critical race theory in both upper division and graduate classes as well as general readers interested in social media, film, school testing, and technology.

Provocative in tone and argument, our collection invites these audiences into further discussions and actions that interrupt racialized whiteness in twenty-first-century culture; as such, our collection promotes rhetorical analyses as a productive means of fostering such discussions and actions.

We three coeditors of *Rhetorics of Whiteness* also coedited a 2004 special edition of *Rhetoric Review* that focused on whiteness studies as an important site for developing antiracist and antiwhiteness tactics. But our scholarly call resulted in only a few scholarly projects, such as Jennifer Trainor's *Rethinking Racism: Emotion, Persuasion, and Literacy Education in an All-White High School*. One result of our collaboration, however, is that we periodically chat about the state of whiteness in U.S. culture. Recently we noted two seemingly contradictory cultural trends that intrigue us: the momentum of whiteness studies as an active research field has waned during the past decade even as the two elections of President Barack Obama have rendered *white* an operative term in mainstream discourses. Given this emergence of *white* in mainstream discourses, the need for whiteness studies as a means for theorizing, analyzing, interpreting, and challenging racialized whiteness seems more urgent than ever. So we decided to create this edited collection, *Rhetorics of Whiteness: Postracial Hauntings in Popular Culture, Social Media, and Education*. We sent out a call for contributors, and the chapters herein are the result.

While contributors were revising their chapters during the summer and fall of 2014, whiteness again exploded in mainstream U.S. discourses immediately after the August 9, 2014, killing of Michael Brown in Ferguson, Missouri. In response to Ferguson, the term *white* flooded the airwaves and internet. The *Huffington Post* declared "White Privilege on the Streets of Ferguson" (Marie). *Alternet.org* noted "12 Things White People Can Now Do Because of Ferguson" (Woods). *MediaMatters.org* analyzed Sunday news shows reporting on Ferguson and concluded that "*Fox News Sunday* Hosts More White People on Ferguson than All Other Broadcast Sunday Shows" (Groch-Begley). And the *Washington Post Opinions* claimed that "Ferguson Isn't about Black Rage against Cops. It's White Rage against Progress" (Anderson).

In an odd synergy, other engagements with whiteness also emerged in 2014 mainstream discourses. Movie theaters promoted *Dear White People*. The *New York Times* Opinionator examined "White Anxiety and the Futility of Black Hope" (Yancy and Sullivan). And a Pinterest board explored "The Incredible Whiteness of Being" (Grayson) in response to a viral video of *Rhetorics of Whiteness* contributor Professor Ersula Ore and an Arizona State

University campus policeman, whose actions CNN described as "Arizona Professor's Jaywalking Arrest Quickly Gets out of Hand" (Lacey-Bordeaux).

As we were finishing this introduction in early 2015, whiteness again emerged in mainstream discourses. *Selma* exposed how racial whiteness haunted U.S. law. In a self-reflective move, NPR aired "Challenging the Whiteness of Public Radio" (Kumanyika). And Fox News' *Fox and Friends* bemoaned *Rhetorics of Whiteness* contributor Lee Bebout's Arizona State University course entitled US Race Theory and the Problem of Whiteness, which resulted in public harassment toward Professor Bebout, with the ASU campus and his neighborhood leafletted by a local white supremacist organization.

Even the 2015 Oscar show generated buzz about whiteness. Host Neil Patrick Harris's opening monologue included the line, "Tonight we celebrate Hollywood's best and whitest . . . sorry, brightest" in reference to the academy's 94 percent white membership and also to the omission of nominations for *Selma* in major categories (McCormack). On the other hand, in Patricia Arquette's Best Supporting Actress acceptance speech, her plea for equal pay for women, which seemed to ignore women of color and LGBTQIA folks, lit up social media with claims that she used the term *women* as if it were coded white, even if that was not her intent (McCormack; Petri). Meanwhile, some viewers thought Common and John Legend got it right in their acceptance speeches for best original song, "Glory," from *Selma* (McCormack), although other viewers felt Legend made "all white people out to . . . be racist" (Harrison). But if one reads their speeches, it becomes apparent that Common noted what we all have in common:

> Recently, John and I got to go to Selma and perform "Glory" on the same bridge that Dr. King and the people of the civil rights movement marched on fifty years ago. This bridge was once a landmark of a divided nation, but now it's a symbol for change. The spirit of this bridge transforms race, gender, religion, sexual orientation, and social status. . . . This bridge was built on hope, welded with compassion, and elevated by love for all human beings. (qtd. in Penn)

Legend simply pointed out differences that still exist:

> We wrote this song for a film that was based on events that happened fifty years ago, but we say that Selma is now because the struggle for justice is right now. . . . We live in the most incarcerated country in the world. There are more black men under correctional control today than were under slavery in 1850. (qtd. in Penn)

These discussions were reignited in September 2015 when Viola Davis became the first African American to win an Emmy for best actress in a drama, *How to Get Away with Murder*. She used her acceptance speech to directly address how white privilege and racism plague Hollywood, drawing on Harriet Tubman's speech to help contextualize their persistence.

"In my mind, I see a line. And over that line, I see green fields and lovely flowers and beautiful white women with their arms stretched out to me, over that line. But I can't seem to get there no how. I can't seem to get over that line."

That was Harriet Tubman in the 1800s. And let me tell you something: The only thing that separates women of color from anyone else is opportunity. (qtd. in Gold)

Regardless of political ideology and despite being months apart, Oscar and Emmy viewers certainly included discussions of whiteness in their Monday morning post mortems of both shows.

But if U.S. citizens are to understand this issue in more depth, these post mortems and other discussions of whiteness need better theoretical grounding and framing. Our collection meets that need and calls for further scholarship. If the elections of Barack Obama in 2008 and 2012 inspired our collection, then the events of Ferguson in 2014 made it even more necessary. For even as *whiteness* reemerged in 2014 and 2015 as a common term in mainstream U.S. discourses, its use has been haunted by competing definitions, unstated assumptions, and troubled histories.

Defining *Haunting Whiteness*

Our collection was originally titled *Haunting Whiteness: Rhetorics of Whiteness in a "Postracial" Era*. Consequently, the term *haunting whiteness* shaped our vision and contributors' thinking and remains an important concept. Our call for chapters invited contributors to make two moves: to contemplate how whiteness haunts twenty-first-century U.S. culture and to submit antiracist and antiwhiteness projects that expose as fantasy the idea that we live in a postracial world. But such a call begs questions of definition. To begin, *haunting whiteness* itself is a troubled phrase. To unpack it, let us look to nineteenth-century U.S. literature wherein it is easy to see how whiteness haunts a term. If a sentence states that a man walks down the street, he is assumed to be white; thus, whiteness haunts the term *man* as a racial identity marker and, thus, functions as an unstated norm. On the other hand, if a sentence needs to show a nonwhite man walking down the

4

street, he is racially marked, for example, as a colored man or an Indian. In the literature of Charles Chesnutt, a biracial novelist and cofounder of the NAACP, all characters, white and nonwhite, carry racial identity markers, but Chesnutt's practice was not the norm. Indeed, whiteness regularly haunted uses of such terms as *man*, *woman*, and *writer* in nineteenth-century U.S. literary and other cultural discourses, a haunting that continues to this day. A more recent example of how a term may be haunted by whiteness (as an assumed norm) appears in this collection's epigraph, a Toni Morrison tweet that reads, "In this country American means white. Everybody else has to hyphenate." Thus, the term *American* is exposed as being haunted by whiteness. But whiteness can haunt more than just a term. It can haunt entire texts and people's actions and their identities as well as cultural sites and events at particular historical moments.

What exactly is this whiteness that haunts? In this collection, *whiteness* is defined as a term functioning as a trope with associated discourses and cultural scripts that socialize people into ways of seeing, thinking, and performing whiteness and nonwhiteness. Both white and nonwhite bodies may perform whiteness, albeit to different ends and often with different success. As such, whiteness has historically been defined in different ways, for example, as a performance of acting white, violence and terror, the drive to consume land and cultures, religious hypocrisy, denial, and ignorance (Ratcliffe, *Rhetorical Listening* 111–31). When people interact with these definitions of *whiteness*, the term functions as an identification, that is, as a moment of thought, observation, or action that instantaneously becomes embodied within a person, either consciously or unconsciously, in ways that inform not only a single person's identity but also the identities of cultural groups, cultural sites, and cultural objects, such as texts and technologies (47–53). The chapters in this collection cull from our myriad identifications associated with whiteness in the twenty-first century in order to make such identifications visible, to analyze and interpret them, and to offer means for interrupting definitions, discourses, and cultural scripts of racial whiteness that lead to oppression.

As an identification, whiteness functions as Sigmund Freud suggests all identifications function: as a ghost, a haunting, that feeds on invisibility, nostalgia, and melancholy. This definition is posited in Freud's 1917 "Mourning and Melancholia" where he conceptualizes identification as a process whereby an individual's ego consumes the lost object in fantasy so as to maintain a connection with it. In his 1921 *Group Psychology and the Analysis of the Ego*, Freud extends identification into the social realm, an idea channeled by sociologist Avery Gordon in her 2008 *Ghostly Matters:*

Haunting and the Sociological Imagination. Gordon posits such haunting as follows: "Haunting raises specters, and it alters the experience of being in time the way we separate the past, the present, and the future" (xvi). From Freud to contemporary writers, psychoanalytic discussions of identification have invoked the powerful metaphor of ghosts and, thus, hauntings.

The term *haunting* also raises a specter of enthymemes, which are rhetorical syllogisms wherein major or minor premises are omitted so that hearers may supply them (Aristotle I.2). In "The Enthymematic Hegemony of Whiteness: The Enthymeme as Antiracist Rhetorical Strategy," Matthew Jackson explains how "racist enthymemes can function to support arguments for white supremacy inconspicuously and indirectly" and often occupy a subterranean and silent discursive space because complete syllogisms—such as, "all fully human men are created equal/all white men are fully human/ all white men are created equal (and its reverse that nonwhites are not fully equal/are not fully human/and are not created equal"—are less acceptable in the twenty-first century (604–6). Jackson uses a news story about a policeman exonerated of any wrongdoing in the death of a nonwhite suspect to lay out the enthymeme: "White men are credible witnesses" (unstated major premise); "the officer is a white policeman" (unstated minor premise); "the officer is a credible witness" (stated conclusion). The reverse is also "true" (605). Ratcliffe argues that Jackson's concept of postmodern enthymeme is important because it "helps us articulate, analyze, negotiate, employ, revise or reject multiple significations of the unstated," with the unstated being not simply an absence but a "gap waiting to be filled with meaning" ("In Search" 277). Tammie M. Kennedy adds that the enthymematic silences Jackson underscores are a product of traditional academic writing that relies on cognitive dimensions of understanding and action (264–65), which Victor Villanueva argues is "insufficient" for sustained, ethical social action and remembering practices (12). Further, twentieth-century whiteness theory highlights that "whiteness, like racism, is always more than one thing, and it's never the same thing twice" (Ellsworth 266). We cannot necessarily understand it away nor "fix it" or "fight it" by hoping ethical action will follow reason (Kennedy 265). Rather, we must be cognizant of its presence and its functions as well as of the critical tools necessary to engage it.

The purpose of *Rhetorics of Whiteness*, then, is twofold. First, the collection as a whole brings a rhetorical lens to help us understand how whiteness haunts a broad array of twenty-first-century discourses and how, via discursive cultural scripts, it inflects identities of bodies, cultural groups, sites, objects, events, and actions. Second, and perhaps more importantly, each chapter in *Rhetorics of Whiteness* offers concepts or tactics as critical tools not just for rhetorically analyzing whiteness but also for interrupting the operations of normative whiteness, operations that remain both visible and invisible as they have sustained and transformed themselves in a new millennium.

Defining *Oxymoronic Whiteness*

How might the trope of *whiteness* be defined in the twenty-first century? The contradictory cultural trends that we note in the opening paragraphs of this introduction appeared to us, at first, to map a simple binary opposition: either people were discussing whiteness (in popular discourses), or they were not (in academic discourses). But we are ever suspicious of simple binary oppositions (right/wrong, good/bad, black/white) because they entrap us within a logic that allows only two options and renders invisible that which the slash signifies as well as that which exceeds the binary spectrum. So we contemplated how to reframe these contradictory trends into a more generative form. Ultimately we concluded that these two trends function not so much as a binary opposition but, rather, more as an oxymoron, as a rhetorical figure in which two apparently opposing terms or ideas are presented in conjunction with one another in order to generate new meanings.

This shift from binary opposition to oxymoron represents not just an academic sleight of hand but rather a fundamental shift in how we think about whiteness. Binary oppositions invite us first to focus on fixed propositions, such as whether someone does or does not invoke the term *white*, and then to judge one decision right and the other wrong. Imagining whiteness as an oxymoron, however, invites us to identify multiple contradictions in discursive uses of whiteness, whether the term is directly employed or serves as a haunting. These contradictions are privileged not in order to judge one right and one wrong but, rather, in order to identify the contradictions, analyze them, generate myriad meanings from them, and then act upon them.

Granted, we are not the first to link whiteness and oxymoron. Kil Ja Kim asserts in her open letter to white antiracists that "there is no such thing as a white anti-racist. The term itself, 'white anti-racist' is an oxymoron." Grounded in this stipulative use of oxymoron, Kim outlines a corollary set of behaviors afforded to white people:

> First, don't call us, we'll call you. If we need your resources, we will contact you. But don't show up, flaunt your power in our faces and then get angry when we resent the fact that you have so many resources we don't and that

7

we are not grateful for this arrangement. And don't get mad because you can't make decisions in the process. Why do you need to? Second, stop speaking for us. We can talk for ourselves. Third, stop trying to point out internal contradictions in our communities, we know what they are, we are struggling around them, and I really don't know how white people can be helpful to non-whites to clear these up. Fourth, don't ever say some shit to me about how you feel silenced, marginalized, discriminated against, or put in your place as a white person. Period. Fifth, stop calling me sister. I will tell you when you are family. Finally, start thinking of what it would mean, in terms of actual structured social arrangements, for whiteness and white identity—even the white antiracist kind (because there really is no redeemable or reformed white identity)—to be destroyed.

We respect Kim's claims and emotions, grounded as they are in the experiences of her body. In this collection, however, we offer a competing use of *oxymoron*, one linked to Ratcliffe's rhetorical listening in ways that enable us to lay Kim's claims alongside ours in order *not* to reify the category *white* and uphold an oppressive social structure of *whiteness* but, rather, to name the terms and engage them as a means of understanding their operations and collaborating in the dismantlement of their oppressions, being always cognizant of power differentials associated with differing cultural locations.

To this end, our collection encourages conversations about whiteness in ways that will help elucidate how racial whiteness (and mixed-race) operates within twenty-first-century U.S. culture, whether within discourses of literature, entertainment, social media, law, education, journalism, or politics. Sometimes twenty-first-century functions of whiteness repeat patterns identified in earlier writings from slave narratives to the essays of James Baldwin and Adrienne Rich to the writings of 1990s–2000s scholarship in whiteness studies. In terms of the latter, this collection is indebted to seminal whiteness studies scholarship by Richard Dyer, Cheryl Harris, bell hooks, Neil Ignatiev, George Lipsitz, Ian Haney-López, Peggy McIntosh, Toni Morrison, Dave Roediger, Lynn Worsham, George Yancy, and others who have written about how whiteness operates within media, literature, history, property, pedagogies, and legal studies as well as across various categories of "differences." At other times, however, twenty-first-century functions of whiteness take on new permutations because of new cultural groups, sites, or texts and technologies, as identified in the more recent work of Michelle Alexander's *The New Jim Crow*, Houston Baker's American Book Award winner *Betrayal: How Black Intellectuals Have Abandoned the Ideals of the*

Civil Rights Era, and Ta-Nehisi Coates's *Between the World and Me*. These new permutations of whiteness require adapted or new concepts and tactics. By providing such concepts and tactics, our collection continues the long struggle to encourage individual and collective work toward social justice.

Operations of Oxymoronic Whiteness

Operations of oxymoronic whiteness abound in contemporary U.S. culture. One appears in the coexisting presence and absence of whiteness as a *racial* category within U.S. culture. As a racial identity marker, whiteness has visibly reemerged during the past decade within discourses of politics, law, education, journalism, social media, literature, and entertainment. As previously noted, the 2008 and 2012 presidential elections exemplify this trend in that mainstream media's preelection polling efforts as well as postelection analyses regularly included "whites" as an operative category of voter demographics. At the same time, mainstream media frequently depicted Obama's candidacies and presidency as clear signs that the U.S. has entered a "postracial" epoch wherein racial identities of candidates and voters no longer matter. The contradiction is glaring. But what does it mean?

Another operation of oxymoronic whiteness emerges in the multiple uses of the term *white* as a *political* (and by association, *economic*) category. For example, conservatives often champion colorblindness, yet for many, whiteness has emerged as a popular category of political value signifying the status quo. According to some conservative media, the status quo or that-which-should-be-the-status-quo has been assaulted by President Obama's elections, and these assaults have been directed at both white people and conservative values, a linkage that posits a close relation between whiteness and conservative values even as not all conservative people are racially marked as white and not all people marked racially as white are conservative. For many in the conservative media, these presidential elections have generated deep apathy toward antiracist policies and have incited sharp vitriol, variously and often, by those who have felt threatened by the changing demographics in the United States, whether the changes are caused by immigration or birth rates. In contrast, many moderates and liberals likewise champion colorblindness, yet for many, whiteness has emerged as a political category that suggests critique. According to moderate/liberal media, Obama's elections signal that the status quo has changed but needs to keep being revised in order to improve society. So regardless of political ideology, *white* and other racial categories are being invoked as having political value to describe demographics and to argue for or against policy development, even as a colorblind logic is often embraced as a means for arguing that we now live in a postracial epoch. These contradictory interpretations of whiteness are glaring, both between conservative, moderate, and liberal ideologies as well as within each. But what do these contradictions mean?

If the aforementioned racial and political/economic operations of whiteness were interpreted as binary oppositions, they would simply trap people (especially mixed-race people and first-generation immigrants) within fixed options: either being angry at others (*others* being defined in relation to whatever cultural location one is situated within) or denying differences among us. If the aforementioned operations of whiteness are interpreted as oxymorons, however, then the contradictions within and among the operations of whiteness would be laid alongside one another to determine what myriad meanings might be generated and what possible actions might be taken in particular situations. Thus, the figure of oxymoron offers whiteness studies a generative interpretive approach that promotes antiracism and antiwhiteness by making visible the hauntings of whiteness. This visibility may, in turn, facilitate productive debates and antiracist/antiwhiteness actions.

Chapter Descriptions

Rhetorics of Whiteness offers five sections that identify and rhetorically analyze cultural sites haunted by whiteness: popular culture, social media, education, pedagogy, and academic theory. Each section is introduced by one or two reflections written by prominent scholars noted for having published at some time in their careers on whiteness studies, critical race studies, or ethnic studies; these scholars include Annette Harris Powell, Catherine Prendergast, Jennifer Trainor, Amy Goodburn, Hui Wu, Victor Villanueva, and Sharon Crowley. These scholars were invited to write short reflections (500–750 words each) on the current state of whiteness studies and on the challenges of redressing the stronghold of whiteness in our contemporary bodies, institutions, lives, and classrooms. These reflections are not intended to summarize each section; rather, they are offered to spur conversations with one another and with section chapters. The sixteen chapters in *Rhetorics of Whiteness* are written by authors ranging from beginning scholars to prominent scholars in rhetoric and composition studies, whiteness studies, or education. These chapters offer rhetorical analyses of how whiteness haunts contemporary culture as well as critical tools, both concepts and tactics, that readers may employ to identify, analyze, interpret, evaluate, and argue about how whiteness haunts our supposedly "postracial" society.

Part one, "Hauntings in Popular Culture," maps how whiteness infiltrates popular fiction, film, television, and news media and also offers means of interruption. Gregory Jay's "Not Everyone's Protest Novel: White Fictions of Anti-Racism from Stowe to Stockett" invokes James Baldwin's famous essay by the same name for "explicating the ambivalent psychology of white racial liberalism" in popular novels, especially as it is intersected by gender. Highlighting how the same story (*The Help*) may be read through different genres (novel and film) to expose different functions of whiteness, Christine Farris's "*The Help* as Noncomplicit Identification and Nostalgic Revision" examines the popular novel and film alongside the historical events of Central High School in Little Rock, Arkansas, to expose how "fantasies of interracial relationships" revise the white complicity inherent in actual historical events. Anita M. DeRouen and M. Shane Grant's "Must(n't) See TV: Hidden Whiteness in Representations of Women of Color" argues that performances of women of color in the TV programs *Suits* and *Scandal* mask rather than disrupt white normativity and, thus, exact a "price" on the main characters. And Kristi McDuffie's "Colorblind Rhetoric in Obama's 2008 'Race Speech': The Appeal to Whiteness and the Disciplining of Racial Rhetorical Studies" argues that neoliberal and colorblind ideologies enable both the mainstream press to deem Obama's speech a success and mainstream rhetorical critics to be "emotionally disciplined" into agreement.

Part two, "Hauntings in Social Media," critiques the relatively new digital terrain of social media to uncover specific practices of white normativity as well as specific practices of resistance. Tim Engles's "Racialized Slacktivism: Social Media Performance of White Antiracism" evaluates performances by "aspiring white allies" and concludes that such allies too often fall victim to slacktivism, or activism characterized by "impulsive, shallow, and solipsistic modes of self-aggrandizing display." Sarah E. Austin's "The Ghost's in the Machine: eHarmony and the Reification of Whiteness and Heteronormativity" demonstrates how dating sites, such as eHarmony, perpetuate whiteness through a "scientific" matching system that privileges personality characteristics traditionally coded white and the notion that race is biology. Jennifer Beech's "Facebook and Absent-Present Rhetorics of Whiteness" claims that the ability to repost or "share" Facebook memes reveals ongoing struggles to maintain white power and de facto segregation in electronic spaces.

Part three, "Hauntings in Education," examines how educational institutions are whitewashed and, as such, must be challenged. Lee Bebout's

"Washing Education White: Arizona's HB 2281 and the Curricular Investment of Whiteness" postulates whiteness as the invisible foundation to the logic and language of Arizona's HB 2281 law, which prohibits schools from teaching courses in ethnic studies because they supposedly promote resentment toward another race or foster solidarity only among like individuals. Cedric Burrows's "How Whiteness Haunts the Textbook Industry: The Reception of Nonwhites in Composition Textbooks" argues that composition textbooks too often frame nonwhite authors with "white" theoretical apparati: for example, Malcolm X and MLK are often anthologized, but their headnotes, introductory reading questions, summary reading questions, and writing assignments often ask students to examine these readings in terms of traditional western rhetorical theories that reinforce patterns of white discourse, not in terms of African American rhetorical theories or practices. Casie Moreland and Keith Miller's "The Triumph of Whiteness: Dual-Credit Courses and Hierarchical Racism in Texas" explores Texas dual-credit curricula, such as Advanced Placement, and exposes how students who benefit from these programs are often the same white students who profit from institutional racism that works to the detriment of nonwhite students.

Part four, "Hauntings in Pedagogies," reflects on multiple pedagogical approaches and tactics for teaching about whiteness and racial oppression. Leda Cooks's "On the Cover of the *Rolling Stone*: Deconstructing Monsters and Terrorism in an Era of Postracial Whiteness" argues that personal storytelling about race and racism can build intergroup alliances, raise awareness on the part of white students, and promote healing, if performed dialogically. Meagan Rodgers's "The Pedagogical Role of a White Instructor's Racial Awareness Narrative" demonstrates how antiracist white teachers can effectively address race and privilege in classrooms populated by white students when their pedagogies include critical tools that acknowledge racial ambivalence and draw on emotional literacy. Alice McIntyre's "Practicing Mindfulness: A Pedagogical Tool for Spotlighting Whiteness" offers mindfulness as a critical pedagogical tool to help address white students' discomfort, anger, insecurity, and resistance when they are asked to reflect on their thinking about whiteness.

Part five, "Problems Haunting Theories of Whiteness," identifies individual and structural problems haunting definitions of *whiteness* and offers concepts for reimagining these problems. Ersula J. Ore's "Whiteness as Racialized Space: Barack Obama and the Rhetorical Constraints of Phenotypical Blackness" defines *whiteness* in terms of racialized space, argues that understanding whiteness as racialized space is a rhetorical necessity for nonwhite rhetors operating in white spaces (as exemplified by Barack Obama's presidency), and concludes that such a rhetorical necessity "belies [our culture's] claims of postraciality." Nicole Ashanti McFarlane and Nicole Snell's "Color-Deafness: White Writing as Palimpsest for African American English in *Breaking Bad* Screen Captions and Video Technologies" exposes the production and consumption of "audist frameworks" and how these support racialized whiteness in media and, by implication, elsewhere. Ronald Kuykendall's "Whiteness as Antidialogical" defines *whiteness* in terms of antidialogicism, arguing that existing whiteness studies scholarship is insufficient to transform the normative practices of white hegemony because the logic of whiteness is inherently antidialogical; instead, he calls for scholarship that fosters a revolutionary social transformation that makes it impossible to be white.

These chapters offer competing arguments and represent myriad purposes. These purposes include: locating the power of racialized whiteness in specific cultural sites of popular culture, social media, education, pedagogy, and academic theory; identifying rhetorics of racialized whiteness, especially white privilege, in various discourses and spaces; defining an *ethos* needed to serve as an antiracist ally; and providing the scholarly and pedagogical tools necessary to contest normative racialized whiteness. While these purposes blur, they also underscore and extend historical approaches used to organize whiteness studies as an academic field.

Rejecting the notion that race no longer matters, *Rhetorics of Whiteness* invites twenty-first-century conversations on racialized whiteness. Although our collection continues scholarly conversations initiated by cultural critics throughout U.S. history and engaged by whiteness studies scholars from the 1990s and early 2000s (many of whom no longer produce scholarship in this area), our collection also acknowledges that racialized whiteness is a complex and dynamic topic that has persisted despite efforts to combat both racism as well as the material and discursive dominance of whiteness. Consequently, this collection challenges scholars, students, and other citizens to explore new epistemological and ontological approaches to understanding whiteness. As such, this collection supplements scholarly journal conversations about intersections among critical race studies, whiteness studies, rhetoric, writing, and literacy practices. Scholarship within this collection, we hope, may generate future research and yet be accessible enough for discussions inside and outside the classroom, discussions about how oxymoronic whiteness haunts not just academic scholarship but all our lives.

Works Cited

Alexander, Michelle. *The New Jim Crow: Mass Incarcerations in the Age of Colorblindness.* 2010. New York: The New P, 2012. Print.

Anderson, Carole. "Ferguson Isn't about Black Rage against Cops. It's White Rage against Progress." *Washington Post Opinions.* 29 Aug. 2014. Web. 14 Feb. 2015.

Aristotle. *On Rhetoric: A Theory of Civic Discourse.* Trans. George Kennedy. New York: Oxford UP, 1980. Print.

Baker, Houston. *Betrayal: How Black Intellectuals Have Abandoned the Ideals of the Civil Rights Era.* New York: Columbia UP, 2008. Print.

Coates, Ta-Nehisi. *Between the World and Me.* New York: Spiegel and Grau, 2015. Print.

Dear White People. Dir. Justin Simien. Perf. Tyler James Williams, Tessa Thompson, Kyle Gallner. Code Red, 2014. Film.

Dyer, Richard. *White: Essays on Race and Culture.* New York: Routledge, 1997. Print.

Ellsworth, Elizabeth. "Double Binds of Whiteness." *Off White: Readings on Race, Power, and Society.* Ed. Michelle Fine et al. New York: Routledge, 1997. 259–69. Print.

Fox and Friends. Fox. 31 Jan. 2015. Television.

Freud, Sigmund. *Group Psychology and the Analysis of the Ego.* 1921. New York: W. W. Norton, 1990. Print.

———. "On Mourning and Melancholia." *The Standard Edition of the Complete Psychological Works of Sigmund Freud.* Trans. James Strachey. London: Hogarth P, 1917. 243–58. Print.

Gold, Michael. "Viola Davis' Emmy Speech." *New York Times* 20 Sept. 2015. Web. 1 Oct. 2015.

Gordon, Avery. *Ghostly Matters: Haunting and the Sociological Imagination.* 2nd ed. Minneapolis: U of Minnesota P, 2008. Print.

Grayson, Rose. "The Incredible Whiteness of Being." *Pinterest.* Web. 25 Feb. 2015. ["It's Time We Treat Police Brutality as a National Crisis" from Gawker.]

Groch-Begley, Hannah. "Fox News Sunday Hosts More White People on Ferguson than All Other Broadcast Sunday Shows." *MediaMatters.org.* 1 Dec. 2014 Web. 14 Feb. 2015.

Haney-López, Ian, ed. *White by Law: The Legal Construction of Race.* 1996. New York: New York UP, 2006. Print.

Harris, Cheryl. "Whiteness as Property." *Harvard Law Review* 106 (June 1993): 1707–91. Print.

Harrison, Lily. "Sean Hannity Slams John Legend's Oscars Speech: 'He Doesn't Know Anything about Politics.'" *Eonline.com*. 23 Feb. 2015. Web. 26 Feb. 2015.

hooks, bell. "Representations of Whiteness." *Black Looks: Race and Representation*. Boston: South End P, 165–78. Print.

Ignatiev, Neil. *How the Irish Became White*. 1995. New York: Routledge, 2009. Print.

Jackson, Matthew. "The Enthymematic Hegemony of Whiteness: The Enthymeme as Antiracist Rhetorical Strategy." *JAC* 26 (2006): 601–41. Print.

Kennedy, Tammie M. "Enthymematical, Epistemic, and Emotional Silence(s) in the Rhetoric of Whiteness." *JAC* 27 (2007): 253–75. Print.

Kennedy, Tammie M., Joyce Irene Middleton, and Krista Ratcliffe. "The Matter of Whiteness: Or, Why Whiteness Studies Is Important to Rhetoric and Composition Studies." *Rhetoric Review* 24 (2005): 359–73. Print.

Kim, Kil Ja (as Tamara K. Nopper). "The White Anti-Racist Is an Oxymoron: An Open Letter to White 'Anti-Racists.'" *Race Traitor*. n.d. Web. 17 July 2013.

Kumanyika, Chenjerai. "Challenging the Whiteness of Public Radio." *All Things Considered*. NPR. 29 Jan. 2015. Radio.

Lacey-Bordeaux, Lacey. "Arizona Professor's Jaywalking Arrest Quickly Gets out of Hand." *Cnn.com*. 30 June 2014. Web. 20 Feb. 2015.

Lipsitz, George. *The Possessive Investment in Whiteness: How White People Profit from Identity Politics*. 1998. Philadelphia: Temple UP, 2006. Print.

Marie, Renita. "White Privilege on the Streets of Ferguson." *Huffington Post*. 2 Oct. 2014. Web. 14 Feb. 2015.

McCormack, Daniella. "Diversity in Media Is an On-Going Effort." *Baycat*. 23 Feb. 2015. Web. 26 Feb. 2015.

McIntosh, Peggy. "White Privilege: Unpacking the Invisible Knapsack." *The National See Project*. 1988. Web. October 2015.

Middleton, Joyce Irene. "Talking about Race and Whiteness in *Crash*." *College English* 69 (Mar. 2007): 321–34. Print.

Morrison, Toni. *Playing in the Dark: Whiteness in the Literary Imagination*. New York: Vintage, 1993. Print.

Morrison, Toni (@MsToniMorrison). "In this country American means white. Everybody else has to hyphenate." *Twitter.com*. 3 Apr. 2013, 5:19 P.M. Tweet.

Penn, Charli. "Common and John Legend Deliver Moving Oscar Acceptance Speech after Win for 'Glory.'" *Essence.com*. 23 Feb. 2015. Web. 26 Feb. 2015.

Petri, Alexandra. "The Trouble with Patricia Arquette's Oscar Speech." *ComPost*. *Washingtonpost.com*. 23 Feb 2015. Web. 26 Feb. 2015.

Ratcliffe, Krista. "In Search of the Unstated: The Enthymeme and/of Whiteness." *JAC* 27 (2007): 275–90. Print.

——. *Rhetorical Listening: Identification, Gender, Whiteness*. Carbondale: Southern Illinois UP, 2005. Print.

Roediger, David, ed. *Black on White: Black Writers on What It Means to Be White*. New York: Schocken, 1999. Print.

——. *The Wages of Whiteness: Race and the Making of the American Working Class*. New York: Verso, 1991, 2007.

Selma. Dir. Ava DuVernay. Perf. David Oyelowo, Carmen Eiggo, Tim Roth, Oprah Winfrey. Studio, 2015. Film.

Trainor, Jennifer Seibor. *Rethinking Racism: Emotion, Persuasion, and Literacy Education in an All-White High School*. Carbondale: Southern Illinois UP, 2008. Print.

Villanueva, Victor, Jr. "*Memoria* Is a Friend of Ours: On the Discourse of Color." *College English* 67.1 (Sept. 2004): 9–19. Print.

Woods, Jane. "12 Things White People Can Now Do Because of Ferguson." *Alternet.org*. 18 Aug. 2014. Web. 14. Feb. 2015.

Worsham, Lynn. "After Words: A Choice of Words Remains." *Feminism and Composition Studies: In Other Words*. New York: MLA, 1998: 329–56. Print.

Yancy, George, and Shannon Sullivan. "White Anxiety and the Futility of Black Hope." *Opinionator. New York Times*. 5 Dec. 2014. Web. 14 Feb. 2015.

PART ONE

HAUNTINGS IN POPULAR CULTURE

REFLECTION

"POSTRACIAL"

Annette Harris Powell

THE DISCUSSION OF race has shifted to a set of coded "postracial" messages designed to move away from race, yet they only exacerbate its significance. This shift occurs over time, so there is a progression from what Ian Haney Lopez refers to as Richard Nixon's "Southern Strategy," "a euphemism that obscures racism," to Ronald Reagan's use of the phrase "Welfare Queen," to George H. W. Bush's use of Willie Horton to stoke fears about the criminality of African Americans and the failure of the government to address it, to Bill Clinton's diss of Sister Souljah. Presidential candidate Donald Trump mines similar ground when he stokes fear and divisiveness through "take America back, make America great again" rhetoric. These neutral depictions send a message about African Americans as naturally subordinated. Advancing this message, public discourse has embraced neutrality, from colorblindness to postracialism. Accordingly, many of the civil rights gains of the 1960s have been dismantled through colorblind policies. The appeal of colorblind neutrality and postracialism rests in the fact that race can be submerged so that any substantive or critical discussion of race is avoided.

President Obama's postracial rhetoric draws directly upon neutrality, liberal individualism, and colorblindness. His rhetoric resonates because he appeals to American society's pluralism and openness. President Obama, in his "A More Perfect Union" speech, underscores concepts that "unite" beyond race. Embracing the commonality and shared values of the American polity, President Obama underscores this unity without referencing race. This colorblind approach is unsuccessful because it acknowledges race in order to ignore it. As critical race theorists recognize, there is really no such thing as colorblindness because race must first be acknowledged, only to then be ignored. Indeed, postracialism, like colorblindness before it, serves to drive any substantive analysis of race underground so that structural or systemic inequality is preserved in the name of neutrality. This is how Obama derives political capital and reinforces his ability to deal with black issues while simultaneously ignoring them. For me, his rhetorical moves are somewhat reminiscent of Clinton's staged Sister Souljah moment. Obama shows that he is not afraid to take African Americans (his own people) to task for their shortcomings, "irresponsibility," and "lack of courage" in controlling their own destiny.

Admittedly I, like many others, am often fatigued by the continuing discussions around race, yet I recognize that these discussions are still quite necessary because, as evidenced by the use of lethal force against people of color in Ferguson, Baltimore, New York, Cleveland, Minnesota, Baton Rouge, and many other places across the country, *race still matters*. Despite the fact that an African American holds the presidency, blackness continues to change the terrain of everything, and having an African American president has made this more evident, not less. So in thinking about whether whiteness studies is still relevant, my response is wholeheartedly yes, but it needs an even more critical edge. Whiteness studies needs to acknowledge the new, widely accepted approach to race (postracialism) that has altered the meaning of race and racial categories. The very fact of how whiteness continues to function in institutional spaces, and the ubiquitous trumpeting of "liberal individualism," makes it clear that we cannot afford to be less vigilant. Whiteness is advanced through the liberal individualistic claim inherent in reverse discrimination lawsuits—the Constitution protects individuals, not racial groups. *Fisher v. University of Texas*, recently argued before the Supreme Court and rooted in Abigail Fisher's claim that she was displaced by an unidentified person of color, is itself a striking example of privilege. Ironically, Fisher's academic credentials would not merit outright admission under the very program she challenges. She nevertheless argues that she was injured because the admissions process was "race-conscious" rather than race neutral. Ultimately, the Supreme Court rejected Fisher's claim, and concluded that race could be considered, as one of many factors, in a holistic admissions review process after race-neutral alternatives proved ineffective in achieving diversity.

Whiteness is the normative principle that defines the American experience historically, socially, and politically. Whiteness studies seeks to move beyond the one-dimensional depictions of how race functions in society to a critical analysis of the manner in which white privilege rationalizes the subordination of oppressed minorities. But this is only part of the story. Whiteness studies shares a common doctrinal foundation with critical race theory, unpacking neutrality and its edifying effects in the preservation of inequality.

I propose that this inquiry be expanded to a more comprehensive analysis of the rhetorical underpinnings of oppression and how whiteness is performed to advance and normalize inequality.

Works Cited

Delgado, Richard, and Jean Stefancic. *Critical Race Theory: An Introduction.* 2nd ed. New York: New York UP, 2012. Print.

Fisher v. University of Texas. Vol. 135 U.S. 2888. Supreme Court of the United States. 2015. *LexisNexis Academic.* Web. 30 Aug. 2015.

———. Vol. 579 U.S. Supreme Court of the United States. 2016. *Westlaw Academic.* Web. 23 June 2016.

Lopez, Ian Haney. *Dog Whistle Politics: How Coded Racial Appeals Have Reinvented Racism and Wrecked the Middle Class.* New York: Oxford UP, 2014. Print.

Obama, Barack. "A More Perfect Union." National Constitution Center, Philadelphia, PA. 18 March 2008. Speech.

"Sister Souljah Moment." C-Span. 13 June 1992. Web. 29 June 2015. http://www.c-span.org/video/?c4460582/sister-souljah-moment.

"Willie Horton 1988 Attack Ad." YouTube. 3 Nov. 2008. Web. 29 June 2015. https://www.youtube.com/watch?v=I09KMSSEZ0Y.

NOT EVERYBODY'S PROTEST NOVEL: WHITE FICTIONS OF ANTIRACISM FROM STOWE TO STOCKETT

Gregory Jay

> Down here, you can't throw a dead cat without hitting an older, well-off
> white person raised by a black woman, and every damn one of them will
> earnestly insist that a reciprocal and equal form of love was exchanged
> between them.   —Sally Mann, *Hold Still*

IN *PLAYING IN* the *Dark: Whiteness and the Literary Imagination*, Toni Morrison examines "the way black people ignite critical moments of discovery or change or emphasis in literature not written by them" (ix). These moments belong to an influential tradition of liberal race fiction that produced yet another best seller in Kathryn Stockett's 2009 novel *The Help*, which was adapted, like its predecessor *To Kill a Mockingbird*, into a hit Hollywood film. Does the popularity of this sympathetic portrayal of black domestics during the height of the civil rights movement provide evidence that we have moved into a "postracial" era? Or does that very success, and the tendency of readers and critics to focus on its white protagonist, suggest that anxieties toward blackness continue to haunt the strategies of progressive fiction and film in the twenty-first century?[1] The genre of white liberal race fiction arguably originates with Harriet Beecher Stowe's *Uncle Tom's Cabin*, which was the target of James Baldwin's famous 1949 essay "Everybody's Protest Novel." Baldwin's critique of Stowe's racial ideology provided one of the founding documents of whiteness studies in the literary realm, as did his 1984 essay "On Being 'White' . . . and Other Lies." That essay famously argued that the "price of the ticket" for European immigrants seeking assimilation "was to become 'white,'" investing in the invention of a mythical racial identity that inevitably dehumanized others: "Because they think they are white, they cannot allow themselves to be tormented by the suspicion that all men are brothers" (178, 180). His analysis, unfortunately, seems relevant again today as we consider the cultural work of *The Help* as well as the ghastly violence that continues against the black body in America. Ta-Nehisi Coates has recently written searingly of that ongoing violence by explicitly taking up Baldwin's critique of whiteness in his award-winning *Between the World and Me*, a title he borrowed from a poem of the same name on lynching by Richard Wright. The upbeat interracial humanism many have found in Stockett's novel, I will argue, overlooks the story's exposure of the violent attempts by those who think they are white to expel the black body. It is a destructive but ultimately futile effort to ensure the superior purity of their fantasized racial identity.

Stockett telegraphs the tradition into which she is inserting her novel when Aibileen (a black maid and one of the novel's three narrators) cannot get books from the local whites-only library in Jackson, Mississippi, and so asks the white heroine Skeeter to check them out for her. What's on Aibileen's list? Not surprisingly, she asks for masterpieces of white liberal antiracism— *Huckleberry Finn* and *To Kill a Mockingbird*—along with W. E. B. Du Bois's *Souls of Black Folk* and some Freud (presumably to figure out why white folks are so "crazy") (179–80). Baldwin's essay will help explain how these supposedly progressive fictions continue to exhibit white fears of blackness and a return of the drive to separate and exclude the people who embody it. My essay's purpose, however, is not once again to denounce or defend either Stowe or Stockett. Rather I intend to extend and complicate Baldwin's analysis by explicating the ambivalent psychology of white racial liberalism these novels express and to consider how gender complicates the story.

According to Baldwin, "*Uncle Tom's Cabin*, that cornerstone of American social protest fiction," casts the Northerner Miss Ophelia as spokeswoman for the proper white moral response to slavery: "'This is perfectly horrible!' she exclaims. 'You ought to be ashamed of yourselves.'" It is, he judges, "a very bad novel," characterized by "self-righteous, virtuous sentimentality . . . the ostentatious parading of excessive and spurious emotion" (13). Baldwin implies that such inauthenticity characterizes much white liberal protest, which creates plenty of self-righteous affect for its practitioners. This sentimentality indulges in depictions of oppression and violence, congratulating itself on its feelings of outrage and redeeming whiteness through the spectacle of black suffering (an analysis recently reiterated in Garcia et al. [8]).

Baldwin's criticism, however, has been countered by Americanist scholars, such as Jane Tompkins and Glenn Hendler, who defend Stowe's turn to "sentimental power" as an antiracist instrument. Marianne Noble, for example, contends:

> Political transformation through feelings was precisely the reaction that sentimental abolitionist authors sought to provoke. Convinced that Americans had become deadened to the pain suffered by victims of heartless public policies because they thought in impersonal abstractions, authors like Stowe sought to restore feelings to dominant modes of cognition. They "cut . . . to the quick" in an effort to pierce through anaesthetizing abstractions and make readers think through the subjective responses of intuition, imagination, and sympathetic extensions to others. (295)

Stowe's recourse to a rhetoric of familial, and especially maternal, emotions and her attachment of them to the antislavery cause was no doubt effective, as the reception of her novel among white abolitionists shows (Southern reviewers complained that her use of emotion was unfair). She makes the separation of mothers from their children the primary example of slavery's evil and sin, using a rhetoric of universal humanism and an appeal to moral sensibility rather than an argument about racism and political economy. The readers whose emotions she targets for sentimental education, however, remain implicitly white, as is the presumed audience of the protest tradition here under scrutiny. This presumption explains why these rehabilitations of sentimental power fail to completely overcome Baldwin's objections. As Hendler argues, the universalizing of sentimental rhetoric obscures its bad faith: "The politics of sympathy is fatally flawed," he contends, "by sentimentalism's drive to turn all differences into equivalences. . . . If I have to be like you and feel like you in order for you to feel for me, sympathy reaches its limits at the moment you recognize that I am not quite like you" (146).

Among the privileges of whiteness, then, lies this assumption of the normative position of white affect, and the implicit claim that nonwhites must perform for those norms in order to deserve white sympathy, as does the beleaguered Uncle Tom. Moreover, this sympathetic logic leads to an ideology of "color-blindness," which both denies the reality of race and reinscribes racial injustice by ignoring how the historical and social construction of racial oppression continues to operate unchecked. Since blacks must become more like whites to deserve sympathy, African Americans become subject to the denigration of their actual bodies and cultural practices, so that the demand for equivalence turns into another motivation for racist actions. I will describe that treatment of blacks by whites, and the consequent subjectivity for whites it produces, through the theory of *abjection*. Baldwin's rejection of Stowe's sentimentalism proceeds from his refusal of the demand for equivalence and his focus on fearful white imaginings of blackness.

In her chapter on "white sympathy" fiction, Jodi Melamed explains that Baldwin's essay "tellingly identified the race protest novel as a primary cultural technology for producing, disseminating, and implanting racial-liberal thinking" and "described how the process of entering into representation through the mediation of official antiracist knowledges was to become subject to . . . destructive normalizing and rationalizing systems" (xi). Melamed reads Baldwin's essay as striking an analogy between Cold War liberalism and its integration of antiracism into a nationalist war strategy, on the one hand, and Stowe's program of moralistic and sentimental tropes for opposing racial labor systems and justifying a civil war on the other. "Baldwin saw *Uncle Tom's Cabin*," she writes, "as evidence that the actual work of sentimental discourses of liberal reform (past and present) was to establish an epistemology that guaranteed white salvation" (xi). The "high cost" of this strategy, she notes, "was that permissible narratives of black experience and subjectivity had to stabilize concepts of exceptional humanity and benevolence of antislavery whites" (xii). Melamed describes how the institutions of publishing and academe, after World War II, promoted an ideology of the antiracist white sympathy novel as a text focused on attitudes and prejudices among whites rather than on the political economies of racism and class exploitation.

A close reading of Baldwin's essay can show how sentimental white salvation in these novels is also linked to a logic of racial abjection. Though grammar dictates that "abjection" takes the form of a noun and has adjectival and adverbial cognates, I intend to extend its use to that of a transitive verb: "to abject." This move is in accord with the term's etymological origins in the late Middle English adaptation of the Latin "abjectus," meaning to reject or throw away. In an interview, Julia Kristeva, the primary contemporary theorist of the abject, explains:

The term in French has a much more violent sense than in English. It means something disgusting. . . . It is an extremely strong feeling which is at once somatic and symbolic, and which is above all a revolt of the person against an external menace from which one wants to keep oneself at a distance, but of which one has the impression that it is not only an external menace but that it may menace us from the inside. (Baruch and Serrano 135–36)

Kristeva's definition well fits the white racist rhetoric that portrays the black body as a cause for disgust, and blackness itself as something that must be segregated out or violently removed. Writes Coates to his son: "'White America' is a syndicate arrayed to protect its exclusive power to dominate and control our bodies" (42). According to Noelle McAfee, the "the abject is what one spits out, rejects, almost violently excludes from oneself," so that processes of psychological abjection and sociopolitical abjection take similar forms and follow parallel rhetorical and affective trajectories (46). Yet what is abjected is "never banished altogether. It hovers at the periphery of one's existence, constantly challenging one's own tenuous borders of selfhood. . . . It remains as both an unconscious and a conscious threat to one's own clean and proper self" (46). This description can be applied to black-white relations in the United States and the psychological process by which whites constitute their identity through the ambivalent abjection of a blackness that continues to haunt them. I am not primarily concerned, here, with analyses of the experience of racial abjection by "minority" subjects, as important as these are, but rather with the imaginary abjection of the Other by the dominant, and the role played by the rejection of the Other in the white subject's racial self-constitution (for a different account, see Scott). As we shall see, an analytic using "to abject" helps emphasize how white denigration of the Other includes feelings of anger, attachment, expulsion, shame, and purgation and includes an association of the Other with the realm of waste. Recognizing those links will get us, in turn, to the subjects of labor and of excrement in *The Help*. It is the blacks, of course, who get assigned the job of cleaning up the dirt and getting rid of the abjected stuff in the lives of those who believe they are white. But by that assignment they are guaranteed to become forever identified with the abjected, and never with what is clean.

Abjection and the Fictions of White Moral Salvation

With these theoretical frameworks in mind, we can return both to Baldwin's essay and various novels of white antiracism to discover how they focus on and exhibit the work of abjection in the constitution of white subjectivity. After excoriating Stowe's sentimental depiction of racial violence, Baldwin asks "what constriction or failure of perception forced her to so depend on the description of brutality—unmotivated, senseless—and to leave unanswered and unnoticed the only important question: what it was, after all, that moved her people to such deeds" ("Everybody's" 14). Given Baldwin's own upbringing, it is not surprising that his analysis focuses on Stowe's fire-and-brimstone Christian metaphysics and its abjection of blackness. Writing of Uncle Tom, Baldwin says that "since he is black, born without the light, it is only through humility, the incessant mortification of the flesh, that he can enter into communion with God or man." Stowe, he claims, is not motivated by "virtuous rage" but "merely by a panic of being hurled into the flames, of being caught in traffic with the devil"—for slavery is sin, and its practitioners devils. Stowe could not embrace the blacks "without purifying them of sin. She must cover their intimidating nakedness, robe them in white, the garments of salvation; only thus could she herself be delivered from ever-present sin" (17–18). Following Baldwin's imagery, we can say that Tom's violent death (reminiscent of the lynching and castration ritually repeated on black men in the decades to follow) is "sentimental" or "sensational" to the degree it belongs to a theological racial imaginary that purges the white world of its fear of darkness, bringing grace to itself at the price of the black man's abjection and sublimation. The "incessant mortification" of Tom's flesh, however, is not a self-chosen ritual of individual piety; it is the torture the white man imposes as a punishment for Tom's resistance—which is to say, for Tom's politics. Tom is never blacker in Legree's eyes than when he refuses to betray Cassy and Emmeline. Legree's enraged response to Tom's black politics gets entangled with a plot thread about Legree's memory of his saintly mother, whose entreaties to reform he violently spurned; he receives a lock of her hair after her death, so that a haunting agony over his rejection of her colors his need to abject Tom. Kristeva had theorized that the primal abjection is the infant's revolt against the body of the mother, from which the child must ambivalently separate to gain autonomous subjectivity and to which it longs to return. This mother/child dynamic within the logic of abjection turns out to uncannily forecast the problems exhibited in the relations of white children to the black women who are assigned their care and feeding, as will be abundantly clear in *The Help*.

Liberal white antiracism, then, emphasizes the attainment of a superior moral consciousness and cleansed subjectivity that pays for its salvation through the abjection of the racial Other. Stowe herself flirted with efforts to solve the American race problem by sending blacks back to Africa in a colonization scheme that was the political equivalent of abjection. Her novel pursues the cultural work of the white reader's sentimental education in a famous effort to "feel right" through sympathy, as she explained in the novel's didactic conclusion:

> There is one thing that every individual can do,—they can see to it that they feel right. An atmosphere of sympathetic influence encircles every human being; and the man or woman who feels strongly, healthily and justly, on the great interests of humanity, is a constant benefactor to the human race. See, then, to your sympathies in this matter! Are they in harmony with the sympathies of Christ? or are they swayed and perverted by the sophistries of worldly policy? (456–57)

This injunction to "feel right" becomes the principal aim and rhetorical design of mainstream white liberal antiracist fiction from Stowe to Stockett. *The Help* resembles white sympathy novels such as *Huckleberry Finn* and *To Kill a Mockingbird* in which the youthful white protagonist's moral education on the subject of race, given in first person, is offered to white readers for identification and edification, and to black readers as a token that their oppression is recognized. These are those "critical moments of discovery or change" Morrison describes (ix).

Such racial uplift novels are explicitly about white people and their positions, as are influential best sellers such as Fannie Hurst's 1933 *Imitation of Life* and Laura Hobson's 1947 *Gentleman's Agreement* (a protest novel against racialized anti-Semitism). In each case the struggling moral consciousness of the adult white protagonist becomes a stand-in for the reader's journey to enlightenment. It's always difficult to prove why a book or film becomes popular. If a series of these kinds of texts, however, that resemble one another in striking ways also resemble one another in popularity, and in popularity with similar white racialized audiences, then the critic has some grounds for speculating on their common patterns of plot, character, form, and ideology. All of these texts offer readers who think they are white literary experiences of moral uplift that may ease as well as disturb their conscience; after all, the recognition of sin and the hope of redemption are preferable to the mere naming of evil as such or to doing something about it. The narrative form enacts a suturing between the protagonist's moments of self-critical moral insight about racism, on the one hand, and the reader's self-aware identification with that insight as a result of appreciating the text itself on the other. As a reader, if I can be like Huck or Scout or Skeeter in declaring that "I'd rather go to hell" than countenance the injustices of racism, then I'm more ready to like their books. My contention is that such books implicitly continue to abject blackness; white readers identify with their superficial antiracism and so experience a salvational sublime in their conviction that they have abjected racism itself.

As Baldwin's essay suggests, the salvation of the white self through sympathy in white antiracist texts usually turns on this abjection and sublimation of a blackness both intimate (as in the figure of the mammy) and cordoned off (see the theme of segregated toilets in Stockett). In Stowe, Tom's abused body becomes the suffering site of that abjection, and his death and heavenly ascent the sublimation. The arc of this sublimation also promises the white reader that blackness will no longer be a source of shame, as slavery makes it, but rather something expelled, either by colonization schemes or hosannas of heavenly forgiveness. In Twain, blackness is abjected into language, the black speech of Jim and the slaves sublimated into the colloquialism of Huck (see Fishkin, *Was Huck Black?*). Once the game of abjection with the reenslaved Jim goes sour, for the readers and the players, Huck seems to have no choice at the end of the novel but to "light out for the Territory," fleeing a blackness whose sublimation cannot be achieved except through language, wherein its incorporation threatens to shame as well as to enlighten.

The absence of the white mother in Huck's life, as for Scout in *To Kill a Mockingbird*, may be linked to the cultural work of separating from, or abjecting, the mammy figure who took her place and who haunts the desires of the white racial subject. In *Imitation of Life*, the white heroine Bea Pullman hires Aunt Delilah, the mammy figure, to supplement her own failing maternal labor as she turns to a career in business built on Delilah's waffle recipe. Here the abject blackness of the domestic is sublimated economically through the waffle-house business (pancakes in the film version); this Aunt Jemima economy offers a nurturing incorporation and transubstantiation of blackness, aligning the legacy of domestic servitude with the rise of mass consumer capitalism and the celebrity economy. The expropriation of the abjected black body under slavery gets updated as this black domestic's recipes are appropriated for profit by the white employer. The working-class white woman's rise to star status combines exquisite sympathy for her help with narcissistic capital accumulation. Delilah's reunion with her own daughter refracts the anguished, fatal separation of a black maid and mother from her tragic mulatto daughter. *Imitation of Life* reminds us how the consumption of black bodies through linguistic, financial, erotic, and cinematic economies appeals to the taste of a sympathizing white audience, as the mammy figure had always been the offer of a consumed black breast and an abundance of black flesh available ambivalently only because of its abjection.

Perhaps the most canonical of white antiracist novels in the modern period is Harper Lee's *To Kill a Mockingbird*, famously dramatized by the Oscar-winning film with Gregory Peck and taught in most American high schools (Jay 487–88). The novel's pedagogical popularity can be directly ascribed to the overtly didactic structure of the narrative, as the white reader is positioned to identify with Scout as she learns the proper lessons of sympathy from her father, though he fails to save an unjustly accused black man from death. As in the previous novels, the rhetorical focus is on uplifting the white moral consciousness even as the black body is once more abjected. Sympathy for the unjustly convicted Tom (that name again) is abetted by a mammy figure (Calpurnia, a domestic unburdened this time by weight) as well as by Harper Lee's preemptive castration of him through the symbolism of his crippled arm. As white liberal lawyer Atticus Finch demonstrates dramatically in court, this damaged appendage proves to any objective observer that Tom never could have raped the white-trash girl Mayella Ewell, who in fact tried to molest him. After his conviction Tom is shot by prison guards while trying to escape, the abjection of his black masculinity a price to be paid for the sublime characterization of the wisdom of the white Atticus, reverence for whom is channeled through the reminiscence of his adoring child, whose narrative interpellates the (white) reader into the proper liberal position. Lee's text further displaces the actual political economies of racism and class exploitation by the abjection of the white-trash family, onto whom is projected the racism that actually originated with the ruling-class merchants, plantation owners, bankers, judges, and—yes—lawyers of the South (and North). Meanwhile the heroic courtroom labors of Thurgood Marshall and other black attorneys who fought lynching and segregation for decades are ignored in favor of the heroic depiction of Atticus as white savior (for a harrowing account of Marshall's courtroom work in the South trying to save black bodies, see King). At the very moment (1960) that African Americans are putting their lives on the line to fight for their rights, *To Kill a Mockingbird* offers a story of black impotence that provides whites an imaginary hero who absolves them of racial guilt and presumptively claims the right to define right action.

Daughters and (M)others in *The Help*

The dramatic events of the civil rights era are the fictional backdrop, rather than compositional context, of Stockett's *The Help*, though like its predecessors it too struggles to balance an antiracist message with a narrative of white moral education and uplift. The sentimental feelings conjured by *The Help*—as with Stowe, largely focused on the separation of mothers from children—are cordoned off from politics, just as the political events of the 1960s are evoked but marginalized in both the book and film. While we are meant to feel the injustices done to the maids, we are, just as importantly, meant to like them, find them funny and admirable and unthreatening. As the stories of these domestic workers get told, one doesn't feel much of a protest taking place in the present, even as protests are shown or alluded to in the texts. Indeed, we may conclude that the emphasis on moral education and the white reader's uplift in the liberal antiracist novel thwarts whatever intention it may have to protest the material conditions of oppression that whites continue to benefit from and would rather not dwell too long upon. Granted, the plot and imagery of *The Help* contains the story of a protest against the abjection of blackness, as the effort to make the maids use segregated bathrooms in white homes symbolizes the South's Jim Crow laws. This protest doesn't come across very well in reading the novel, given the usurpation of the black workers' story by the tale of the white writer and the confusion of the lives and careers of the fictional Skeeter and the actual author Stockett. In the film, however, the problematic representation of the maids and their voices in the novel gets partially remedied by the acting of Octavia Spencer and Viola Davis, who easily overshadow Emma Stone's Skeeter. The cinema, and the visual presence of powerful black actresses, allows the symbolic tale of abjection and its rejection to be seen more clearly and to be protested against through the casting and performance of Spencer and Davis.

As with previous texts in the tradition, *The Help* solicits popular investment in its moral pedagogy through the deft employment of narrative forms supportive of racial liberalism. Stockett puts the stories of Aibileen and Minny into first-person present discourse, as if they were writing in a daily journal or speaking across the kitchen table to us after work. For example, Minny says of her employer Celia Foote: "It's really starting to irritate me how she never leaves the house, how she smiles like the maid walking in every morning is the best part of her day" (59). This use of the present tense places us, the readers, into the unfolding of a story whose literal and moral ends are yet to be arrived at or known, which serves as a proper formal framework for the mysteries the novel pursues (Why does Celia stay in bed all day? Will Skeeter develop a moral consciousness strong enough to oppose Hilly?). This discourse creates a sense of intimacy, revelation, and sharing between the speaker/writer and the reader, again closing the gap between Aibileen and Minny and their mostly white audience and at the same time giving voice to their criticisms of the ways of white folks. Formally, the structure foreshadows the stories told to Skeeter later on by the black maids that become the material of her book (titled *Help*). But the stories we are reading are *not* from that book, at least not literally; these chapters by Aibileen and Minny recount incidents that take place *before* Skeeter convinces them to tell their stories. If these were the stories they told to Skeeter, they would not be in the present tense, nor would they be so unknowing of the mysteries they speak about. The above passage would have been, in Skeeter's manuscript, something like this: "It really started to irritate me how she never left the house, since I had no idea then about her fear of another miscarriage." The presentist technique includes accounts of life at home, as when Minny refers to what her daughter Kindra said to her "last night" (60). Readers are positioned as secret sharers of these maids; we feel trusted by them in this sharing, just as Skeeter will later be. This parallel between the reader's position and Skeeter's reinforces, I believe, the conclusion that the assumed audience for the book is white, since the revelations about racial oppression they offer will not be news to most African American readers, though they may appreciate seeing them in mainstream texts. Many black readers (and later movie viewers) appreciated *The Help* for the prominence it gave to the lives of women rarely pictured or celebrated in the dominant media. (Davis and Spencer expressed this view in defending the film to a critical Tavis Smiley.)

The voicing of resistance in the text comes through in two primary modes: *(1)* in conversations between the black characters, in which they express their ideas and feelings about the white people in their lives and the conditions of their work, and *(2)* in the frequent contrast between what a black character says to a white person and what she thinks to herself. The first mode comes early and often, as in Minny's recollection of how, when she began her first job as a maid at age fourteen, her mother sat her down to learn the seven "rules for working in a White Lady's house," including "Remember one thing: white people are not your friends" and "don't you *ever* let that White Lady find you sitting on her toilet," and the one Minny can never follow: "No sass-mouthing" (46). Mode number two can be seen when Celia Foote complains to Minny that she wishes she could take better care of her azalea bushes, which prompts within Minny sarcastic thoughts about Scarlett O'Hara, *Gone with the Wind*, and the organ of excrement:

A Deft commercial comes on and Miss Celia stares out the back window at the colored man raking up the leaves. She's got so many azalea bushes, her yard's going to look like *Gone with the Wind* come spring. I don't like azaleas and I sure didn't like that movie, the way they made slavery look like a big happy tea party. If I'd played Mammy, I'd of told Scarlett to stick those green draperies up her white little pooper. Make her own damn man-catching dress. (58–59)

While this passage is important for expressing Minny's conscious rejection of the mammy stereotype and her countermemory of the truth of slavery days, the narrative form also dramatizes the "black mask," how African American characters regularly think one thing and say another, hiding their thoughts from the whites around them. As readers we are drawn into this drama of double consciousness, invited into the space of black interiority to share and appreciate its true feelings and thoughts. Minny's sarcastic reference to Scarlett's "white little pooper" resonates with the novel's thematics of toilets and abjection, and it foreshadows the way she tricks Hilly Holbrook into ingesting the blackness she despises, which Minny has hidden in a pie. If we are white readers, the text's critique of whites may hold up an uncomfortably accurate mirror of us, but this negative view meets a contrary perspective in the passages of secret thought we are allowed to share. Affectively, we feel better as we occupy the space of deconstructive knowledge with Minny, our whiteness momentarily blacked out by an identification with her epistemological standpoint. The attachment we feel to that standpoint is strengthened, moreover, by our appreciation of her strength and sassy language, which entertains even as it critiques. Furthermore, the plot, carries forward this narrative lesson about listening empathetically to the Other into the story of Skeeter's moral awakening. When she explains her book project idea to Miss Stein on the phone, "showing the point of view of the help," she seems to have almost listened in on Minny's thoughts: "Everyone knows how we white people feel, the glorified Mammy figure who dedicates her whole life to a white family. Margaret Mitchell covered that. But no one ever asked Mammy how she felt about it" (123). Stockett has said much the same thing in recalling how no one in her family thought about how their "domestic," Demetrie, lived or what she thought of them and her situation (Evans).

It appears that Skeeter's character is meant to channel a politically correct liberal progressivism for the white audience, a position with which they can identify and thus feel good about. Her narrative, however, lacks the depiction of intellectual or moral growth typical of white antiracist sympathy novels such as *Huckleberry Finn* or *Gentleman's Agreement* or *To Kill a Mockingbird*. Unlike Huck, she doesn't go through a crisis of conscience, or give voice to substantive ethical or political reflections. She's naive, young, and a bit shallow. We see her reporting but not learning much. In trying to make the maids' stories the book's real focus, and not her story, Skeeter (or Stockett) empties her own individual drama of its complexity, at least on the surface, though as we will see, symptoms of her psychological struggles abound and are tied back to abjection, blackness, and the (m)other. The problem of regression is common to the tradition: Huck's decision to help Jim doesn't stop him, or Twain, from using the word *nigger* over two hundred times, reinscribing the ex-slave's abjection; Bea's affection and championing of Delilah's cooking skills doesn't stop her from exploiting her financially; Atticus admits from the start that he can't save Tom, nor does his tolerance of his queer tomboy daughter awaken a conscious critique of gender norms.

In the central plot of Stockett's novel, the comically transparent abjection of blackness is embodied in Hilly Holbrook's "Home Help Sanitation Initiative," a campaign to mandate that every white house have a separate toilet for "the help." Hilly also wants to get rid of her mother's maid, Minny, who is too strong and opinionated for her taste. Hilly sends her mother to a nursing home and gives Minny notice; she spreads false rumors that Minny has stolen from the Holbrooks, effectively blocking Minny from other jobs until she is hired by the marginalized and desperate Celia Foote, whose counternormative form of rural whiteness and sexual display is abjected by the middle-class matrons of Jackson. In revenge for Hilly's treatment, Minny prepares a pie into which she has baked her own feces. Far from a trivial act, Minny's culinary revenge evokes the many tales of plantation masters being sickened or poisoned by their enslaved African American cooks, and so reinforces the novel's comparison of 1960s domestic labor in the South to the system of antebellum slavery. Thus, this hilariously literal episode of making white people eat shit becomes the vehicle for a more serious exposure of the political economy of abjection, as the segregated and expelled blackness returns to its source. One could argue that Stockett's transference of the civil rights movement from the protest against segregated bussing (also led by domestic workers and referenced early in the novel in an aside about Rosa Parks) to the protest against segregated toilets is not a depoliticization of antiracism, but instead a psychologically astute defamiliarization of the economy of abjection so vital to the profitability of white supremacy. In having Skeeter abscond with and study a pamphlet on Jim Crow laws, Stockett bluntly makes the case that the toilet plot is an effective way of encapsulating a complex historical drama whose huge sociopolitical systematicity is hard to grasp without the aid of such an allegorical plot. The shame, humiliation, and mental and physical oppression imposed by the Sanitation Initiative makes the personal political. There remains, however, the disturbing implication that the sublimation of black abjection still plays out as a subject position only for white people, in this case Stockett's stand-in, Skeeter, who rides the success of the maids' stories to a profitable career in New York publishing, effectively telling her old sorority sisters that they can eat shit when it comes to her as well. Skeeter gets out of Jackson; indeed, the maids convince her she has no alternative. Perhaps sensitive to the implications of Skeeter's success, Stockett gives the final authorial role to Aibileen, narrator of the last chapter. Hilly contrives to get Aibileen fired in revenge for the shit pie and its inclusion in Skeeter's book. Aibileen had been secretly supplying the substance of Skeeter's home-care columns for the local newspaper, and now gets the job herself, though her authorship can't be revealed. "Maybe I ought to keep writing," she thinks, "not just for the paper, but something else, about all the people I know and the things I seen" (522). With these words Aibileen becomes the fictional inaugural figure of that renaissance of black women's writing that begins in the early 1960s and would include Toni Cade Bambara, Gayle Jones, Alice Walker, Toni Morrison, and many others. The abjection of black women is best countered, the text (and history) suggest, by the coming to voice of these women.

Why, beyond the obvious humor, does Stockett make the shit-eating pie so central to the book? Logically, it exactly reverses the segregation of bodies that the whites would mandate with their separate bathrooms. The white culture's abjection of the black body is reversed by a surreptitious act of incorporation—emphasis on corpora. Yet the reversal is also a revelation, commenting as it does on the white child's feeding at the black breast. The necessity of abjecting the mother, as theorized by psychoanalysis, becomes caught up in the white child's primal attachment to, and socially demanded rejection of, the black (m)other, usually figured as the mammy. In this relationship and its ambivalence is modeled white society's ambivalence toward the blackness it at once feeds upon and repudiates, keeps intimately close and yet segregates. Noble summarizes Kristeva as follows: "Abjected entities—such as wounds, pus, feces, corpses and the mother's body . . . represent the ecstatic promise of a recaptured sensation of a lost sense of continuity with one's mother and 'the all' that she represents" (306). Dependence and separation infuse this relationship to blackness with ambivalence; the requirement to abject the mother in order to establish a separate selfhood plays out redoubled with racial animus and desire in the white child's abjection of the black (m)other. Traditionally the mammy figure feeds the white child and white culture, literally and figuratively. White culture's abjection of the black body tries to deny this relation of dependency and this primal incorporation. Minny's perverse kitchen act reinscribes the reality of that dependency and the always already incorporated place of the black body within the white body and its political and psychological economies. Skeeter's own joke on Hilly—having the used toilets delivered to the Holbrooks' front lawn—is funny, but it also carries forward the logic of the text's treatment of abjection, racism, and whiteness. To borrow from Freud, this "return of the repressed" puts the shit back where it came from, in the white house.

The separation of mothers from children, as I have noted above, occupies a central part of sentimental literature's attack on slavery. For Stowe, the threat of little Harry's sale is what precipitates his mother Eliza's flight at the start, and her reunion with her mother Cassy brings the novel full circle in the end. The fundamental immorality of the slave institution gets argued through the mother-child plot, which circumvents political or scientific-racist rationales for slavery by cutting, literally, to the heart of the matter. Mother-daughter plots are also central to exposing the oppression of the maids in *The Help*, as one would expect of a modern sentimental novel whose black-white relations remain close to those characteristic of slavery. We are reminded more than once of how careers as domestic workers separate the black maids from their own children. More problematically, these women often express their sentimental affection for the white children that they raise, creating scenes many readers will find offensively similar to past mammy caricatures. Aibileen, contradicting stereotypical accounts of the mammy's undying love for her white charges, tells us that she regularly has to move on from a family once the child grows up, not wanting to stay around to watch their affection turn to oppression as the child learns the Jim Crow ways of abjecting blackness and identifies with the racism of its elders. Thus the emotion evoked by the separation of the domestic worker from the child is used to motivate the audience's moral alienation from the racist structure of the new plantation economy of domestic servitude. Presumably white readers will be affected by the loss these scenes dramatize, while black audiences may feel very differently as they share Aibileen's cold realism about the inevitability of white racism.

Two other major plotlines reinforce the connections of whiteness and racism to an ambivalent separation from (m)others: the mystery of the disappearance of Constantine, Skeeter's childhood maid, and the portrayal of Charlotte, Skeeter's mother. These episodes expose Skeeter's color-blind humanism. Constantine was separated from her own daughter, Lulabelle, when she was four. We are told Skeeter realizes that "Constantine's love for me began with missing her own child. Perhaps that's what made it so unique, so deep. It didn't matter that I was white. While she was wanting her own daughter back, I was longing for Mother not to be disappointed with me" (424). As her name obviously suggests, Constantine embodies the enduring love and commitment of the mammy/mother figure, as well as the bitter irony of how structural racism interrupts this constancy through alienation. Constantine was Skeeter's family's domestic worker, her nanny and maid, and questions about her disappearance during Skeeter's time away at college nag at her through much of the book. Skeeter's separation from this mother figure, it turns out, is doubled by the facts of Constantine's own story: we learn that she gave up her light-skinned daughter to an orphanage in Chicago (the tragic mulatto plot again), and later tried to get her back (see *Imitation of Life* for a similar plot). The involvement of Charlotte in Constantine's tragedy is revealed during the same narrative time in the novel as is the exposition of Mrs. Phelan's near-fatal illness, thus reinforcing the reader's attention to the loss of mothers and the alienation of daughters. Having read Aibileen's account of how Charlotte drove Constantine away, Skeeter confronts her mother and forces her to tell the story. When Lulabelle returned at age twenty-five, we now learn, she entered the Phelan house during Charlotte's meeting of the "DAR"—Daughters of the American Revolution. An angry exchange erupted as Charlotte ordered Lulabelle to leave by the back door and commanded Constantine to, again, break off relations with her daughter. "She hadn't seen her daughter in twenty years" replies Skeeter. "You can't . . . tell a person they can't see their child" (428). Skeeter, like Stowe, relies on an emotional and moral truth that is color-blind, while her mother Charlotte sticks to the racial rhetoric of difference: "They are not like regular *people*," replies Charlotte, echoing slave owners who discounted the pain felt when enslaved families were separated. The rhetoric of this episode intends to contrast Skeeter's color-blindness—"It didn't matter that I was white"—with Charlotte Phelan's insistence on racial difference. Unfortunately, color-blindness is an ideology that obfuscates white privilege and makes the rooting out of racial injustices more, rather than less, difficult, while at the same time providing the white subject with the affect of moral superiority. These thoughts by Skeeter are offensive because they lead to the denial of her own whiteness, a color-blind "humanism," which wipes out the fact of white economic exploitation of black workers. In this sentimental fantasy the black nannies and maids are transformed from laborers, caught in a carefully designed system of oppression, into mothers in a natural system of caretaking love. Skeeter seems to forget Aibileen's point, that the black maid doesn't just see her racial charges as colorless children, but instead can never forget their whiteness and their power over her future, which is why Aibileen must leave them. She is not their mother, but an other. What we must always be on the lookout for in reading the sentimental white race novel, from Stowe to Stockett, is this sublimation of political economy into the fantasy of a color-blind, domesticated humanism with its trappings of moral uplift. Stowe pioneered the strategy with her Christian version, a novel in which the temptation of color-blindness takes the form of casting her major mother-daughter characters as so light-skinned they could pass.

Why is Charlotte Phelan's illness entwined by Stockett with Skeeter's telling of Constantine's story, and this graphic detail: "The toilet water rushes through the house, filled with a little more of my mother's body," as Mrs. Phelan coughs up her insides (425). It seems more than a coincidence that this scene of the mother's imagined abjection involves a toilet. I would speculate that this episode expresses Skeeter's barely repressed aggression toward her mother, and offers more evidence that at the book's heart is Skeeter's need to separate herself from her mother's repressive power and the regime of whiteness for which she speaks—either to cough up what she has incorporated from her white mother or to witness that mother's death. Given the racial and historical dynamics of the scene, I would also interpret it as signifying the expression of Skeeter's anger against the white mother who has abandoned the white child by turning it over to the care of the black worker.

Skeeter does finally separate herself from her resuscitated mother (who is still dying of cancer) by taking the job at Harper and Row in New York, which she earns by ventriloquizing the voices of the black maids and mothers and identifying through sympathy with them. She thus restores her position as their figural daughter, and by rhetorically "blacking-up" achieves the abjection of the suffocatingly judgmental Mrs. Phelan. Throughout the novel Mrs. Phelan criticizes Skeeter for her failure to embody normative white femininity: she's too tall, too opinionated, too interested in a career, not interested in marriage, dresses unattractively, and has curly hair (as if to mark her genetically as a bit black and wooly headed). Skeeter thus feels driven to take up the ultimately nonnormative position of symbolic blackness as a dark fulfillment of her mother's fears, and in compliance with the fantasy that Constantine is her real mother. In the harshest interpretation, one could argue that the abjection of blackness is instrumentalized by Skeeter to enable white self-identity and a profitable future.

Yet the popularity of *The Help* suggests that it exercises a sentimental power to which we (many whites and a surprising number of African Americans) are still drawn, and find useful. As with Stowe, the manipulation of affect does open up possibilities for transgressing the boundaries set by institutional racism. The centrality of gender to such antiracist texts, moreover, leads to a profound ambivalence toward the norms of the dominant patriarchal culture and its reliance on a logic of abjection. White mothers are made to stand, like the DAR, for the national motherland and obligated to oversee the development of children into obedient players of racial performance. Black mothers can only support their families at the cost of caring for their own children and becoming affectively tied to the very white youth who will eventually be the next generation of their oppressors. These (m)other plots teach that whiteness is always already gendered, and that mothers and daughters, black and white, are psychologically and socially constructed to participate in a regime at once rewarding and alienating, redolent of natural emotions, and corrupted by capitalist practices. We may conclude that racial abjection is not separable, after all, from the abjection of gender, and that women caught in these twin plots would do well to find alliances that give expression to their joint entanglement.

Critical race theorist Sumi Cho writes that

> post-racialism in its current iteration is a twenty-first century ideology that reflects a belief that due to the significant progress that has been made, the state need not engage in race-based decision making or adopt race-based remedies, and that civil society should eschew race as a central organizing principle of social action. (1593)

Given that *The Help* retrospectively celebrates the revolt of the civil rights movement against Jim Crow, as practiced by government and public agencies as well as by private citizens, and gives voice to the stinging critiques of whiteness articulated by the maids, Stockett's book fits uneasily into the postracialist camp, at least insofar as we understand that its challenges to racism apply to our own moment and not simply to the past. Yet the book's recourse to a plot and rhetoric of sentimental education moves the emphasis emphatically from civil society to the personal realm and asks the white reader, via Skeeter, to *feel* right rather than *do* right. The color-blind humanism Skeeter articulates, insofar as it overlooks the real material conditions of black life and sentimentalizes the capital-labor oppression governing race relations, falls back into the temptations of a postracial rhetoric. An insistence that race or color "doesn't matter" is belied by the ongoing abjection of blackness. Qualifying this conservatism, however, is the plot's almost equally anguished treatment of gender oppression, white and black, and the uplifting fable of black and white women making an alliance against white patriarchy. This latter tale, and the affective interpersonal boundary-crossing it idealistically promotes, may be one of the main reasons for the popularity of the book and film, and perhaps enough reason to find their study of continued interest in explicating how race and gender persistently cross in cultural works concerned with whiteness and social justice.

Note

1. For such a critique of *The Help* see "An Open Statement" by the Association of Black Women Historians (Jones), the denunciation by bell hooks in "Help Wanted," and the essays collected in Garcia et al.

Works Cited

Baldwin, James. "Everybody's Protest Novel." *Notes of a Native Son*. Boston: Beacon P, 1955. 13–23. Print.

———. "On Being 'White' . . . and Other Lies." *Black on White: Black Writers on What It Means to Be White*. Ed. David Roediger. New York: Random House, 1998. 177–80. Print.

Baruch, Elaine, and Lucienne J. Serrano, eds. "Julia Kristeva." *Women Analyze Women in France, England, and the United States*. New York: New York UP, 1988. 129–48. Print.

Cho, Sumi. "Post-Racialism." *Iowa Law Review* 94 (2009): 1589–645. Print.

Coates, Ta-Nehisi. *Between the World and Me*. New York: Spiegel and Grau, 2015. Print.

Davis, Viola, and Octavia Spencer. Interview with Travis Smiley. *PBS*. 9 Feb. 2012. Web. 29 Jan. 2016.

Evans, Joni. "*The Help*: Today's *To Kill a Mockingbird*? With Author Kathryn Stockett." *Women on the Web*. 12 Apr. 2010. Web. 20 Aug. 2014.

Fishkin, Shelley Fisher. *Was Huck Black? Mark Twain and African-American Voices*. New York: Oxford UP, 1993. Print.

Garcia, Claire Oberon, Vershawn Ashanti Young, and Charise Pimental, eds. *From "Uncle Tom's Cabin" to "The Help": Critical Perspectives on White-Authored Narratives of Black Life*. New York: Palgrave Macmillan, 2014. Print.

Hendler, Glenn. "The Structure of Sentimental Experience." *Yale Journal of Criticism* 12.1 (1999): 145–53. Print.

Hobson, Laura. *Gentleman's Agreement*. 1947. Marietta, GA: Cherokee Publishing Co., 2007. Print.

hooks, bell. "Help Wanted: Re-imagining the Past." *Writing beyond Race: Living Theory and Practice*. New York: Routledge, 2013. 58–70. Print.

Hurst, Fannie. *Imitation of Life*. Ed. David Itzkovitz. 1933. Durham: Duke UP, 2004. Print.

Jay, Gregory. "Queer Children and Representative Men: Harper Lee, Racial Liberalism, and the Dilemma of *To Kill a Mockingbird*." *American Literary History* 27.3 (2015). 487–522. Print.

Jones, Ida E., et al. "An Open Letter to the Fans of *The Help*." Association of Black Women Historians. n.d. Web. 20 Aug. 2014.

Lee, Harper. *To Kill a Mockingbird*. 1960. New York: Grand Central P, 1988. Print.

Mann, Sally. *Hold Still: A Memoir with Photographs*. New York: Little Brown, 2015. Print.

McAfee, Noelle. *Julia Kristeva*. New York: Routledge, 2004. Print.

Melamed, Jodi. *Represent and Destroy: Rationalizing Violence in the New Racial Capitalism*. Minneapolis: U of Minnesota P, 2011. Print.

Morrison, Toni. *Playing in the Dark: Whiteness and the Literary Imagination*. New York: Random House, 1992. Print.

Noble, Marianne. "The Ecstasies of Sentimental Wounding in *Uncle Tom's Cabin*." *Yale Journal of Criticism* 10.2 (1997): 295–320. Print.

Scott, Darieck. *Extravagant Abjection: Blackness, Power, and Sexuality in the African American Literary Imagination*. New York: New York UP, 2010. Print.

Stockett, Kathryn. *The Help*. New York: Amy Einhorn Books, 2009. Print.

Stowe, Harriet Beecher. *Uncle Tom's Cabin*. 1852. Ed. Kenneth S. Lynn. Cambridge, MA: Belknap P, 1962. Print.

Tompkins, Jane P. *Sensational Designs: The Cultural Work of American Fiction, 1790–1860*. New York: Oxford UP, 1985. Print.

Twain, Mark. *The Adventures of Huckleberry Finn*. 1885. Mineola, NY: Dover P, 1994.

THE HELP AS NONCOMPLICIT IDENTIFICATION AND NOSTALGIC REVISION

Christine Farris

"So's we the same. Just a different color," say that little colored girl. The little white girl she agreed and they was friends. The End. Baby Girl just look at me. Law, that was a sorry story if I ever heard one. Wasn't even no plot to it. But Mae Mobley, she smile and say, "Tell it again."
                                                    —Kathryn Stockett, *The Help*

True reconciliation can occur only when we honestly acknowledge our painful, but shared, past.   —Elizabeth Eckford, of the Little Rock Nine

RHETORICIANS, ALONG WITH literary and cultural critics, have studied for some time the discourse of American civil rights struggles. Literary representations of disenfranchisement that perpetuate racial stereotypes and construct whites as heroic agents can be traced to Harriet Beecher Stowe's 1852 novel *Uncle Tom's Cabin*, which persuaded white audiences toward abolitionism as a matter of moral justice and cross-racial maternal sensibility. A reliance on faulty analogy between the disempowerment of free white women and blacks (Wiegman 194) and what Daniel Itzkovitz calls "a condescending kindness toward the black community" (viii) have characterized sentimental representations of race relations ever since. Following the election of the first African American U.S. president, the overwhelming success of Kathryn Stockett's 2009 novel *The Help* (along with the 2011 film version) raises questions about how the contemporary American public understands responsibility for segregation and the actions that began to turn things around. What does Kathryn Stockett's *The Help* encourage audiences to see as the individual and systemic barriers to civil rights? In its melodramatic focus on women's interracial relationships, with whom does it encourage audiences to identify? This chapter will examine how *The Help* extends and revises commonplaces that amount to a fantasy of interracial relationships, one already sentimentalized in Fannie Hurst's 1933 novel *Imitation of Life*, which was also adapted to film in 1934 and 1959. *The Help* is more than a melodrama or a story of condescending kindness. It is also a nostalgic revision of white complicity in actual historical racial events. *The Help* achieves in fiction a reconciliation attempted unsuccessfully in real life by the two Southern women—one black, one white—represented in the iconic photographs of the 1957 desegregation of Central High School in Little Rock, Arkansas. The story of Elizabeth Eckford and Hazel Bryan, which began with hateful, but soundless, words captured in an instant by the camera, sent around the world, and preserved as artifact, is also a Southern narrative of the civil rights era that begs and, ultimately, resists the forgiveness and historical revision sought by Kathryn Stockett.

Stockett's *The Help* tells the story of black domestic workers and their white employers in Jackson, Mississippi, between the years 1962 and 1964. While there are chapters written from the first-person perspective of two black characters, at the center of the novel is Eugenia Phelan, nicknamed Skeeter, a white graduate of Ole Miss, who returns home to Jackson to find that the beloved family maid Constantine has mysteriously left town. Eventually she finds Aibileen and Minny, who continue the work begun by Constantine: awakening the privileged Miss Skeeter to racial injustice and authorizing her career breakthrough, a tell-all book on the lived experiences of black maids.

Not surprisingly, as Martha Southgate points out, *The Help* is framed by a trope that American popular culture can't seem to outgrow: "that a white character is somehow crucial or even necessary to tell this particular tale of black liberation" (Southgate 38). In this case, it is a trope within a trope, in that idealistic Skeeter, not noble Aibileen or feisty Minny, secures the book contract with Harper and Row that will make the maids' anonymous stories public. We are led to believe that this intervention by a white woman of privilege would have been necessary in 1963 Jackson, where, in fact, black women were active politically and, like Anne Moody (*Coming of Age in Mississippi*), capable of telling their own stories.

While it presumes to be a narrative of collective action for social change, *The Help* is framed in such a way as to minimize the political tension of factual events. Stockett shoves off to the side the real-life murder in Jackson of black civil rights leader Medgar Evers, regional field secretary of the NAACP. In the first published edition of the novel, Stockett, a native of Jackson, mistakenly has Evers "bludgeoned" to death, rather than shot. A correction had to be made to subsequent editions. Despite historical evidence of repeated clashes between the local NAACP and the White Citizens Council, the characters who interact with the fictional Skeeter are presented as apolitical, if not comical. Aibileen and Minny make light of lunch-counter sit-ins, in which their fellow church members participate. Skeeter's beau Stuart and his senator father are good ol' boy alcoholics who go-along-to-get-along with real-life segregationist Governor Ross Barnett. It was Barnett who arrested and imprisoned the Freedom Riders in 1961 and, in defiance of a federal court order, opposed James Meredith's enrollment at University of Mississippi in 1962. Consistent with black male caricature, Aibileen's absent husband is a cheat. Minny's husband Leroy is both an emasculated wife-beater and a running gag.

What agency there is in *The Help* lies not so much with the men as with the women, who are fueled by their common resistance to the manipulative racist queen bee Hilly Holbrook, advocate of the Home Health Initiative for separate toilets. Eventually, the women become angry enough to "cross the line" and take action. Minny bakes feces into a chocolate pie of revenge. Skeeter has toilets moved from the dump to Hilly's front lawn. Hilly's villainy, however, functions as a buffer. While white readers and viewers feel for Aibileen and Minny, the "courageous" actions of Skeeter permit, in historical hindsight, a sense of noncomplicity in racist actions or systems that permit them, particularly if Hilly is what racism looks like. It is possible to identify with good scout Skeeter and generous Celia, whose identification with the black characters works metaphorically, "privileg[ing] commonalities more than differences" (Ratcliffe 67). Stockett presents their outsider status and attempts to cross gender and class lines as parallel to those of their long-suffering, loyal black employees, suggesting, in a tradition of American literature and film, a universality of struggle, if not a "transcendence of racism by compassionate individuals" (Berlant 99).

The Help is certainly not the first popular American work that attempts to bridge racial difference and transform institutions through melodrama and comedy about common unjust circumstances. Cultural theorist Lauren Berlant, writing on sentimental politics in Harriet Beecher Stowe's

Uncle Tom's Cabin and Edna Ferber's *Showboat*, points to a literary and cinematic tradition of white appropriation of the history and experience of suffering by nonwhites. "The culture industry," according to Berlant, "uses these events to publicize progress in the dismantling of antiblack racism . . . laminating the structure of romantic fantasy and its conventions of overcoming obstacles onto the history and posthistory of slavery" (99). Skeeter, who barely noticed when James Meredith integrated her alma mater Ole Miss, struggles after college to enter the male domain of journalism and publishing, defying expectations that she will find a man and settle down. As she tests her independence, Skeeter must suffer fools and their biases wherever she turns. The editor at the *Jackson Journal* deems her fit by virtue of her gender to take over the column on housekeeping hints. "I assume you know how to clean?" he asks, after remarking on her looks and dating potential. "Clean? I'm not here to clean. I'm here to *write*," she insists (Stockett 86).

The only one of her fellow sorority sisters to not yet marry and have children, Skeeter is forced by her conventional mother to conk her frizzy blonde hair, straightening it with chemicals before her blind date with the senator's son. Traumatized as ugly by her mother and childhood bullies, Skeeter had turned repeatedly to the woman by whom she claims she was raised, the maid Constantine, who assured her that she need not internalize the prejudice of others, nor let her female body stand in the way of options in life. "Ugly live up on the inside," Constantine said. "Ever morning until you dead in the ground . . . you gone have to ask yourself, Am I gone believe what them fools say bout me today?" (Stockett 73). At age thirteen, Skeeter "was just smart enough to realize she meant white people" (73–74). Constantine's wisdom comes from a life of racial oppression, but Skeeter takes comfort in the analogy.

With Constantine as a substitute mother who loves her for what she is, Skeeter is able to view herself as a substitute *daughter*, crossing racial lines, "something besides my mother's white child." "All my life," she says, "I'd been told what to believe about politics, coloreds, being a girl. But with Constantine's thumb pressed in my hand, I realized I actually had a choice in what I could believe" (Stockett 74). Even before she learns the truth about Constantine's actual mixed-race daughter, Lulabelle, who was banished to live in Chicago, Skeeter is positioned as the replacement. Skeeter is not, however, the perfect white child of Toni Morrison's *The Bluest Eye*, looked after by the black domestic servant Pauline and envied by her daughter Pecola. Both Skeeter and her younger version, Mae Mobley, Aibileen's "baby girl" in the home of Skeeter's best friend Elizabeth, are constructed as imperfect, victims themselves of prejudice, in need of compassion from those who have suffered greater adversity.

Another needy "outsider" in the melodrama is the blonde, curvaceous Celia Foote, who comes not from the better homes of Jackson but a shack in nearby Sugar Ditch. Celia has married Johnny, Hilly's former boyfriend. Though white, her efforts to integrate herself into Jackson's elite are unsuccessful. When she comes to call, she is made to stand humiliated on the front porch, while members of the bridge club she cannot join pretend she is not there. Her exclusion and naivete with regard to race and class boundaries make possible a unique relationship with her maid Minny—a bond of empowerment rooted in their having both been seriously misread and wronged by Hilly and her minions. Celia is not a Skeeter, the empathetic white liberal do-gooder who breaks the rules. She is rather another version of the *tabula rasa* innocent child (a la Shirley Temple in *The Little Colonel*) who, by virtue of her outsider status, somehow never learned the rules of Jim Crow, and, thus, can share lunch and miseries with her maid. Celia and Minny's relationship, a mutual rescue from bad cooking, indignity, and assault (domestic and yard invasion by a peeping Tom), is perhaps the novel's most sentimental and fantastical.

"The political tradition of sentimentality," according to Berlant, "ultimately equates the vernacular with the human: in its imaginary, crises of the heart and of the body's dignity produce events that can topple great nations and other patriarchal institutions if an effective and redemptive linkage can be constructed between the privileged and the socially abject" (40). In popular representations of collective pain and supposed transcendence of racism, however, stereotypes typically remain intact. The connection that the garish but lonely Celia finally makes with the sassy, no-nonsense Minny reinforces the sentimental notion that underneath, as Stockett's characters say, "we are all alike." In response, audiences may, as Berlant claims, identify against their own interests (40). Nevertheless, the bond established by a sentimental political text is as likely to justify the power structure in place as it is to "give form and language to impulses toward resistance" (41). Berlant points, for example, to the Rodgers and Hammerstein musical *The King and I*, which includes *Uncle Tom's Cabin* as a satirical play-within-a-play. The King of Siam is a slaveholder, polygamist, and tyrant, but one who is caught up in his destiny, vulnerable, and ultimately deserving of sympathy and compassion from the women around him, including the tutor Anna, and from the audience (Berlant 41).

Similarly, most readers, sympathetic to the relationship Celia is able to forge, don't question whether her wealthy and loving husband Johnny Foote (who promises a lifetime job for Minny's loyalty) belongs to the Jackson White Citizen's Council, or if he will, after all that's been exposed, be moved to take any political action against it. Though feared by both Celia and Minny for most of the novel, Johnny, according to Minny, is reading *To Kill a Mockingbird*, as is Skeeter. Are we to think that a seed is planted, similar to that of Stowe's novel in the court of Siam? It is far more likely that white privilege and the paternalistic power structure will be maintained.

Hazel Carby has analyzed the ways in which a nineteenth-century work like Harriet Beecher Stowe's *Uncle Tom's Cabin* and a contemporary film about cross-racial relationships like Lawrence Kasdan's *Grand Canyon*, both produced in response to a moment of perceived racial crises, "appeal to the hearts and minds of the privileged to intervene in the lives of those less fortunate than themselves" (237). "Acts of patronage are appealing," says Carby, "because 'the power of the patron is secured at the same moment that those subjected to patronage are confirmed in their powerlessness'" (237). According to Carby, as was the case with Stowe's novel, "fear of what will happen in the present as a consequence of the slavery of the past" can inspire a reconstruction of the past "in order to imagine an alternative national future . . . in which a paternalistic racial formation can be maintained" (238).

One might say that not all narratives of race relations need to argue for the social reorganization of power or take as their subject the high drama of big-history in the style of Lee Daniels's film *The Butler*, based on the life of Eugene Allen, White House domestic worker for thirty-four years. However, in its characterization of the ordinary citizens of Jackson, *The Help* is a revision of a historical moment for an anxious contemporary Obama-era audience. *The Help*'s reframing of history and its comfortable scenarios of personal interracial relationships depend on the binaries and safe caricatures of melodrama that run deep in popular American culture and secure the identity and position of the white characters. *The Help*'s use of distorted images and inattention to historical accuracy moved the Association of Black Women Historians to issue an open statement to fans that concluded:

> In the end, *The Help* is not a story about the millions of hardworking and dignified black women who labored in white homes to support their families and communities. Rather it is the coming-of-age-story of a white protagonist, who uses myths about the lives of black women to make sense of her own. ("Open Statement to the Fans of *The Help*")

Skeeter's open-mindedness that contrasts with the evil racism of "mean girl" Hilly can be traced, not to her overbearing mother Charlotte, but to Constantine, the "wise mammy" family maid, invested in her success. Similarly, we are led to believe, Skeeter's doppelgänger, Mae Mobley, will rise above the racism and timid conformity of her mother, thanks to the loving guidance of Aibileen, who, like Constantine, has lost her actual child.

The needless death of Aibileen's son, Treelore, whose original idea it was to write a book about working conditions, "planted a seed" of racial bitterness in his mother that becomes, in the hands of Skeeter, a collaboration to document the maids' experiences. Potentially, Skeeter's and Aibileen's book project could have opened up what Krista Ratcliffe would call a space of nonidentification, in which parties, positioned differently in terms of history, race, and power, might work toward understanding how differently they have experienced some of the same things (73). Skeeter interviews the maids that Aibileen recruits and listens to stories that finally *do not* confirm her expectations of loving cross-racial relationships between the help and the white families they work for. Then, from new understanding and identifications, presumably might have come action in the white as well as the black community. But those lived experiences of the maids—filled with more abuse than affection—are not really the center of the novel or the film. Rather, *The Help*—including the story within the story—is framed and driven by Skeeter's nostalgia for her "mammy," her efforts to unravel the mystery of Constantine, and her hope to confirm, despite complications, the truth of her own recollections, which hinge on her unconscious identification with black women who replace her own demanding mother. In a series of cross-identifications, Skeeter's coming-of-age remains intertwined with the unconditional love of the loyal mammy and the mammy's identification with her white employer, for whom the mammy feels—true to the myth—genuine affection and the need to sacrifice.

The mission that becomes the book project is finally Skeeter's white version—simultaneously a nostalgic tribute to Constantine and an appropriation of all the maids' work. In this regard, both Kathryn Stockett and her protagonist Skeeter come uncomfortably close to fitting Micki McElya's characterization of Southern white women as the keepers of an imaginary pre–Civil War history. McElya found, in her research in the archives of the United Daughters of the Confederacy, that members felt their white memories of slavery constituted a "specialized racial knowledge" (64) that authorized performances in blackface and dialect and support in 1923 for the erection of a national monument in Washington, D.C., to commemorate the affection between white children and their mammies and "defen[d] a Southern utopia" (Horwitz). The idea for the mammy monument and the senate bill that supported it died under pressure from the black community and from activists, including W. E. B. Du Bois.

Apparently haunted by the death of her real childhood maid Demetrie when she was sixteen, Kathryn Stockett grew up in the 1970s, not the 1950s or the 1960s, much less the 1860s. Nevertheless, she "takes her stand" in Dixie. Such noncomplicit identifications and distractions from accountability for history are nothing new in American popular culture. *The Help* is, in many ways, a nostalgic revision of Fannie Hurst's 1933 melodrama *Imitation of Life*, in which a white woman struggles to achieve economic success and fame while living with a black housekeeper who raises the neglected daughter, provides the commodity they turn to profit, and remains a faithful servant, even after they earn enough money to go their separate ways. Just as *The Help* traces Skeeter's coming into her own, Hurst's novel and director John Stahl's 1934 film adaptation, starring Claudette Colbert and Louise Beavers, represent the rising career of Bea Pullman, who opens a successful waffle franchise from the recipe, labor, and trademark face of her maid, Delilah. In the 1959 film version, director Douglas Sirk turns Bea from a tycoon into actress Lora Meredith, played by Lana Turner. Lora is subjected not to the glass ceiling of the male-dominated business world but to the humiliation of the casting couch and the trials of fulfilling her dreams on the Broadway stage and in Hollywood.

Like *The Help*, all three versions of *Imitation of Life* present a momentary place of identification and possibility in which hierarchies could be renegotiated: two single mothers—one white, one black—share a domestic space and work side by side. As her empire expands, however, Bea grows more alienated—not only from what she produces, but from Delilah, her daughter Jessie, and her own physical needs. Bea (Lora in the later version) postpones maternal and romantic intimacies to concentrate on work. Bea is incognizant of how her economic freedom has come off the back of faithful Delilah, who begs to stay on in servitude. In the parallel, but more tragic, strain of the melodrama, smiling Delilah, domestic icon to millions who have consumed her "brand," grows ill from a cancerous tumor she has neglected, but dies from a broken heart when her light-skinned daughter Peola renounces her to pass for white. Peola eventually marries a former unsuspecting loyal customer of Delilah's and leaves with him for Bolivia.

Only in the 1959 Douglas Sirk version are the dots connected and the white protagonist Lora's unconsciousness of her white privilege made explicit.

The Peola character, renamed Sarah Jane, parodies in dialect a subservient maid when Miss Lora asks her to help her mother serve at a Hollywood party. In perhaps the film's most memorable scene, the dying maid, named Annie in this version, plans her funeral, as did Delilah in the earlier versions, to be attended by hundreds from her church and the various lodges to which she belongs. Lora tells Annie she didn't know she had this separate life and so many friends. "Miss Lora," Annie replies, "you never asked."

In this respect, *The Help* could be regarded as a somewhat more progressive revision of *Imitation of Life*. Miss Skeeter, the writer, in fact, *does* "ask"; she even builds partial awareness of white privilege into her pitch to the New York editor, Miss Stein. Ironically, while the maids are privy to the details of their employers' lives, she tells Miss Stein, the white employers know nothing of theirs. But, finally, what we learn of the maids' lives is that which intersects with Skeeter and her friends, meaning their work for white people. Skeeter's awareness of her white privilege is subsumed into her angst over her break-up with Stuart, who learns of Skeeter's involvement with the antiracist project in much the same way Sarah Jane's white boyfriend in *Imitation of Life* learns she is "passing."

At the urging of her editor, Skeeter also contributes a chapter on her relationship with the family maid Constantine, but not the revelation that Constantine had been forced to give up her biracial daughter Lulabelle for adoption or that her own mother Charlotte had fired Constantine after a racist confrontation with the now-grown militant Lulabelle, on her return to Jackson. In the novel, Lulabelle dares to pass for white at a meeting of Charlotte's chapter of the DAR, when she comes looking for her mother. In the film version, Constantine's daughter, "Rachel," merely tries to enter by the front door the house in which her mother has worked for decades. In only a slightly new take on the mammy and tragic mulatto tropes of *Imitation of Life*, the fired Constantine and Lulabelle are reunited, but banished once again to Chicago, where Constantine soon dies.

Not having sacrificed her true story as the maids had done, Skeeter, identifying with Lulabelle, as Constantine's "real" daughter, like the biracial daughters in *Imitation of Life*, must suffer. She is losing her mother Charlotte to cancer. Her mother's eventual death will break much of Skeeter's connection to the Southern traditions she has revised and protected in the book that launches her career and her emancipation from Jackson, Mississippi—where the maids must go on living with the consequences. Skeeter's omission of her mother's racism and complicity in Constantine's misery from her contribution to the book signifies what is most troubling about *The*

Help—the seamless unity with which the novel and the film minimize racial difference, conflict, and accountability. The faithful servants have sacrificed their stories, risked their jobs and safety. Skeeter and the maids now identify as one, endorsed and celebrated by the black church members. After having been falsely accused of stealing by Hilly and fired by Elizabeth, Aibileen now thinks she is more free than Hilly. When the past can be pleasantly rewritten and rectified, it would appear that all is forgiven and no action need be taken.

The pressure for racial redemption and forgiveness functions not only in popular fiction and film but also in the stories of real life civil rights events such as the Little Rock, Arkansas, school desegregation on September 4, 1957. Captured in an iconic newspaper photograph taken by Will Counts, fifteen-year-old African American Elizabeth Eckford, one of a group of students referred to as the Little Rock Nine, attempts to enter Central High School while a fifteen-year-old white student, Hazel Bryan, part of an angry mob, screams racial epithets at her back. As David Margolick recounts in his book *Elizabeth and Hazel: Two Women of Little Rock*, the eminent civil rights activist Daisy Bates had assembled the other students at her home to walk together, escorted by clergymen. The Eckford family did not have a telephone, so Bates was unable to inform Elizabeth of the plan; thus, she walked alone (Margolick 32). Elizabeth's way was blocked by the National Guard, protestors, and the press. Some in the crowd spit on her and yelled "Go home, nigger. Go back to Africa" (37). The harassment did not end for Elizabeth with her admission to Central High; it was, according to Margolick, only the beginning.

Forever framed in that photograph, both Elizabeth and Hazel have spent much of their lives in a cycle of blame, apology, and reconciliation. Six years later, in 1963, the year in which *The Help* is set, Hazel Bryan called Elizabeth Eckford on the telephone, confessed that she was the girl in the picture, and apologized. Elizabeth accepted her apology, but it gave her little comfort. Traumatized by the event and the daily torment in the high school years that followed, Elizabeth lived for years with depression. She served in the military, raised two boys alone, and took a job as a probation officer after years of unemployment and disability. Hazel Bryan worked for a number of years counseling black teenage mothers, according to her husband, to atone for what she did. She was active in the peace movement. However, she said, the press "want to keep me where I am in that picture" (Margolick 194).

As the fortieth anniversary of the Little Rock school desegregation approached, with plans for a speech by President Clinton, Hazel was eager to make a public apology and to be forgiven. "There's more to me than that one moment," she said (Margolick 193). In 1997, the original photographer Will Counts, a retired photojournalism professor at Indiana University, staged that reconciliation between Elizabeth and Hazel. Counts's new photograph of the two in front of their former school was made into a poster with the caption "Reconciliation" and sold in the Central High School Museum. In a second printing of the poster, Elizabeth insisted it include a sticker with a disclaimer: "True reconciliation can occur only when we honestly acknowledge our painful, but shared, past" (Margolick 262).

After the anniversary, Elizabeth and Hazel became friends for a time, profiting from appearances and lecture tours, but now, despite many shared interests, they do not speak. Falling out of the frame of the happy ending for Little Rock, Elizabeth and Hazel grew to mistrust one another. Preserved in a photograph recirculated around the world, reproduced in newspapers, documentaries, textbooks, and archived at Indiana University, Hazel has faced criticism from other white Central High students for both her original actions and her apology as the representative of a racism they choose to minimize or disclaim. Many felt that she did not or does not speak for them.

Hazel embodies the hatred of Jim Crow that she feels needs to be let go, but Elizabeth refuses to fulfill that dream for her. According to Margolick, despite, or maybe because of, getting to know her, Elizabeth thinks Hazel's story is inconsistent, that perhaps she did not act spontaneously on that day. She wants Hazel to own up to more of her racist past, including the influence of her parents' bigotry (Margolick 232–33). For Elizabeth, there is always more work to do in recognizing the differences in their experiences. While a photograph may not fully represent a historical moment, it offers evidence that something happened that demands more than metaphorical attention and commodification. Perhaps Elizabeth Eckford equates reconciliation with oversimplification of a history too complicated for simple identifications and easy apologies, with actions that are complex and irreparable.

Works Cited

Berlant, Lauren. *The Female Complaint: The Unfinished Business of Sentimentality in American Culture*. Durham: Duke UP, 2008. Print.

The Butler. Dir. Lee Daniels. Perf. David Oyelowo, Forest Whitaker, Oprah Winfrey. Weinstein, 2013. Film.

Carby, Hazel V. "Encoding White Resentment: Grand Canyon—A Narrative for Our Times." *Race, Identity, and Representation in Education*. Ed. Cameron McCarthy and Warren Crichlow. New York: Routledge, 1993. 236–47. Print.

The Help. Dir. Tate Taylor. Perf. Viola Davis, Octavia Spencer, and Emma Stone. Touchstone, 2011. Film.

Horwitz, Tony. "The Mammy Washington Almost Had." *Atlantic*. The Atlantic Monthly Group, 31 May 2013. Web. 23 Feb. 2014.

Hurst, Fannie. *Imitation of Life*. 1933. Ed. Daniel Itzkovitz. Durham: Duke UP, 2004. Print.

Itzkovitz, Daniel. "Introduction." *Imitation of Life*. By Fannie Hurst. Durham: Duke UP. 2004. vi–xlv. Print.

The Little Colonel. Dir. David Butler. Perf. Lionel Barrymore, Bill Robinson, and Shirley Temple. Fox, 1935. Film.

Margolick, David. *Elizabeth and Hazel: Two Women of Little Rock*. New Haven: Yale UP, 2011. Print.

McElya, Micki. *Clinging to Mammy: The Faithful Slave in Twentieth-Century America*. Cambridge: Harvard UP, 2007. Print.

Moody, Anne. *Coming of Age in Mississippi*. New York: Doubleday, 1968. Print.

Morrison, Toni. *The Bluest Eye*. 1970. New York: Vintage, 2007. Print.

"An Open Statement to the Fans of *The Help*." *Association of Black Women Historians*. ABWH, 17 Jan. 2012. Web. 6 Jan. 2016.

Ratcliffe, Krista. *Rhetorical Listening: Identification, Gender, Whiteness*. Carbondale: Southern Illinois UP, 2005. Print.

Southgate, Martha. "The Truth about the Civil Rights Era." *Entertainment Weekly*. 12 Aug. 2011, 38. Print.

Stockett, Kathryn. *The Help*. New York: Berkley, 2009. Print.

Wiegman, Robyn. *American Anatomies: Theorizing Race and Gender*. Durham: Duke UP, 1995. Print.

MUST(N'T) SEE TV:
HIDDEN WHITENESS IN REPRESENTATIONS
OF WOMEN OF COLOR

Anita M. DeRouen and M. Shane Grant

> From what political perspective do we dream, look, create, and take
> action?   —bell hooks, *Black Looks: Race and Representation*

OVER THE PAST several years, television dramas featuring women of color
(WOC) in leading or narratively central roles have been on the rise. The
USA cable network gave us Gina Torres in the legal thriller *Suits* (2010),
ABC brought us the divine Kerri Washington as a Washington, D.C., fixer
in ABC's *Scandal* (2012), CBS chimed in when they cast Lucy Liu as the
Watson figure in *Elementary* (2012), and NBC hopped on the bandwagon
with their short-lived crime drama *Deception* (2013), starring Meagan Goode
(who then reappeared in the fall of 2015 on Fox in the television adaptation
of the film *Minority Report*). Additionally, in 2013, Fox placed Nicole Beharie
as a detective opposite a recently revived Ichabod Crane in the supernatural
cop drama *Sleepy Hollow*, while the fall 2014 season brought us the highly an-
ticipated Viola Davis vehicle *How to Get Away with Murder* (ABC). It would
appear that the second decade of the twenty-first century is a much better
time to be a WOC in mainstream media than it has in previous decades.

In *Shaded Lives: African-American Women and Television*, Beretta E.
Smith-Shomade examines the representation of black women in mainstream
television from 1980 to 2001. As she traces the historical representation of

WOC early in the book, she says of Christie Love (Teresa Graves), the lead character in the 1974 dramatic series *Get Christie Love!*, "She provided nothing new. Her character did, however, provide a modicum of empowerment to those who rarely saw physically strong and attractive Black women in visual culture" (15). Thirty-eight years passed before a network took on another drama featuring a black female lead. Smith-Shomade's work traces the representation of black women in situation comedy, the music industry, and the newsroom, but is necessarily silent on the issue of the drama given the lack of material on which to comment. Her work underscores, though, the need for continued attention to representations of black women in mainstream media as a means of "deconstruct[ing], or at least decenter[ing], systems of power" (187). She calls for "vigilance, control of vision, direction, and distribution" as the means for black women to "begin to consistently resist, reposition, or possibly even escape objectification and assume sustained and affirming agency" (187).

Given the abundance of female characters of color in dramatic series today, we might think that Smith-Shomade's 2002 desires have been met. On the surface it appears that WOC no longer find themselves relegated to the drama's background, playing domestics, secretaries, or guest-starring in episodes that feature them only for a single episode or brief story arc. It would seem that WOC are finally finding their own space in mainstream television representation. Deeper analysis, however, reveals that these characters continue to serve the needs of normative whiteness.

To make this examination, we limit our focus to the shows *Suits* and *Scandal*. We selected these two series for their similar circumstances—the stories of two black female attorneys at the helm of powerful institutions who must frequently use their power to protect whiteness from itself and others—and for their divergent circumstances—the foregrounding of an interracial relationship in one, a white coded heteronormative marriage in the other. The distinctly different races and genders of their respective creators—one (Aaron Korsh—*Suits*) naively unaware of his property's narrative implications in the discourse on whiteness, the other (Shonda Rhimes—*Scandal*) acutely so—also make these shows ideal partners for analysis. Doing so provides the opportunity to interrogate WOC as envisioned by both a white male producer (Korsh) and a black female producer (Rhimes). Unlike Shonda Rhimes's placement of Olivia Pope (Kerry Washington) at the very center of the show's narrative, Aaron Korsh does not anchor his narrative around his prominent black female character, Jessica Pearson (Gina Torres). Our intent here is to display how, even though at the center of the narrative, Olivia Pope still becomes marginalized in the service of whiteness in her own story, much in the same way Jessica Pearson lacks centrality in the narrative that centers on the law firm she owns and runs.

This comparison allows us to argue that the characters we examine serve the interests of white men as well as the further deployment of systemic whiteness instead of challenging or revealing the power and privilege whiteness confers. Our exploration reveals how these characters pay what bell hooks calls the "price" for "[assimilation] into the dominant culture" by their "[collusion] in supporting the thinking and practice of white supremacy" (*Writing* 24). Jessica and Olivia provide evidence of an openness to new images and voices on the part of media creators. However, their narrative contexts actually deploy each to strengthen whiteness and the hegemonic power structures frequently seen as oppressive to marginalized communities.

We begin with a grounding in the individual shows' narratives. Next, we interrogate the personal lives of the two WOC featured in these shows and how their personal relationships enact either the dream of multiracial harmony or the horror of interracial sexual reproduction. We argue that both instances, whether implicit as in the case of Jessica Pearson or explicit as that for Olivia Pope, come at the cost of personal fulfillment. We also reveal how the characters' professional worlds echo their loss of narrative centrality. Finally, we discuss their creators' subject positions as establishing their ability to engage or not in transformative dialogue around whiteness. Ultimately, we see these characters embracing hegemonic normativity as opposed to fighting either systemic racism or white privilege, or both.

Aaron Korsh's *Suits* follows the personal and professional lives of a group of lawyers at the top-tier New York City law firm of Pearson Hardman, run by WOC Jessica Pearson. The show's premise focuses on her boy Friday, Harvey Specter (Gabriel Macht), and his new hire/mentee Mike Ross (Patrick J. Bateman). The primary source of the show's early conflicts results from Mike's hiring because he never attended law school or took the state bar exam. In the pilot episode, Mike, who has agreed to complete a marijuana drop for his drug-dealing roommate, finds himself in the hotel in which Harvey conducts interviews. Thinking he is being followed by an undercover officer, Mike ducks into the room where other applicants wait for their interview. Playing along, Mike aces the interview and finds himself working as an attorney under Harvey's guidance, who knows of and hides Mike's lack of credentials ("Pilot").

Scandal, produced by Shonda Rhimes, follows Olivia Pope and her team of "gladiators in suits" as they help the wealthy and powerful hide or minimize the scandals in which they find themselves. The show's primary tension exists between Olivia and the current Republican president, Fitzgerald Grant (Tony Goldwyn), with whom she began an affair while serving on his election team. In part to extricate herself from the affair, Olivia declines a place on the president's staff, instead creating her own firm. However, many of her clients serve as either federal employees or elected officials, so Olivia finds herself continually redrawn to Fitz—the subject of her own personal scandal.

In order to help illuminate how these two WOC become defined as white, we look to a combination of queer and whiteness theories so that we may expose how the employment of normative sexual narratives can be used to negate the racial otherness of central roles embodied by WOC. Although both Jessica and Olivia clearly identify as heterosexual, Michael Warner points out that the term "queer" need not apply only to individuals with same-sex desires. In his seminal text *The Trouble with Normal: Sex, Politics, and the Ethics of Queer Life* (1999), Warner claims that a queer outlook is one in which individuals find themselves at odds with the rigid sexual mandates of straight culture—the notion that sex and sexual desire should lead to acts committed only by married people of the opposite sex in a dark room utilizing the missionary position with the intent of producing a child (37–38).

Questions of heterosexual queerness remain a rich field of study. In her 2012 book *Rereading Heterosexuality: Feminism, Queer Theory, and Contemporary Fiction*, Rachel Carroll continues the heterosexual queer tradition. As part of her framework she employs the notion that "heterosexuality as an institution continues to have immense normative power; while this power impacts most explicitly on non-heterosexual identities it also extends to heterosexual identities which do not conform to familial, marital or reproductive norms—norms which have a particular impact on female identities" (1). These notions of heterosexual queerness imply that any character at odds with heterosexual ideals bears the potential for queer readings. For example, a heterosexual character who engages in sex with three different characters, one of whom is married, can be read as queer due to their failure to abide by the strict, and therefore easily broken, heterosexual ideal.

Warner's notion that we can queerly read heterosexuality ties in with whiteness theory when coupled with the work of Richard Dyer, who discusses the issue of whiteness and sexuality in his groundbreaking work *White* (1997). Early in his first chapter, Dyer rather accurately notes that whiteness, and therefore the privilege and power it conveys, is mutable, stating,

A shifting border and internal hierarchies of whiteness suggest that the category of whiteness is unclear and unstable . . . the sense of a border that might be crossed and a hierarchy that might be climbed has produced a dynamic that has enthralled people who have had any chance of participating in it. (19–20)

This notion of a whiteness hierarchy implies that one white person can be more white than another white person. Presumably, the more white you are the more power and privilege you have to enact and deploy. To help solidify this claim, Dyer makes use of the different ways in which Jewish people and the Irish have been seen as sometimes "purely" white and at others linked visually to primates—most often chimpanzees and apes—during different times and places during the nineteenth century (52–57).[1] Something similar can be said for queerness and the heterosexual ideal. A person who has sex outside of marriage but only in the dark with a partner of the opposite sex could be conceived of as less queer (or more normative) than a person who has sex with a person of the opposite sex on the floor in the kitchen with the lights on and vice versa depending on the specific discursive narratives regarding sex and deviance at any given time and place. This hierarchy of queerness/heteronormativity mirrors Dyer's hierarchy of whiteness in a way that allows us to analyze the romantic and sexual lives of Jessica Pearson and Olivia Pope—the ways in which they maintain, are denied, or employ white privilege and power. To summarize, the more heteronormative their sexual behavior and desires, the more they conform to normative ideals; the more they conform to normative ideals, the more potential they have to ascend within the whiteness hierarchy.

In her 2004 book *The Twilight of Equality*, Lisa Duggan discusses the relationship between the heteronormative ideal and neoliberal economic politics. Duggan claims that staying in line with normative rules helps to achieve a neoliberal economy "in ways supportive of upward redistribution of a range of resources, and tolerant of widening inequalities of many kinds" (ix). In short, these characters' engagements with heteronormativity place them in a position to succeed professionally at the expense or oppression of others. In a similar vein, Jane Ward examines the function of white normativity in LGBT organizations that actively seek to be and to be seen as racially diverse communities in her 2012 article "White Normativity: The Cultural Dimensions of Whiteness in a Racially Diverse LGBT Organization." Ward contends that "white hegemony in the broader culture 'trickles down' into organizations, producing whiteness as the standard by which 'normal' people, ideas, and practices are often measured, even within racially diverse organizations" ("White Normativity" 564). This insertion of "external norms produce[s] rewards for organizations that have white normative cultures and, conversely, produce[s] constraints for those organizations that attempt to operate outside of a cultural framework that is familiar to whites" ("White Normativity" 565). As power brokers working within such organizations, both Olivia and Jessica are subjected to the normalizing function of whiteness, tying whiteness to their success and their ability to appease the external demands of the hegemonic culture's attitudes on sexuality. Furthermore, in her book *Not Gay: Sex between Straight White Men* (2015), Jane Ward goes on to say, "Whiteness continues to function—even in an allegedly 'postracial' era—as a stand-in for normal sexuality" (21). For both characters, creating or maintaining a heteronormative, and therefore whiter, public image affords them professional opportunities that embrace a neoliberal political economy. Being successful black women who appear as sexually normative as possible to the other characters on the show allows them to participate and benefit from the very systems that support the upward redistribution of resources and widening inequalities Duggan identifies.

Whether in their personal or professional lives, Jessica and Olivia operate from the sphere of whiteness, their racial identities textually invisible until the point where they can no longer be treated as such. At these moments they are thrown into a narrative crisis that requires they uphold whiteness even to the denial of their own identity. That they are in positions of power that might upend the hegemonic structures of their TV narrative to the betterment of the marginalized populations they represent never seems to be at issue. Instead, the plight of the marginalized seems all but hidden in the weekly challenges faced by their clients. In *Suits*, WOC characters rarely speak from their racial identity position, while in *Scandal* even those characters who do speak from the margins continue to advance whiteness agendas. For example, Olivia Pope's extremely powerful father, Eli (Joe Morton), repeatedly speaks from the margin, exposing whiteness. In this way, we might see him as a character speaking marginalized truth to normative power. He speaks about the need for Olivia to remember her raced self, reminding the audience, too, of the disparities faced by marginalized people trying to engage with the American meritocracy. However, Eli is known by the codename "Control," the powerful commander of a shadow security organization B316. In this role, he completes illegal security operations in the interest of preserving the political status quo. No matter how much Eli remains aware of that dominant structure, his life's work is wrapped up in protecting it, the duty to protect the "white" nation trumping any obligation to uphold its most sacred values—actual equality for all ("It's Handled"; "A Door").

While these women have, in a sense, free reign in the working world, their power is nonetheless undermined by and reinforced through their dealings with heterosexual/heteronormative culture as well as a racialized culture. To the extent that they have been able to adopt and negotiate whiteness, they have achieved success. To maintain that success they must continue to capitulate to the necessity and power of whiteness in their dealings. For example, in the last half of the second season in *Suits*, Jessica's firm becomes so vulnerable that it must fight a losing battle against being bought out by another firm. This forces Jessica to wait, like a princess in a fairy tale, for a white Prince Charming to rescue her from the sinister (and most likely perverted) clutches of the villain. This threat of "losing it all" appears once again midway through season five when a former partner in the firm works to wiggle his way back in by attempting to oust Jessica. In the case of Olivia Pope, capitulating to whiteness means increasingly erasing parts of her own African American life story to support Fitzgerald Grant's presidency. Each woman is placed (by herself or others) into what Erica Chito Childs calls "a new color-blind and multiracial packaging" where "whiteness is protected and privileged, while maintaining that racism is a thing of the past" (187). These programs end up reinforcing white supremacist power structures while devising a sterile role for black women in the power structure. If faced with this claim, Jessica and Olivia would likely respond quite differently. Early in season one, Olivia tells Fitz that she refuses to play Sally Hemmings to his Thomas Jefferson; she clearly sees at least some of the narrative problems within their relationship and would probably stew privately about her concerns over an expensive glass of red wine ("Happy Birthday"). Unlike Olivia, Jessica likely would adamantly, vocally, and loudly insist that the broader racial implications of her actions and story line are of no import: her wealth and much more importantly her power are what matter, despite how tenuous her power may be since it comes so frequently under threat.

In her 2002 article, "Intimate Publics: Race, Property, and Personhood," Robyn Wiegman draws a distinction between a multiracial and interracial vision for our future that proves useful in a discussion about how Olivia and Jessica both experience and promote white supremacy in their personal lives. Wiegman examines actual and fictional cases of a sterile multiracial family construction to argue that reproductive technologies allow for the formation of multiracial family and kinship without the need for actual interracial sex. In this way, technology through surrogacy protects and upholds hegemonic structures and "white masculine power" by making it possible for a white male to lay claim to a multiracial child without actually having to engage in the physical act of production. This notion of a clean-and-progressive paternity is most readily seen in *Suits'* primary family unit, the "marriage" of Jessica Pearson and Harvey Specter and the "birth/adoption" of their "child," Mike Ross. Mike serves as the character with whom the audience is supposed to identify. He is introduced to the audience as a hustler; his connection to the firm removes him from this life with its implied racialized connections. Harvey and Jessica's "adoption" of Mike provides the nurturing family stability that he needs to successfully enact his new fully white identity, to save him from a life of street hustle.

Jessica's discovery of Mike's illegitimacy brings the growing "marriage" with Harvey into narrative focus; until the end of the first season, Jessica is a benign narrative presence. Harvey is her closer, they have a sort of mentor-mentee relationship, and she protects her firm, but not to the extent that she'll condone unethical or harmful behavior. Jessica ultimately agrees to cover for Mike as Harvey claims he will prove an asset as they fight against the return of a formerly ousted partner ("She Knows"). The characters enter the second season, then, as a surrogate family, bound together by the knowledge of Mike's illegitimacy and the need to maintain control of the firm in order to keep the secret safe.

Jessica's lack of any consistent romantic or sexual partners, as well as her remaining childless, reinforces the notion that she and Harvey are engaged in a relationship akin to an interracial marriage. In order to fully cement their heteronormativity as a coded couple, and the power it confirms upon them, they require offspring—the physical embodiment of a legacy who can act to ensure their success beyond retirement/death. Upon learning about Mike's illegitimacy as an actual lawyer, Jessica's decision to keep Mike's secret and retain him as an employee creates a pseudo family unit. Harvey and Jessica serve as Mike's "parents" and he as their wunderkind, a notion Jessica herself introduces when she tells Harvey that Mike is "a total package. Maybe even the best of both of [them]" ("She Knows").

In addition, throughout the battle for control of the firm in the second and third seasons, characters use the language of courtship, marriage, and divorce as they examine and deal with the repercussions of the engagements Jessica alternately fights off, considers, and accepts. In all of this maneuvering, protecting Mike—their dirty family secret—keeps Jessica tethered to Harvey as much as her reliance on his whiteness does. She can't maintain control of the firm without him, and the price of his allegiance is her acceptance of Mike as their "child." Coding Harvey and Jessica as parents of Mike allows them to shore up/protect whiteness from the threat Mike presents to white hegemony and power as enacted and embodied by both Harvey and Jessica. The multiracial but nonsexual couple/parents are able to act as such without having to "dirty" whiteness or its power through the "filthy" notion of interracial sex acts. In remaining chaste with each other they enact a white purity by not "dirtying" themselves physically, both through the sex act itself and the further "dirtiness" of sex between a white man and a WOC.

While the coded heteronormative family in *Suits* supports a depoliticized multiracial ideal, the romantic relationship between Olivia Pope and Fitzgerald Grant on *Scandal* creates the potential for an interracial horror of the sort Robyn Wiegman calls "founding U.S. culture on the actual act of interracial generative (hetero)sex" (862). If Harvey and Jessica enter into a sexless marriage to protect their power, their legacy, and their surrogate offspring, enacting a sort of socially palatable if ethically unpleasant multiracial future, the specter of an actual offspring from Olivia and Fitz's affair in *Scandal* evokes Wiegman's image of a horrific interraciality.

Olivia and Fitz's relationship becomes monstrous as the show progresses, suggesting that Weigman's reading of the "horror" of interracial sex in the context of U.S. culture extends to the present day and evokes the argument posed by Julian B. Carter in his 2007 book, *The Heart of Whiteness.* Carter discusses the discursive conflation of whiteness and white heteronormative marriage ideals from 1880 to 1940 to craft a picture of "normal" that has political and cultural implications. Through the public crafting of a marriage ideal grounded in white heteronormativity, such a marriage "became the privileged site for the literal and metaphorical reproduction of white civilization" (loc 153); Carter goes on to suggest that "normal Americans, by definition, were whites who used their respectably reproductive sexuality for the betterment of race and nation" (loc 261). The romance at the center of *Scandal*, then, has the potential to upset not just one household but the polis itself, and by press time, the viewing audience has witnessed the horror imagined by both Weigman and Carter. The relationship has caused the dissolution of the First Family, hazarded the impeachment of the president and the exposure of his use of his office to serve Olivia's needs, and the assumed abortion of the illegitimate offspring of this interracial union. Throughout the impeachment investigations in particular, the marriage of the president becomes understood as a vital component of national security; to overcome this obstacle and protect both president and nation, Olivia reinstates the shadowy power—her father and his secret organization—that she has long sought to contain.

Given the connection between the personal and political that Weigman and Carter posit, it is not surprising that these women's personal lives merge with their professional worlds. Olivia and Jessica are most successful at deploying their whiteness during these mergers when they become erased or sidelined within their own narratives by minimalizing their sexuality. In the *Suits* season-two episode "All In," Jessica is surprised by the appearance of a former classmate, Ella Fullman nee Madieros (Rachel Crawford), now the judge assigned to a thorny fraud case involving Harvey. Fullman has denied what should be an automatically granted motion, and when Jessica confronts her about this denial, Fullman indicates that there are more personal matters at play. Later, in a conversation with Harvey, Jessica confesses the nature of Ella's grudge:

JESSICA: There was a prank.

HARVEY: How bad was it?

JESSICA: We went to law school together and I got her drunk.

HARVEY: So?

JESSICA: So she woke up in front of the entire Con Law class—

HARVEY: That's recoverable.

JESSICA: She might have been naked.

HARVEY: Might have been?

JESSICA: Was.

HARVEY: We're screwed.

JESSICA: Come on, Harvey. She was uptight. I just straightened her out. That's what you do with uptight people. ("All In")

This scene reveals the lengths to which Jessica will go to maintain her position of power: not only does she knowingly subject a woman of color to ridicule, she does so by getting her drunk and literally exposing her naked body to her professor and classmates, an act of sexual violence that she laughs off with Harvey as·a "prank." Their conversation also reveals that she has done the same to Louis Litt (Rick Hoffman), a junior partner in her firm, and that she has allowed Harvey to take the fall for that particular prank, in an effort to, for all three parties, "straighten them out" because they're "too uptight."

We find it curious that her desire is to "straighten them out"—as opposed to "loosening them up"—as the phrase suggests their uptight path is one too crooked to help them achieve success. In this way, we might see Jessica as a figure poised to stabilize patriarchal norms, her actions making her the alpha male in her sphere. This "straightening" is achieved through the performance of sexual violence on characters explicitly and implicitly feminized—and, in one case, the performance itself is attributed to Harvey, the character whose white masculinity Jessica relies upon for the continued success of the firm. This suggests that their uptightness is the transgression, one that must be punished in such a manner as to expose their vulnerability. And, as Ward claims in *Not Gay*, sexualized forms of hazing are almost always deployed in part to increase the bond between individuals in white systems or organizations (151–52). As the scene continues and Jessica and Harvey swap their respective tales of "pranks" against their lesser, the viewer is encouraged to see this bit of bonding as evidence of Jessica's power and ease in a white, masculine environment.

Instead of becoming masculine, Olivia constantly erases herself from her own romantic narrative. In a meeting with Fitz and his wife Mellie (Bellamy Young) the three actively and consciously reconstruct the narrative of Olivia and Fitz's affair to present to the press. This negotiation ultimately marginalizes Olivia's significance to Fitz. When Olivia endorses Fitz's suggestion that he simply tell the truth, Mellie objects:

MELLIE: If you try to tell that disgusting [true] fairy tale to the press, I will make such a scene. . . .

OLIVIA: How many times?

MELLIE: What?

OLIVIA: How many times did Fitz and I sleep together? Three? Five? How many would you be okay with?

MELLIE: Two.   ("It's Handled")

Following Olivia's capitulation to Mellie's wishes, Mellie continues to lay out the specific and largely fictitious details about their actual affair. Mellie's narrative for the press, and the world, effectively erases Olivia's significance by negating Fitz's love for her. By framing and agreeing to work within the boundaries of this plan, Olivia complies with her own erasure, securing her access to Fitz's power and position by agreeing to do what it takes to keep him in the White House. This narrative action is repeated in the show's most recent arc, with Olivia's race deftly negated in the season-five episodes

"Dog-Whistle Politics" and "You Got Served." Using the frame of the news exposé, the show plays out the ramifications of the public knowledge of Fitz and Olivia's affair; Olivia's life is put under the media microscope, and the viewer witnesses the racialization of her background. A reporter notes that her father wanted "to raise an African American girl who felt as fully entitled to own the world as any white man" and suggests that she "[felt] so entitled to the brass ring of power that she simply took it instead of earning it" ("Dog-Whistle Politics"). Olivia overcomes this narrative construction by eliding the racialized aspects of her identity and appearing on live television to appeal to the painful power of love, suggesting that while she wishes she had never met the president, thereby removing herself as the cause of much personal and national pain, she has met him and can do nothing to undo what is done. ("You Got Served"). By this point, race is no longer an issue in the narrative arc, and Olivia is installed in the White House as the presumptive heir to the role of First Lady, a role quickly cast by the show as a marginalizing step down for a woman of her talents.

Finally, we must engage and identify the function of personal subjectivity on the part of the creators of these two shows, not to engage in a simplistic search for authorial intention but, rather, to acknowledge the subject positions these two producers occupy as vital to our understanding of the products they create. It is of consequence that Aaron Korsh is a white male, a graduate of the Wharton School of Business who spent five years as an investment banker before leaving that realm to pursue a newfound passion for television writing and production (Robbins). Mike Ross, the main character in *Suits*, is a stand-in for Korsh who says "he didn't work hard but got away with it because he was smart" (Robbins). While Korsh aligns himself with Mike's "fraudulent" behavior in the series, he does not appear to do so with any awareness of Mike's successful ruse as possible because of his whiteness. When asked about the implausibility of the premise—that Mike is able to step in almost seamlessly to the highly educated community of Harvard-trained lawyers at the firm—he says, "It's a legitimate critique," but "you have to make the buy. And if you want to, you will" (Robbins).

Viewers have made the buy. *Suits* recently premiered its sixth season, remaining a solid performer for the USA network for several years. The central narrative tension still surrounds Mike's lack of an appropriate professional genealogy, and the issue of his race—or, rather, the invisibility that it confers upon him to continue the ruse—is as absent from the show's explicit narrative as it was in the pilot episode.[2] To the oppositional viewer, the show is naive in its commentary on Mike's unearned position, Korsh's production blissfully unaware of how it capitalizes on white normativity to make the central tension plausible. Mike can put on a suit in the pilot episode to make a drug run, hide out in a hotel room full of potential law associates, and talk himself right into a job for which he is not legally credentialed. His white body in a suit marks him as a member of a class to which he does not belong, literally opening the door for his success.

In this way we can see Korsh's work as operating in the white normative space. In her article "Becoming a Writerly Self: College Writers Engaging Black Feminist Essays," Juanita Rodgers Comfort examines the ways student writers can become more sensitive to their subject positions through the examination of personal writings by black women, enabling them to establish a "rhetorical identity"—a "presence invested in the text, developed by the writer to accomplish particular persuasive effects in the minds of readers" (556). Comfort also notes that "the advantage vested in whiteness lies in its ability to mask its own power and privilege—to render them normative, even invisible, in the minds of most whites" (549). While Comfort's work on writerly identity deals with the student essayist, she rehearses a familiar understanding of the role of the rhetor in the communication triangle, his or her need to establish ethos for audience buy-in a key component to the successful receipt of his or her message. In this way, we can consider Korsh's seemingly unreflective consideration of the product of his creation as complicit in furthering the normative whiteness that he appears to have neither engaged nor questioned.

Shonda Rhimes, on the other hand, is constantly confronted with her blackness. In an October 2014 interview with Lacey Rose of the *Hollywood Reporter*, Rhimes expresses her frustration with the media's constant attention to this aspect of her identity, stating that she "find[s] race and gender to be terribly important . . . to who [she is]. But there's something about the need for everybody else to spend time talking about it . . . that pisses [her] off" (Rose). While the frustration with the constant pointing is evident, she is well aware of the role of her race and gender in shaping her worldview and informing her approach to writing. Of Rhimes's work with her mentor Debra Martin Chase, an African American producer, Rose writes, "The pair . . . shared a strong desire to expand [the media] marketplace to include a more multicultural world that wasn't being represented." Rhimes is, therefore, in a different position with regard to her subjectivity than Korsh (at least as represented through their public personas); she operates in the more transformative and transgressive space imagined by bell hooks:

For those of us who dare to desire differently, who seek to look away from the conventional ways of seeing blackness and ourselves, the issue of race and representation is not just a question of critiquing the status quo. It is also about transforming the image, creating alternatives, asking ourselves questions about what types of images subvert, pose critical alternatives, and transform our worldviews and move us away from dualistic thinking about good and bad. Making a space for the transgressive image, the outlaw rebel vision, is essential to any effort to create a context for transformation. (*Black Looks* 4)

While Olivia continues to uphold whiteness structures, it is clear that Rhimes is more willing and able to draw the audience's attention to her blackness as an identity category. In "Dog-Whistle Politics," Rhimes foregrounds the typical narrative constructions of black womanhood as the press investigates Olivia; the character is framed as a Jezebel figure, a potential Sapphire, and a golddigger. When the reporter narrating the televised exposé that frames the episode asks, "Is Olivia Pope still seeking to gain her father's dream?" the viewing audience is expected to understand that nothing could be further from the truth for a character who has consistently struggled to escape her father's expectations. Rhimes's work challenges viewers both to grapple with the status quo and to long for a change, if for no other reason than to release the narrative's protagonist from the agony of her troubled relationship.[3]

We can see Rhimes, too, as connected to the lineage of what Veronica T. Watson calls the literature of white estrangement. In her 2013 book, *The Souls of White Folk: African American Writers Theorize Whiteness*, Watson argues that there is a long and rich tradition of African American writers using literary texts focused on white life to interrogate the functions of whiteness through a black person's lens. These novels, often marginalized within the tradition of African American literature, "represent Whiteness as a positionality, or perspective, which refuses to acknowledge its own narrowness, its alarmingly consistent history of oppression, its contradictions and failures" (5). Watson's work to recuperate and connect a string of marginalized texts helps us to see the work that Shonda Rhimes has done with *Scandal* as part of continuing this lineage through the use of popular drama, her story a serial narrative through which such a critique of whiteness plays out before its vast audience on a weekly basis. As do the novels in Watson's study, Rhimes's work in *Scandal* "makes visible the unseen, unspoken, and unevaluated nature of Whiteness." Like the authors Watson examines, Rhimes "challenge[s] the myths and mythologies of Whiteness and the meanings that are ascribed to it within American society . . . by forcing readers to confront the regressive, destructive, and often uncivilized 'nature' of Whiteness as it is constructed in their worlds" (5).

It is this distinct difference in subjective worldview that we find most appealing as we examine these two television narratives. Korsh's *Suits*, a product of unexamined whiteness, and Rhimes's more critically aware *Scandal* provide a productive space in which to tease out the ways in which our popular narratives can present strong WOC while still operating within unproductive alignments with white normativity. What we discover in the end is that it is not enough to engage in mere representation of WOC in mainstream narratives; instead, social transformation can only come about if we, the audience, are provided both the knowledge of and the tools to dismantle white hegemony. As the two shows continue to develop their storylines, we see no evidence of any further awareness on the part of Korsh's *Suits*; the characters remain unrelentingly oblivious to their collusion in the maintenance of normative whiteness. Rhimes's *Scandal*, however, has begun to open outward to a more critical focus. By 2014, episodes reveal Olivia's burgeoning crisis of conscience as she becomes increasingly aware of the structural oppression that she has worked to uphold. This development encourages us to more readily see Rhimes's text as representative of the literature of white estrangement. We hope for a continuation of this trend.

Notes

1. Historian Nell Irvin Painter recounts the history of the assignment of white identity to various groups in the United States in her 2012 work, *The History of White People*; after identifying four distinct "enlargements of whiteness" in U.S. culture, she concludes that "the fundamental black/white binary endures, even though the category of whiteness—or we might say more precisely, a category of nonblackness—effectively expands" (396).

2. It is worth noting that, as of press time, Mike has been arrested for fraud. However, the specifics of the charge have not been revealed. The episode in which this occurred was the midseason finale, and new episodes have not yet aired. It is possible that Mike's secret is about to be revealed. It is equally possible that this is an outsider's legal maneuver to displace Jessica or Harvey so that control of the firm might be wrestled from them.

3. While *Scandal* may not bring us to a character seeking to empower the masses, Rhimes's subsequent show, *How to Get Away with Murder*, dramatizes a woman of color educating a sexually, racially, and gender-diverse group while working as a defense attorney whose cases typically serve to protect individuals from marginalized groups.

Works Cited

"All In." *Suits: Season Two*. Writ. Karla Nappi. Dir. John Scott. Universal Studios, 2013. DVD.

Carroll, Rachel. *Rereading Heterosexuality: Feminism, Queer Theory, and Contemporary Fiction*. Edinburgh: Edinburgh UP, 2012. Print.

Carter, Julian B. *The Heart of Whiteness: Normal Sexuality and Race in America, 1880–1940*. Durham, NC: Duke UP, 2007. Kindle file.

Childs, Erica Chito. *Fade to Black and White: Interracial Images in Popular Culture*. Lanham, MD: Rowman and Littlefield, 2009. Print.

Comfort, Juanita Rodgers. "Becoming a Writerly Self: College Writers Engaging Black Feminist Essays." *College Composition and Communication* 51.4 (2000): 540–59. JSTOR. Web. 2 Nov. 2014.

"Dog-Whistle Politics." *Scandal Season 5*. Writ. Mark Fish. Dir. Zetna Fuentes. ABC Studios, 2015. Web.

"A Door Marked Exit." *Scandal Season 3*. Writ. Zahir McGhee. Dir. Tom Verica. ABC Studios, 2013. Web.

Duggan, Lisa. *The Twilight of Equality: Neoliberalism, Cultural Politics, and the Attack on Democracy*. Boston: Beacon P, 2004. Print.

Dyer, Richard. *White: Essays on Race and Culture*. London: Routledge, 1997. Print.

"Grant: For the People." *Scandal: The Complete First Season*. Writ. Shonda Rhimes. Dir. Roxann Dawson. ABC Studios, 2012. DVD.

"Happy Birthday, Mr. President." *Scandal: The Complete Second Season*. Writ. Shonda Rhimes. Dir. Oliver Bokelberg. Buena Vista Home Entertainment, 2013. DVD.

hooks, bell. *Black Looks: Race and Representation*. Boston: South End P, 1992. Print.

———. *Writing beyond Race: Living Theory and Practice*. New York: Routledge, 2012. Kindle file.

"It's Handled." *Scandal Season 3*. Writ. Shonda Rhimes. Dir. Tom Verica. ABC Studios, 2013. Web.

"Pilot." *Suits: Season One*. Writ. Aaron Korsh. Dir. Kevin Bray. Universal Studios, 2012. DVD.

Robbins, Stephanie. "Ignoring His Gut '*Suits*' Korsh Well." *NewBay Media*. n.p. 18 Feb. 2013. Web. 2 Nov. 2014.

Rose, Lacey. "Shonda Rhimes Opens Up about 'Angry Black Woman' Flap, Messy *Grey's Anatomy* Chapter and the *Scandal* Impact." *Hollywood Reporter*. 8 Oct. 2014. Web. 2 Nov. 2014.

"She Knows." *Suits: Season Two*. Writ. Aaron Korsh. Dir. Michael Smith. Universal Studios, 2013. DVD.

Smith-Shomade, Beretta. *Shaded Lives: African-American Women and Television*. New Brunswick, NJ: Rutgers UP, 2002. Kindle file.

"War." *Suits: Season Two*. Writ. Aaron Korsh. Dir. John Scott. Universal Studios, 2013. DVD.

Ward, Jane. *Not Gay: Sex between Straight White Men*. New York: New York UP, 2015. Print.

———. "White Normativity: The Cultural Dimensions of Whiteness in a Racially Diverse LGBT Organization." *Sociological Perspectives* 51.3 (Aug. 2008): 563–86. Print.

Warner, Michael. *The Trouble with Normal: Sex, Politics, and the Ethics of Queer Life*. New Haven, CT: Harvard UP, 1999. Print.

Watson, Veronica T. *The Souls of White Folk: African-American Writers Theorize Whiteness*. Jackson: UP of Mississippi, 2013. Kindle file.

Wiegman, Robyn. "Intimate Publics: Race, Property, and Personhood." *American Literature* 74.4 (2006): 859–85. Print.

"You Got Served." *Scandal Season 5*. Writ. Zahir McGhee. Dir. Kevin Bray. ABC Studios, 2015. Web.

COLOR-BLIND RHETORIC IN OBAMA'S 2008 "RACE SPEECH": THE APPEAL TO WHITENESS AND THE DISCIPLINING OF RACIAL RHETORICAL STUDIES

Kristi McDuffie

ALTHOUGH PRESIDENT BARACK Obama is the first black[1] President of the United States, he is considerably mum on issues of race. As authors such as Tim Wise and Eduardo Bonilla-Silva note, Obama seems to tread lightly with race-related issues in order to avoid being seen as controversial and threatening (Wise 36–62; Bonilla-Silva 255–300). Consider, for example, Obama's veiled response to the shooting of Trayvon Martin, a highly racialized event in the public discourse in 2012: "If I had a son, he would look like Trayvon" (qtd. in Stein). This response, while eliciting considerable media attention, is still more subtle than an earlier comment in 2009, when Obama called white police officers "stupid" for arresting Henry Louis Gates Jr. for breaking into his own home (Graham). Obama received considerable criticism for that comment and ultimately invited both Gates and the arresting officer for beers at the White House in an attempt to make amends (Feller). The Gates moment remains one of Obama's few overtly racial comments, even in an environment where his every comment and action are considered in light of his race.

For example, after the police shooting of unarmed Michael Brown in Ferguson, Missouri, in August 2014, which underwent federal investigation for potential police misconduct, President Obama's tempered remarks came under criticism from both conservative and liberal African American and white audiences. In explaining why Obama said so little in response to the shooting of Michael Brown and ensuing riots, writer Jamelle Bouie posits that Obama has learned that minor comments, such as the "stupid" comment to the Gates episode mentioned earlier, significantly hurts his approval ratings with white voters. Five years later, despite being known for raceless rhetorical strategies in academic and some intellectual circles (Bonilla-Silva 255–300; Wise 36–62), Obama is nonetheless "thoroughly racialized. There's nothing he can say on race that won't lead to rancor, fractured on racial lines" (Bouie). In order to not make things worse, as Obama winds down the remainder of his presidential term, it appears that "he avoids the subject" of race as much as possible (Bouie).

Obama's racial rhetorics during his two presidential terms demonstrate that avoiding racial topics is necessary for him to stay in favor with white voters; in fact, appealing to white voters through rhetorics of color blindness was necessary for Obama to gain favor with enough white voters to win the presidency in the first place. In contrast, African American politicians who confront racial inequalities explicitly and often, such as Al Sharpton and Jesse Jackson, reach a glass ceiling related to political office (Bonilla-Silva 223). There is one particular moment in Obama's presidential campaign, however, that is memorialized as the most overtly racialized event of his candidacy and ensuing presidency: his "A More Perfect Union" speech in 2008, given to diffuse public outrage about comments made by Obama's pastor, Reverend Jeremiah Wright. The speech was hailed as successful for dispelling indignation about Reverend Wright's racialized and so-called unpatriotic rhetoric, and subsequent rhetorical analyses have investigated reasons why the speech was rhetorically effective.

Despite race and whiteness studies work highlighting Obama's colorblind race rhetorics in the writings of Eduardo Bonilla-Silva, David Frank and Mark Lawrence McPhail, and Tim Wise, rhetorical studies have not significantly integrated these critiques into their investigations of Obama's race rhetorics, perhaps because, as I argue in this chapter, rhetoric scholars have come to equate any direct confrontation with race as evidence of progress on race relations in the United States, even though I find that the speech appeals to white privilege through color-blind rhetorical strategies. Ostensibly for this same reason, or simply because researchers were interested in different aspects of his work, numerous rhetoric scholars who analyze Obama's rhetorical prowess, from David A. Frank to Robert E. Terrill, do not incorporate critical whiteness studies scholarship into their examinations. In this chapter, I reread the speech through a whiteness studies framework and, specifically, in light of color-blind rhetorical strategies that appeal to white supremacy and white privilege, in order to demonstrate that Obama's most racialized rhetorics are actually steeped in whiteness logics. I argue that by not considering the speech's compliance in color blindness and white hegemony, the existing rhetorical scholarship on this speech remains complicit in such ideologies and the racial status quo that both the speech and the resulting analyses claim to disrupt. I find that the pattern of rhetorical studies on Obama's 2008 "race speech" suggests that rhetorical studies has been emotionally disciplined (Worsham) to reproduce neoliberal and color-blind ideologies because those ideologies were deemed successful by a mainstream audience. Instead of reproducing those values, rhetorical analyses should incorporate critical whiteness scholarship in order to intervene in the ramifications of whiteness in U.S. political and scholarly discourses.

In this way, this chapter extends examinations of whiteness studies in rhetoric and composition, such as those by AnaLouise Keating; Tammie Kennedy, Joyce Middleton, and Krista Ratcliffe; Matthew Jackson; and Wendy Ryden and Ian Marshall, into political discourses and problematizes the lack of attention to whiteness studies in rhetorical scholarship about Obama's racial rhetorics in general and about his "A More Perfect Union" speech in particular. Rhetoricians and other interested parties studying Obama's racial rhetorics, from journalists to pundits to everyday citizens, should consider the effects of neoliberalism and color-blind racial rhetorics in speeches such as these in order to avoid participating in the maintenance of white supremacy and white privilege.

The Rhetorical Situation of the 2008 Speech

Barack Obama, a U.S. senator from Illinois, was running for the Democratic Party nomination for president in 2007 and 2008. In March 2008, the ABC show *Good Morning America* released several excerpts from 2001 and 2003 sermons from Obama's pastor, Reverend Jeremiah Wright from the Trinity United Church of Christ in Chicago. The media and public were outraged at remarks that they perceived to be inflammatory, racist, anti-Christian, and anti-American (Frank 168). Statements condemning the United States for its treatment of blacks, along with those implicating the United States in the 9/11 attacks because of its "terrorism" against other countries, were repeated as sound bites at large in the news (Ross). Obama was implicated by his association with Wright and tried to distance himself from these attacks through public statements, but the media frenzy continued. This moment was pivotal in Obama's presidential campaign, as a black candidate in need of white voter support, so in a larger, more concentrated response, Obama gave a speech in Philadelphia later in March titled "A More Perfect Union" (an allusion to the preamble to the Constitution). Aside from several conservative critics, most audiences, including the same media outlets that were playing the sound bites, responded positively to the speech (Frank 168). For example, a *New York Times* editorial called the speech a "Profile in Courage" and lauded Obama for his show of character in the way he handled the controversy ("Mr. Obama's"). Soon after this speech, Obama became the front-runner of the Democratic candidates and ultimately won the presidency in November. While there are numerous reasons for Obama's party nomination, there is no doubt about the positive role that this speech played in his candidacy (Rowland and Jones 144), and I find that it is because of Obama's appeals to whiteness within the speech that made it so effective for mainstream audiences.

Responses to the Speech in Rhetorical Scholarship

Several rhetoricians studying political rhetoric have provided positive explanations for the rhetorical effectiveness of Obama's "A More Perfect Union" speech, explanations that often value Obama's neoliberalism and color-blind ideologies at the expense of erasing and minimizing forthright discussions of racial realities and inequities. David A. Frank analyzes the speech as displaying a prophetic tradition mimicking Martin Luther King Jr.'s rhetoric, a tradition based on reference to Bible stories, to African origins of Christianity, and to a pairing of anger and hope (172–73). Frank notes the difficult challenge that Obama faced in addressing Wright's accusations: "Obama's burden was to place America's sins and promise into relationship, to put black anger and white anxiety into perspective, to offer himself as an embodiment of the country's contradictions, and to narrate a story of hope his audience could adopt better to fulfill a prophetic commitment to others" (Frank 178–79). Frank finds Obama's claim that white racism is not endemic to be unsupported by scholarship (179), but finds Obama's discussion of racial injustice emerging out of the "American republic and its laws" (Frank 182) and legalized discrimination to be progressive (183). Frank also finds Obama's legitimization of white anger and claims of reverse racism to be a unifying tactic and ultimately calls the speech "a masterpiece with small flaws" (190).

Robert E. Terrill analyzes Obama's speech in light of W. E. B. Du Bois's concept of double consciousness, finding that Obama embodies double consciousness and encourages Americans to also do so as a productive means of discussing race. As Terrill argues, Obama's double consciousness emerges out of his own racial background, while his audience's double consciousness can happen by considering each other's grievances—by whites considering African Americans' anger and African Americans considering whites' feelings on reverse discrimination. Ultimately, Terrill finds the speech and Obama's rhetorical eloquence as holding possibilities for contemporary public discourse (363–86). Terrill, like the other scholars I describe, thus values Obama's rhetorical success without accounting for the negative ramifications of appealing to whiteness through color blindness as I will demonstrate in my own reading of the "A More Perfect Union" speech later in the chapter. Although each of these individual readings certainly has merit, together, they demonstrate a pattern of not considering the ways in which Obama's racial rhetorics in this speech contribute to the maintenance of white supremacy and white privilege.

Robert Rowland and John M. Jones similarly explore why there was "almost universal praise" for Obama's speech (126). Rowland and Jones claim that Obama was successful because he "contextualized the problem of race in a sacred religious narrative" and, more importantly, connected that narrative to the most powerful narrative of the American Dream (127), which is linked to classic American liberalism (132). Rowland and Jones write that Obama claims both that race problems persist because all Americans do not have access to the Dream and also that race problems can be solved by making the Dream universally available. Rowland and Jones find that Obama did not "paper over racial conflict or the racial injustice that remained a major problem in the United States" (134) but rather united people under a universal appeal to the American Dream (147). In a separate article, Paul Lynch also finds Obama's unification strategies to be the reason for the speech's success, although Lynch explains Obama as unifying blacks and whites through a rhetoric of friendship (1–7).

Next, Judy L. Isaksen discusses the movement of Obama's campaign tactics from making race (and arguably racialized whiteness) invisible earlier in the campaign to critically engaging race during the March 2008 race speech. Before that speech, Obama's tactics erased and disavowed race (457). Isaksen explains Obama's behavior with black polarity theory and critical race theory. Black polarity theory details two polar stereotypes for black males: the bad black man and the good black man. Isaksen sees Obama's initial reluctance to address race as a negotiation of these polarities because Obama wants to be seen as good and nonthreatening and avoid the angry black man stereotype. Critical race theory (CRT) is comprised of legal scholars who "view the law and its legal rhetoric as complicitous in sustaining both White normativity and White supremacy" and "work to expose the ways in which the law is an interested, ideologically driven force that sustains asymmetric power relations" (463). Obama engaged in CRT because he "did not point an accusatory finger at the citizens of America as the responsible agents, but at our government and the legal system" (464). Isaksen also tracks Obama's associations with CRT through his work on the *Harvard Law Review*, his professor Derrick Bell (a well-known CRT theorist), and the courses he taught at the University of Chicago. While Isaksen incorporates CRT into her analysis of Obama's racial rhetorics, she, too, is not critical enough in deconstructing Obama's appeals to whiteness through his color-blind and neoliberal rhetorical strategies. Isaksen cites Obama's credentials with CRT and explains how Obama acknowledges systemic racism in his "A More Perfect Union" speech but that he does so in a way that allows white listeners to maintain postracial mentalities as well as white privilege. Specifically, Obama mentions discriminatory institutional practices to legitimize white resentment, not in order to point out persistent racial inequalities between whites and people of color. Furthermore, Obama's legal background and associations with critical race theory, and ostensibly critical whiteness studies, outside of this speech are not evidence of ethical or progressive rhetoric on race and whiteness.

Most recently, in 2012, Susanna Dilliplane finds the speech to be significant because of the rhetorical challenges of the situation, the rhetorical strategies Obama used to address those challenges, and how those rhetorical strategies fit into his campaign as a whole. The primary rhetorical challenges Obama faced were his need to reject Wright's statements without rejecting Wright's symbolism to the black community (129) and his need to convey a black perspective without only representing black interests (130). Obama invoked unification themes in order to meet those challenges, and those themes were evident in Obama's campaign overall.

In contrast to these positive analyses of Obama's racial rhetorics, there are some more critical articles that evaluate Obama's race rhetorics in other situations. In an article on an earlier speech, the 2004 Democratic National Convention speech that introduced Senator Barack Obama to the nation, Mark Lawrence McPhail engages in a dialogue with David Frank. Frank gives a complimentary reading of the speech as demonstrating a rhetorical approach of consilience that can bring reconciliation. McPhail, on the other hand, found the speech problematic in its "racelessness" with a message that ignores and obscures America's racial history and current racial realities (Frank and McPhail 572–73). Further, McPhail notes that Obama invokes the "resources of whiteness and its dominant rhetorical tropes: innocence, race neutrality, and positive self-presentation" (583) and actually "eliminates any need for Americans to address the symbolic and social pathologies of white privilege and power" (573). Despite McPhail's explanation of Obama's appeal to whiteness, however, McPhail's critiques do not seem to inform subsequent work on Obama's race rhetorics.

Color Blindness and Whiteness

Taken as a whole, this sampling of scholars analyzing "A More Perfect Union" shows considerable attention to the "effectiveness" of the speech given the positive public response to it and Obama's subsequent political wins. Most of the scholars described above also find Obama's engagement with race to be progressive. However, none of the rhetoricians question these measures of success or the way this speech appeals to whiteness through color-blind and neoliberal rhetorical strategies, which would be considerably different if they included goals of critical whiteness studies. Critical whiteness studies include efforts to destabilize, deconstruct, and redress whiteness by "examining what it means to be white, how whiteness becomes established legally, how certain groups moved in and out of the white race, 'passing,' the phenomenon of white power and white supremacy, and the group of privileges that come with membership in the dominant race" (Delgado and Stefancic 83). This chapter rereads this speech with those goals in mind, analyzing how Obama utilizes rhetorical strategies of color blindness in order to keep white voters assured of their power and privilege.

Bonilla-Silva is a sociologist who investigates why whites do not think race has any substantial effect on people's lives in contemporary U.S. society, despite the significant economic disparities that continue between whites, blacks, and other people of color. Compared to the Jim Crow era, when racism was built on biological differences, the current post–civil rights racial ideology is based on more subtle cultural racism and blame-the-victim tropes. Today, most whites in the United States claim that they "don't see any color, just people," that discrimination no longer significantly affects minorities' lives, and that minorities are themselves responsible for any ongoing racial conflicts (Bonilla-Silva 1). Bonilla-Silva continues stating that most whites believe that "if blacks and other minorities would just stop thinking about the past, work hard, and complain less (particularly about racial discrimination), then Americans of all hues could 'all get along'" (1). To investigate the frames and linguistic strategies of this color-blind racial ideology, Bonilla-Silva analyzes survey and interview data from two studies, one of college students from three U.S. universities and another of Detroit residents. Ultimately he determines that "most whites endorse the ideology of color blindness and that this ideology is central to the maintenance of white privilege" (14). Bonilla-Silva categorizes his findings into four central frames that convey color blindness: abstract liberalism, which invokes liberal tenets of individualism and bootstrap mentality to claim equal opportunity and deny inequities; naturalization, which suggests that race segregation is "natural" and by choice, rather than constructed; cultural racism, which blames cultural differences, such as character failings and social choices, for causing inequalities; and minimization of racism, where whites deny the effect of race because they can (74).

Although Bonilla-Silva's work is not normally considered part of critical whiteness studies, I argue for its use in whiteness studies because of the way that he details the rhetorical strategies that facilitate the maintenance of whiteness in a postracial era. Bonilla-Silva's four frames, along with numerous linguistic strategies that he identifies, allow people to justify racial inequalities today using facially race-neutral language while in actuality sustaining white supremacy and white privilege. These strategies are thus discursive building blocks of whiteness, blocks that must be identified, understood, and redressed as part of deconstructing whiteness. Whiteness (not synonymous with white people) is a sociocultural construction that situates whites as superior to other races and entitled to greater benefits (Feagin; Smedley and Smedley). Whiteness emerged out of a historical context privileging wealthy white economic interests (Smedley and Smedley) and today is "associated with the unjust social system and resistance to change, with the denial of accountability, with closure, with silence, with hypocrisy, and with ignorance of other cultures" (Keating 427). Color-blind racial ideology has been taken up in rhetoric and composition by David G. Holmes, who analyzes color-blind racial rhetorics in the Kennedy-Nixon presidential debates to argue that race-neutral language like "equal opportunity" actually disenfranchises people of color, as does Aja Y. Martinez, who discusses how Chicano students engage in color-blind rhetorical strategies to assimilate into the academy. This chapter builds upon that work, as well as other inquiries into whiteness rhetorics (Jackson; Ryden and Marshall) by reading Obama's speech as informed by whiteness generally and color blindness specifically.

A Rereading of the Speech

Since the rhetoricians listed above review Obama's speech in detail, this analysis will be a focused rereading of the speech, rather than an extensive analysis, focused on illustrating Obama's color-blind racial rhetorics within the speech. To begin, Obama appeals to one of the strongest ideologies in U.S. history: liberalism. Bonilla-Silva explains that liberalism is the strongest tenet of color-blind racial ideology and uses ideas of *equal opportunity*, *choice*, and *individualism* to justify racial inequalities by arguing that it is minorities' own faults that they have not succeeded (28). For example, abstract liberalism allows whites to oppose affirmative action on the basis that everyone has equal opportunities in education and employment while ignoring vast differences between whites and minorities in income, wealth, education, and employment levels (Bonilla-Silva 28).

Obama's "A More Perfect Union" speech appeals heavily to liberalism values, beginning with its reference to the Constitution and its "ideal of equal citizenship under the law; a Constitution that promised its people liberty and justice" (Obama). Obama also speaks to a deep-seated ideology in American culture that all Americans are equal and deserve equal opportunities. Rather than demonstrating awareness of the ways that liberalism functions in maintaining hegemonic whiteness, however, the rhetoric scholars who analyzed this speech previously, and particularly Rowland and Jones, find the speech rhetorically effective largely *because* of Obama's liberalism tropes, such as his appeal to the mythical American Dream.

Another primary way that Obama appeals to liberalism is through the trope of individualism. Obama asks that every individual take responsibility for solving racial discord, which includes "taking full responsibility for [their] own lives" (Obama). Part of the individualism trope within the liberalism frame is that individuals are responsible for their own destinies and that systematic and institutional influences are minimal. Even in discussing the history of racism, Obama focuses on the individual: "What's remarkable is not how many failed in the face of discrimination, but how many men and women overcame the odds; how many were able to make a way out of no way, for those like me who would come after them" (Obama). Obama's attention to individual effort, versus sustained, collective efforts both for and against change, is remarkable given the pervasive, systemic ways that racism (and responding activism) permeates U.S. history. Finally, even the anecdote that concludes the speech reinforces individualism. Obama offers an emotional appeal by describing a young white woman, Ashley, who participated in his campaign because she wanted to improve conditions for low-income people (Obama). As a child, Ashley told her mother that she preferred mustard and relish sandwiches because she knew her mother could not afford better food (Obama). After hearing this story, an older black man claimed that he was participating in the campaign "because of Ashley," which illustrates how two individuals can transcend race (Obama). This emotionally entreating story also appeals to whites' value of liberalism without confronting racism as systemic, which is a foundational way race scholars approach race and racism today, and it refers to the way that racial bias is built into our institutions and organizations, from schools to governments to places of worship, to benefit whites and disadvantage people of color ("Moving the Race Conversation").

Obama does address systemic racism in his speech, but in a misleading way. While he acknowledges that discrimination exists within the legal system and other institutions, he denies the existence of systemic white racism. Obama says that Wright's remarks "expressed a profoundly distorted view of this country—a view that sees white racism as endemic" (Obama). As some of the rhetoric scholars discussed above admit, race and whiteness studies scholars have written extensively on the endemic nature of white racism. Bonilla-Silva, for example, writes that Obama's comment "should be surprising to race scholars around the nation who regard racism as indeed 'endemic' and know that race has been a 'divisive' matter in America since the 17th century!" (220). Thus, Obama mentions discrimination within institutions without expressing systemic racism as being based in white racism in order to advantage whites and disenfranchise people of color. The rhetorical effect of Obama's maneuvering is to seem like he is directly confronting race while still appealing to whites' color-blind racial ideologies. Another aspect of color-blind ideology is its claims of reverse racism, which fail to acknowledge persistent racial inequalities between whites and people of color and the power dynamics of white supremacy, and reverse racism is evident in this speech as Obama grants legitimacy to whites' feelings of reverse discrimination. He says,

> Most working- and middle-class white Americans don't feel that they have been particularly privileged by their race. . . . And in an era of stagnant wages and global competition, opportunity comes to be seen as a zero sum game, in which your dreams come at my expense . . . resentment builds over time. (Obama)

Instead of acknowledging white racism, Obama blames white resentment on "a corporate culture rife with inside dealing, questionable accounting practices, and short-term greed; a Washington dominated by lobbyists and special interests; economic policies that favor the few over the many" (Obama). Although not all whites experience privilege to the same degree, if at all, race and whiteness scholars identify such institutional factors as maintaining white privilege rather than causing white resentment. The effect of naming such factors unproductively refocuses discussions from race to class, a tactic that creates differences between whites rather than acknowledges white racism (Beech 173). Furthermore, Obama's phrase conveys that race is getting in the way of focusing on "real" problems that prevent everyone from achieving the American Dream, a maneuver evident throughout Obama's campaign (Bonilla-Silva 219). Minimizing the impact of race and racial whiteness on social outcomes in the United States adheres to the minimization of racism frame of color-blind racial ideology, one that appeals to whiteness by denying white participation in racism and reproduces whiteness.

Implications for Rhetorical Studies

My reading of "A More Perfect Union" contrasts sharply with the previously cited rhetoricians. Rowland and Jones's contention that Obama did not "paper over racial conflict" is unfounded in my reading, which highlights several instances where Obama's appeals to liberalism, individualism, and reverse racism indeed paper over racial inequalities, systemic racism, and white privilege. Rowland and Jones, conversely, praise Obama's rhetoric for appealing to liberalism through the American Dream mythology and do not consider the role that liberalism plays in maintaining hegemonic whiteness today. Terrill, who values Obama's use of African American rhetorical traditions, nonetheless also does not consider any of the ways that the speech maintains rather than challenges existing racial structures. Although Isaksen incorporates critical race theory into her analysis, she, too, does not identify Obama's appeals to whiteness through his use of color-blind rhetorical strategies and neoliberalism in particular. While Dilliplane's analysis discusses race directly, such as by explaining how the rhetorical situation of the speech required Obama to address the racialized accusations of Wright's statements as well as Obama's own racial identity, she reports on these challenges without problematizing them. For example, she explains that Obama had to distance himself from being the "black candidate" focused on "black interests" in order to appeal to white voters (132) but does not critique the political and social culture that makes being black and having black interests a problem. She does not note the hypocrisy of white candidates not needing to disavow white interests in order to achieve public office. In this way, Dilliplane reports on these events from a raceless standpoint, one that comments on race rhetorics without considering how those rhetorics support white racism, racial inequalities, and reproduce white privilege.

These rhetorical analyses and their common oversights together demonstrate an affective disciplining of the field of racial rhetoric. Julie Jung discusses disciplinary debates in rhetoric and composition and outlines how those debates discipline scholarly identity. She explains that "conventional readings of reflections on the debate sponsor an economy of emotion whereby teacher-scholars working in rhetoric and composition are repeatedly hailed to recognize themselves as subjects who are identifying 'correctly'" (n.p.). This disciplining is based on Lynn Worsham's concept of the schooling of emotion, where people are pedagogically disciplined to have particular affective responses to certain events, often including a denouncement of emotion in favor of liberal rationality (216). The schooling of emotion also causes us to perceive acts of violence as individualized, aberrational events rather than as emerging from particular social, political, and economic structures (219).

I offer that a similar disciplining is evident in the rhetorical analyses on the Obama speech. The rhetorical analyses on "A More Perfect Union" suggest that rhetoric studies has been affectively disciplined to see any political discourse on race, especially that by a minority politician, and especially any that attempt to unite rather than divide, as progressive. Obama's election to the presidency has symbolically represented progress for racial relations in the United States, so rhetoricians may be emotionally disciplined to support such progress, regardless of whether the details of his campaign and presidency, such as the racial rhetorics in his speeches, are racially progressive.[2] The analyses also suggest that rhetoricians are disciplined to focus on analyzing rhetoric that was judged to be successful by an external metric (in this case, numerous media outlets and white voters). By taking the success of the speech for granted, rhetoricians focus on explaining how Obama's rhetoric was effective for a broad, hegemonic audience without considering how the speech might affect marginalized populations, such as disenfranchised people of color. The assumption of success also excuses rhetoricians from a more thorough inquiry into whose opinion counts in labeling the speech a success . . . or even who gets to speak within political discourse.

It is considerably difficult for African American politicians and other politicians of color to attain high political office, but I advocate that we can celebrate the United States, electing a black President while still problematizing the race and whiteness rhetorics influencing and emerging from a political and social system placing such successes neatly within white racial ideologies. Rather than analyze race and whiteness rhetorics in a whitewashed framework, we should examine how color-blind rhetorics support white hegemony through increasingly covert means. Furthermore, examining those color-blind rhetorical positions means opening possibilities for redressing whiteness and its stronghold in our social and political landscape. In this way, rhetorical studies can engage in racial justice rather than remaining complicit in existing race relations.

Notes

1. Obama is the son of a white woman from the United States and a black man from Kenya and self-identifies as black; for example, he marked (only) African American on the 2010 census even though it allowed for more than one option (Harris-Perry).

2. Bonilla-Silva argues that, in addition to fitting a manufactured minority politician persona, Obama's politics reveal that he is quite conservative, or at least a centrist (214–15).

Works Cited

Beech, Jennifer. "Redneck and Hillbilly Discourse in the Writing Classroom: Classifying Critical Pedagogies of Whiteness." *College English* 67.2 (2004): 172–86. Print.

Bonilla-Silva, Eduardo. *Racism without Racists: Color-Blind Racism and the Persistence of Racial Inequality in America*. 4th ed. Lanham, MD: Rowman and Littlefield, 2013. Print.

Bouie, Jamelle. "Why Did Obama Say So Little about Ferguson?" *Slate*. The Slate Group, 26 Aug. 2014. Web. 15 Sept. 2014.

Delgado, Richard, and Jean Stefancic. *Critical Race Theory: An Introduction*. 2nd ed. New York: New York UP, 2012. Print.

Dilliplane, Susanna. "Race, Rhetoric, and Running for President: Unpacking the Significance of Barack Obama's 'A More Perfect Union' Speech." *Rhetoric and Public Affairs* 15.1 (2012): 127–52. Print.

Feller, Ben. "Beer Summit Begins: Obama Sits Down with Crowley, Gates." *Huffington Post*. TheHuffingtonPost.com, Inc., 30 Jul. 2009. Web. 8 Nov. 2013.

Frank, David A. "The Prophetic Voice and the Face of the Other in Barack Obama's 'A More Perfect Union' Address, March 18, 2008." *Rhetoric and Public Affairs* 12.2 (2009): 167–94. Print.

Frank, David A., and Mark Lawrence McPhail. "Barack Obama's Address to the 2004 Democratic National Convention: Trauma, Compromise, Consilience, and the (Im)possibility of Racial Reconciliation." *Rhetoric and Public Affairs* 8.4 (2005): 571–94. Print.

Graham, Nicholas. "Obama on Skip Gates Arrest: Police Acted 'Stupidly.'" *Huffington Post*. TheHuffingtonPost.com, Inc., 22 Aug. 2009. Web. 8 Nov. 2013.

Harris-Perry, Melissa. "Black by Choice: The First Black President Has Created a Definitional Crisis for Whiteness." *Nation*. The Nation, 15 Apr. 2010. Web. 8 Nov. 2013.

Holmes, David G. "Affirmative Reaction: Kennedy, Nixon, King, and the Evolution of Color-Blind Rhetoric." *Rhetoric Review* 26.1 (2007): 25–41. Print.

Isaksen, Judy L. "Obama's Rhetorical Shift: Insights for Communication Studies." *Communication Studies* 62.4 (2011): 456–71. Print.

Jackson, Matthew. "The Enthymematic Hegemony of Whiteness: The Enthymeme as Antiracist Rhetorical Strategy." *JAC* 26.3–4 (2006): 601–41. Print.

Jung, Julie. "Rhetoric and Composition's Emotional Economy of Identification." *Enculturation: A Journal of Rhetoric, Writing, and Culture*. Enculturation, 12 Aug. 2010. Web. 8 Nov. 2013.

Keating, AnaLouise. "Interrogating 'Whiteness,' (De)constructing 'Race.'" *College English* 57.8 (1995): 901–18. Print.

Kennedy, Tammie M., Joyce Irene Middleton, and Krista Ratcliffe, "Symposium: The Matter of Whiteness; Or, Why Whiteness Studies Is Important to Rhetoric and Composition Studies." *Rhetoric Review* 24.4 (2005): 359–73. Print.

Lynch, Paul. "Not to Shy Away: Barack Obama's Rhetoric of Friendship." *Present Tense: A Journal of Rhetoric in Society*. The Present Tense, 2.1 (2011): 1–7. Web. 8 Nov. 2013.

Martinez, Aja Y. "'The American Way': Resisting the Empire of Force and Color-Blind Racism." *College English* 71.6 (2009): 584–95. Print.

"Moving the Race Conversation Forward: How the Media Covers Racism, and Other Barriers to Productive Racial Discourse." *Race Forward: The Center for Racial Justice Innovation*. Raceforward, 22 Jan. 2014. Web. 14 Sept. 2014.

"Mr. Obama's Profile in Courage." *New York Times*. The New York Times Co., 19 Mar. 2008. Web. 13 Dec. 2011.

Obama, Barack. "A More Perfect Union Speech." *NPR*. NPR, 18 Mar. 2008. Web. 8 Nov. 2013.

Ross, Brian. "Obama's Pastor: God Damn America, U.S. to Blame for 9/11." *ABC News*. Disney-ABC News Group, 13 Mar. 2008. Web. 13 Dec. 2011.

Rowland, Robert C., and John M. Jones. "One Dream: Barack Obama, Race, and the American Dream." *Rhetoric and Public Affairs* 14.1 (2011): 125–54. Print.

Ryden, Wendy, and Ian Marshall. *Reading, Writing, and the Rhetorics of Whiteness.* New York: Routledge, 2012. Print.

Shapiro, Ari. "Obama Warms to Speaking Personally about Race." *NPR.* NPR, 3 Aug. 2013. Web. 8 Nov. 2013.

Smedley, Audrey, and Brian D. Smedley. *Race in North America: Origin and Evolution of a Worldview.* 4th ed. Boulder, CO: Westview P, 2012. Print.

Stein, Sam. "Obama on Trayvon Martin Case: 'If I Had a Son, He'd Look Like Trayvon.'" *Huffington Post.* TheHuffingtonPost.com, Inc., 23 Mar. 2012. Web. 8 Nov. 2013.

Terrill, Robert E. "Unity and Duality in Barack Obama's 'A More Perfect Union.'" *Quarterly Journal of Speech* 95.4 (2009): 363–86. Print.

Wise, Tim. *Color-Blind: The Rise of Post-Racial Politics and the Retreat from Racial Equity.* San Francisco: City Lights Books, 2010. Print.

Worsham, Lynn. "Going Postal: Pedagogic Violence and the Schooling of Emotion." *JAC* 18.2 (1998): 213–45. Print.

PART TWO

HAUNTINGS IN SOCIAL MEDIA

REFLECTION

BEFORE #BLACKLIVESMATTER

Catherine Prendergast

THE REVOLUTION WOULD not be televised but it would be tweeted. After August 9, 2014, when Mike Brown was shot by Darren Wilson in Ferguson, Missouri, protestors hit both the streets and the internet, claiming the hashtag #BlackLivesMatter as a counter to mass-media disregard to blacks murdered by police. This hashtag would, as we now know, prove all too reusable with each new police shooting over the next year. But that wasn't the beginning of what would be black protest via Twitter.

On December 20, 2013, the hashtag #HasJustineLandedYet marked the time between the moment Justine Sacco, head of corporate communications for media conglomerate IAC, tweeted "Going to Africa. Hope I don't get AIDS. Just kidding. I'm white!" and twelve hours later, when she landed and logged on to find that she had outraged thousands and lost her job.

Much could be said about the "haunting whiteness" that allowed Sacco the privilege of joking about AIDS and its victims, while announcing her fictive racial exemption from the disease. One could imagine Sacco making such remarks as a casual aside at a country club and suffering no consequences as a result. But Twitter, a public interface whereon what is tweeted (if not locked) can be read by 7 billion people, is no country club. Perhaps that is exactly why African Americans have chosen Twitter as a premiere site of rhetorical activism: according to the Pew Research Center, more African American internet users than white internet users use Twitter (Smith).

While there is nothing new about African Americans calling out whiteness in any media, Twitter has brought unprecedented networking, speed, and fast consequences to rhetorical action.

More Examples

When on August 17, 2012, patrons at a showing of the film *The Butler* at Regal Cinema in Silver Spring, Maryland, were greeted by armed guards, a woman tweeted the incident and the phone number of the cinema, bringing all to the attention of ABC News.

Just a week after Justine Sacco landed, social media pressure forced musician Ani DiFranco to cancel her feminist writing retreat on a Southern plantation. A Twitter meme under the hashtag #AniDiFrancoRetreatIdeas drew parallels between the proposed retreat and vacationing at Dachau.

In 2012 Tressie McMillan Cottom (now an assistant professor at Virginia Commonwealth University, whose Twitter profile when she was a graduate student used to read, "I tried shutting up once. It ended badly for all concerned") started a successful online petition to convince the *Chronicle of Higher Education* to fire Naomi Schaefer Riley, a journalist who had argued, based on reading a few dissertation titles, that universities should discontinue programs in African American Studies.

Not only have black Americans been finding in Twitter an effective platform for public protest, they have been using it as a springboard to raising their voice to other venues. Since the Schaefer Riley affair, Cottom, published in *Slate*, *Salon*, the *New York Times*, and the *Atlantic* and has appeared on the Dan Rather show. Aspiring director Justin Simien, who circulated a trailer of his film *Dear White People* on Twitter as part of a successful Kickstarter campaign to fund its production, premiered his film at the 2014 Sundance Festival. (Full disclosure [but no apologies]: I contributed to Simien's Kickstarter campaign.)

Not all view the fast mobilization of activists on Twitter as an unalloyed good. After the Sacco affair, commentators Roxane Gay in *Salon* and Nick Bilton in the Bits blog of the *New York Times* expressed unease that Sacco lost her job and faced death threats over one tweet. Sacco, they argued, was an ordinary person whose life was ruined by complete strangers in twelve short hours. Her punishment was out of proportion with the impact of her opinion.

No one should receive death threats over a tweet (or anything else). I would argue, however, that if your joke relies upon the death of millions as the source of its humor, death threats are not an unimaginable response. Yes, Justine Sacco is ordinary. But so is whiteness. It is completely mundane. It's the water we swim in. It is so unspectacular to us that only its exceptional exhibition (as in the form of Sacco's AIDS tweet) will engender any sanction. At all.

Rarely considered in discussions of the consequences of Twitter activism are the consequences of squelching it. Given business as usual, whiteness assures that those already in power keep their powerful jobs, using their money and privilege for the most part to promote primarily the interests of white people. That assurance must be considered in any evaluation of the power of Twitter.

If Twitter knows no country club, it knows no "hush harbor" (Nunley) either. Twitter has become the new rhetoric of protest to whiteness, marked not by silent presence but by rapid-fire speech and quick counters to mainstream media's misrepresentation or no representation whatsoever. Whiteness, be on notice: the hashtags might change but the movement will not diminish. Black Twitter is haunting you.

Works Cited

Bilton, Nick. "Is the Internet a Mob without Consequence?" *New York Times* 24 Dec. 2013. Web. 30 Dec. 2013.

Cottom, Tressie McMillan. "The Case of the *Chronicle of Higher Education*." Blog. *Tressiemcc.com*. 14 May 2012. Web. 30 Dec. 2013.

Gay, Roxane. "The Cost of Twitter Outrage." *Salon.com*. 23 Dec. 2013. Web. 30 Dec. 2013.

Nunley, Vorris. *Keepin' It Hushed: The Barbershop and African American Hush Harbor Rhetoric*. Detroit, MI: Wayne State UP, 2011. Print.

Smith, Aaron. "African Americans and Technology Use: A Demographic Portrait." Pew Research Center. 6 Jan. 2014. Web.

Smith, Aaron, and Joanna Bremmer. "Twitter Use 2012." Pew Research Center. 31 May 2012. Web. 30 Dec. 2013.

RACIALIZED SLACKTIVISM: SOCIAL MEDIA PERFORMANCES OF WHITE ANTIRACISM

Tim Engles

> What exactly it means to be white seems to elude no one as fully as it
> eludes those of us who are white. . . . We do not know ourselves, and,
> worse, we seem only occasionally to know that we do not know ourselves.
> —Eula Biss, *Notes from No Man's Land*

IN 2012 TWO racially charged events provoked enormous amounts of social media controversy—the killing of Trayvon Martin by George Zimmerman and the posting by Invisible Children, Inc. of a thirty-minute video that immediately went viral, "Kony 2012." In both cases many white netizens felt driven to post immediate expressions of solidarity with black victims and to portray their own actions as effective modes of social-justice activism. In innumerable online performances, such respondents demonstrated the common white tendency of projecting seemingly heartfelt antiracist feelings in order to distance oneself implicitly from other, racist white people; at a deeper level, they also distanced themselves from a shamefully racist identity that continually haunted their self-reflexive performances of antiracism. In many ways, social media have become requisite platforms for race-related activism. As Lisa Nakamura and Peter Chow-White point out, "the digital turn has changed the game," and in response, "critical race scholarship, that is to say scholarship that investigates the shifting meanings of race and how it works in society, and proposes interventions in the name of social justice, must expand its scope to digital media and computer-based technologies" (5). Perhaps because the advent of Web 2.0 and its widespread usage are relatively recent phenomena, few studies of online performances of white identities exist.[1]

This essay addresses the dubious efficacy of common white efforts to combat racism via social media. As Malcolm Gladwell points out, the "weak ties" that online interaction promotes "seldom lead to high-risk activism," leading all too often instead to "the kind of commitment that will bring only social acknowledgement and praise" ("Small Change"). More specifically, this study addresses whether the inherently self-declarative element of social media interaction necessarily limits even self-aware presentations of white antiracism to ineffectual narcissism; some probable root causes of such racial narcissism; and ultimately whether it is always the case, as Kil Ja Kim argues in a widely cited "open letter to white anti-racists" published on the *Race Traitor* journal's website, that "the white anti-racist is an oxymoron." On a more positive note, this study also reveals that while aspiring white allies often demonstrate in social media the same poorly considered motivations, assumptions, and understandings that many of them do in real-world advocacy, social media interaction does allow for immediate and effective critique of such performances by more racially cognizant netizens, primarily people of color, and, at times, white commentators as well. As I will demonstrate with reference to online discourse that arose in response to the killing of Trayvon Martin and to the posting of the video "Kony 2012," and to recent scholarship on racially whitened proclivities, social media interaction often triggers certain commonly inculcated feelings and inclinations in aspiring white allies. It tends to inspire impulsive, shallow, and solipsistic modes of self-aggrandizing display, steering aspiring white allies all that much more strongly toward "slacktivism," rather than to effective activism.[2]

"I Am Trayvon Martin" and "Kony 2012"

On February 26, 2012, seventeen-year-old Trayvon Martin stepped out of his aunt's Florida home to buy his younger brother a snack. As he was returning through a largely white gated community, carrying only his phone, a can of iced tea, and a bag of Skittles while wearing a hoodie, Martin was confronted by twenty-eight-year-old George Zimmerman, a white Hispanic man who was volunteering as a neighborhood guardian. As Martin continued walking, Zimmerman called a 911 dispatcher to voice his concerns: "This guy looks like he's up to no good or he's on drugs or something. It's raining and he's just walking around looking about" (Yancy and Jones 3). Zimmerman then left his car, pursued Martin, and after a scuffle, shot him through the heart. Allegations of racist police misconduct arose when Zimmerman was only briefly detained and superficially interrogated by police, and then was not subsequently arrested and charged with second-degree murder until April 11, seven weeks later.

Martin's death and Zimmerman's prolonged freedom incited a flurry of online responses, both in condemnation and defense of Zimmerman's actions. Among those who expressed outrage, Martin's murder stood as a particularly stark example of the widespread targeting of innocent black men, who repeatedly suffer surveillance, abuse, and death for nothing more provocative than being present in public spaces. Such events, including the superficial detainment and questioning of Zimmerman and the length of time that he went without being formally arrested and accused of murder, exemplify Ruth Wilson Gilmore's trenchant definition of contemporary racism as "the state-sanctioned or extralegal production and exploitation of group-differentiated vulnerability to premature death" (247). Common social media expressions by white people of sorrow and outrage in response to Martin's death included tweeted commentary and links, Facebook reposts of news articles and video reportage, petition signings and distribution, and self-written comments and articles on personal blogs and Tumblrs. Of particular interest for the ways it revealed certain common and limiting white tendencies toward social justice activism was the "I am Trayvon Martin" campaign. This movement of sorts echoed similar expressions of solidarity in the 2011 "I am Troy Davis" campaign, which arose in response to the apparently racist conviction and execution of a black man named Troy Davis in Butts County, Georgia. In both cases innumerable white slacktivists took to producing photos, t-shirts, bumper stickers, flyers, and posters that nominally supplanted their own identities with that of an African American victim of racism.[3]

In response to the death of Trayvon Martin, white netizens who claimed identification with a young black man perceived a particularly visual opportunity for self-declaration because Martin was wearing a hoodie, a racially coded item of clothing that may have exacerbated the seemingly racist vigilance of his killer.[4] As the length of Zimmerman's freedom grew, citizens, celebrities and politicians donned hoodies as a public sign of solidarity and protest. Protesters organized a Million Hoodie March in New York City, Representative Bobby Rush was ejected from the congressional floor for wearing one during a speech, and Fox News personality Geraldo Rivera was credited with instigating it all by claiming that "the hoodie is as much responsible for Trayvon Martin's death . . . as George Zimmerman was" (Castellanos). In social media, people of all races posted photos of themselves wearing hoodies, often above the words "I am Trayvon Martin," while others wore newly purchased t-shirts emblazoned with the phrase.

Other, primarily nonwhite netizens who agreed that Martin's killing was an especially egregious manifestation of the continued vigor of American racism nevertheless objected to such photos and sloganeering when posted by white people. In a widely reposted commentary, blogger "curiously cool" did not object so much to white people's donning of a hoodie, despite its racial connotations, as to their accompanying usage of the phrase "I am Trayvon Martin," since "white people are not Trayvon. . . . They are protected by the system that persecutes people like Trayvon and I. The phrase becomes useless and loses its symbolism when co-opted by them."[5] On March 31, "13emcha," a young white woman, posted "I AM NOT TRAYVON MARTIN," a YouTube video of herself reading a statement to other white activists in which she declared,

> I know you wear that shirt to stand in solidarity with Trayvon, Troy, and other victims of injustice. The purpose of those shirts is to humanize these victims of our society, by likening them to the middle-class white activist wearing it. . . . A more accurate t-shirt to display on my white body would be "I AM GEORGE ZIMMERMAN." Zimmerman and I were indoctrinated in the same American discourse where we learned that the "other," particularly black men like Trayvon and Troy, were less human and were to be feared. . . . Realizing that you more closely resemble a homicidal oppressive force than a helpless victim is a really uncomfortable thing to do, I know. But wanting to identify with the victim is weak, and immature when it is not an accurate representation of reality. Real change is effected when we own up to our actions, our privilege, and our complicity with the system that murdered Trayvon and countless others.

In her response to other self-declaring white allies, 13emcha runs the risk, as indeed this chapter and this entire volume focused on whiteness do as well, of recentering whiteness, and thus of distracting from efforts to ameliorate the costs for nonwhite people of de facto white supremacy. Nevertheless, effective efforts to counter white supremacy's effects surely include analysis of the workings of whiteness, including those within white people themselves, and 13emcha's vlog effectively critiques the decontextualized nature of narcissistic white activism. As many of the comments below the video suggest, such critique can help to nudge aspiring white allies toward more self-aware, risky, and efficacious activism. I will address 13emcha's performance more fully later and posit as well some potential sources for the common white tendencies toward righteous self-display that she critiques. These tendencies were also enacted in response to Invisible Children, Inc.'s March 5 posting of a thirty-minute video about a fugitive Ugandan criminal, Joseph Kony.

In a vividly emotional manner, the "Kony 2012" video calls for collective interracial netizen action in pursuit of the murderous, child-kidnapping leader of the Lord's Resistance Army, and tens of millions responded. However, the video also struck many as a dismayingly white-framed, white-centered, and financially suspicious narrative about yet another Western man's patronizing adventures in Africa. Jason Russell, cofounder of Invisible Children, Inc., narrates and stars in "Kony 2012," which begins with the birth of Russell's own child. Russell includes footage of himself later telling his four-year-old son about Kony and of his initial meetings with Jacob, a Ugandan youth, who then says on camera that his brother was killed by Kony's henchmen. Russell recounts his organization's earlier efforts to "give a voice" to Africa's abused children, which he credits Invisible Children with doing by rallying American youth support via social media, to the point where meetings with politicians culminated in Barack Obama's deployment in 2011 of U.S. troops to central Africa. The video shows Russell and his cohorts celebrating this news, despite his own recollection earlier of warnings from "everyone in Washington we talked to," who said that "there is no way that the United States will ever get involved in a conflict where our national security or financial interests are not at stake." Russell returns to footage of himself telling his son that Kony is also "invisible," because so few people in America know of him and his crimes. The video's proposed solution is for legions of social media users to "make Kony famous," which they could do by badgering celebrities and policymakers into talking publicly about Kony, and by buying Invisible Children's thirty-dollar "action kits." "If the [U.S.] government doesn't believe the people care about arresting Kony," Russell says, "the [American troops'] mission will be canceled. In order for the people to care, they have to know. And they will only know if Kony's name is everywhere." The video then announces a "Cover the Night" campaign, telling Invisible Children donors to use the stickers and posters in their action kits on a particular night in April to "blanket every street in every city until the sun comes up"; staged footage in this segment shows young people covering their faces with bandanas and dashing through dark streets and tunnels, seemingly eluding police in a dangerous but exciting effort to topple Kony by making him famous. The film ends by claiming that thanks to social media, ordinary people can easily band together and produce change: "We are living in a new world, Facebook World . . . a global community bigger than the U.S." The film then describes immediate actions that viewers can take: they can acquire the action kit by donating money to Invisible Children, Inc., and "above all," they should "share this movie online."

"Kony 2012" quickly became the most rapidly spread online video by that point in time, garnering 100 million views in six days as millions of netizens responded, especially, to the directive to share the movie. Innumerable white westerners also seized "Kony 2012" as a chance to identify themselves online as social justice activists—by Tweeting links to the video, by creating their own reaction videos, and by reposting it on their blogs, Tumblrs, and Facebook pages, along with stylized visual and written expressions of anguish and outrage. That identifying themselves as activists was precisely the main point for many netizens was explicitly recognized by Invisible Children's website, where ad copy in the "SHOP" section (now available only in archives) declared, "People will think you're an advocate of awesome with this official Action Kit. Since KONY 2012 is a yearlong campaign, you can decorate yourself and the town all year long with this one-stop shop" (Invisible Children). Along with "Kony 2012" posters and stickers (which undoubtedly appeared more often in bedrooms and dorm rooms and on laptops and spiral notebooks than in public spaces),[6] the kit included a t-shirt, bracelets, buttons, stickers, and posters, all emblazoned with Kony's name. Those with thirty dollars to "donate" by buying the action kit helped make Kony famous by "decorating" themselves with these declarative adornments and then by posting selfies in the usual social media spaces.[7] As with the "I am Trayvon Martin" hoodie photos, white netizens stirred into activism seized these accoutrements as a chance to forward themselves against a black (alternately "urban" and "African") backdrop as "advocates of awesome." As they did so, they became the center-staged protagonists in personalized versions of what has come to be known as the White Savior Complex, a contemporary iteration of the colonialist White Man's Burden.

As the fame of both Joseph Kony and Jason Russell spread beyond social media to become a multiperspectival "polymedia event,"[8] more skeptical netizens began investigating and critiquing not only the underlying intentions and potential effects of the campaign but also the likely motives of ordinary white participants. Blogger Martin Wagner pointed out that

Russell has been criticized most heavily for playing the "white savior" role, which happens when privileged white Westerners decide they have some duty to impose their presence upon struggling developing nations and underprivileged peoples and Fix Everything with their magical Whiteness rays. "White savior" behavior is usually marked by not-entirely-honest motives, and an oafish refusal to make sure you have all your facts in order and a sensible game plan in mind before donning your cape and flying in. It is . . . all about doing good in order to be seen doing good.

In a series of tweets that grew into an incisive blog post at the *Atlantic*, Nigerian American novelist Teju Cole addressed the larger context of what he termed "the White Savior Industrial Complex": "The white savior supports brutal policies in the morning, founds charities in the afternoon, and receives awards in the evening. . . . The White Savior Industrial Complex is not about justice. It is about having a big emotional experience that validates privilege."[9] At the individual level, when white netizens responded to Russell's call to band together with others in a collective effort to get Joseph Kony (by buying action kits and by reposting the video, linking to it, and tweeting their support of it), many undoubtedly felt motivated to do so because they seemed to be taking part in a "big emotional experience." Ultimately, though, the lack of real-world efficacy of their efforts, and the apparent unwillingness of most to go any further than such limited and self-aggrandizing steps, suggests that mere validation of white racial privilege was indeed the most significant outcome.

In addition to an emotional appeal implicitly aimed (whether intentionally or not) primarily at young white viewers, the argument of "Kony 2012" contained an array of other fallacies. As the video succeeded in making Joseph Kony famous, a plethora of commenters from across the globe, including many from Uganda, began using social media to point out its gaps and oversights, problems that might have given pause to aspiring white allies were they to overcome the common white tendency to ignore insights on offer by racial others by pausing long enough to find and consider them. Ugandan prime minister Amama Mbabazi delivered via YouTube a direct response to what he termed a "slick video," mainly to say that although "Kony 2012" struck him as "inspiring," and although Kony and his army continued to commit horrific acts, those acts were no longer occurring in Uganda because its military had already forced Kony and his Lord's Resistance Army out six years earlier. In an implicit rejection of the film's simplistic dichotomy of good Western order versus bad African disorder, Mbabazi also emphasized that Uganda is now a "modern, developing country, which enjoys peace, stability, and security." Like many other online critics, Ugandan video blogger and journalist Rosebell Kagumire objected to the cartoonish narrowing of a complex set of problems and conflicts to "just one bad guy," and she too called out the video's echoes of colonialist assumptions:

> If you are showing me as voiceless, as hopeless . . . you shouldn't be telling my story if you don't believe that I also have the power to change what is going on. And this video seems to say that the power lies in America, and [that] it does not lie with my government [and] with local initiatives on the ground.

Again, had those white netizens who felt inspired by Invisible Children, Inc.'s video to take some form of action paused to google and consider such criticisms offered from perspectives other than their own, their subsequent actions might have taken less self-aggrandizing and more effective forms.

As Cole notes in his *Atlantic* blog post, Joseph Kony had become "no longer the threat he was, but he is a convenient villain for those who need a convenient villain." Why, then, did so many white netizens feel a "need" to react to such a reductively individualized, and yet decidedly black, villain? And why did so many others identify in the "I am Trayvon Martin" campaign with such a similarly figured victim? More generally, what motivations and tendencies prompt many white activists to act so quickly, and so superficially, and in ways that ironically assert as well their own primacy over nonwhite people?

The White Shame and Happiness Complex

As Sherri Grasmuck notes in an analysis of ethno-racial identity displays in social media, "we still know relatively little about what it means to construct identity in environments where visual cues about race, through photographs for example, are offered to the audience" (161). Nevertheless, the use of heuristics that have arisen from an extensive corpus of work on common white racial proclivities, and on the emotions that often drive them, can provide tentative explanations of the motives and feelings that drive common iterations of antiracist white identity. As Sara Ahmed argues, white antiracism efforts often result in little more than a "re-turning" back toward oneself, a self-congratulatory feeling of accomplishment for having performed a properly antiracist stance that ultimately fails to produce effective antiracist action ("Declarations"). Worse yet, this kind of racialized solipsism can ironically contribute to a "new discourse of white pride," as antiracism gestures become merely "a matter of generating a positive white identity, an identity that makes the white subject feel good about itself." Ahmed identifies this phenomenon in broader terms as "the non-performativity of anti-racism" ("Declarations"), and as other researchers have demonstrated, while white participants in various antiracism discourse communities get to feel good about themselves, their efforts often contribute little toward amelioration of the de facto white supremacy faced by people of color, largely because their primary motivations are ultimately self-reflexive. This is not to say that collective antiracism efforts via social media that include white netizens never produce real-world change; indeed, the "I am Trayvon Martin" campaign was primarily organized to pressure police in Florida to arrest George Zimmerman, a collectivist pressure that apparently produced the desired result. While the term "white antiracist," then, may not be entirely oxymoronic, a common lack of racial self-awareness often does lead white people to "return" inward, as they simultaneously move, online and in real-world space, outward into interaction with people who are and are not white. As they oscillate in these contrary directions, they unwittingly enact an array of common white tendencies, including the perceived need to feel ashamed about being white in the face of injustice imposed on particular racial "others," and a need to move beyond this shame into some form of immediate action, and thereby to return to a relieved state of relative, normative happiness, even while performing ostensibly purposeful social justice activism.

Since the encouragement of more effective activism is clearly a worthy goal, such common white emotions deserve closer attention. In her discussion of negative affects as potential motivators toward collective antiracist activism, Alexis Shotwell describes shame as the sense of being "haunted" by an undesirable version of oneself:

> Shame represents being thrown into the self you are that you repudiate, a self you don't want to be. . . . [The] experience of shame in the face of racism— one's own or other people's—discloses both present racism and also potential for antiracist praxis, embedded in the desire to deny the racist self. (93–94)

For Shotwell, perception of the self you don't want to be implies as well "a self you also are, a self you want to be" (93). And yet, in terms of activism involving racial difference, if one does not recognize the significance of one's self *as a white self*, ontologically nonsensical replacements of the haunting bad white self with a nonwhite other can occur. An initial perception of one's self as a shamefully complacent white self, and then a rejection of or fleeing from that identity, rather than acknowledgment and examination of it, likely accounts for many white appropriations of another haunting presence, the ghostly identity of Trayvon Martin.[10] In such cases as the white netizen's donning of a hoodie and declaring solidarity with Trayvon Martin by declaring that he or she *is* Trayvon Martin (or Troy Davis), such a repudiation of self is all too thorough. In contrast, more self-aware white activists, such as video blogger 13emcha, maintain recognition of the shameful version of their white selves; it no longer "haunts" them because they acknowledge and foreground it, by recognizing the constitutive context of historical and ongoing white supremacy and thus, as 13emcha puts it in her video, their "complicity with the system that murdered Trayvon and countless others."

As 13emcha also points out, for whites with antiracist inclinations to acknowledge that they "more closely resemble a homicidal oppressive force than a helpless victim is a really uncomfortable thing to do." Activists of color often express frustration with a common white desire to avoid feeling uncomfortable when discussing race, racial whiteness, or working against racism. Indeed, feeling good about oneself and one's actions aligns all too neatly with a broader, foundational (and in a sociohistorical sense, particularly white) American emphasis on happiness, and on a "right" to the pursuit of it, even before the pursuit of something like justice, and even *while* pursuing justice. Evident in many of the self-declarative performances by white clicktivists in both the "I am Trayvon Martin" and "Kony 2012" campaigns is a sense of something akin to joy, as much as principled drive or determination. As Mirca Madianou points out about Invisible Children's efforts to make anti-Kony donations and activism appealing, "The slogan of the campaign, 'Make Kony Famous,' is ironic. . . . Irony, playfulness and pastiche marked the whole campaign. . . . The bracelets of the campaign evoke those worn by concert-goers while the documentary score is high-energy electronica" (257).[11] If this projected feeling of happiness did exist within those white netizens who responded, many likely achieved it trying to leave a shamefully complacent white self behind in pursuit of a better self, one that emphasizes a largely imagined and unearned sense of solidarity with people of color. The aspiring white ally's failure here is that of not recognizing that whiteness cannot be left behind because the United States is a thoroughly racialized society that continues to respond differently to white people, and more to the point, that any white person is necessarily embedded and implicated in an overarching system of de facto white supremacy. Accordingly, as 13emcha distinguishes her contextually cognizant, consciously white self from naive, unwittingly white ones by recognizing that she is more like Zimmerman than Martin, her affective demeanor—unsmiling, staunchly determined and frowning—is a marked contrast to theirs as well. In this sense, her message regarding obliviously appropriative white performances of antiracism in the "I am Trayvon Martin" campaign also conveys rejection of the common white projection of an assumed right to personal ease and happiness, a presentation of self that can be jarring and discordant in spaces where others may well feel less reason for, and entitlement to, such emotions.

Similarly, in response to self-centering white slacktivist reactions to "Kony 2012," an anonymous satirist clearly chose the photograph below at quickmeme.com, where visitors can add text to selected photos, in order to produce an image of projected satisfaction with a job well, and all too easily, done (figure 5.1). Shotwell aptly notes that there is a "widespread refusal and avoidance of negative affects in many social spaces in North America in particular, and an implicit idea that the purpose of life is to be endlessly comfortable and at ease" (80). Such a conception of "the purpose of life" is more readily adopted in the United States by middle-class white people, who, thanks to their race and class memberships, tend to live relatively less-encumbered lives; as a result, having fewer categorically induced hardships to deal with makes mainstream culture's emphasis on comfort, ease, and general contentment seem that much more suited to people like oneself. As Barbara Karens explains in an online commentary on the common white antiracist activist's emphasis on spreading awareness of particular issues and events, and too little else, "as members of the white collective, we can 'be aware' of many things but not change our actions to fit our claimed awareness. . . . White people's need to feel comfortable and good through self-image management, deception and make-believe goes really, really deep." As Christian Lander put it in "Awareness," one of the earliest posts (23 January 2008) on his popular satirical blog "Stuff White People Like," spreading awareness of injustice, and also indicating that one is responsibly aware of it, can strike such well-meaning white people as ends, rather than means, as well as ways to regain any temporary loss of happiness:

> An interesting fact about white people is that they firmly believe that all of the world's problems can be solved through "awareness." Meaning the process of making other people aware of problems, and then magically someone else like the government will fix it. This belief allows them to feel that sweet self-satisfaction without actually having to solve anything or face any difficult challenges.

Writing four years prior to Jason Russell's primary suggested method for making Joseph Kony famous—"Above all, share this movie online"—Lander continued, "Raising awareness is also awesome because once you raise aware-ness to an acceptable, arbitrary level, you can just back off and say 'Bam! did my part. Now it's your turn. Fix it.'"[12] In addition to achieving so easily "that sweet self-satisfaction," and as with other performances of antiracist activism described above, white purveyors of awareness succeed in identify-ing themselves as properly concerned and caring, and perhaps as that much better than other less-caring white people as well.

Figure 5.1. "Become Social Activist" meme

Social media interaction encourages whitened habits of being and action in these terms by providing immediate forms of seemingly effective and self-fashioning action, including a projection of oneself as not only an admirably caring "activist" but also as one who is achieving, in this way too, a white middle-class version of happiness. This emotional state is a feeling, a "good" feeling. One way aspiring white activists often seek to achieve happiness when bad feelings arise in response to the sufferings of nonwhite others—bad feel-ings not only about such suffering but also more vaguely bad feelings, such as shame, about one's own potential complicity in it—is to move beyond those feelings, their sources, and their implications, toward doing something that seems good for nonwhite others. And the sooner one does it, the sooner one can go back to feeling relatively good, and happy, and satisfied with a sense of oneself as a "good," though still rather shameful, and yet nonracist, person. As Ahmed writes, "The white subject that is shamed by its racism is hence also a white subject that is proud *about* its shame. The very claim to feel bad . . . also involves a self-perception as 'good'" ("The Politics" 81). Accordingly, while white people who become aware of racial injustice can feel bad about themselves as a shamefully complicit white person, they can also quickly move on toward a self-conception as a good person, and thus away from feeling bad, by doing something that at least seems antiracist—and thus, something that seems to shift them back into the usual, comfortable category of "good person." As a consequence, the common white tendencies enacted during interactions with racial others of skipping over explanatory context and ignoring the differing perspectives of people of color in pursuit of immediate (but often ineffectual) action are thereby exacerbated.

I do not seek to reduce common white psychological and emotional phenomena to a monolithic and constant pursuit of easeful happiness. Such feelings and the striving for them exist differently in different people, and they continually intermingle not only with white racial shame but also with the feelings brought about by one's daily life and interactions, by one's social class, personal history, physical condition, and so on. And if comfort and happiness are motivating goals, so for many is a sense, a sometimes nagging sense, of social responsibility. If well-meaning white North Americans have some awareness not only of the problems suffered by nonwhite others but also, however dimly, of their own complicity in them (which I would argue is a prime, shame-inducing motivator of much white antiracism activism), then doing something to ameliorate that suffering feels like a responsibility. The rapid rise of social media makes it easier than ever to do such a "something" quickly, and perhaps the quickest way to satisfy this felt obligation toward others is to at least become aware of their problems, and then to spread this awareness by forwarding and tweeting articles, videos, quotations, memes, and so on. Such actions via social media—like those of posting photos of oneself wearing a hoodie, or a t-shirt emblazoned with an antiracist message—exemplify how white antiracist slacktivism all too often carries a sense of responsibility only as far as self-aggrandizing *expressions* of solidarity, expressions that do not actually contribute to collective, and thus more effectively counterhegemonic, forms of activism.[13]

Given these common tendencies even among white people who see racism and hope to counter it, yet often end up doing little more than projecting a seemingly antiracist image of themselves and easing their own discomfort and guilt, can aspiring white allies escape such intricate and varied re-turnings toward their white selves? Can they make effective antiracism contributions? As a white scholar, I hesitate to even ask such questions since, as Ahmed points out, white people too often ask nonwhite scholars and activists such as herself, "What can white people do?" Ahmed contin-ues, "The sheer solipsism of this response must be challenged," because to ask such a question "is not only to return to the place of the white subject, but it is also to locate agency in this place. It is also to reposition the white subject as somewhere other than implicated in the critique" ("A Phenom-enology" 164–65). Ahmed nearly affirms Kil Ja Kim's claim, that "the white anti-racist is an oxymoron," and perhaps all I should do in closing, despite my conviction as a scholar and educator that knowledge can be a form of power, is acknowledge that Kim may well be right and that white people should simply stop trying to fight racism, including talking and writing about it. However, as Ahmed goes on to imply, and as 13emcha argues (and demonstrates), the fact that aspiring white activists often act in impulsive, naive, and even damaging ways does not mean there are no effective modes of white antiracism action. As Barbara Applebaum argues in her recent dis-cussion of self-aware white racial "vigilance" and the vexed responses and feelings expressed by white students in justice-oriented classrooms, becoming and remaining cognizant to the extent one can of the effects of privileged racial positionality, and acting accordingly, are crucial, and so is resistance to cultural injunctions regarding the individualistic pursuit of constant comfort and happiness: "Vigilance is a form of critique that is willing to stay in the anxiety of vulnerability and remain open to the unsettlement of anger" (33).[14] Surely such vigilance, in which aspiring white allies maintain a seriously principled attitude and self-awareness, can foster not only a more general white racial circumspection, but also humility, reserve, and a more genuine respect toward enlightened activists, particularly those of color who have the patience and willingness to point white people who would like to help in more communal and productive directions.

I would like to thank Zavi Kang Engles and the Youth Coalition for Com-munity Action, whose invitation to speak at Pitzer College on common white modes of social justice activism was the initial impetus for this chapter.

Notes

1. Related studies include Naomi W. Nishi et al. on "the projection of on-line personae via white avatars," in "Exposing the White Avatar" (2015); Aisha

Durham on virtual white performances of blackface in racist imitation of Trayvon Martin, in "_____ While Black" (2015); danah boyd on racial divides in social media, in *It's Complicated* (2014), and on "white flight" from Myspace to Facebook, in "White Flight in Networked Publics" (2012); Jessie Daniels on online white supremacist advocacy, in *Cyber Racism: White Supremacy Online and the New Attack on Civil Rights* (2009); Sherri Grasmuck et al. on "strategies of racelessness" deployed by white Facebook users, in "Ethno-racial Identity Displays on Facebook" (2009); Dara N. Byrne on declarations of white identity on minority-focused sites, in "The Future of (the) 'Race': Identity, Discourse, and the Rise of Computer-Mediated Public Spheres" (2008); Margaret Chon's early discussion of whiteness as "the predominant racial norm on the Internet" (241), in "Erasing Race? A Critical Race Feminist View of Internet Identity Shifting" (2003); and Lisa Nakamura's early analysis of "identity tourism," in *Cybertypes: Race, Ethnicity, and Identity on the Internet* (2002).

2. As H. S. Christensen writes, "slacktivism" is generally understood to describe not all forms of online-based activism (e.g., clicktivism), many of which can be effective, but rather "political activities that have no impact on real-life political outcomes, but only serve to increase the feel-good factor of the participants."

3. Also worth noting are the racist personae that other white netizens performed in response to Martin's death, one form of white-identity performance that those who made antiracism gestures sought to distinguish themselves from. As Aisha Durham explains, these reactions included mocking forms of humor and play revolving around dead black male bodies, such as the posting of not only blackface photos but also of depictions of "Trayvoning" (a form of planking in which white youth stage and embody recreations of Martin's death scene) and an online game entitled "Angry Trayvon," in which players don Martin's persona as an avenging urban vigilante in order to "express White rage" by killing virtual inner-city residents (256).

4. As Douglas L. Keene and Rita R. Handrich note, "assumptions about the 'hoodie' reflect stereotypes and biases. The hoodie wearer is seen as a delinquent, as dangerous, as probably black, as untrustworthy, and as 'suspicious.'" When asked by the 911 dispatcher to describe the clothing of Martin, whom he had already described as "suspicious," Zimmerman focused first on Martin's hoodie ("Transcript"); also see Castellanos.

5. As reblogged by "aprilzosia: at *queer.not confused*, 27 March 2012.

6. Regarding the failure of Invisible Children, Inc.'s "Cover the Night" campaign, see Rory Carroll, "Kony 2012 Cover the Night Fails to Move from the Internet to the Streets" (2013). As Graham Meikle also notes, "'Cover the

Night' was not a call to collaborative, shared creativity, but rather to consumption of a prepackaged campaign product" (379).

7. Though such analysis is beyond the scope of this study, there is much to say here as well about the common diffusion in social media of activist impulses into commodified, and thus relatively neutralized, activism. See, for instance, Jodi Dean on "communicative capitalism" in *Blog Theory: Feedback and Capture in the Circuits of Drive* (3–4, 2010); Graham Murdock, "Producing Consumerism: Commodities, Ideologies, Practices" (2013); and Steven Miles, "Young People, 'Flawed Protestors,' and the Commodification of Resistance" (2014). In his analysis of the "insulated" and "benevolent" whiteness pervading the Kony 2012 campaign, David J. Leonard observes,

> The pleasure of clicktivism and its related consumerism, which given the power in dollars and credit cards is more like swipetivism, emanates from its distance and insulation from criticism. It results from not only financial privilege but also a technology that allows for participation without the burden or responsibility of being challenged or examining one's own complicity in injustice.

It seems likely that in several ways, middle-class white activists are more susceptible than others to the seduction of this form of coopted dissent.

8. Mirca Madianou describes polymedia events as a phenomenon in which "an event triggered by the media generates a series of reactions or related events which are played out in different media platforms." They are "unplanned, transnational, and decentralized in the sense that there is no shared official or central narrative; polymedia events are marked by parallel or clashing narratives" (261).

9. It should be noted as well that this "big emotional experience" often comes at the state-sponsored expense of others who are conceptualized in opposing terms: "The white saviour complex imagines black violence as a threat to civilisation. Thus, any form of state violence, whether international war or the prison industrial complex, is repositioned as 'saving' and 'civilising'" (Leonard, n.p.).

10. As Zeus Leonardo and Michalinos Zembylas explain in their analysis of "technologies of whiteness" and affect,

> Whites have built anti-racist understandings that construct the racist as always someone else, the problem residing elsewhere in other Whites. In some instances, this alibi is a white subject's former self. In a recuperative logic, whiteness is able to bifurcate "whites" into good and "bad" subjects, sometimes within the same body or person . . . (151)

11. Perhaps this particular emphasis on happiness accounts as well for the popularity among white American activists of a quotation typically attributed to Emma Goldman: "If I can't dance, I don't want to be part of your revolution."

12. Ironically, while Landers's blog and its offshoot books offer some insightful critiques of a certain form of bohemian whiteness, among several problems with its popularity was that some white readers used it to merely laugh at common white tendencies. More generally, as Grzanka and Maher point out, *Stuff White People Like* "does explicitly name Whiteness, but this act of exposition is simultaneously undercut with its reframing of Whiteness," the power of which "is downplayed as it is consistently incorporated into the framework of neoliberal multiculturalism. Whiteness is rendered ridiculous, but ultimately inconsequential" (388). For a more favorable reading of the blog's analytical utility, see Rosenblatt, "Stuff the Professional-Managerial Class Likes: 'Distinction' for an Egalitarian Elite" (2013).

13. As Amy Schiller writes in her more general analysis of "Kony 2012" and other examples of ultimately self-serving "faux-lanthropy," social media can discourage

> a more sober form of solidarity in the public sphere. The self displaces the communal at the center of this broad range of activities that compose "philanthropy." Rather than enduring institutions, or norms of obligation and gratitude, the main motivators for giving of time and/or money are the sympathetic recognition from others onto oneself, and the allure of one's emotions being strong enough to bring about world change. (581)

14. As Peggy McIntosh points out in her foundational analysis of white privilege, another benefit of white racial membership is that it shields white people "from having to be angry" (294).

Works Cited

Ahmed, Sara. "Declarations of Whiteness: The Non-Performativity of Anti-Racism." *Borderlands E-journal* 3.2 (2004): n.p. Web. 12 Dec. 2015.

———. "A Phenomenology of Whiteness." *Feminist Theory* 8.2 (2007): 149–68. Print.

———. "The Politics of Good Feeling." *Australian Journal of Critical Race and Whiteness Studies* 1.1 (2005): 72–85. Web. 12 Dec. 2015.

Applebaum, Barbara. "Vigilance as a Response to White Complicity." *Educational Theory* 63.1 (2013): 17–34. Print.

aprilzosia. "oddityball asked . . ." *queer.not confused.* aprilzosia.tumblr.com, 27 Mar. 2012. Web. 20 June 2014.

Biss, Eula. *Notes from No Man's Land: American Essays*. Minneapolis: Graywolf P, 2009. Print.

Boyd, Danah. *It's Complicated: The Social Lives of Networked Teens*. New Haven, CT: Yale UP, 2014. Print.

———. "White Flight in Networked Publics: How Race and Class Shaped American Teen Engagement with MySpace and Facebook." *Race after the Internet*. Ed. Lisa Nakamura and Peter A. Chow-White. New York: Routledge, 2012. 203–22. Print.

Byrne, Dara N. "The Future of (the) 'Race': Identity, Discourse, and the Rise of Computer—Mediated Public Spheres." *Learning Race and Ethnicity: Youth and Digital Media*. Ed. Anna Everett. Cambridge: MIT P, 2008. 15–38. Print.

Carroll, Rory. "Kony 2012 Cover the Night Fails to Move from the Internet to the Streets." *Guardian*. theguardian.com, 21 Apr. 2012. Web. 16 Dec. 2015.

Castellanos, Dalina. "Geraldo Rivera: Hoodie Responsible for Trayvon Martin's Death." *Los Angeles Times*. latimes.com, 23 Mar. 2012. Web. 16 Dec. 2015.

Chon, Margaret. "Erasing Race? A Critical Race Feminist View of Internet Identity Shifting." *Critical Race Feminism: A Reader*. Ed. Adrien Katherine Wing. New York: New York UP, 2003. 238–49. Print.

Christensen, H. S. "Political Activities on the Internet: Slacktivism or Political Participation by Other Means?" *First Monday*. U of Illinois at Chicago, 7 Feb. 2011. Web. 16 Dec. 2015.

Cole, Teju. "The White Savior Industrial Complex." *Atlantic*. theatlantic.com, 21 Mar. 2012. Web. 14 Mar. 2013.

"College Freshman: WATCH ONE THIRTY MINUTE VIDEO BECOME SOCIAL ACTIVIST." *Quickmeme*. quickmeme.com, n.d. Web. 12 Dec. 2015.

Daniels, Jessie. *Cyber Racism: White Supremacy Online and the New Attack on Civil Rights*. New York: Rowman and Littlefield, 2009. Print.

Dean, Jodi. *Blog Theory: Feedback and Capture in the Circuits of Drive*. Cambridge, UK: Polity P, 2010. Print.

Durham, Aisha. "____While Black: Millennial Race Plan and the Post Hip-Hop Generation." *Cultural Studies <=> Critical Methodologies* 15.4 (Aug. 2015): 253–58. Print.

Gilmore, Ruth Wilson. *Golden Gulag: Prisons, Surplus, Crisis, and Opposition in Globalizing California*. Berkeley: U of California P, 2007. Print.

Gladwell, Malcolm. "Small Change: Why the Revolution Will Not Be Tweeted." *New Yorker*. newyorker.com, 4 Oct. 2010. Web. 17 June 2014.

Grasmuck, Sherri, et al. "Ethno-Racial Identity Displays on Facebook." *Journal of Computer-Mediated Communication* 15 (2009): 158–88. Print.

Grzanka, Patrick R., and Justin Maher. "Different, Like Everyone Else: *Stuff White People Like* and the Marketplace of Diversity." *Symbolic Interaction* 35.3 (2012): 368–93. Print.

Invisible Children. "KONY 2012 ACTION KIT." *SHOP*. Internet Archive/Wayback Machine. n.d. Web. 23 Jan. 2016.

Kagumire, Rosebell. "My Response to KONY2012." Online video clip. *YouTube*. Google Inc., 17 Mar. 2012. Web. 19 July 2013.

Karens, Barbara. "The White Collective (a Blinding Glimpse of the Obvious)." *Colors of Resistance Archive*. coloursofresistance.org, Mar. 2006. Web. 17 July 2013.

Keene, Douglas L., and Rita R. Handrich. "The 'Hoodie Effect': George, Trayvon and How It Might Have Happened." *Jury Expert* 24.3 (May 2012): n.p. Web. 15 July 2013.

Kim, Kil Ja (as Tamara K. Nopper). "The White Anti-Racist Is an Oxymoron: An Open Letter to White 'Anti-Racists.'" *Race Traitor*. n.d. Web. 17 July 2013.

Lander, Christian. "#18 Awareness." *Stuff White People Like*. 23 Jan. 2008. Web. 16 Dec. 2015.

Leonard, David J. "Remixing the Burden: Kony 2012 and the Wages of Whiteness." *Critical Race and Whiteness Studies* 11.1 (2015): 1–22. Web. 3 Dec. 2015.

Leonardo, Zeus, and Michalinos Zembylas. "Whiteness as Technology of Affect: Implications for Educational Praxis." *Equity and Excellence in Education* 46.1 (2013): 150–65. Print.

Madianou, Mirca. "Humanitarian Campaigns in Social Media: Network Architectures and Polymedia Events." *Journalism Studies* 14.2 (2013): 249–66. Print.

Mbabazi, Amama. "Right Honourable Amama Mbabazi, Prime Minister of Uganda.mov." Online video clip. *YouTube*. Google Inc., 17 Mar. 2012. Web. 12 Dec. 2015.

McIntosh, Peggy. "White Privilege and Male Privilege: A Personal Account of Coming to See Correspondences through Work in Women's Studies." *Critical White Studies: Looking Behind the Mirror*. Eds. R. Delgado and J. Stefancic. 1988. Philadelphia: Temple UP, 1997. 291–99. Print.

Meikle, Graham. "Social Media, Visibility, and Activism: The *Kony 2012* Campaign." *DIY Citizenship: Critical Making and Social Media*. Eds. Matt Ratto et al. Cambridge: MIT P, 2014. 373–84. Print.

Miles, Steven. "Young People, 'Flawed Protestors,' and the Commodification of Resistance." *Critical Arts: A South-North Journal of Cultural and Media Studies* 28.1 (2014): 76–87. Web. 18 June 2014.

Murdock, Graham. "Producing Consumerism: Commodities, Ideologies, Practices." *Critique, Social Media, and the Information Society.* Eds. Christian Fuchs and Marisol Sandoval. New York: Routledge, 2013. 109–24. Print.

Nakamura, Lisa. *Cybertypes: Race, Ethnicity, and Identity on the Internet.* New York: Routledge, 2002. Print.

Nakamura, Lisa, and Peter Chow-White. "Introduction." *Race after the Internet.* Eds. Lisa Nakamura and Peter Chow-White. New York: Routledge, 2012. 1–18. Print.

Nishi, Naomi, et al. "Exposing the White Avatar: Projections, Justifications, and the Ever-Evolving American Racism." *Social Identities: Journal for the Study of Race, Nation, and Culture* 21.5 (2015): 459–73. Print.

Rosenblatt, Daniel. "Stuff the Professional-Managerial Class Likes: 'Distinction' for an Egalitarian Elite." *Anthropological Quarterly* 86.2 (2013): 589–624. Print.

Schiller, Amy. "Philanthropy as Political Liquidation." *Society* 52.6 (2015): 580–84. *EBSCOhost.* Web. 12 Dec. 2015.

Shotwell, Alexis. *Knowing Otherwise: Race, Gender, and Implicit Understanding.* University Park: Pennsylvania State UP: 2011. Print.

13emcha. "I AM NOT TRAYVON MARTIN." Online video clip. *YouTube.* Google Inc., 31 Mar. 2012. Web. 12 Dec. 2015.

"Transcript of George Zimmerman's Call to the Police." *Mother Jones.* n.d. Web. 3 Dec. 2015.

Wagner, Martin. "Evangelical Narcissism: or, Jason Russell *Really* Is an Epic Douchebag." *Atheist Experience.* freethoughtblogs.com, 18 Mar. 2012. Web. 9 July 2013.

Yancy, George, and Janine Jones. "Introduction." *Pursuing Trayvon Martin: Historical Contexts and Contemporary Manifestations of Racial Dynamics.* Eds. George Yancy and Janine Jones. Lexington, UK: Lexington Books, 2012. 1–24. Print.

THE GHOST'S IN THE MACHINE: EHARMONY AND THE REIFICATION OF WHITENESS AND HETERONORMATIVITY

Sarah E. Austin

IT HAS BEEN well-established that race is not based in a human's genetic makeup but, rather, that it is a social construct that has been used to segregate, discriminate against, enslave, and even euthanize the nonwhite Other (Bell; Bonham; hooks; Knowles; Morrison; Painter). Despite the very plain racial and ethnic discrimination and hatred occurring in U.S. society at this moment in the form of recent violent arrests of black Americans, including Arizona State University professor Ersula Ore, shootings of unarmed nonwhite individuals, religiously focused attacks on health-care providers, and the burning of black churches, the notion that the United States is postracial has somehow spread. U.S. society has been able to successfully "e-race" the othering of nonwhites through the strategic and often unchallenged placement of social, political, and economic structures, all of which were brought to the forefront through various symposia, publication collections, and special issues, such as Tammie Kennedy et al.'s *Rhetoric Review* 2005 Symposium on Whiteness Studies; Shona Hunter et al.'s *Social Politics'* 2010 special issue on reproducing and resisting whiteness; Krista Ratcliffe's *Rhetorical Listening: Identification, Gender, Whiteness*; and Aileen Moreton-Robinson et al.'s *Transnational Whiteness Matters: Mythunderstanding*, to name a few.

These publications affirm the reality that race is socially constructed and systematically perpetuated. Recently, given the amount of racially motivated violence, such publications undergird (rather than negate) the need to examine the ways in which whiteness has become synonymous with "neutral" and "normal" in our culture during an age of so-called postracism. Furthermore, while it might be argued that the internet has allowed more access to knowledge, the reality of the web demonstrates that it is inextricably linked to the prison-military-industrial complex by its very inception (Fernandez 526), and so an analysis of our digital culture is imperative in this discussion. It is a complex that, like electronic media theory and technoscience and computer science fields, is populated mostly by white, middle-class males who unknowingly (in most cases) "mistake 'European' and 'North American' for 'universal' and as a result develop . . . criteria that marginalize and exclude the distinctive characteristics of other cultures" (Fernandez 524).

Richard Dyer outlined the need for whiteness studies as a way to respond to demands from nonwhite intellectuals, notably Patricia Williams, who in her 1997 Reith Lecture calls on whites to recognize and investigate their whiteness and begin to reexamine their own complicity in systems of hegemony, hierarchy, and oppression. Not to do so, Dyer argued, would be "to assume [that] we have no 'racial' identity, as if other, nonwhite people are raced, but we whites are just people" (qtd. in "Seeing the White").

Dyer's conviction has recently been corroborated by Christian Rudder, founder of OkCupid, a popular online dating site discussed in his book *Dataclysm*. Rudder set out to utilize his site's glut of information to see what patterns emerged about humanity and found, unsurprisingly, that the "data on race . . . could've been from the 1950s." Here is how he describes the book on amazon.com:

> [I] unpacked three separate databases and found that in every one white people gave black people the short-shrift. . . . Asians and Latinos apply the same penalty to African Americans that white folks do, which says something about how even (relatively) recent additions to the "American experience" have acquired its biases. (Q&A with Christian Rudder)

This reinforcement of white as a desirable, invisible, natural state is strengthened by the rhetorical moves and visual structures utilized on websites. This analysis seeks to illuminate such moves and structures in order to decenter whiteness, to draw attention to the fact that it is an aspect of humanity that is taken for granted as ordinary and that, in functioning as such, it solidifies and perpetuates hegemonic structures, power inequities, and discrimination.

Likewise, heteronormativity has become aligned with whiteness and, thus, is also the default norm. Specifically, because of the increasing reliance on the web for gathering and distributing news and information, connecting with family and friends, and finding potential significant others, it is necessary to scrutinize how the space works to reproduce the social norms of whiteness and heterosexuality. While there has been much research conducted on the ways in which gender is selective and exclusionary both in traditional and online dating forums (Feliciano et al.; Murr; Robnett and Feliciano; Tsunoki et al.; Wilson et al.; Yancey.), little research has been conducted to show how websites perpetuate the status quo of whiteness and heterosexuality as neutral and normal. As a result, we have become further ensconced in a racialized, engendered society, which continuously allows groups to be "othered" in ways that sustain problematic hierarchies. This chapter's visual and rhetorical analysis will focus on the perpetuation of whiteness as it is explicitly connected to heterosexuality in the present-day social media site, eHarmony.

Such an analysis makes apparent the ways in which whiteness and heteronormativity together are able to more insidiously persist and even thrive within a society that has labeled itself postracial. Although it is unlikely that eHarmony will alter its visual and rhetorical mindset regarding white as preferable and the male-female binary as natural given its founder's overtly conservative, Christian values, which are inherently and historically imbued with a sense of whiteness ("Neil Clark Warren"), this analysis hopes to make clear how the hegemonic structures of race and gender work together and flourish in online spaces. Ideally, sites will slowly, thanks to recent changes in U.S. legislation, adapt to the increased social acceptance of those othered by such structures.

In order to show that eHarmony linguistically and rhetorically embraces and fosters whiteness as neutral and heteronormative, the analysis will provide a qualitative discussion of the rhetorical moves made via the website and the accompanying questionnaire's visual selections, design aesthetics, and linguistic choices (headings, content, word choice, etc.). Similarly, the "29 Dimensions of Compatibility," which are broken down into two categories—Core Traits and Vital Attributes (Why eHarmony: 29 Dimensions of Capability)—will be rhetorically analyzed in order to determine the linguistic and cultural ways that these categories reaffirm whiteness and heterosexuality as normal and desirable, and in fact, allow this normality to be continually invisible.

The Website

The homepage for eHarmony appears as depicted in figure 6.1. The gender selections indicated on the homepage are found in a dropdown menu format; once registered, the gender choices are represented by the male/female signs, complete with corresponding background colors or, in other cases, by bathroom door iconography: a male silhouette in blue and a female silhouette displayed in a pink dress (figure 6.2). Either way, this representation is highly heteronormative given that there are individuals who are seeking both men and women or individuals who do not identify as strictly male or female: cross-dressers, intersex individuals, those who have not had a physical sex change but identify as a gender other than the one they appear to be, among others.

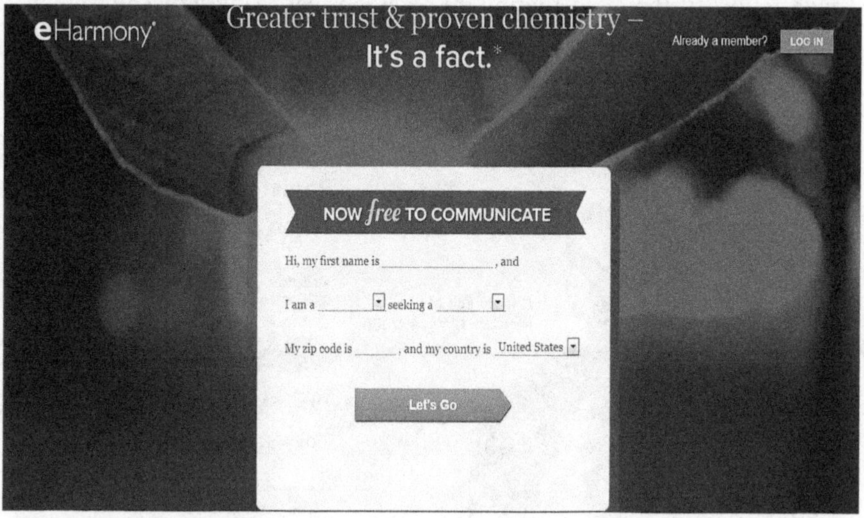

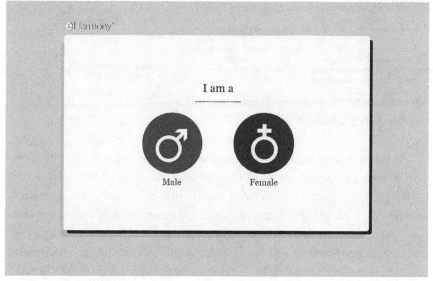

Figure 6.1. eHarmony splash page

Figure 6.2. Gender choices

The website does not allow the user to identify as both male and female, nor does it allow a choice of neither; likewise, it does not allow one to search for people of both genders at the same time, as depicted by the drop-down menu when registering (figure 6.3). Similarly, one cannot specify that s/he looks like one gender but identifies as the other. In fact, when one types in his/her name and selects, for example, "I am a Woman," the box that asks what the user is seeking automatically selects "Man." This implies a societal expectation, further perpetuating the heteronormative myth that all women want men and further that this space is not welcoming to anyone who does not fit into (or buy into) a strictly heteronormative, gendered system that is steeped in whiteness.

Figure 6.3. Gender binaries

This discrimination was reinforced when eHarmony was sued in 2008 because of its unwillingness to cater in any way to LGBTQ individuals ("Neil Clark Warren"). Because of the lawsuit, the website did add these categories; however, as I focus on later in the chapter, these categories are not part of the main page, nor easily accessed from it, further relegating nonwhite, nonhetero groups to the physical margins of the site. And while American society seems to be shifting toward a more multiracial, homosexual inclusivity as highlighted by the election of an African American president in 2008, the U.S. military's repeal of Don't Ask Don't Tell in 2011, and the passage of marriage equality laws by the U.S. Supreme Court for same-sex couples in 2014, eHarmony is unlikely to reflect this trend in the near future given its conservative religious focus. It is unclear at what point not embracing such societal shifts will be financially detrimental to the company, if ever. However, the lawsuit, coupled with the website's clear intent to cater to white, hetero individuals, means it's likely that they will lose customers to more identity-specific sites like Grinder.com or blacksingles. com, which cater to more diverse users. Further, even if eHarmony did add a "gay" or "multiracial" option, the underpinnings of the site's values are overtly articulated by its perpetuation of white, heteronormative ideologies.

Not surprisingly, the color and central location of the gender-identity box draws the eye, exemplifying what Robin Williams, a well-known author of web design books, coined the CRAP principle, which outlines the most effective visual arrangement for internet sites. Her principle, which is utilized almost uniformly across U.S. college campuses in order to teach web design, states that for any visual design to be viewed as organized, unified, analytic, and professional, it must pay attention to Contrast, Repetition, Alignment, and Proximity (CRAP) (Rundle). However, it is important to note, as Anne Wysocki does in her article "The Sticky Embrace of Beauty," that form is part of content, not completely separated from it, and that how a design is constructed is as telling as what is being assembled (149). Likewise, the adjectives Williams attaches to an organized layout are not in fact, neutral, as she implies. Rather, these adjectives ascribe value to a specific way of viewing, and this value has become so ingrained that it has become the norm for formatting pages whether they are online or in print. Much like whiteness and heteronormativity, this way of viewing texts has been rendered invisible by its pervasiveness, and only those who carefully consider the ways that values shape action via such methods as visual rhetorical analysis are immune (151). In reality, the ways in which certain visual designs are privileged, constructed, and maintained are identical to the ways in which U.S. society creates media that reflect race and gender norms that are perpetuated and systematized through historical acts of discrimination and hierarchical decision-making.

White people are only ever able to talk about the Other as an abstract aspect of a fossilized society (hence, the insistence that one black president equals a postracial society); one without material consequences for those at the top of the power structure, since their seeing or not seeing their own whiteness in no way effects their predominance in the job market, politics, or education ("Seeing the White" 1). Yet we cannot escape "somehow being shaped by the viewing" in which we are participating (Wysocki 152). This is exactly why white skin has become the invisible default (especially in the eyes of those who identify or pass to a general public as white) for viewing and discussing human beings and why hetero relationships are deemed natural. The ability to permanently shape how individuals view one another enables a societal hierarchy to exist that privileges those in power. Online media like eHarmony and others simply mirror the larger societal norms and recreate the othering that has already been fully accepted and rendered invisible.

As Rudder's work details, and Wysocki's and Williams's work reveal, online profiles that are built to attract romantic partners divulge humans' inherently undiscussed and often unconscious biases around race and gender. In the deliberately crafted world of eHarmony's website, what "we see before our eyes exhibits a particular perspective, centered upon the self. It takes time and effort to learn to compensate for the one-sidedness of the egocentric view; and throughout a person's life there persists a tendency to reserve for the self the largest possible share of power to organize the surroundings around itself at the center" (Arnheim 4–5), in this case, preferences about what one should find attractive and desirable: white, hetero. Further, these analyses (Rudders, and those derived from Wysocki's and Williams's work) disclose a more disturbing reality, that the indoctrination of white and hetero being ordinary, best, most attractive, have become so normalized that, in fact, individuals represent these biases during their most vulnerable and private moments, moments when they thought no one was watching.

Like Wysocki's rhetorical analysis of the visual, Arnheim's observation articulates exactly the appeal of hegemonic structures to an individual brought up unaware that American society's capitalist, racist, and sexist values are constructed. Focusing on one's own goals and desires, whether they are romantic—as is the case with eHarmony users—or otherwise, negates any focus on the community and exacerbates the reality that "othering" has become the norm. Such individual focus casts aside the empathy and compassion necessary to undermine systems of racism and sexism, among other hegemonies, precisely because individuals are not aware of their own preferences, or, if they are, they are so unwilling to share them that they only reveal them in instances where they believe no one is paying attention.

Nowhere is this "othering" more apropos than on a dating site where an individual is primarily focused on his or her own happiness. Thus, it is in spaces where we are prone to the solipsistic world of our inner selfish desires and unaware of an audience that tropes of whiteness and heteronormativity are most likely to show themselves. Whiteness and heteronormativity are the central tenets of eHarmony's website because they are its most prominent and repetitive features. The website carefully follows the visual design principles put forth by Robin Williams and dissected using Wysocki's methods and, in so doing, reinscribes societal norms as natural to humans' ways of being.

How a website is constructed may appear benign and unintentional. However, humans make meaning out of shapes and the placement of objects in a space, whether that space is two or three dimensional. The placement of shapes on a page automatically implies energy, status and values (Bang 58). The elements of visual composition take on and reflect meanings of human experience, directionality, and embodiment because positioning in space reflects our positioning in reality and the meanings that are attached to those positions (Kress 136). And since eHarmony is one of the most widely used dating websites and reflects hegemonic/normative structures of our current society, it is an important social site of investigation. Analyzing its visual rhetorical structures and moves is particularly prescient and kairotic as we claim to be in a postracial society. It is a Western visual tradition that space and directionality are a semiotic resource of culture. As such, the systems we carry forward through our conceptual "tools" and in conceptual and real spaces are those that we value and, thus, must always be studied, cross-examined, and questioned (199).

The box, lightly colored and crisply shaped, contrasts well with the fuzzy, dark, slightly abstract background picture of the happy white couple (see figure 6.1). Because the picture is intentionally out of focus and zoomed in too far, the couple is not personally identifiable; it is only their positioning, as a hetero, white couple presumably in love (because they're holding hands), that is used to comfort the user in a space that may seem scary or foreign. While participating in online dating is becoming more socially acceptable, it still carries a certain amount of attached stigma ("Online Dating"); those who decide to join need constant reinforcement as to their decision to participate, and thus the rhetorical moves of the site have to be white, hetero default settings that emphasize to individuals identifying as such that they are welcome. Subsequently, these default settings also communicate loudly to those who do not identify as white/hetero that they are not. In this way, the image of the couple ideally aligns with the CRAP principle as it is an unassuming and unintrusive backdrop for recruiting those people the site wants. The translucent white box subtly but forcibly directs the user to identify as a man or woman and to clarify who s/he is seeking so that the participant may "get on with" finding his or her "perfect match" with relative ease. The white box allows the website to more efficiently sell its product to its target audience: white, hetero individuals.

Following the CRAP principle, the web page is deceptive in its scope. At first glance it appears to be occupied only by this single backdrop photo, the translucent box and the little red banner welcoming users to the site. However, the P in CRAP stands for proximity; the user may decide to scroll down the page and will discover much more content than is initially evident. Such "standards" only serve to further white heteronormativity, which is also considered ordinary and typical because of the literacies it inherently privileges. The content of the obscured aspects of the page uphold the R and P of the CRAP principle: the proximity of objects makes logical sense to the user, and the user can always navigate to more than one section of the site with ease, assuming, as the site does, that the individuals joining the page are conditioned to see left-to-right, top-to-bottom, and proximity as a measure of importance as logical and normal. Such assumptions, made most often by the creators of pages who are overwhelmingly white males (Miller), reinforce that white and heterosexual are the norms for this online society in a way that, like the obscured aspects of the page, obfuscate hegemonies, which may be unintended but exist and communicate nonetheless.

Recall that the top of the homepage has the phrase, "Greater Trust and Proven Chemistry: It's a fact*." The first five words are in bold, white, Georgia 24 font to give maximum contrast to the dark backdrop and for ease of reading. The words: "It's a fact*" are slightly smaller, positioned just below the initial phrase about trust and are in gold. Thus, the positionality of the phrases themselves highlights and privileges the Trust and Chemistry of the site's methodology and underscores the "fact" that underpins that trust.

It's the trust aspect of the site that Seth Godin questions in his book *The Icarus Deception: How High Will You Fly?* Godin focuses on Trust and Permission. He is referring to the trust that consumers put into sites when we allow access to our Facebook pages or contact lists, and when we entrust our personal and financial information with the belief that our information will be secure. Such trust is given willingly and is an aspect of privilege.

Godin says, "Media is cheap, sure, attention is filtered, and it's virtually impossible to be heard unless the consumer gives us the ability to be heard. The more valuable someone's attention is, the harder it is to earn" (2). Because consumers listen to those they trust and seek out people who tell them stories that emotionally appeal and intellectually resonate, Godin asserts that websites work hard to craft an aura of remarkability and freshness, something "worth listening to" (2). Thus, eHarmony, by boldly asserting on the front page that it is trustworthy, manages to create an interface not of carefully chosen and crafted images and words but a comfortable, safe space for connecting with friends and meeting would-be significant others. In doing so, the machine brilliantly and completely disappears behind the curtain. It's an interesting juxtaposition—as humans we are attracted to things that we deem risky and fresh but also perceive to be safe and trustworthy. Consequently, the creator of the site must be edgy, fresh, and exhilarating while simultaneously maintaining a level of familiarity that resonates as trust. Such familiarity is earned on the basis of its ability to reiterate hegemonic principles of whiteness and heterosexuality, as they are subconsciously felt to be trustworthy.

The homepage of the website achieves this familiarity by including a place to follow eHarmony on Facebook, Twitter, and YouTube as well as four subcategories for those who are not quite ready to decide that they are "seeking" a significant other: "About eHarmony," "Why eHarmony," "eHarmony Tour," and "Success Stories." The site also advertises that it is part of the Better Business Bureau, Trust-e certified, and secured by Norton. All of these icons, littered at or around the bottom of the homepage, serve as reminders that this space is "normal" and "familiar," which comforts the would-be consumer and coaxes him or her to further utilize the site (figure 6.4). Similarly, the "success stories" serve to reassure the user that this is a safe, comfortable space in which s/he might find love. In order to support that ethos, the site appeals to the users' emotions by proving the site's effectiveness. The success story page, which can be accessed via the homepage, features polaroid-esque photos depicting entirely heterosexual relationships (see figure 6.3). Only one of seven pictured individuals could even remotely be construed as anything other than "white." The page seems to say, "See? This isn't scary. This is exactly how the world looks, how the world should look." And in so doing, it effectively relaxes many of its users while also perpetuating whiteness as neutral and heteronormative. This is oppressive to people who are not white and straight and serves to perpetuate the idea that only straight white people deserve love and representation.

Figure 6.4. Ethos of trust

If one looks carefully, there are subpages available for "samesex couples," and "country-specific pages," but they are not easy to find via the standard CRAP principle guidelines. That is, they are not accessible via the main webpage nor are they in close proximity to the "eye-catching" aspects of the website. This rhetorical obfuscation on the part of the web designer suggests (because they are relegated to non-CRAP spaces) that such groups are not mainstream enough to warrant repetition or attention in the same way that the white, heteronormative pages are. Thus, the message is that white heteronormativity is saleable, and other lifestyles, preferences, and appearances are less desirable and should be silenced. The implication is that they aren't good enough to occupy the same privileged space as the white heterosexuals.

Should one be curious enough to scroll down to the bottom of the homepage, the reason for the asterisk that accompanies the word "fact*" is explained: it denotes a 2009 study done by Harris Interactive, a research team that eHarmony hired to conduct surveys of the site, its matchmaking capabilities, and its successes. So, while eHarmony allows users a feeling of safety via its trustworthy algorithms and recognizable, obedient, white, heteronormative frames, it also allows for a limited amount of variation in order to reach out to a slightly broader, although still "normal," obedient, and contained "other." This further exemplifies the silent but deliberate ways that the site utilizes rhetorical moves and web design to further its neoliberal values, perpetuating whiteness and heterosexuality as acceptable imperatives, and relegating nonwhite, nonheterosexual groups to the margins (literally and figuratively).

Godin asserts that websites must always be changing and evolving in order to keep their consumers' attention, "because attention and trust must be earned, not acquired" (3). Hence, the appeal of eHarmony is that it allows users to be in a safe, contained space that is "research-based." Once ensconced in the space, individuals can sift through a manageable number of choices that have been garnered using a specific questionnaire designed to limit their matches to categories with which the consumers (and the site) are comfortable. The attraction of an unknown significant other found online is risky enough even with the safety of screened individuals. If the webpage then also imbues the consumer's "matches" with people that fail to live up to their physical, ethnic, racial, and sexual comfort zones, the website may very likely go out of business. eHarmony users are trained systematically to have hegemonic preferences and eHarmony both caters to and perpetuates those preferences.

As Godin posits, the website must earn the trust and permission of its users and cannot afford to upset the status quo of its largest consumer base. Judging by the white, hetero norms perpetuated on the site, eHarmony's biggest demographic must consist largely of white, heterosexual men and women. eHarmony and its users are stuck in a racist/sexist, sexual orientation-ist feedback loop in which the very set-up of the site is flawed by its privileging of whiteness and heterosexuality, and so attracts users who are also flawed in their need to seek those hegemonic systems out. The result is that they feed off of each other.

The attentions individuals garner via the eHarmony website are those they themselves have predetermined to be acceptable with the website's and questionnaire's help. In theory, the algorithm used by the website is doing what Godin says only human artists can do: identify the magical story worth telling (3). And while the "matches" are algorithmically generated, the success stories that are posted on the website accentuate the human element of finding love. However, in this case, the only love worth finding is that of white heterosexuals. The photos chosen to grace eHarmony's pages and the additional content are selected by (one assumes) marketing experts who then "tell" the success stories and spread their own magic via the corporate machine of the World Wide Web and, in so doing, continue to further the fairytale that only those who look like Cinderella and her white, male prince deserve the kind of love offered at eHarmony.

About eHarmony

One of the site's subtabs is called Company Overview: the background of the page is white with a blue header. To the right is a "fun fact" that utilizes Social Security Administration statistics to show that since 2000 (the year eHarmony was launched) the use of the name Harmony increased 47 percent, implying that eHarmony's launch must have been the cause for this, which further supports the initial claim that the website is trustworthy. There are blue hyperlinks to eHarmony affiliates (labs and advice) as well as information about the board of directors.

There are only two people listed on the Board of Directors page: Dr. Neil Clark Warren and Greg Penner. Dr. Warren, an older gentleman and clinical psychologist, is the founder of the site. He is most often referred to as Dr. Warren in order to reassure users that he is qualified to find them "matches." Greg Penner is a partner in an investment banking firm and the director of Walmart, Hyatt, and eHarmony, among other corporations. Both are white, hetero men. The "fun fact," one of eHarmony's rhetorical moves designed to hook the audience both emotionally and ethically, appears on the Board of Directors page. One fact claims that on average 438 members of eHarmony marry daily in the United States thanks to the website's "match-making" capabilities. This fun fact has a montage of sixteen happy couples' wedding pictures (all hetero, five featuring all-white couples, three featuring one white partner and one light-skinned Asian, African American, or Latino partner, three Asian couples, and two African American couples). There is also a link back to the sign-in page so the convinced users may quickly navigate back to the main page and begin the process of finding their own "perfect match," which will invariably be a white, hetero one.

The "Management" tab lists the names and titles of those who "manage" the eHarmony company. Each name is clickable and shows a bio of the individual listed. The fun fact on this page says that those individuals who star in eHarmony's commercials are actual couples who were successfully matched on the site and highlights Julia and Adam, a successful match who happen to be white and hetero.

The "Shareholders" page, the last tab under "About," lists three shareholding companies and gives basic information about who they are, their overall interests, and when they became part of eHarmony. There are hyperlinks to one of the shareholders' sites and a fun fact included (figure 6.5). Figure 6.5's message that success is equivalent to being a hetero, white couple is impossible to misconstrue.

eHarmony's Shareholders

In addition to our founders and employees, we have the following major shareholders:

Technology Crossover Ventures

Technology Crossover Ventures (TCV) became an investor in eHarmony in 2004. TCV, founded in 1995, is a leading provider of growth capital to technology companies, providing funds to later-stage private and public companies. With $7.7 billion in capital under management, TCV has made growth equity and recapitalization investments in over 160 companies leading to 45 initial public offerings and more than 30 strategic sales or mergers. In addition to eHarmony, representative investments include Altiris, Expedia, Fandango, Liquidnet, Netflix, RealNetworks, Redback Networks, Solect Technology, TechTarget, Travelport, Webroot, and Zillow. TCV has 11 partners and is headquartered in Palo Alto, California.

Sequoia Capital

Sequoia Capital became an investor in eHarmony in 2004. Sequoia Capital provides venture capital funding to founders of startups who want to turn business ideas into enduring companies. As the "Entrepreneurs Behind the Entrepreneurs", Sequoia Capital's Partners have worked with innovators such as Steve Jobs of Apple Computer, Larry Ellison of Oracle, Bob Swanson of Linear Technology, Sandy Lerner and Len Bozack of Cisco Systems, Dan Warmenhoven of NetApp, Jerry Yang and David Filo of Yahoo!, Jen-Hsun Huang of NVIDIA, Michael Marks of Flextronics, Larry Page and Sergey Brin of Google, Chad Hurley and Steve Chen of YouTube, Dominic Orr and Keerti Melkote of Aruba Wireless Networks, Jonathan Kaplan of Pure Digital, Tony Hsieh of Zappos and Omar Hamoui of Admob. To learn more about Sequoia Capital visit www.sequoiacap.com/us/internet.

Fun Fact

eHarmony's first known Success Couple was married on **Feb. 17, 2001.**

Figure 6.5. Facts about eHarmony shareholders

On the "Newsroom" page there are rotating news articles featuring eHarmony. It is adorned by the same fun fact as figure 6.5, with the same white, hetero silhouette. It includes hyperlinks to the eHarmony main page at the very top in large blue and gray lettering and to the lesser-advertised country and minority pages. The links to countries' pages and to alternative dating pages are in tiny white script at the very bottom of this page (figure 6.6).

Figure 6.6. More information about eHarmony and other dating sites

In order to get to these pages, one has to scroll all the way down past the news reel. It is difficult to come upon these pages accidentally. That these categories are considered anathema to the "main" site is further evidence that what has become normalized is white and heterosexual and, arguably, American.

The 29 Dimensions of Compatibility that form the underpinnings of eHarmony's dating philosophy are the cornerstones of the site's perpetuation of whiteness and heteronormativity as neutral. According to the website, the Dimensions of Compatibility are made up of two categories, "Core Traits" and "Vital Attributes." The Core Traits, which are identified as those aspects of an individual that do not change throughout adulthood are Emotional Temperament, Social Style, Cognitive Mode, and Physicality. Additionally, the Vital Attributes, those characteristics that are learned, are more likely to be malleable. These attributes are Relationship Skills, Values and Beliefs, and Key Experiences. Each subcategory has an icon next to it.

The icons are all light blue rectangles with rounded edges, but the symbol inside the rectangle varies by trait or attribute. A few are noteworthy given the focus of this paper: Social Style is accented by a light blue square with an orange male figurine (much like the bathroom icon) centrally located in the rectangle and in front of two darker blue female figurines, one on each side and behind the male icon (figure 6.7). This image location suggests, given Wysocki's, Kress's, Bang's, and others' theories of positionality, that the male is the focus of social style and that women are plentiful, assuming one is white.

Married: May 28, 2006

Core Traits

Emotional Temperament
How do you feel about yourself and about the world? While specific day-to-day and moment-to-moment events play a major role in our emotions, deep-seated patterns of emotion are also a fundamental part of who you are and how people perceive you. The following dimensions are considered part of your Emotional Temperament: *Self Concept, Emotional Status, Energy: Emotional, Obstreperousness, and Passion: Romantic.*

Social Style
How do you relate to other people? Do you crave company, or prefer to be alone? Are you more comfortable leading, or do you prefer to go along with the group? Basic feelings such as these comprise an important aspect of who you are and who you will be most compatible with. The dimensions which define your Social Style are: *Character, Kindness, Dominance, Sociability, Autonomy, and Adaptability.*

Cognitive Mode
How do you think about the world around you? Are you motivated by an insatiable curiosity about the world and events around you? Are you constantly looking for intellectual challenges? Do you find humor to be your favorite coping strategy when dealing with the world? Although Emotional Temperament and Social Style can impact on this trait, your Cognitive Mode is an important separate aspect of who you are, and defines a lot of the ways in which you interact with people. The dimensions which define your dominant Cognitive Mode are: *Intellect, Curiosity, Humor, and Artistic Passion.*

Physicality
How do you relate physically with the world? How do you relate physically with yourself? Are you energetic, athletic and constantly in motion? Or are you more comfortable and happy walking than running? Feelings and thoughts which revolve around your physical life form an important aspect of who you are. The dimensions which deal with your Physicality include: *Energy: Physical, Passion: Sexual, Vitality and Security, Industry, and Appearance.*

Figure 6.7. Core traits

Another notable icon is the Values and Beliefs icon (figure 6.8) that pictures, foregrounded on the same light blue rectangle as every other icon on this part of the page, what looks like three darker blue books. Two are next to one another, with the third leaning against the upright two, as books on a shelf. The first one says in white lettering on the spine of the "book": "Ambition." The second "book" is titled "Spirituality" and the third is blank. This suggests that individuals should focus on finding significant others who

Vital Attributes

Relationship Skills
The amount of effort and skill that you devote to making a relationship work are key elements of who you are, and what type of person you are most likely to succeed with in a relationship. The dimensions that identify your Relationship Skills are: *Communication Style, Emotion Management, Conflict Resolution.*

Values and Beliefs
Values and Beliefs are at the center of most of our life experiences. How we feel about spirituality, religion, family and even politics influence how we think about the world and who we are going to be most comfortable sharing our lives with. The dimensions that determine your Values and Beliefs are: *Spirituality, Family Goals, Traditionalism, Ambition, and Altruism.*

Key Experiences
All of your life experiences combine to affect who you are and how you relate to the world. Although many of the effects of these experiences are represented by the other Core Traits and Vital Attributes, the following dimensions are considered part of your Key Experiences: *Family Background, Family Status, and Education.*

Figure 6.8. Vital attributes

are spiritual and ambitious, the former of which is often equated with heteronormativity and the latter of which is often associated with masculinity.

Similarly, the values and beliefs are listed in bold lettering at the end of the description of this category: spirituality, family goals, traditionalism, ambition, and altruism (see figure 6.8). While furthering altruism would improve the social hierarchies present in social media such as eHarmony, advancing traditional values could be identified as one reason why whiteness is seen as neutral and normal, and heteronormativity as desirable.

Lastly, the icon next to Key Experiences shows a yellow oval wearing an orange graduation cap complete with tassel. This is also foregrounded against the light blue rectangle. The bolded key experiences are: Family Background, Family Status, and Education. Interestingly, where someone "comes from," her family's status, and her education have historically been ways of segregating and "othering" nonwhite and nonmale populations. In fact, "gender, race, and class are interacting systems of domination that affect access to power and privileges" (Chow). For example, despite decades of effort, school and residential segregation continue to be problems in the United States, and racial segregation is often inextricably linked to class segregation (Frankenberg 67). In addition, women tend to earn less money than their male counterparts for the same job, and this inequality is more pronounced for black or Hispanic women (Cotter 444).

Once users decide to embark upon the lengthy process of filling out the eHarmony questionnaire, they are initially asked to enter their name. The next screen then says, "Hi, [your name here]. It's nice to meet you," and attempts to ease the user's fears by assuring him or her that the process is "a breeze." The effort to comfort the person embarking on the journey is further punctuated using *pathos* by backdropping the page with a serene nature shot and by beginning with easy questions, with the first question asking if the user is a male or female.

However, there are no alternatives to the two choices, nor is one able to click both the male and female categories. Further emphasizing the binary, the male and female symbols, conveniently demarcated in blue and pink, are positioned directly below the category. If the layout of the pages, the photo and verbiage choices of web design itself, and the above question were not sufficient to convince the user that this site privileges white heteronormativity, the following few questions should. After asking for the user's birthdate and quickly calculating and posting in large letters what the user's age should be based on the information, then determining the user's geographic location (where do you live?), the questionnaire proceeds to the questions. And, just to be absolutely sure to make the point that this means white, hetero relationships, the icon above the question consists of interlocking circles of red and blue, one with a white silhouette of a woman, the other a white silhouette of a man (figure 6.9).

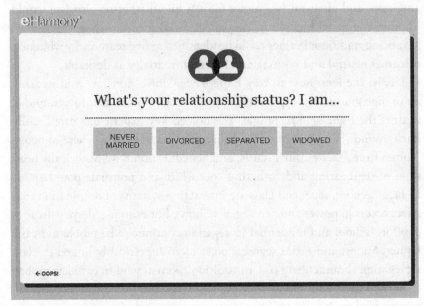

Figure 6.9. Relationship status

Immediately following the intense questioning, the 90 percent finished screen appears. The site appeals to the user's emotions by telling her or him how amazing her or his story is and that the only part of the questionnaire left is the part where they must rank by importance the categories of physical appearance, race, religion, daily habits, education, and financial status. This screen is backgrounded with a photo of an older white man and white woman (based upon their dress, as their faces are not shown), again zoomed in so only their torsos are visible. They are holding hands (figure 6.10). Again eHarmony perpetuates whiteness to the detriment of nonwhite people.

It is these connections between people that eHarmony purports to build on its website. And it is these bridges that reinforce, silently and with positive intentions, the status quos of heteronormativity, racism, and whiteness as normal and invisible. What makes the internet so intriguing is that it has the ability to communicate and perpetuate norms while it simultaneously subverts, creates, confounds, and challenges them. It is not sufficient to simply become aware of the systems that serve to exclude, segregate, and oppress others. Instead, analyses like this one need to find their way into

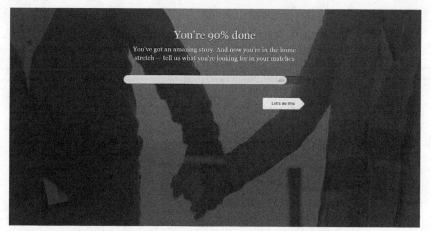

You're 90% done

You've got an amazing story. And now you're in the home
stretch — tell us what you're looking for in your matches

Let's do this

Figure 6.10. Heteronormative representations of affection

our classrooms, our conversations, our daily lives. If we are able to utilize critical pedagogies in our classrooms and foster public intellectualism and scrutiny through our media, perhaps we can move beyond simply naming whiteness and heteronormativity, beyond simply making them visible, and instead begin to subvert, dismantle, and transform them. Then, we may become part of a new revolution instead of simply being the perpetuators of discriminatory hegemonic structures.

Works Cited

Arnheim, Rudolf. *The Power of the Center: A Study of Composition in the Visual Arts.* Berkeley: U of California P, 1983. Print.

Bang, Molly. *Picture This: Perception and Composition.* San Francisco: Chronicle Books, 2000. Print.

Bell, Derrick. *Faces at the Bottom of the Well: The Permanence of Racism.* New York: Basic Books, 1992. Print.

Bonham, Vence, Jr. "Viewpoint: Race and Genomics: A Challenge to Medical Educators." National Human Genome Research Institute. n.d. Web. 29 Jan. 2016.

Chow, Esther Ngan-Ling. "Introduction: Transforming Knowledgement: Race, Class, and Gender." *Race, Class, and Gender: Common Bonds, Different Voices.* Ed. Esther Ngan-Ling Chow, Doris Wilkinson, and Maxine Baca Zinn. Thousand Oaks, CA: Sage P, 1996. xix–xxvi. Print.

Cotter, David A., Joan M. Hermsen, and Reeve Vanneman. "Systems of Gender, Race and Class Inequality: Multilevel Analyses." *Social Forces* 78.2 (Dec. 1999): 433–60. eHarmony © 2000–13. 11 Nov. 2013. Web. 7 Aug. 2014.

Feliciano, Cynthia, Belinda Robnett, and Golnaz Komaie. "Gendered Racial Exclusion among White Daters." *Social Science Research* 38 (2009): 39–54. Print.

Fernandez, Maria. "Postcolonial Media Theory." *The Feminism and Visual Culture Reader*. Ed. Amelia Jones. London: Routledge, 2003. 520–28. Print.

Frankenberg, Erica, Chungmei Lee, and Gary Orfield. "A Multiracial Society with Segregated Schools: Are We Losing the Dream?" *The Civil Rights Project*. Harvard University. Jan. 2003. PDF file.

Godin, Seth. *The Icarus Deception: How High Will You Fly?* London: Penguin Books, 2012. Print.

hooks, bell. "Representation of Whiteness in the Black Imagination." *Black Looks: Race and Representation*. Boston: South End P, 1992. Print.

Hunter, Shona, Elaine Swan, and Diane Grimes. "Introduction: Reproducing and Resisting Whiteness in Organizations, Policies, and Places." *Social Politics* 17.4 (2010): 407–22.

Kennedy, Tammie M., Joyce Irene Middleton, and Krista Ratcliffe. "Whiteness Studies" Symposium. *Rhetoric Review* 24.4 (2005): 359–402. Print.

Knowles, Caroline. *Race and Social Analysis*. Thousand Oaks, CA: Sage. 2003. Print.

Kress, Gunther, and Theo van Leeuwen. *Reading Images: The Grammar of Visual Design*. New York: Routledge, 1996. Print.

Miller, Claire Cain. "Technology's Man Problem." *New York Times*. Technology, 5 Apr. 2014. Web. 14 Sept. 2014.

Moreton-Robinson, Aileen, Maryrose Casey, and Fiona Nicoll, eds. *Transnational Whiteness Matters: Mythunderstanding*. Lanham, MD: Rowman and Littlefield P, 2008. Print.

Morrison, Toni. *Playing in the Dark: Whiteness and the Literary Imagination*. New York: Vintage, 1992. Print.

Murr, Andrew. "Dating the White Way." *Newsweek* 144.6 (2004): 9. Print.

"Neil Clark Warren, eHarmony Founder, Says Gay Marriage 'Damaged His Company.'" *Huffington Post*. TheHuffingtonPost.com, Inc. 15 Feb. 2013. Web. 14 Sept. 2014.

"Online Dating and Relationships." Senior Researcher Aaron Smith and Assistant Researcher Maeve Duggan. *Pew Internet Project*. Washington, DC: Pew Research Center. 21 Oct. 2013. Web. 14 Sept. 2014.

Painter, Nell Irvin. *The History of White People*. New York: Norton, 2010. Print.

Q&A with Christian Rudder, cofounder of OkCupid and author of *Dataclysm*. *Amazon.com*. n.d. Web. 14 Sept. 2014.

Ratcliffe, Krista. *Rhetorical Listening: Identification, Gender, Whiteness.* Carbondale: Southern Illinois UP, 2006. Print.

Robnett, Belinda, and Cynthia Feliciano. "Patterns of Racial-Ethnic Exclusion by Internet Daters." *Social Forces* 89.3 (Mar. 2011): 807–28. Print.

Rundle, Mike. "How C.R.A.P. Is Your Design?" *Treehouse Blog.* 26 Oct. 2013. Web. 14 Sept. 2014.

"Seeing the White." *Times Higher Education.* 30 June 1997. Web. 12 Sept. 2014.

Tsunokai, Glenn T., Augustine J. Kposowa, and Michele A. Adams. "Racial Preferences in Internet Dating: A Comparison of Four Birth Cohorts." *Western Journal of Black Studies* 33.1 (2009): 1–15. Print.

Williams, Patricia. *The Reith Lectures 1997: The Genealogy of Race.* Lecture 3: "The Distribution of Distress." Transmission: 11. *BBC.* March 1997. Radio.

Wilson, Shauna B., William D. McIntosh, and Salvatore P. Insana II. "Dating across Race: An Examination of African American Internet Personal Advertisements." *Journal of Black Studies* 37 (2007): 964–82. Print.

Wysocki, Anne Frances. "The Sticky Embrace of Beauty: On Some Formal Problems in Teaching about the Visual Aspects of Texts." *Writing New Media.* Ed. Anne Frances Wysocki et al. Logan: Utah State UP, 2004. 147–98. Print.

Yancey, George. "Crossracial Differences in the Racial Preferences of Potential Dating Partners: A Test of the Alienation of African Americans and Social Dominance Orientation." *Sociological Quarterly* 50 (2009): 121–43. Print.

7

FACEBOOK AND ABSENT-PRESENT RHETORICS OF WHITENESS

Jennifer Beech

IN THE EARLY 1990s Mary Louise Pratt gave us the concept of contact zones: "social spaces where cultures meet, clash, and grapple with each other, often in contexts of highly asymmetrical relations of power, such as colonialism, slavery, or their aftermaths as they are lived out in parts of the world today" (34). Although Pratt originally employed the concept to examine writings developed in situations of conquest over indigenous people, the term has come to be used to examine educational institutions, public spaces, and other locales—with various contact zones generally considered separate physical spaces that we might circulate ourselves within and between, and as we do, we encounter different discourse communities in each place. With the advent of the internet, our notion of contact zones as separate physical spaces gets complicated as a user's ability to place oneself within only one zone at a time becomes nearly impossible.

Consider, for instance, Facebook as a contact zone where we are brought into contact with—via our friends list but also via the friends of friends—people from diverse educational, social, and cultural backgrounds, and people from diverse races, classes, sexual orientations, and religions, among others. Yet even as the nature of social networking disallows users to associate solely with the like-minded, we might observe how in the absence of de jure segregation some Facebook users make efforts toward de facto segregation—not simply through limiting their friends lists but also by recirculating memes that (not so) subtly invoke what legal scholar Thomas Ross has identified as a rhetoric of white innocence and black abstraction. Living in a so-called politically correct culture, few Facebook users are comfortable making posts that they would categorize as overtly racist. Instead, what often operates is an absent-present racist discourse that hinges upon a combination of what is and what is not said or pictured to offer coded racist messages designed to maintain a sense of white superiority. Rather than critique Pratt's concept, this chapter provides a kairotic examination of contemporary manifestations of contact zones, now in the form of online social networking interactions.

This chapter works at the intersection of whiteness and cultural studies by analyzing a representative Facebook meme for the ways its circulators participate in varying degrees of explicit to implicit rhetorics of whiteness. However, contrary to previous cultural studies methods of exploring the tripartite schema of production, circulation, and reception, I want us as cultural analysts to consider how, with the ease and ability to simply repost or "share" Facebook memes, we must initially shift the weight given to production (many producers are unidentified and immaterial in this social-networking culture) and, instead, give extra weight to recirculation and reception (particularly given the phenomenon of the "like" button). Beyond the larger interdisciplinary fields of whiteness studies, the work of Kennedy, Middleton, and Ratcliffe—among other rhetoricians—is important for helping us interrogate how whiteness functions as a trope that codes and privileges some bodies as white and for understanding that "all bodies in the US are socialized by whiteness as a racial category" (363). As we take on roles as antiracist critical thinkers or pedagogues, we must renew our efforts to help fellow users become more critical about the productive aspects of Facebook memes—particularly when memes perpetuate racist construc-tions that maintain white privilege and serve to subjugate people of color.

Coding and the Rhetoric of White Innocence and Black Abstraction

> When we create arguments, when we act as rhetoricians, we reveal
> ourselves by the words and ideas we choose to employ.
> —Thomas Ross, "Innocence and Affirmative Action"

Race theorists call our attention to the rhetorical facets of all acts of com-munication, noting that racist discourse often operates "subtextually with the familiar 'code-word' phenomenon" (Winant 7) and often hinges upon a "rhetoric of innocence" (Ross 27). Ross explains that when whites employ a rhetoric of innocence (be it with respect to discussions of affirmative action or other situations in which they perceive they are being taken advantage of), they simultaneously invoke a sense of black abstraction and an implied sense of blacks as the defilers of white innocence ("Innocence" and "The Rhetorical Tapestry of Race"). As Ross goes on to point out in "The Rhetorical Tapestry of Race," a rhetoric of black abstraction portrays "the black outside of any real and rich social context" (90) and works "to deny, or obscure, the humanness of blacks" (90). Participants circulating and receiving memes on Facebook are well-versed in decoding the absent-present racist subtextual messages intended by producers and by those who recirculate the messages.

By way of example, let us consider the following text, originally written as a letter to the editor of the *Clarion Ledger*, a Jackson, Mississippi, newspaper, and later turned into a Facebook meme and recirculated first by the organization 100 Percent FED Up in the following form, along with a photo of the author:

Dear Mr. President:

During my shift in the Emergency Room last night, I had the pleasure of evaluating a patient whose smile revealed an expensive Shiny gold tooth, whose body was adorned with a wide assortment of elaborate and costly tattoos, who wore a very expensive Brand of tennis shoes and who chatted on a new cellular telephone equipped with a popular R&B ringtone.

While glancing over her Patient chart, I happened to notice that her payer status was listed as "Medic . . . aid"! During my examination of her, the patient informed me that she smokes more than one costly pack of cigarettes every day and somehow still has money to buy pretzels and beer.

And, you and our Congress expect me to pay for this woman's health care?

I contend that our nation's "health care crisis" is not the result of a shortage of quality hospitals, doctors or nurses. Rather, it is the result of a "crisis of culture," a culture in which it is perfectly acceptable to spend money on luxuries and vices while refusing to take care of one's self or, heaven forbid, purchase health insurance.

It is a culture based on the irresponsible credo that "I can do whatever I want to because someone else will always take care of me." Once you fix this "culture crisis" that rewards irresponsibility and dependency, you'll be amazed at how quickly our nation's health care difficulties will disappear.

Respectfully,

STARNER JONES, MD

Although the newspaper did not include a photo of Jones, the Facebook meme pictures him as a clean-cut, smiling white man in green scrubs with "Starner Jones, M.D. Emergency Medicine" written over the pocket on the left side of his shirt. Hence, we need to consider how the photo works in conjunction with the text to figure a rhetoric of white innocence and black abstraction, coding blacks as the supposed defiler of government programs and coding white tax payers as the innocent victims of these defilers. Toni Morrison's groundbreaking work *Playing in the Dark: Whiteness in the Literary Imagination* was integral to our differentiation between victimized raced bodies to "racializing bodies as the perpetuators of racism" (17). Whereas Starner's letter figures the coded black body as defiler of white innocence, Morrison's work helps us, as critical race theorists, recognize Starner's pictured white body as a perpetuator of racism.

On their Facebook profile sticker, 100 Percent FED Up describes themselves as fed up with "corrupt politicians, political correctness, overreaching government, mainstream media propagandists." From a cultural studies perspective, one editorial change from the original newspaper letter is particularly notable: the meme reads "equipped with a popular R&B ringtone," whereas the original read "her favorite tune for a ring tone." Jones's major step to code the patient as nonwhite is his careful first description of the patient's "gold tooth" before describing any other aspects of the person's physical self-presentation that might simply be read as youthful. As an emergency room doctor, Jones attends to many patients weekly. Surely, at least one of the patients he has perceived to have spent money on "luxuries" (instead of on health insurance) has been white—perhaps, like many patients, he or she has sported less easily spotted porcelain veneers. However, just in case Facebook users miss Jones's subtext, 100 Percent FED Up piles on the coding when they revise Jones's final description to denote a specific genre of music that is meant to be decoded as music listened to by abstract black persons. The inclusion of the photo of Jones—clearly a white doctor—is key to solidifying a message of white innocence. Facebook users are supposed to read the good white doctor—a named and specific human being—as the purveyor of current realities. The unnamed, yet coded, black patient is abstracted from any real context. Facebook users do not need to know who she is, for in this rhetorical framework, she stands in for the abstracted (black) welfare queen. No matter that—as Allison Linn's article title, "The Myth of the Modern Welfare Queen" makes clear—the supposed welfare queen that Ronald Reagan so decried in the late 1970s is just that: a myth. Yet, as Melanie Bush posits, "without the means to explicitly express feelings of blame, racialized coding has become a routine part of mainstream discourse" (6). What this meme represents then is what Cameron McCarthy et al., who build upon the work of Frederick Nietzsche and Robert Solomon, identify as racism thinly disguised as bourgeois resentment (167). Clearly there are class dimensions to this meme. In this case, however, white people with insurance define their identity by negating the identity of the imagined uninsured, abstracted, poor black other. The mythic poor black welfare queen stands in for supposedly everything that's wrong with the system. (It is no accident that 100 Percent FED Up did not assign the woman a Willie Nelson ring tone.)

Interrogating Our Roles as Antiracist Intellectuals on Facebook

I have personally seen this meme recirculated by whites ranging from far right-wing conservatives to those more moderate in their political orientations. With a little web research, I easily discovered that after Jones's letter was published in the newspaper, it quickly went viral as others recirculated it in e-mails and via the Facebook meme. I would like to say that I only became aware of this meme when alerted to it by one of my antiracist activist friends. Unfortunately, three persons from my friends list have recirculated the meme—one to my great surprise. As a self-identified working-class intellectual, I consider it important to maintain connections with friends, family, and loved ones from my home community—even as these connections often present me with others whose cultural habits sometimes prompt them to trade class for race privilege. I currently have around 170 Facebook friends, ranging from high school dropouts to those with some education, to others with four-year degrees, masters, and doctorates. About half of my friends have less than a four-year college degree. As with my case, your Facebook universe is likely a diverse contact zone as well. Indeed, Facebook is the twenty-first-century embodiment of Pratt's contact zone.

In the particular instances where I have privately asked people who have recirculated the Jones meme about their affiliation with the group 100 Percent FED Up, all have disclosed that they really know nothing about the group and have no affiliation with it; they simply recirculated the meme from another friend's post. The ability to simply "share" memes produced by others without the perceived need to interrogate the background or intentions of the original producers creates a situation in which recirculation overrides the original productive aspect of cultural artifacts that originally fascinated cultural studies critics. Indeed, we all likely observe Facebook users whose posts consist almost entirely of recirculated memes—ranging from innocuous or humorous memes about pets or romantic relationships to posts intended to oppress nondominant groups. Apps, like Status Shuffle, remove the labor of producing original intelligent, witty, thoughtful, or ethical status updates. In the contact zone of Facebook, recirculation has become production. Yet, as our discussion highlights, these recirculated productions are not without consequence.

As I have participated in this social networking site over the last several years, and particularly as racial and class tensions have escalated during President Obama's second term and with the introduction of the Afford-able Care Act, I have actively reflected upon the degree to which I should speak up and enact my role as an intellectual—particularly considering the ways that Italian theorist Antonio Gramsci has defined intellectuals and particularly in light of more recent critical studies of whiteness. And prob-ably most especially when I and others have spoken up to engage difference have I pondered whether or not it were better to only befriend or engage like-minded individuals or better to bridge academic and more popular discourse conventions.

I have become ever mindful of James Zappen's suggestion that

the nature of communication online "is something more than an interaction between speaker and audience in the traditional sense but, rather, a complex negotiation between various versions of our online and our real selves . . . between our many selves and the computer structure and operations through which we represent these selves to others." (Grabill and Pigg 103)

Further, as Jeff Grabill and Stacey Pigg posit, when we enter online forums, we bring with us our already embodied identities, but we also enact identity performances (like those related to race, class, gender, and sexuality). Citing the work of Charles Antaki and Sue Widdicombe, Grabill and Pigg assert that "identity [perhaps, especially in these online spaces] is understood as an 'emergent product rather than the pre-existing source of linguistic and other semiotic practices'" (102). Grabill and Pigg observe various moves that participants in an online science forum make to either build a writer's identity or build a community identity as a way to gain rhetorical agency in online forums; the authors are particularly interested in identity perfor-mances that "enable rhetorical agency by moving the conversation" along, as opposed to agonistic posts where participants seemed more concerned with merely "making one's own point" (115). The authors discuss how nonspe-cialists often gain rhetorical agency through the articulation of shared roles and experiences; one participant, for instance, gained rhetorical agency by invoking her role as a young woman infected with the particular virus under discussion. Although Grabill and Pigg do not draw class implications, when reading that part of their article, I immediately related their findings to a number of ethnographic studies where researchers have observed working-class communities holding in higher esteem the authority of lived experience, as opposed to the citation of expert authority that we hold so dear in academe. My friend Lisa, a mother of two, let me know fairly quickly that my role in any conversation about child rearing was as a listener. She nixed my attempt to cite a recent article I'd read by an adolescent psychologist, telling me, "When you have children of your own, you'll get what we're talking about. Till then, just listen, girlfriend."

Let's consider how rhetorical agency and notions of intellectual authority seem to be developing in online forums. In "Blogging and Mass Politics," Michael Keren identifies a new kind of "intellectual" emerging. He terms him the "mass man," whose discourse, he says, "lacks discursive structure, moderate style, and introspection . . . [and who is] characterized by the engagement in an intellectual activity without exerting [what the academy would recognize as] the needed qualifications [of restrictions, courtesy, inductive and deductive reasoning, and notions of justice]" (9). The mass man's posts are backed by passionate expression of emotion, ignoring generally accepted notions of civilized discourse. While his "mass man" might sound more like what is commonly referred to as a "troll," Keren asserts that the proliferation of such discourse in online forums subtly affects participants' notions of what constitutes authority and intellectual activity—especially when such discourse is validated through the mechanism of the "like" button in a forum like Facebook. (Until recently, there was no "dislike" button.)

I would add that the mechanism of the "share" button seemingly removes the need for careful thought, research, crafting of arguments or sentences, or even keyboarding. Users can simply hit "share" to participate in online discourse. While we might posit that the ability to share gives users a false sense of productivity, as people who study rhetoric, we would do well to attend to the ways that powerful and punitive discourses continue to reproduce power structures when recirculated. The Facebook share button potentially becomes a powerful tool for those who feel squeezed out by discourse of political correctness. Mass man does not have to be able to independently produce articulate prose or possess the ability to design persuasive texts; mass man simply needs to find a meme to repost. And while we, as trained rhetoricians and race theorists, might find it easy to identify such misuses of rhetoric, we often find it far more difficult to engage with our "mass man" friends in ways that work for productive change.

Now, let's consider the mass man intellectual in relation to two other types of intellectuals—those whom Gramsci terms "traditional" and "organic." In his *Prison Notebooks*, Gramsci writes that "all men are intellectuals . . . but not all men have in society the function of intellectuals" (304). Contemporary traditional intellectuals still fall under those Gramsci identified as professors, clergy, and the occasional independent scholar—all who too often incorrectly imagine themselves as working outside of hegemony. Organic intellectuals, as scholar of race, class, and rhetoric Victor Villanueva Jr. differentiates, "are those whose work remains tied to the classes from which they originated, even if they work outside their original communities" (129). Villanueva goes on to say that "organic intellectuals might function within more traditional intellectual organizations, like the university, yet remain organic if the functions they undertake have them conceptualizing and articulating the social, economic, and political interests of the group or class from which they came" (129). The following quote from the *Prison Notebooks* is particularly provocative when related to the proliferation of discourse on the web from so many different factions of society:

> There is no human activity from which every form of intellectual participation can be excluded. . . . [Everyone] carries out some form of intellectual activity . . . , participates in a particular conception of the world, has a conscious line of moral conduct, and therefore contributes to sustain a conception of the world to modify it, that is to bring into being new modes of thought. (321)

Hence, as antiracist rhetoricians, we might each ask: What then should be my role or roles on Facebook? Should I simply friend like-minded intellectuals and liberals from outside academe? If I keep my current friends list, what is my job when faced with racist or other damaging posts? Should I engage such posts from an "organic" intellectual position, invoking, perhaps, the authority of lived experience, while also sneaking in some traditional academic authority? Likewise, to what degree should we encourage friends and peers to move between their roles as bourgeoning intellectuals and as common folks? Like Kirsten Uszkalo and Darren Harkess, I am intrigued by the ways that our cyborg identities take shape and shape us and allow us to occupy new online spaces. They write, "If the body is the 'original prosthesis,' then social media can be seen as an additional prosthesis we learn to manipulate as a way of extending our consciousness" (34).

Beyond Preaching to the Choir or Simple Finger-Pointing

As antiracist intellectuals, we have a responsibility to move beyond simple classroom-based cultural studies critique, which itself is a valuable endeavor for making whiteness visible to students and dispelling what Barbara Flagg terms the "transparency phenomenon" (629), for exposing the problems with what many whiteness scholars identify as color blindness, and for exposing "race-neutral 'masks and other disguises'" (Brown 644). Facebook offers us a chance to address the challenge Bush poses in her final chapter: "Locating 'cracks in the wall of whiteness' helps to uncover and affirm hope and optimism about the possibilities for challenging the vast historical inequalities and injustices systematically structured throughout our society and sustained by dominant ideological narratives that reinforce and reproduce racialized patterns" (219). Although Bush is not addressing social networking at all, I like the coincidental pun as we consider ways to locate "cracks in the [Facebook] wall of whiteness." Like Bush, I agree that "identifying the processes by which race is constructed on an everyday basis allows us to determine the means by which to interrupt them" (220). If we limit our friends list or hide posts from friends that we come to expect to be offensive, then we simply preach to the choir as we occupy false positions of intellectual superiority. Instead, we need to capitalize on the potentially powerful opportunities Facebook offers us for interruption.

As we look for such opportunities to create new forms of intellectual exchange on Facebook, we can learn from other scholars' work with university students whose teachers have attempted to enact race-based critical pedagogies. For instance, Jennifer Trainor has observed that critical pedagogies of whiteness falter when they offer white students only two subject positions: the guilty white position or the innocent position of the disenfranchised working-class white. Neither perspective, Trainor contends, allows for the complex subjectivities of white students, and neither figures a position from which white students may imagine themselves as "legitimate social actors" (634). Likewise, as Bush found when studying students at Brooklyn College of the City University of New York, "most whites appear to be more concerned about being called a racist than about the impact of racism or about the possibility that they might not understand or know something" (224). Bush observed a rhetorical pattern among participants in her study that we would do well to consider as we attempt to engage others on Facebook: "Another tendency among whites was to be defensive when accused of racism, consider the accusation, and then return to a self-defense [of white innocence], as though the process of consideration clears one's name" (225). When we apply these observations to our encounters with racist posts on Facebook, we might conclude how ineffective it is to simply call out others as racist; such finger-pointing is unproductive, as it works first at a level of shame and tends to create more resentment. Simply calling out every post we perceive as racist is likely to result in a limited friends lists for us—returning us to preaching to the choir.

Again, let's apply to Facebook the ideas of another scholar who was originally not concerned specifically with online spaces. In her article "Segregation, Whiteness, and Transformation," legal scholar Martha R. Mahoney writes, "Breaking down the walls of exclusion helps break down white dominance as well as making white spaces less white" (655). Following from Mahoney, I assert that we need to make our Facebook universes less white. While we cannot import our friends' comments to the walls of friends who may hold explicit or implicit racist beliefs, we can work to ensure that what our friends encounter on our own walls is a range of thoughtful discourse by diverse friends who are able to exchange difference in rhetorically savvy ways. At points, I've been privately asked by other friends to come over to a more public discussion on their wall and help them out; in turn, I might later ask that friend to help me. And by help, I do not mean intellectual bullying. When, for instance, my German, Afro-Caribbean, Jewish, and Latina friends contribute at different points, they help to disrupt the notion of the "property right in whiteness" (Mahoney 655); that is, they help disrupt any notions of Facebook—at least on my page—as a "whites-only setting" (Bush 224) where whites may make unexamined or thinly coded racist comments.

While we might work to more thoughtfully shape the space and discourse at work on our own walls, our participation on others' walls is a bit more tenuous. In 1992 bell hooks observed,

> Since most white people do not have to "see" black people (constantly appearing on billboards, television, movies, in magazines, etc.) and they do not need to be ever on guard nor to observe black people to be safe, they can live as though black people are invisible, and they can imagine that they are also invisible to blacks. (42)

Now, over twenty years later, with our first African American president completing his second term, people recognize (some in disdain, others in overly optimistic ways that imagine we live in a postracial era) that the racial landscape of America is changing. And, in response, some folks attempt to enact de facto segregation via limiting their friends list. The tactics I describe above help dispel the notion of Facebook as a white property right, but those can only work if we allow ourselves to be friends with people whose views do not easily align with our own, and those tactics do not necessarily disrupt the imagined white spaces others build on their own walls. What then is our role as a participant on the walls of others? How might we break down walls, as opposed to building (de)fences?

Perhaps, an answer lies in a return to Grabill and Pigg's notion of identity-in-use and a reminder of the value that folks from diverse backgrounds place in the authority of lived experience. When I participate in conversations with friends of friends who do not personally know me, my identity as an academic can easily be discerned by hovering over my profile picture. Without any prior contact, knowledge of my profession may preconstruct my ethos as "one of those liberal professors." With this in mind, I usually take steps to find some community interests with participants on a friend's page, be it a shared love of pets or cooking or an expression of support for a grieving friend. As Grabill and Pigg make clear, identity-in-use is "shaped at the micro level through discursive negotiations and interactions that happen in [ongoing online] conversation" (108). Having established over time some sort of thoughtful ethos, only then might I attempt to intervene in troubling discussions. Often, when I do, I take one of three approaches: *(1)* a quasi-Socratic approach, mainly asking the participant to clarify comments and stances; *(2)* an approach—following from Bush's suggestion—that draws attention to "multiple realities and incongruous attitudes" (233); or *(3)* an approach that mixes gentle sarcasm with self-effacing humor.

For instance, one of the same friends who recirculated the Jones meme recently posted two juxtaposed pictures of a "young Nancy Reagan" and a "young Michelle Obama." As a scholar trained in feminist, class, and race theories, I could have easily offered a scathing critique of the image. Instead, I enlisted the help of my spouse, who has a longer standing relationship with this particular friend. First, he acknowledged the attractiveness of Reagan's photo while also contextualizing it as a retouched publicity photo. Next, he observed that the photo of Obama appeared to be one of those school photos captured during an awkward adolescent phase. At this point, I dug up a rather unflattering high school photo of my own and posted it to our friend's wall—as well as to my own—with the caption "A Young Jennifer Beech." Our friend liked my post on her wall, as well as the one on my wall, and briefly acknowledged the context of Reagan's picture. Even though this example seems rather simple, over time such seemingly silly discussions can work to disrupt notions of Facebook as a white space. At other points I have asked this same friend to explain the nature of her objections to liberation theology (which a meme she posted accused Obama's relatives of espousing), to account for her stance as a Christian as she evokes the mythic welfare queen, and to say what she admired about a bell hooks saying she had recirculated (after which, she promptly removed the post).

Even as my paragraph above offers one friend by way of example, I want to caution against seeing racism on individual terms. Like many race theorists, I believe we all fall somewhere along a racist continuum and that many of our racist beliefs are implicit. I am not so much concerned with demonizing the doctor who initially penned that letter to the editor as I am with the fact that those on Facebook extended his racial coding and that his letter went viral—through recirculation designed mostly to reinforce white innocence and privilege and black abstraction.

Although this analysis focuses primarily on one cultural artifact, we can apply these same heuristics when considering encounters in other social media and even with face-to-face interactions in our daily lives. As antiracist intellectuals, we must not simply preach to the choir (a different type of absent positioning) or finger point (an in-your-face unproductive present positioning). As we move in and out of online contact zones, we need to take up the challenge of critically examining efficacious ways to reposition ourselves as intellectuals in hopes of maintaining old and forging new connections that forward productive race relations.

Works Cited

Brown, Eleanor Marie. "Confronting Racelessness." Delgado and Stefancic 644–45. Print.

Bush, Melanie E. L. *Breaking the Code of Good Intentions: Everyday Forms of Whiteness*. New York: Rowman and Littlefield, 2004. Print.

Delgado, Richard, and Jean Stefancic, eds. *Critical Whiteness Studies: Looking behind the Mirror*. Philadelphia: Temple UP, 1997. Print.

Fine, Michelle, et al., eds. *Off White: Readings on Power, Privilege, and Resistance*. 2nd ed. New York: Routledge, 2004.

Flagg, Barbara J. "'Was Blind, but Now I See': White Race Consciousness and the Requirement of Discriminatory Intent." Delgado and Stefancic 27–32. Print.

Grabill, Jeff, and Stacey Pigg. "Messy Rhetoric: Identity Performance as Rhetorical Agency in Online Public Forums." *Rhetoric Society Quarterly* 42.2 (2012): 99–119. Print.

Gramsci, Antonio. "Intellectuals and Education." From *Prison Notebooks*. Rpt. in *The Antonio Gramsci Reader: Selected Writings 1916–1935*. Ed. David Forgacs. New York: New York UP, 2000. 300–322. Print.

hooks, bell. "Representations of Whiteness in the Black Imagination." *Black on White: Black Writers on What It Means to Be White*. Ed. David R. Roediger. New York: Schocken, 1998. 38–53. Print.

Jones, Starner. Letter. *Jackson (MS) Clarion-Ledger*. *USA Today* Network, 23 Aug. 2009. Web. 24 Sept. 2014.

Kennedy, Tammie M., Joyce Irene Middleton, and Krista Ratcliffe. "The Matter of Whiteness: Or, Why Whiteness Studies Is Important to Rhetoric and Composition Studies." *Rhetoric Review* 24.4 (2005): 359–73. Print.

Keren, Michael. "Blogging and Mass Politics." *Biography* 33.1 (2010): 110–26. Print.

Linn, Allison. "The Myth of the Modern Welfare Queen." *CNBC*. NBC Universal, 21 Aug. 2013. Web. 16 Nov. 2013.

Mahoney, Martha R. "Segregation, Whiteness, and Transformation." Delgado and Stefancic 654–57. Print.

McCarthy, Cameron, et al. "Race, Suburban Resentment, and the Representation of Inner City in Contemporary Film and Television." Fine et al. 163–74. Print.

Morrison, Toni. *Playing in the Dark: Whiteness in the Literary Imagination*. New York: Vintage, 1992. Print.

Pratt, Mary Louise. "Arts of the Contact Zone." *Profession* 91 (1991): 33–40. Print.

Ross, Thomas. "Innocence and Affirmative Action." Delgado and Stefancic 27–32. Print.

———. "The Rhetorical Tapestry of Race." Delgado and Stefancic 89–97. Print.

Trainor, Jennifer Seibel. "Critical Pedagogy's 'Other': Constructions of Whiteness in Education for Social Change." *College Composition and Communication* 53 (2002): 631–50. Print.

Uszkaolo, Kristen C., and Darren James. "Consider the Source: Critical Considerations of the Medium of Social Media." *From Text to Txting: New Media in the Classroom*. Ed. Paul Budra and Cling Burnham. Bloomington: U of Indiana P, 2012. 15–42. Print.

Villanueva, Victor, Jr. *Bootstraps: From an American Academic of Color*. Urbana, IL: NCTE, 1993. Print.

Winant, Howard. "Behind Blue Eyes: Whiteness and Contemporary U.S. Racial Politics." Fine et al. 3–16. Print.

PART THREE

HAUNTINGS IN EDUCATION

REFLECTIONS

A DWINDLING FOCUS ON WHITENESS

Jennifer Seibel Trainor

I HAVEN'T COMPLETED a thorough investigation, but I'm fairly certain that I wrote the last essay that *College Composition and Communication* has published on whiteness. It came out in 2008. A quick search of the last few years' CCCC conference programs confirms this dwindling focus on whiteness studies in composition: in 2012 there were a few sessions that addressed whiteness, including mine; in 2013, there were none (this is not to say there were no sessions on race or racism or privilege, only that the specific term, "whiteness," does not appear). Has the field moved on? Should it move on? In what follows, I detail what I consider to be the most important insight I learned from my research on whiteness, and how it haunts me as I survey the field of education today.

My research on whiteness focused on efforts to address racism in the classroom, particularly white students' sometimes racially charged assertions, their defensiveness, and the difficulty they sometimes have in exploring issues of racial justice. This led me to several research projects that investigated how white students respond to matters of race, culminating with a year-long ethnographic project at a suburban high school—97 percent white—located outside a midsized city in the Northeast. Of the insights about the workings of racism and the potential for antiracist pedagogies gleaned from this work, the one that haunts me is this: we don't teach students about race only in those moments when we assign a multicultural text or include a unit that critiques whiteness or privilege. As Amanda Lewis writes, schools may not teach racial identity in the way that they teach multiplication or punctuation, but schools are settings where students acquire some version of the "rules of racial classification" and of their own racial identity. Lewis argued, in 2003, that we haven't fully grappled with how students learn about race in the context of everyday interactions in school. In my own research I saw powerful evidence of Lewis's argument, as I began to uncover how tacit, unexamined lessons, rituals, and practices in school exerted a powerful influence on students' responses to matters of race. To take a quick example: the high school where I did my research pervasively valued "positive thinking." Students were exhorted constantly by teachers and administrators to "look on the bright side," "focus on the positive," and "keep up a good attitude." There were bright yellow beanbags with smiley faces sitting along one wall of the classroom. The student aid who recited the pledge of allegiance each day over the PA system always added "Have a great day!" at the end of her recitation. This focus on positive thinking predisposed students to look negatively upon fictional characters, real individuals, or groups of people who did not appear to present a positive outlook on life, which in turn fueled sometimes hostile or racist responses to critiques of racism. These critiques were perceived as whining or complaining. My research suggested that teaching students about social justice was not so much a matter of finding the right argument, the right assignment or reading that would convince students to give up problematic racial beliefs. Instead, we need to think about how schools unknowingly persuade students to believe in certain ways about race. Kenneth Burke writes that persuasion takes place not through "one particular address, but [through] a general body of identifications that owe their convincingness much more to trivial repetition and dull daily reinforcement" (qtd. in Trainor "Talking Back").

These seemingly trivial practices, taken-for-granted values, and daily reinforced routines of schooling are sometimes referred to as "the hidden curriculum." The hidden curriculum is a kind of lens—a way of bringing into view the values, beliefs, emotional rules and norms that schools impart by virtue of taken for granted institutional and pedagogical practices. Unwittingly, schools teach students what it means to be raced in a particular way; schools teach students how to view themselves and others as racialized beings. Schools employ what James Berlin called "technologies of self-formation," and they are intimately involved in the shaping of "particular kinds of subject formations in young people" (190).

In the late 1990s and early 2000s, when I was doing my research and trying to uncover this racialized hidden curriculum, No Child Left Behind was not yet a law. There was no standards movement, no reform movement, no common core, and no high-stakes testing. "Assessment" was rarely a concern. We did not focus on learning outcomes. In the years since, discourses of education reform, including discourses of accountability, performance, and measurement, have become a pervasive and dominant aspect of school culture, and this school culture, like any, has its hidden dimension, its tacit, unexamined lessons. Indeed, in Amanda Walker Johnson's new book, *Objectifying Measures: The Dominance of High-Stakes Testing and the Politics of Schooling*, she describes "the testing regimes' method of statistical objectification," a method which masks and worsens educational segregation and inequality (143). Her book uncovers the hidden connections between the seemingly neutral educational reform movement and the politics of race. Although not billed as "whiteness studies," *Objectifying Measures* shows how education reform reinforces privilege and hurts students of color. It's a haunting notion, and it strongly argues that for scholars in whiteness studies, there is yet work to be done.

Works Cited

Berlin, James A. *Rhetorics, Poetics, Cultures: Refiguring College English Studies*. West Lafayette, IN: Parlor P, 2003. Print.

Johnson, Amanda Walker. *Objectifying Measures: The Dominance of High-Stakes Testing and the Politics of Schooling*. Temple UP, 2009. Print.

Lewis, Amanda E. "'What Group'? Studying Whites and Whiteness in the Era of 'Color-Blindness.'" *Sociological Theory* 22.4 (Dec. 2004): 623–46. Print.

Trainor, Jennifer Seibel. "The Emotioned Power of Racism: An Ethnographic Portrait of an All-White High School." *College Composition and Communication* 60.1 (Sept. 2008): 82–112. Print.

———. "Talking Back to Contemporary Multicultural and Whiteness and Pedagogies." Invited Blog. CCCC Diversity blog. Web. 23 Oct. 2008.

ADMINISTERING WHITENESS STUDIES

Amy Goodburn

When I was originally asked to write this contribution, I was reluctant to do so. I responded,

> While my work as a teacher/administrator/scholar is informed by attending to/probing the implications and consequences of white privilege and especially attending to difference for social justice in education, I haven't been publishing or presenting on research within the whiteness studies community. . . . I'm happy to try to generate something—but it would probably be more local/rooted in my own experience as a teacher/administrator rather than a commentary on the movement as a whole. (e-mail, August 1, 2013)

As I reread my response months later, I'm struck by several assumptions that contributed to my somewhat apologetic tone: that there is "a whiteness community" to whom I would be responding, that "what counts" in whiteness studies is research publication in this community, and that my authority would be questioned because I haven't been actively publishing. Although I haven't published in whiteness studies discourse lately, I have been immersed in utilizing discourses of critical race theory and whiteness studies to support student access and success. For me, the value of whiteness studies in the twenty-first century lies in its use by antiracist educators to disrupt white power and privilege and promote social justice.

As associate vice chancellor of Academic Affairs at the University of Nebraska–Lincoln (UNL), I oversee undergraduate student success initiatives such as learning communities, academic advising, career services, early outreach, first-year experiences, and so on. This work focuses on one primary goal: improving UNL undergraduates' six-year graduation rates.

So where does whiteness studies come in? As I reviewed UNL's six-year graduation rates, it became clear that the rates for students of color, particularly African American males, are significantly lower than those of their white counterparts. Coupled with this disparity is a growing dissatisfaction with the campus climate for students of color. Two years ago the campus saw a series of racist events initiated by white students—"Around the World," Homecoming skits that disparaged Muslims and Mexican Americans, a white student senator using the "n-word" in a public debate about ethical language use, Halloween costumes that mocked ethnic groups, and an African American columnist for the school newspaper who described his daily struggle to feel included on campus. In response, the director of UNL's Multicultural Center held a campus forum for students, faculty, and staff "to join in a discussion about minority student retention, campus climate, and cross-cultural awareness." Follow-up actions included a rally titled "Not Here, Not Now, Not Ever" and a task force on improving campus climate.

But tensions remain. In the wake of protests about race across college campuses in fall 2015, UNL students held a "Black Lives Matter" rally and presented a list of demands to university administrators including required multicultural training for freshmen, new curriculum about race relations, and "a letter fully acknowledging that racism and racist acts—using those exact words—have occurred on the campus of UNL and that something will be done."

Antiracist work is never easy, and our institution clearly has much work to do to change the conditions that students of color experience in their daily lives on campus. But whiteness studies has provided me concepts and strategies to do the following: (1) name and acknowledge the problems caused by racism and racist attitudes and beliefs, (2) unlearn habits of mind that view racist behavior as normalized, (3) carefully listen to and learn from others without denying or appropriating their pain, and (4) identify structures and processes that I can disrupt and remake to better support all UNL students' educational experiences. Robin DiAngelo's book *What Does It Mean to Be White? Developing White Racial Literacy* is one of many texts that I've been drawing upon to sponsor my thinking and action as an administrator. For instance, I'm working with the directors of the honors and undergraduate research programs to understand how current guidelines and application processes might be discouraging students of color from participating. The Retention Advisory Committee is exploring a new outreach program for first-year students of color in conjunction with the Multicultural Center and an orientation program that sponsors conversations about whiteness and privilege for incoming first-year students. I'm disseminating results from UNL's participation in the 2013 National Survey of Student Engagement to encourage instructors to promote more discussions about race in the classroom. For me, the future of whiteness studies lies in providing tools and strategies for teachers and administrators to use daily to enact change.

I am also sympathetic to scholars in black studies, ethnic studies, and critical race theory who are critical of the project of whiteness studies. As Maulana Karenga notes, "Focusing on Whiteness as a concept can degenerate into a project that results in treating Whiteness as simply an intellectual problem of abnormal and contradictory thought and 'invention' rather than a social problem of domination, unequal wealth and power, injustice and unfreedom." For whiteness studies to remain relevant and useful, it must engage with these other conversations and communities. As a white administrator at a predominantly white research institution, I need to remain conscious and reflective about my blind spots, the experiences that I do not bring to the table, the questions that I don't ask or that don't even occur to me to ask. Similarly, scholars in whiteness studies need to be engaged with others in the larger antiracist project of creating a socially just society. I wish whiteness studies were not necessary in the twenty-first century. But given the daily struggles and injustices I see playing out on my campus, I believe whiteness studies will continue to play an important role working in concert with other antiracist scholars across disciplines to address the injustices and unfreedoms that Karenga outlines.

Works Cited

DiAngelo, Robin. *What Does It Mean to Be White? Developing White Racial Literacy.* New York: Lang, 2012. Print.

Karenga, Maulana. "Whiteness Studies: Deceptive or Welcome Discourse?" *Black Issues.* DiverseEducation.com 20 Nov. 2013. Web. 2 Dec. 2013.

WASHING EDUCATION WHITE: ARIZONA'S HB 2281 AND THE CURRICULAR INVESTMENT IN WHITENESS

Lee Bebout

IN 2010, THEN Arizona state superintendent and eventual attorney general Tom Horne and former state representative and later state superintendent John Huppenthal drafted and advanced HB 2281, a bill that outlawed courses that promoted the overthrow of the U.S. government, instilled racial resentment, were designed for students of a particular ethnic group, or advocated ethnic solidarity.[1] Governor Jan Brewer signed the legislation into law three weeks after its more famous legislative kin, SB 1070. While written to broadly target any racially oriented and potentially seditious courses, HB 2281 (now Arizona Revised Statute 15-112) was used to specifically mark Tucson Unified School District's (TUSD) Mexican American Studies (MAS) courses that Horne and Huppenthal had long railed against. Later, when Superintendent Huppenthal declared the courses in violation of the law, the TUSD governing board initially supported the MAS program. However, amid a series of lawsuits and the pressure of losing significant levels of state funding, the board acquiesced: courses were suspended, books were boxed up and shipped out, curriculum was banned, and teachers and administrative support staff were relocated or fired. Today, TUSD has instituted new "culturally relevant" ethnic studies courses to replace the MAS curricula and meet the conditions of a decades-old court-mandated desegregation order. Moreover, the lawsuit filed by MAS students continues to wind its way through the U.S. court system.

Perhaps unsurprisingly these tactics sparked an outcry among the Tucson and national Chicana/o communities and allies. Notably, students and local activists organized protests well before the district suspended classes. Once Huppenthal succeeded in threatening to choke off funds, local organizing efforts gained national attention. On April 26, 2011, students from UNIDOS (United Non-Discriminatory Individuals Demanding Our Studies) engaged in direct action, chaining themselves to the seats of the TUSD governing board and shutting down a meeting in which the board was set to vote to change MAS courses to electives (Huicochea). MAS educators, administrators, and students formed Save Ethnic Studies to gain political and financial support for MAS. Dos Vatos Films released *Precious Knowledge*, a documentary on the MAS controversy, which aired on PBS. Houston-based journalist and radio host Tony Díaz organized Librotraficante, a political protest caravan that traveled to Tucson, featuring several speakers whose books were part of the banned curriculum. Arizona Ethnic Studies Network held a read-in at the Arizona Capitol with members taking time to lobby their representatives in support of ethnic studies. The National Association for Chicana and Chicano Studies filed an amicus brief in support of the MAS program. For logical reasons, each of these efforts framed the legislation as an attack on ethnic studies in general and MAS in particular. Moreover, these efforts, drawing upon the logics of the 1960s educational activism, rendered HB 2281 as an attack on communities of color. Significantly, much of the academic response to HB 2281 has followed a similar tack, arguing that the ethnic studies ban targets communities of color in an attempt to forge neoliberal consumer-citizens and reproduce dominant ideologies of color blindness, individualism, and American exceptionalism (Clark and Reed 38; Cacho 29–31; Winkler-Morey 51–52).

Through engaging critical whiteness scholarship, this essay builds upon and extends these previous critiques, exposing how the unrecognized norm of whiteness lurks just below the surface of the HB 2281 debates. Importantly, both proponents and opponents of HB 2281 have largely agreed that MAS and ethnic studies are educational projects fashioned for aggrieved racialized communities. Such an argument may underscore the importance of ethnic studies for people of color, but it simultaneously leaves the complex workings of whiteness invisible. Drawing upon a survey of newspaper coverage, court findings, and other discursive manifestations, this chapter offers a critique of the situation that demonstrates how whiteness functions as the invisible foundation to the logic and language at the core of HB 2281. Following this analysis, this essay identifies two rhetorical tactics—curricular investment in whiteness and strategic color blindness—that have been deployed by HB 2281 proponents and opponents respectively. Once identified and made visible, these tactics may be contested to expose the fallacies at the heart of postracial thinking. Critically, this study does more than illustrate yet another moment of racial inequality in the post-Obama era. Rather, these rhetorical tactics may be transferred to other post-2008 analyses. Indeed, doing so will open more effective avenues for political articulation, greater potential for coalition building, and the envisioning of a stronger curricular reform.

Whiteness at the Heart of HB 2281

To recognize how MAS supporters share discursive ground with HB 2281 advocates and the inherent danger therein, one must first make legible the workings of whiteness at the heart of HB 2281. As David Roediger and other whiteness scholars have noted, explicitly racist language has gone out of fashion in the post–civil rights movement era (44). Evidencing what Eduardo Bonilla-Silva has termed color-blind racism, HB 2281 proponents deploy the logics of whiteness through a series of interrelated rhetorical moves: *(1)* they render MAS supporters as radical people of color bent on an anti-American crusade, *(2)* they position whiteness as the norm, *(3)* they embrace abstract liberalism in the form of individualism and meritocracy, and *(4)* finally they claim whites as victims of people of color. Together, these rhetorical moves frame ethnic studies as the territory of (radical) people of color that work against a seemingly universal curriculum that is home to "innocent" and "meritocratic" whites. As I contend later, because these rhetorical moves have not been addressed and critiqued directly, MAS advocates have been limited in their political articulation by deploying a strategic color blindness.

Perhaps the most racially overt and pervasive rhetorical strategy that HB 2281 proponents employ in the construction of a logic of whiteness haunting HB 2281 is that they readily depict MAS supporters as racially and politically radical. For instance, consider the open letter Tom Horne wrote to the citizens of Tucson prior to the drafting of HB 2281. Horne opened by asserting his belief that those of "all mainstream political ideologies" would be concerned if they only knew what was happening in their local schools (1). Horne contended that MAS classes were breeding disruptive students and "a kind of destructive ethnic chauvinism" that had led to the mistreatment of whites and moderate Hispanics (2). To support this, Horne offered an evidentiary litany of radicalism. Rather than translating "raza" as "people," Horne used a literal translation as "race" to depict MAS advocates as racially separatist. He cited one textbook's discussion of José Angel Gutiérrez's metaphorical declaration to "kill the gringo" as a literal endorsement of race violence, and he drew on the MEChA student group's use of "El Plan Espiritual de Aztlán" ("The Spiritual Plan of Aztlán") to tap into fears of a Reconquista (reconquest) (2–3). These are just a few examples of how Horne's letter depicted MAS as racially and politically radical.

Importantly, the construction of MAS as racially and politically radical permeates the vast majority of pro–HB 2281 discourse. Indeed, the construction of MAS as a manifestation of race radicalism appears in the language of the bill itself. To be in violation of the law, schools must promote the overthrow of the government, instill racial resentment, segregate students by race, or develop within students a form of ethnic solidarity. These components are not simply flexible strawmen that can be used to target any curriculum the state Department of Education sees fit. Rather, the wording positions violators as racial radicals and political subversives. Here, the law embodies a common trope of color-blind conservatism where culturally rooted activism is depicted as a minority version of and equivalent to white supremacist analogs like the Aryan Nation (e.g., Buchanan 109). Moreover, as education scholar Richard Orozco has demonstrated, MAS supporters are fashioned to be potential traitors to the nation, drawing upon the trope that has long scripted Mexican Americans as "perpetually foreign" (Orozco 51–54; Rocco). Even after a curricular audit cleared MAS of each of these charges, the rhetoric has persisted and continues today. A columnist for Phoenix's *Arizona Republic*, Doug MacEachern has been an early and consistent voice against the MAS program. Central to his writings, MacEachern regularly framed MAS as racially and politically radical. He and the editorial board at the *Arizona Republic* have described MAS educators as "purveyors of bitterness" ("The Issue") "who make no effort to hide their contempt for traditional American history, civics and the literature of 'dead White males'" ("Roosevelt") and who select literature "for its revolutionary fervor first and its value as fine writing a distant second" ("Tucson's"). Clearly, the rhetoric of HB 2281 advocates characterizes MAS curriculum and its supporters as out of step with the "mainstream" (read: white normativity). Such an effort goes beyond a simple set of ad homonym attacks. Rather, casting MAS and its supporters as racially and politically radical frames and crystalizes HB 2281 opponents as a threatening Mexican American *Other*. Moreover, this implicit, simultaneous construction of a mainstream as under threat from MAS radicals exposes how HB 2281 is not simply an attack on people of color but also an effort to shore up whiteness in the contemporary era.

While the depiction of MAS as a politically, racially radical force is quite overt, the rhetorical strategy of claiming white normativity relies on language-coding. That is, in an era marked by claims of postracialism, rather than explicitly claiming whiteness as the standard for curriculum, HB 2281 proponents position themselves and the curriculum as race neutral and mainstream. For example, while Horne sought to convince people of "all mainstream political ideologies" that MAS was a serious threat, John Huppenthal argued that his decision to find TUSD's MAS program out of compliance was "not about politics, it is about education" (Huppenthal). As has become ubiquitous in the field, whiteness wields its power in part because it positions itself as the norm or universal, occluding its particularity and subjectivity, especially from those who wield it (Dyer 2). Thus, whiteness as a racialized identity and ideological formation becomes invisible to its bearers. Here pro–HB 2281 discourse mirrors and evidences such logic. In asserting that MAS is a biased, racial, and political project, HB 2281 advocates render themselves neutral, colorless, and apolitical. Interestingly, whiteness in this case also takes on a nationalist framework. Consider the way in which MacEachern and others depicted MAS courses as radical, biased, or minoritarian and thus not within the purview of "real" teachers of "traditional" American history and literature classes (MacEachern, "Roosevelt"; "Ethnic-Studies Bullies"; Editorial Board, "Open"). Not only does this move seek to delegitimize MAS as minoritarian but it also leaves unexplored what is "traditional American." In each of these cases, "real" teachers, "traditional" American history, and "mainstream" ideas function as stand-ins for white normativity, a category that dare not speak its name.

Significantly, these coded assertions of white normativity were also manifested through letters to the editor. In one letter, a Phoenix resident contended that "high-schoolers should be learning about our Constitution, government, geography and economics. They should be taught American history, not the Texas version or the Hispanic version, but the basics of how this country was created by mostly European settlers" (Zanzucchi). In distinct ways, each of these rhetorical moves signals HB 2281 as a rallying cry to defend an unbiased, race-neutral curriculum against racial and political biases. Of course, as this letter indicates, the race-neutral "American history" is coded white because of its centralizing of "mostly European settlers." Robin Dale Jacobson provides a lens for understanding this juxtaposition of MAS supporters' racial radicalism to the color-blind gestures of HB 2281 advocates. Jacobson contends that such rhetorical moves evidence what she terms a "defensive bridge" between racial-realist and race-neutral discourses. Through the defensive bridge, HB 2281 advocates "suggest they would like to see a world without racial divisions or that they are in fact color-blind. It is others . . . who perpetuate a system of racial categories" (40). In this vein Horne, Huppenthal, MacEachern, and others see themselves as merely defending themselves against the hostilities of race radicals. Such rhetorical moves do not simply render MAS a threat but they also occlude HB 2281 advocates from the critical gaze, a move that is central to the workings of whiteness.

Proponents of HB 2281 also rely upon and reinforce the logics of whiteness through the rhetorical embrace of abstract liberalism in the forms of a raceless individualism and meritocracy (Clark and Reed; Winkler-Morey). While the law specifically targeted curriculum that advanced racial resentment and ethnic solidarity, HB 2281 proponents elaborated their belief in the centrality of individualism on the pages of local newspapers. In his subtly titled February 2007 editorial "Racist Views Are Poor Use of School Funding," Horne rejected the notion that opposition to ethnic studies was an embrace of white supremacy. Rather, he contended that opposition to ethnic studies "stems from an ideal: that what counts is the individual, not the group; that what matters about people is what they know; what they can do; what beauty they can appreciate; what is their character; not into which group they happen to be born." Unsurprisingly, Horne then went on to argue that he was influenced by and is working as a caretaker for Martin Luther King's dream of a color-blind America. Bonilla-Silva has argued that such articulations of abstract liberalism undergird the cultural logics of color-blind racism (31). Moreover, this logic creates a disparate impact through race-neutral language: "If minority groups face group-based discrimination and whites have group-based advantages, demanding individual treatment for all can only benefit the advantaged group" (36). Likewise, this romance of individualism is an expression of whiteness.[2] As noted earlier, whiteness often renders itself invisible to its bearers. Thus, seeing themselves as raceless individuals—as opposed to a differentially racialized group—positions whites to view individuality as an ideal and racial identification as a strange, retrograde choice.

Moreover, strict adherence to the myth of raceless individualism supports and is supported by belief in meritocracy. That is, if whites are seen as individuals and not racialized bearers of privilege, those psychic and material advantages of privileges are conceptualized as earned rights. In a 2008 column, Robert Robb invokes meritocracy in his rejection of MAS curriculum as victimization studies:

The last thing these students need is to be taught that they are helpless victims of the system and that, short of overturning that system, they have no chance. In reality, if students in any school in this state pay attention to their teachers and do what their teachers tell them to do, they will earn a ticket to the American middle class and a standard of living that is beyond the hope of 90 percent of the world's population.

In her foundational essay, Peggy McIntosh contended that the myth of meritocracy occludes and undergirds white privilege (180). Read in this light, calls for individualism and meritocracy by HB 2281 advocates should not be seen as solely the conflict between color blindness versus racial realism. Rather, these calls function as unrecognized expressions of white racial identity. Indeed, they work in tandem with depictions of their opponents as racial and political radicals to stoke the flames of white victimization.

While critical of MAS as indoctrinating students into an ideology of victimization, HB 2281 proponents have also deployed a discourse of victimhood. Here, one cannot ignore the irony of such a move as their white victimization courses just below the rhetorical surface. Positioning MAS and its allies as racially, politically radical does not simply solidify claims to political neutrality as explored earlier. Rather, because these renderings of MAS radicalism are married to images and discourses of un-Americanness, they are simultaneously rendered a threat while "traditional" (white) "Americanness" is characterized as under siege (Winkler-Morey 51). This rhetorical move takes on greater significance as HB 2281 advocates assert the attacks on great American myths of upward mobility, meritocracy, and American exceptionalism. This deployment of victimization bears significance for the workings of whiteness in two ways.

First, rhetorically, it depends on the simultaneous discrediting of MAS as victimization studies. At the surface, such a move seems contradictory where the logic would read like this: "they" teach about victimization and that is wrong, but "we" are being victimized.[3] However, this move simultaneously seeks to delegitimize some forms of victimhood while claiming others. This rhetorical move functions as a strategic appropriation of pain where the grievances of others are denied and subordinated so that whiteness can be shielded from assertions of racism (Bebout 301; Williams 64).

Second, these articulations of a potential or ongoing white victimhood pay psychological dividends. Despite claims to the contrary, MAS curriculum is not the widespread fomentation of revolution. But it does not need to be to serve the rhetorical and psychological needs of whiteness. As George Lipsitz has suggested, these fears and anxieties of a cultural and political takeover need not be based in fact. Rather, they undergird fantasies that justify "recreational hate." By depicting MAS as an attack on whiteness and Americanness, HB 2281 advocates express a sense of "besieged solidarity," and belonging is one of the key assets of whiteness (50). Importantly, the logics of whiteness identified above are not discrete and isolated. They interpenetrate and work in mutually reinforcing ways. White normativity is dependent upon assertions of racial and political radicalism just as abstract liberalism undergirds claims of white victimhood. These discursive moves circulate widely in the supposedly postracial era, but in the case of HB 2281 and other educational debates, they form a curricular investment in whiteness.

A Curricular Investment in Whiteness and Cognitive Gated Communities

While HB 2281 and its supportive discourses are organized by general tropes and serve the needs of whiteness in the post-civil-rights-movement era, HB 2281 also forges a particular manifestation of race power, what I am calling a "curricular investment in whiteness." Here, I am readily drawing upon the scholarship of George Lipsitz. Contending that racism and white privilege are not simply aberrant leftovers from bygone eras, Lipsitz shows how recent and current social and economic policies propel a disparate valuing of white lives. For example, housing and immigration policies both ascribe financial, psychic, and symbolic value to whiteness. Recognizing HB 2281 as a curricular investment in whiteness turns Lipsitz's theorization to a powerful site of social and ideological reproduction: the schools. Of course, U.S. schools have long reproduced racial and economic inequality, from de facto and de jure segregation to curriculum that privileges Anglo American contributions and dominant US narratives. The end of formal segregation and the rise of multicultural education underwrite the myth of postracialism. In this vein, HB 2281 seeks to negate the potential curricular gains of the 1970s and the advance of multicultural education.[4] Reading HB 2281 as a curricular investment in whiteness suggests that it is part of an old white supremacist tactic repackaged for the discursive and political exigencies of the twenty-first century.

Framing HB 2281 as a curricular investment forges a link between the structural analysis of Lipsitz and the often psychological, cognitive analyses of whiteness offered by many others in critical whiteness studies. Notably, Charles Mills has contended that white supremacy fosters in whites "an inverted epistemology, an epistemology of ignorance, a particular pattern of localized and global cognitive dysfunctions (which are psychologically and socially functional), producing the ironic outcome that whites will in general be unable to understand the world they themselves have made" (18). Recently, Mills expounded upon this notion of "white lies" and "cognitive dysfunction" by describing whiteness as a "cognitive gated community" ("White Lies"). While Mills and other scholars have explored the epistemological effects of white ideology, these are often examined as individual acts of cognitive dysfunction and unwitnessing—individual acts that become communal in their pervasiveness. HB 2281 exposes how such a cognitive dysfunction is codified by law and reproduced in the schools. Horne, Huppenthal, and the state Department of Education work as guards in this cognitive gated community, with their allies policing which ideas belong in schools and which must be described as "untruths" and "un-American" so as to delegitimize those other worldviews. Of course it is critical to note that HB 2281 is not a new move in educational censorship or the curricular investment in whiteness. For example, according to Joe Lockard, nineteenth-century school readers excluded discussions of slavery in order to achieve a broader, national U.S. market by not alienating Southerners. Recently, Darius Echeverría has demonstrated that in the early to mid-twentieth century Arizona Mexican Americans were tracked into Americanization courses. These disparate examples point to the long-standing curricular investment in whiteness.

Critically, particularly in the post-civil-rights era, this curricular investment in whiteness must not be seen as simply "protecting" the minds that inhabit white bodies. Rather, such a curricular investment serves the interests of white supremacy by reaching out and "shielding" students of all colors from the potentially dangerous and subversive ideas. Importantly, however, these protective gestures may target all students, but in discrete and overlapping ways. Regarding white students, HB 2281 advocates contended that MAS curriculum would turn them into targets and victims of racial resentment. Such an assertion was supported in one of the court cases. Mary Stevenson testified that her "daughter told her that the [MAS government] class presented 'how the Anglo-Saxons had treated other people badly, particularly Chicano people'" and "that by 'the end of the class . . . most of the other students would not talk to her at all, except the students who were not of Hispanic background'" (TUSD v. Arizona Dept. of Ed. 32).

While the parent's testimony seeks to link the curriculum to her daughter's experiences of lost friendships, reading this as a strictly causative relationship forecloses other possibilities. Might the broken relationships be caused by other interpersonal issues and communication troubles? Might the daughter be at least partially culpable and not be read as whitely innocent? Could frictive relationships sparked by difficult discussions be productive in the long run? These are not simply unanswerable questions. Through a curricular investment in whiteness, they are unaskable. Notably, MacEachern and other HB 2281 advocates also expressed a fear that dissenting Hispanics were being targeted by MAS educators. In a repeated trope, Doug MacEachern has argued that race should have no bearing on education and politics only to also assert that some Hispanic teachers did not agree with the MAS curriculum ("Racism"). Here, MacEachern's shift from race-neutral to racial-realist discourses is significant because it advances his claims of MAS radicalism and the potential for victimization. Moreover, it gives whiteness a multicultural guise.

When discussing Mexican American students, however, HB 2281 advocates echo the discourse of the White Man's Burden, paternalistically claiming to be working on behalf of minority students by protecting their access to the curriculum—ideologies and myths—of whiteness and American exceptionalism. In the column cited earlier, Robert Robb suggested that by sewing racial resentment and radical ideology, MAS students (read: Mexican Americans) would only see themselves as victims and would not be able to actively shape their own lives. Moreover, in an editorial, Constance D'Ambrosio Steele-Young argued that the "sense of victimization and alienation" that ethnic studies fostered would not be "good soil from which to grow citizens who love and appreciate their country." The arguments of HB 2281 advocates to protect the access of students of color to dominant myths suggests how the curricular investment in whiteness has reconfigured itself in the face of the civil rights movements and their educational gains. Here, whiteness puts on its best multicultural face. The curricular investment seeks to reproduce and reinforce white supremacy by constituting students of color into good white-minded citizens.

Notably, this argument takes up and advances two other related critical interventions. First, Jodi Melamed and others have argued that corporate multiculturalism does not work toward social justice but forms a way of knowing and containing the other while severing discussions of race from material conditions (xvii). Second, Lipstiz contends that white supremacy is not simply for whites. Pointing to Clarence Thomas and Joe Clark, Lipsitz explores the need for white supremacy to build allies from marginalized communities. Lipsitz rightly concludes that the lesson should be that politics should not derive solely from identity, but one's identity should come from her politics (140–58). Moreover, such an insight suggests that if white supremacy can find allies of color, then it is imperative to forge alliances with white antiracists, or whites with antiracist potential. Of course, this is an old tack in U.S. racial justice movements. However, this discourse of white allies has been largely absent from the HB 2281 debate. And while not a panacea for racial justice, it has the potential to make legible and diminish the force of the curricular investment in whiteness.

With Liberty and Critical Ethnic Studies for All

From the debate, it is clear that MAS and ethnic studies advocates seek to disrupt and dismantle the machinations of white supremacy. Indeed, their efforts to address historic and contemporary racial disparities have led to the targeting of MAS as radical and subversive. However, MAS advocates have also ceded crucial discursive ground in framing MAS curriculum in two distinct ways: as essential for Mexican American students and open to *all* students. The first frame is a racial realist designation, and the second is a form of strategic color blindness, a tactic deployed to meet specific ends but which ultimately fails in making the curricular investment in whiteness legible. The assumption that MAS serves the needs of Mexican American students is completely logical when one considers that the MAS program was developed in response to a desegregation case (Collom). Because the district needed to remedy the disparate levels of academic success as tracked by ethnoracial groups, it is unsurprising that remediations be framed through and targeted toward aggrieved communities. That is, if Mexican Americans graduated at lower rates, it would make sense that MAS contended that the program would help Mexican Americans graduate. Moreover, the argument for developing Chicana/o studies to foster a positive self-image for Mexican American students has a long history in the field. As a founding document in the field of study, the 1969 Plan de Santa Barbara argued for Chicano studies as essential to Chicano community uplift (CCCHE). Likewise, Rodolfo Acuña's first edition of *Occupied America* articulates the psychological effects of colonization and offers Chicano history as a corrective to heal the Chicano mind (1). In this way, pro-MAS statements about the need to protect Mexican American, "minority," or "our" history emerge from and align with the goals of the Chicano movement broadly and the desegregation case in particular (Leong; Ramirez; Robinson; Romero).

However, this claim to racial realism violates the tenets of the seemingly race neutral, color-blind HB 2281. By recognizing Mexican Americans as an aggrieved community—not underachieving raceless individuals—pro-MAS advocates may rightly point to social injustice, but they also acquiesce to the framing of MAS as for Mexican Americans, victim studies, and discrete from "traditional" American history and literature. Moreover, both the Cambium report and Judge Kowal noted the racial realist discourse designating the curriculum for Mexican Americans or deploying us/them rhetorical moves as clearly incongruent with the law. While the Cambium report suggested a language change, Judge Kowal used the language to justify his finding of MAS out of compliance with the law and maintain the withholding of state funds from TUSD (Cambium 59, 66; TUSD v. Arizona Dept. of Ed. 34).

Notably, however, pro-MAS writers have also deployed a rhetoric of strategic color blindness, contending that MAS is for *all* students (Carlile; Rosendorf; Valdez). While this move seems to be an honest effort to articulate the importance of Chicana/o studies as a critical area of study—like "traditional" history—it also works against pro–HB 2281 claims of MAS as minoritarian and supplemental. However, as it is underdeveloped, claims of MAS for all seem ineffective. A cognitive friction emerges between the pairing of rhetorical claims to "our" Mexican American history and its importance for all students. If it is truly "our" history, can it be for all? While I would suggest that the answer is clearly yes, the seeming incongruity needs to be addressed. Because the curricular justification for MAS is framed for Mexican American students—self-confidence, graduation rates—the reasons for white students to take these classes are often left unsubstantiated and the claims of MAS for all rings hollow.

But white people need critical ethnic studies too. In his study of Los Angeles high schools, John Wills uncovered how white students were unable to make sense of current racial dynamics because of the ways in which African American history was emplotted within the "traditional" American history curriculum. That is, according to Wills, because incorporating diversity often means addressing slavery before the Civil War and Jim Crow in the early twentieth century, white students are unable to interrogate present-day racial dynamics (385–86). In this way, diversity curriculum is additive in nature, merely spicing up the grand narratives of U.S. history—progress and exceptionalism. Clearly, Wills's description of high school curriculum evidences the curricular investment in whiteness that this paper seeks to identify. Moreover, the inability of white students to meaningfully engage contemporary racial dynamics suggest the cognitive dysfunction Mills and others have explored. Importantly, however, Wills identifies these curricular failures in order to argue for their undoing. He rightly contends that the 1960s model of ethnic studies for the sole purpose of self-esteem building is short sighted. White students need ethnic studies if they are to come to the table and engage in meaningful conversation about the world in which they live. Significantly, such an argument is not the same as the strategically color-blind articulation that all people need ethnic studies, for it roots the necessity in specific racial and social contexts.

Rather than echoing pro–HB 2281 assertions of color blindness and universality, MAS advocates and ethnic studies allies can make a more concrete, specific articulation than MAS for all. While the vast majority of surveyed pro-MAS discourse framed the program as targeted for Mexican American students or for all students, playing into the rhetoric and logics of color blindness, there have been significant moments where students racialized as white are imagined to be equal participants in an ethnic studies education, and potential allies in the building of a more just, multiracial future. For example, in one court case, contesting the notion that MAS is solely for Mexican Americans, educational policy professor Jeffery Millem testified that ethnic studies builds disequilibrium in white students (TUSD v. Arizona Dept. of Ed. 17–18). This notion of disequilibrium suggests that white double-consciousness developed as the cognitive dysfunction, and the cognitive gated community is breached by the experiences and worldviews of others. Here the curriculum works in two ways simultaneously. For Chicano students, MAS can function as a "mirror" to build positive self-identification, and for non-Latinos "the model serves as a window into cultural, historical, and social understanding" (Cambium 61). While this mirror/window paradigm has long been part of the MAS philosophy, the rhetoric responding to HB 2281 has largely focused on the mirror, with little attention to the transformative power of the window.

The significance of ethnic studies for white students and the ability to build transracial alliances is further evidenced in a small section of the Cambium Report. The auditors included passages from group interviews with members of different target communities: students, teachers, administrators, staff, and community members. In one section, an unnamed white high school MAS participant stated the importance of the classes and their ability to reach white students: "Being an Anglo Student in those classes, it doesn't even make a significant difference. I still relate to all the topics even though I am not Mexican American; it's still my community where I live and I'm part of that" (58). The statement is anonymous and brief. What can be gleaned from it? Potentially two things: This student does not see himself as a victim or victimizer. Moreover, he sees himself as part of the community. So much for sowing seeds of "destructive ethnic chauvinism" (Horne "Open Letter").

Paying greater rhetorical and pedagogical attention to white students' need for MAS and ethnic studies can perform critical work in advancing the case for MAS and other formations of ethnic studies. First, it avoids the trap of color blindness, which acquiesces to logics of whiteness and abstract liberalism. Second, it voids the limiting claims that Mexican American history and culture is solely of interest and importance for Mexican American students, which not only violates the letter of the law but also self-marginalizes the curriculum. Here, a note of clarification is needed: pointing to the need of white students for ethnic studies does not suggest that they are the primary audience for ethnic studies. Rather, as suggested by the window and mirror model, ethnic studies provides the words and cognitive frames for students of diverse backgrounds to engage each other and the world in which they live, something that many ethnic studies advocates have suggested and support.

Of course, a critical question remains: will this rhetorical strategy be more effective? Perhaps; perhaps not. Articulations of how ethnic studies meets crucial needs of white students may well stoke the fears of Horne, Huppenthal, MacEachern, and other HB 2281 proponents. After all, it violates the central tenet of contemporary whiteness, for it makes whiteness visible. Significantly, however, vocal HB 2281 proponents should not be the audience. The target audience should be both ethnic studies advocates and those who can be converted into allies. Critically, this strategy will not cede ground from the outset. It names whiteness, and perhaps that alone is a win. Moreover, it specifically works to expose how white people have "skin in the game." They may continue to support the curricular investment in whiteness or they may travel outside their cognitive gated communities, divest in whiteness, and invest in a critically conscious humanity.

Notes

1. In November 2010 Horne became attorney general of Arizona and Huppenthal became state superintendent. In August 2014 both men lost their respective Republican primary races.

2. While examining nineteenth-century U.S. literature in her influential *Playing in the Dark*, Toni Morrison contended that the American romance of individualism has long been rooted in an oppositional relationship to an Africanist presence (44). In many ways, this echoes Charles Mills's assertions that Enlightenment thinkers constructed the autonomous individual subject of universal man against rhetorically constructed subperson Others. The case of HB 2281 evidences that a romance of a seemingly raceless individualism

pervades into the twenty-first century. Two aspects must be noted, however. First, this fashioning of whiteness does not occur solely through antiblack racialization. That is, outside the intellectual preview of Morrison, U.S. whiteness has long been constructed against a vast array of Others and not simply along the axis of a black/white binary. Second, in the late twentieth and early twenty-first centuries, we must recognize that the romance of individualism is an old trope, abundant with racial meaning and affect, readily available for the appropriation of civil rights discourses and the rollback of previous gains in the fights for social justice.

3. Such a move also brackets off what is imagined to be taught in these classes. By classifying MAS as victim studies, the potential curricular emphasis on Mexican American agency found in cultural and political contributions is erased.

4. Of course multicultural education has its own limits. For an excellent examination of the regressive potential in multicultural curriculum, see Jodi Melamed's *Represent and Destroy*.

Works Cited

Acuña, Rodolfo. *Occupied America: The Chicano's Struggle toward Liberation.* San Francisco: Canefield P, 1972. Print.

Bebout, Lee. "The Nativist Aztlán: Fantasies and Anxieties of Whiteness on the Border." *Latino Studies* 10.3 (Autumn 2012): 290–313. Print.

Bonilla-Silva, Eduardo. *Racism without Racists: Color-Blind Racism and the Persistence of Inequality in America.* 3rd ed. New York: Rowman and Littlefield Publishers, 2009. Print.

Buchanan, Patrick J. *State of Emergency: The Third World Invasion and Conquest of America.* New York: Thomas Dunne Books, 2006. Print.

Cacho, Lisa Marie. "But Some of Us Are Wise: Academic Illegitimacy and the Affective Value of Ethnic Studies." *Black Scholar* 40.4 (2010): 28–36. Print.

Cambium Learning, Inc. "Curriculum Audit, Mexican American Studies Department, Tucson Unified School District." 2 May 2011. Web.

Carlile, William. "Horne's Ethnic-Studies Fight a Shock." Letter. *Arizona Republic* 19 June 2009: B.4. Web. 9 Aug. 2013.

Chicano Coordinating Council on Higher Education (CCCHE). *El Plan de Santa Barbara: A Chicano Plan for Higher Education.* Oakland: La Causa Publications, 1969. Print.

Clark, D. Anthony, and Tamilia D. Reed. "A Future We Wish to See: Racialized Communities Studies after White Racial Anxiety and Resentment." *Black Scholar* 40.4 (2010): 37–49. Print.

Collom, Lindsey. "Ethnic Studies Limits Upheld." *Arizona Republic* 12 Mar 2013: A.1. Web. 9 Aug. 2013.

Dyer, Richard. *White: Essays on Race and Culture*. London: Routledge, 1997. Print.

Echeverría, Darius V. *Aztlán Arizona: Mexican American Educational Empowerment, 1968–1978*. Tucson: U of Arizona P, 2014.

Editorial Board. "Open the Program to Public Scrutiny" Editorial. *Arizona Republic* 14 Oct. 2010: B4. Web. *ProQuest*. 9 Aug. 2013.

Horne, Tom. "Racist Views Are a Poor Use of School Funding." Editorial. *Arizona Republic* 3 Feb. 2007: B.7. *ProQuest*. Web. 9 Aug. 2013.

———. "An Open Letter to the Citizens of Tucson." *Arizona Republic* 11 June 2007. *ProQuest*. Web. 09 Aug. 2013.

Huicochea, Alexis. "A Closer Look at Group That Halted TUSD Vote." *Arizona Daily Star* 28 Apr. 2011. Web. 9 Aug. 2013.

Huppenthal, John. "Superintendent of Public Instruction John Huppenthal Rules Tucson Unified School District out of Compliance with A.R.S. 15-112." *azed.gov* 15 June 2011. Web. 27 Aug. 2013.

Jacobson, Robin Dale. *The New Nativism: Proposition 187 and the Debate over Immigration*. Minneapolis: U of Minnesota P, 2008. Print.

Leong, Karen. "Ethnic Studies Books Challenge Preconceptions." Editorial. *Arizona Republic* 28 Feb. 2012: B.9. Web. 9 Aug. 2013.

Lipsitz, George. *The Possessive Investment in Whiteness: How White People Profit from Identity Politics*. Exp. and rev. ed. Philadelphia: Temple UP, 2006. Print.

Lockard, Joe. *Slavery's Silencing: Censorship and Antislavery Dissent*. Forthcoming. Manuscript.

MacEachern, Doug. "Ethnic-Studies Bullies Gaining Clout in Tucson." Editorial. *Arizona Republic* 9 May 2010: B11. *ProQuest*. Web. 9 Aug. 2013.

———. "The Issue: Teaching Tucson's Teachers." Editorial. *Arizona Republic* 14 July 2008: B.8. *ProQuest*. Web. 9 Aug. 2013.

———. "Racism, Distrust of U.S. Being Ingrained by Tucson Raza Studies." Editorial. *Arizona Republic* 3 February 2008: V.1. *ProQuest*. Web. 9 Aug. 2013.

———. "Roosevelt Educator Makes Big Difference." Editorial. *Arizona Republic* 4 Oct. 2009: B11. *ProQuest*. Web. 9 Aug. 2013.

———. "Tucson's Ethnic Studies, Despite Denials, Remain Mystery to Most." Editorial. *Arizona Republic* 24 October 2012: B11. *ProQuest*. Web. 9 Aug. 2013.

McIntosh, Peggy. "White Privilege: Unpacking the Invisible Knapsack." *Race, Class, and Gender in the United States: An Integrated Study*. 7th ed. Ed. Paula S. Rothberg. New York: Worth Publishers, 2007. 177–82. Print.

Melamed, Jodi. *Represent and Destroy: Rationalizing Violence in the New Racial Capitalism*. Minneapolis: U of Minnesota P, 2011. Print.

Mills, Charles W. *The Racial Contract*. Ithaca: Cornell UP, 1997. Print.

———. "White Lies and the Making of the World." Address at Lying: The Making of the World Conference. Arizona State University, Tempe, AZ, 18–20 Oct. 2012.

Morrison, Toni. *Playing in the Dark: Whiteness and the Literary Imagination*. New York: Vintage, 1992. Print.

Orozco, Richard. "Racism and Power: Arizona's Politicians' Use of the Discourse of Anti-Americanism against Mexican American Studies." *Hispanic Journal of Behavioral Sciences* 34.1 (2012): 43–60. Print.

Ramirez, Denise. "The Treaty of Guadalupe Hidalgo." Editorial. *Arizona Daily Star* 10 Feb. 2011. Web. 21 Aug. 2013.

Robb, Robert. "If It Spews Lies, Halt the Schools' Program." Editorial. *Arizona Republic* 15 June 2008: V.5. Web. 9 Aug. 2013.

Robinson, Eugene. "Law Targeting Ethnic-Studies Program is Chilling, Reflects Fear." Editorial. *Arizona Daily Star* 15 May 2010. Web. 20 Aug. 2013.

Rocco, Raymond. "Transforming Citizenship: Membership, Strategies of Containment, and the Public Sphere in Latino Communities." *Latino Studies* 2.1 (April 2004): 4–25. Print.

Roediger, David. "White Looks: Hairy Apes, True Stories, and Limbaugh's Laughs." *Whiteness: A Critical Reader*. Ed. Mike Hill. New York: New York UP, 1997. 35–46. Print.

Romero, Augustine. "At War with the State in Order to Save the Lives of Our Children: The Battle to Save Ethnic Studies in Arizona." *Black Scholar* 40.4 (2010): 7–15. Print.

Rosendorf, Neal M. Letter. "Arizona Schools Ignore Much Hispanic History." *Arizona Republic* 21 June 2010: B.7. Web. 9 Aug. 2013.

Steele-Young, Constance D'Ambrosio. "Ethnic Studies Keep Immigrants from Fully Integrating." Letter. *Arizona Republic* 23 July 2010: 31. Web. 9 Aug. 2013.

TUSD (Tucson Unified School District) No. 1 v. Arizona Department of Education. Administrative Law No. 11F-002-ADE. Judge Decision. Office of Administrative Hearings. Phoenix, AZ. Judge Lewis D. Kowal. 16 Dec. 2011.

Valdez, Linda. "Let's Ditch the '50s Mentality: Ethnic Studies Aren't 'Frivolous' but Important to Our Children's Education." Editorial. *Arizona Republic* 29 Jan. 2007: B.5. Web. 9 Aug. 2013.

Williams, Patricia. *The Alchemy of Race and Rights: Diary of a Law Professor*. Cambridge: Harvard UP, 1991. Print.

Wills, John. "Who Needs Multicultural Education? White Students, U.S. History, and the Construction of a Usable Past." *Anthropology and Education Quarterly* 27.3 (1996): 365–89. Print.

Winkler-Morey, Anne. "The War on History: Defending Ethnic Studies." *Black Scholar* 40.4 (2010): 51–56. Print.

Zanzucchi, Joe. "U.S. History Outranks Latino Studies." Letter. *Arizona Republic* 13 June 2010: B10. Web. 9 Aug. 2013.

HOW WHITENESS HAUNTS THE TEXTBOOK INDUSTRY: THE RECEPTION OF NONWHITES IN COMPOSITION TEXTBOOKS

Cedric Burrows

WHEN I WAS a graduate student working as assistant to the director of a first-year composition program at a large state university, my duties included serving on a composition textbook selection committee. What started out as service soon generated a series of research questions that undergirded my dissertation and that are informing its current revision into a book manuscript. After perusing several textbooks I noticed that many composition readers replicated the texts of Martin Luther King's "I Have a Dream" speech from the March on Washington and Malcolm X's "Learning to Read," an excerpt from his autobiography. Initially I wondered: Why are these exact same excerpts from King and Malcolm X repeated from reader to reader? (For those of you unfamiliar with the genre, readers are composition textbooks comprised of famous essays that serve as genre models, as research materials for students' paper topics, or as repositories of rhetorical tactics that students may identify and then transfer to their own writings.) But the question of replication soon became more complicated, resulting in the questions, "What identity construction emerges for King and Malcolm X in these readers?" and "What are the reception effects for students reading these textbooks?" With these selections, King and Malcolm X were rendered palpable to student readers who could happily echo that the content of one's character matters more than race and that learning to read is a good way to transform one's life. But both men are more complicated, and more activist, than these whitewashed representations in readers. Ultimately I asked myself, "What motivates the selection and receptions of these oft-repeated texts in readers?" And the answer became obvious to me: whiteness haunts the textbook industry.

I begin with two examples that illustrate how whiteness haunts the textbook industry in the twenty-first century. The first situation occurred with the alterations of two mainstays in middle school and high school reading lists. On February 1, 2011, New South Books released Mark Twain's *Adventures of Tom Sawyer* and *Huckleberry Finn* in one volume. What distinguishes this work from other versions is that the new edition replaces "nigger"—which appears in *Huckleberry Finn* 219 times and 9 times in *Tom Sawyer*—with "slave" and switches "injun" to "Indian" in *Tom Sawyer*. During his conversation with teachers in Montgomery, Alabama, book editor Alan Gribben learned that teachers were hesitant to use *Huckleberry Finn* because, "in the new classroom, it's not really acceptable" (Schultz). Based on these talks, Gribben decided to edit the novel as an alternative for both grade-school classrooms and general readers who wanted to appreciate the novel within a twenty-first-century context. New South Books' publisher Suzanne LaRosa agreed with Gribben, stating that the editors noticed "a market for a book in which the n-word was switched out for something less hurtful, less controversial" (Schultz).

The other situation involves what happens when textbooks question the haunting of whiteness. In 2014, the Texas State Board of Education voted on several proposed history, geography, and government textbooks for grades 6–12. However, the watchdog group Texas Freedom Network found that forty-three of the proposed textbooks contained what they deemed to be problematic material. Among the problems include the incorporation of neo-Confederate ideology stating that "states' rights" was the cause of the Civil War, and the outdated usage of Negro and Caucasoid to describe African Americans and whites. In response, spokespersons from Pearson and McGraw Hill state that they will consider the recommendations and critiques while being diligent "to ensure its instructional materials are compliant with Texas standards" (Klein).

The examples of *Huckleberry Finn* and *Tom Sawyer* as well as the Texas State Board of Education illustrate how the textbook industry and the dominant discourses of whiteness intersect within the twenty-first century. On one end of the audience spectrum, textbook publishers are responding to well-meaning groups who want to discuss race in a society that elected its first African American president but euphemistically says "the n-word" because *nigger* is too uncomfortable to say. Instead of fully investigating the racially loaded language created by the dominant discourses of whiteness, the textbooks produce works that alter the language to make the readings more appealing to students; simultaneously, they eliminate the need to think about how whiteness haunts the racially loaded words in the works. On the other end of the audience spectrum, publishers are creating textbooks for those groups who do not want to talk about race because they feel that their whiteness is threatened. They see curricula that focus on nonwhites as a menace that espouses antiwhite messages; as a result, this group wants textbooks that alter historical narratives and reinforce their whiteness. Interestingly, for both audiences, whiteness haunts the textbooks because the textbooks neither fully challenge how whiteness shapes the literature that students read nor do they examine how whiteness created the need for curricula that reflects the communities of nonwhite groups. The result is an oxymoronic whiteness as described in the introduction to this book, an oxymoronic whiteness whose contradictions need to be both identified and challenged.

This oxymoronic whiteness is particularly evident in composition readers. Created during the turn of the twentieth century, readers offer students models for effective academic writing, models that are usually written by white male authors. By the late 1980s and early 1990s, readers began including more writings by women and nonwhites while also providing historical and cultural contexts to situate the readings. Although recent textbooks contain more writings from nonwhite and women writers, how readers use those writings poses other problems. Scholars, such as Jay Jordan, Sandra Jamieson, Michael Kleine, Lester Faigley, Lizbeth A. Bryant, and Yameng Liu, have argued that although readers include writers from various racial, ethnic, and gender groups, they still uphold a dominant pedagogy that reinforces traditional ideologies of which writings are and are not acceptable in the academy. Moreover, Lynn Bloom contends that when framed within an "extensive rhetorical matrix" of biographical headnotes, discussion questions, and suggestions for reading and writing, the text in the reader develops into another meaning that strips the essay of its historical content (418). What is missing in their arguments is a discussion on how whiteness shapes the reframed text of a nonwhite author in readers to make it appealing for a white audience. I contend that readers uphold an oxymoronic whiteness when placing the nonwhite subject in these textbooks. By using the examples of Dr. Martin Luther King Jr. and Malcolm X—two highly anthologized African American men whose historical narratives have been haunted by whiteness—I argue that readers create oxymoronic whiteness via the following rhetorical moves: *(1)* altering the subject's biographical narrative to make it more racially nonthreatening; *(2)* modifying the selection to make the reading racially palpable for a broad audience; and *(3)* creating discussion questions that propagate a white discourse.

Oxymoronic Whiteness in Biographical Headnotes

Oxymoronic whiteness when anthologizing the nonwhite subject begins with the biographical headnotes. The subject's life is narrated around events that are connected to his or her racial background. In the process, any event that is not related to the subject's race is eliminated. This elimination results in the subject's being limited to a raced identity and forced into becoming a racial spokesperson in the textbook. For instance, in *The Bedford Reader*'s overview of King's life, the reader highlights King as a tragic martyr whose career was to save African Americans:

> Martin Luther King, Jr. (1929–68) was born in Atlanta, the son of a Baptist minister, and was himself ordained in the same denomination. Stepping to the forefront of the civil rights movement in 1955, King led African Americans in a boycott of segregated city buses in Montgomery, Alabama; became the first president of the Southern Christian Leadership Conference; and staged sit-ins and mass marches that helped bring about the Civil Rights Act passed by Congress in 1964 and the Voting Rights Act of 1965. He received the Nobel Peace Prize in 1964. While King preached "nonviolent resistance," he was himself the target of violence. He was stabbed in New York, pelted with stones in Chicago; his home in Montgomery was bombed; and ultimately he was assassinated in Memphis by a sniper. On his tombstone near Atlanta's Ebenezer Baptist Church are these words from the spiritual he quotes at the conclusion of "I Have a Dream": "Free at last, free at last, thank God almighty, I'm free at last." Martin Luther King's birthday, January 15, is now a national holiday. (Kennedy 614)

Notice that in the beginning that the biography mentions that King led African Americans in the Montgomery Bus Boycott. By adding that phrase in the beginning of a series of events, the textbook wants students to focus on King as a leader for African Americans and gives the impression that he led African Americans through all the subsequent events listed in the sentence. Also, what is notable about this biography is the elimination of King's efforts to protest the Vietnam War or King's Poor People's Campaign, which involved a coalition of various ethnic groups to occupy Washington, D.C., to fight for economic justice. This omission of King's later career is convenient for the biography because it allows King to remain as a raced individual who can only speak about racial issues instead of other topics related to their careers.

This elimination of any mention of other topics is similar to how the biography of Malcolm X is framed in *Rereading America*. While the biography gives more of an overview of his career as an activist, it also highlights him only as an African American leader:

> Born Malcolm Little on May 19, 1925, Malcolm X was one of the most articulate and powerful leaders of black America during the 1960s. A street hustler convicted of robbery in 1946, he spent seven years in prison, where he educated himself and became a disciple of Elijah Muhammad, founder of the Nation of Islam. In the days of the civil rights movement, Malcolm X emerged as the leading spokesman for black separatism, a philosophy that urged black Americans to cut political, social, and economic ties with the white community. After a pilgrimage to Mecca, the capital of the Muslim world, in 1964, he became an orthodox Muslim, adopted the Muslim name El Hajj Malik El-Shabazz, and distanced himself from the teachings of the black Muslims. He was assassinated in 1965. (Columbo et al. 210)

The first sentence of the biography sets the tone for the rest of the narrative by highlighting Malcolm X as the spokesperson for *black* America. By placing the adjective before America, *Rereading America* gives the impression that Malcolm X's ideas are limited to African Americans and should be confined within one group. As with King, any part of Malcolm X's identity that is not related to being an African American is ignored. For instance, Malcolm X grew up in an integrated neighborhood and attended integrated schools as an adolescent and had an encounter with a white teacher who discouraged him from pursing his dream of being a lawyer. If that information was available, students would learn about how whiteness haunts academic institutions and shapes Malcolm X's early philosophy. Likewise, although the biography focuses on Malcolm X's days with the Nation of Islam and his philosophy of black separatism, there is only a vague explanation of his philosophy after he separated from the Nation of Islam. His views about being a human rights advocate rather than a civil rights leader are hidden in the text in ways that privilege a raced identity and thus narrows the scope of readers' understanding Malcolm X.

Whitening the Selections and Discussion Questions

These headnotes discussed above show the first stage of how oxymoronic whiteness manifests itself in the biographical headnotes. The readers add King and Malcolm X to increase the diversity of their authors. But, when their biographies are placed in readers, the focus of their narratives becomes more about their African American identity rather than a comprehensive view of their ideologies. Students, therefore, will read their biographies and focus more on their identities as African Americans rather than on their identities as writers and speakers, which then frames the readings as a *black* text instead of a text that is written by an African American.

The other steps of creating oxymoronic whiteness in readers occur when the textbooks whiten the text by selective excerpting and by creating discussion questions that either fit into a white standard of communication or reiterate stereotypes of the nonwhite subject. Therefore, whiteness haunts the text by providing a white discourse that is deemed safe for the reader (read: white readers).

For instance, in terms of selective excerpting, many readers represent King's "I Have a Dream" as a written document rather than an oral text delivered to a listening audience. The process results in a speech that is framed within a Western, white rhetorical tradition that favors formality, distance, and restraint. One excerpt from the speech as printed in *The Conscious Reader* and *The Bedford Reader* reads:

> I have a dream that one day the state of Alabama, whose governor's lips are presently dripping with the words of interposition and nullification, will be transformed into a situation where little black boys and black girls will be able to join hands with little white boys and white girls and walk together as sisters and brothers.
>
> I have a dream today. (Shrodes et al. 802; Kennedy et al. 617)

Situated in this framework, the reader does not understand King's pauses, elongation of words, or the responses emoted by the audience. King's passion is lost along with his ethos as a Southern, African American Baptist preacher. Consequently, students learn nothing about conventions of African American rhetorics.

Compare the textbooks' version with a transcription by Clayborne Carson that appears in *A Call to Conscious: The Landmark Speeches of Martin Luther King, Jr.*:

I have a dream that one day down in Alabama, with its vicious racists, with its governor having his lips dripping with the words of "interposition" and "nullification" (Yes,) one day right there in Alabama little black boys and black girls will be able to join hands with little white boys and white girls as sisters and brothers. I have a dream today. [Applause] (85)

Note that in Carson's speech, there are brackets that frame when the audience responds to King's message. Here, Carson shows how King employs call-and-response, an African American rhetorical device in which both the speaker and audience engage with each other on an equal basis. Instead of presenting the information as one in which King talks to a silent audience, Carson gives readers more of a sense for King's preaching style. King, as rendered in Carson's version, gives more of an informal conversation than the one presented in the readers. Likewise, replacing the word "down," a more informal word, with "the state of" suggests that the textbooks are changing King's tone into what they feel is a more formal (i.e., "white") style, and deleting the phrase "with its vicious racists" softens the delivery to one less harsh in tone, as if it would offend the student reading the text.

While whiteness haunts King's speech as a whitened version of his original version, whiteness haunts Malcolm X in textbooks by framing him as the stereotypical black male who lands in prison. The most frequently anthologized work by Malcolm X in readers is a condensed version of the chapter "Saved" found in his autobiography. In its completed version, "Saved" details how Malcolm uses the literacy he gains in prison to persuade other inmates to join the Nation of Islam and to engage in prison debates. He critically engages with the texts he reads to gain a newfound knowledge of his spirituality and of world history. However, whiteness haunts the textbook version by constructing Malcolm X as the illiterate black man who uses prison as a way to acquire an education. This theme is seen through the alternate titles of the readings: "A Homemade Education" in *The Conscious Reader* (Shrodes et al.) and "Learning to Read" in *Rereading America* (Columbo et al.). The result is that these readers focus more on his self-education and erase how white institutions led him to educate himself in prison, an erasure that is further emphasized by the discussion questions. For example, when *The Conscious Reader* asks students to explain the significance of Malcolm X's "homemade education," the teacher's guide for the textbook provides a suggested answer:

In discussing Malcolm's term "homemade education," you might ask students to reflect on the word "homemade." Like a pie baked at home, what is done according to one's own taste and efforts may be most satisfying. Malcolm's "home" during his adult education is a prison, where he can read widely and without the distractions that a real college involves. (Di Paolo 200)

Implicitly, the answer suggests that prison is better than a "real" college, but it does not offer any significant context for students to understand how whiteness played a part in Malcolm X receiving his homemade education. Malcolm X was an exceptional student in middle school but was discouraged to follow his goal of being a lawyer because of race. Also, while in prison, Malcolm X enrolled in correspondence classes for English and Latin. Without this information, the textbook creates Malcolm X's education in prison as something that is crude and haphazardly created without understanding how whiteness shaped and haunted his education and his message.

Because the textbooks do not fully investigate how whiteness structures his background and education, students will not be able to understand why Malcolm X used certain words to reach his message to other converts. Throughout the text, Malcolm X uses words such as "devil" and "white man," which serves as a rhetorical strategy because the wording is vague and allows potential converts to create particular images for themselves of who that person may be. However, in *Rereading America*, the textbook does not ask students to think about how whiteness constructed Malcolm X's language. Instead, it makes Malcolm X the victim whose views have to be justified or defended: "Some readers are offended by the strength of Malcolm X's accusations and by his grouping of all members of a given race into 'collectives.' Given the history of racial injustice he recounts here, do you feel he is justified in taking such a position?" (Columbo et al. 251). As with the previous sections, Malcolm X's views are the ones that are being critiqued instead of the invisible whiteness that created Malcolm X and the language he used to discuss injustices aimed at African Americans. As a result, students risk seeing the nonwhite subject as an unnecessary critic of racism while never having to research how the institutions that uphold whiteness make the subject critical of those institutions.

By using the examples of how King and Malcolm X are positioned in popular readers, I demonstrate how oxymoronic whiteness creates irony when nonwhites are placed within composition textbooks. When nonwhite subjects are placed within these readers, their biographies are framed to place a heavier emphasis on their race. However, in their texts and subsequent discussion questions, their identity becomes haunted by a white standard of discourse that makes it more palpable for mainstream students, but also creates the unspoken assumption that the best forms of communication are constructed in a white standard. These texts also fail to contextualize how whiteness and its systemic power shape these men in terms of their experiences and rhetorical practices.

This ironic, indeed oxymoronic viewpoint became evident to me several years ago when I taught a first-year writing course. The first unit in the class focused on education and literacy with readings by Mark Edmundson, Henry Adams, Carter G. Woodson, and Malcolm X. During the end of the unit, I asked the class to list and describe several themes from the selections. While reading the responses, I came across one that really stood out, and not because of the themes listed. Instead, the student wrote that while she like reading Edmundson and Adams, she had a harder time with Woodson and Malcolm X. Throughout the note, she stated that while she was not racist, she felt that there were too many "black readings" and that the only reason the texts were included was because of diversity. I thought about those comments for a while. Why did the student mark the African American writings in the textbook as different? And what made the student react in that manner? I addressed her response by writing on her paper, explaining my rationale for the readings, feeling as though I had to justify discussing race in the class, as though it really was an intrusion into the student's education.

However, as I realized that my comments were about to spill over into the next page, I decided to ask the student to meet with me during office hours. During our meeting, I expressed my concerns about her comments and asked why she felt disconnected to the readings by Woodson and Malcolm X. She responded, "Reading about race and racism is hard for me because I never had to think about it. I never thought about being white as a race and I don't understand what those other readings have anything to do with me." When I explained my choice of readings and the need to gain various perspectives for critical literacy, she stated, "Again, what does race have to do with me? I don't understand why people just can't get over it. Why should I have to read about it?"

Another situation occurred at the end of the semester; I was in my office receiving the final portfolios when a student appeared. He was African American, an athlete who, while quiet at first, gradually spoke more as the semester progressed. The young man, after handing me his portfolio, extended his hand. After I shook it, he stated, "Thank you for this semester. I often had to read white stuff in my English class, and it felt good to read something written by someone who looks like me and understands my experiences."

I have often thought about the consequences embodied within those representative students for the textbook industry. The first consequence affects the textbook industry because it, in turn, affects students, particularly their lexicon for discussing *black* and *white*. The first student never used the term "white" but placed a lot of emphasis on "black," marking blackness as different, an intrusion into what she felt was the standard. While she never said what the standard was, one could assume that the norm meant "white," considering that she never expressed any issue with the white authors. When the second student said "white," his utterance marked the word as standard, but a standard forced upon him as acceptable. However, as he mentioned the writings by African Americans, he noted that while it was out of the norm from what he traditionally read in school, he embraced it more as something to enhance his education rather than a disruption.

The second consequence affects the educational system itself—how textbooks reinforce the educational system's creation of this duality of reading blackness as different while reading whiteness as the unspoken, default standard to uphold. Like these students, textbooks face a sense of irony with whiteness at the beginning of the twenty-first century. In one part of society are groups who believe that—with the election of the country's first African American president and the prominence of nonwhites in the media—America is a postracial society where little attention should be given to race. Therefore, they challenge why racism has to be discussed in textbooks or other educational materials. On the other end, there is another component of society who believes that—with the haunting of whiteness in the election of the first African American president, the conflicts in Ferguson, Missouri, the death of Trayvon Martin, and other reports of police brutality—racism is alive and that a curriculum needs to be in place to explore these issues. Placed in the center of these groups is the educational system and how information should be constructed in textbooks. If teaching materials are to truly reflect the experiences of all the voices that come into the classroom, they should remember not to mark nonwhite subjects as different for students but instead create a situation where every group's voices are named, represented equally, and framed as important to everyone's education. In this regard whiteness will not haunt textbooks but will appear at the forefront to make students aware of its manifestations. Even though the conversations may be painful, they are needed in order to make whiteness and its presence rife for interrogation and understanding.

Works Cited

Bloom, Lynn Z. "The Essay Canon." *College English* 61 (March 1999): 401–30. Print.

Bryant, Lizbeth. "A Textbook's Theory: Current Composition Theory in Argument Textbooks." Olsen et al. 113–33. Print.

Carson, Clayborne, and Kris Shepard, eds. *A Call to Conscience: The Landmark Speeches of Dr. Martin Luther King, Jr.* New York: Warner, 2001. Print.

Columbo, Gary, Robert Cullen, and Bonnie Lisle, eds. *Rereading America: Cultural Context for Critical Thinking and Writing.* 7th ed. Boston: Bedford/ St. Martin's, 2007. Print.

Di Paolo, Marc F. *The Instructor's Manual to Accompany "The Conscious Reader."* 11th ed. New York: Pearson, 2009. Print.

Faigley, Lester. *Fragments of Rationality: Postmodernity and the Subject of Composition.* U of Pittsburgh P, 1992. Print.

Jamieson, Sandra. "Composition Readers and the Construction of Identity." *Writing in Multicultural Settings.* Ed. Carol Severino, Juan C. Guerra, and Johnnella E. Butler. New York: MLA, 1997. 150–71. Print.

Jordan, Jay. "Rereading the Multicultural Reader: Toward More 'Infectious' Practices in Multicultural Composition." *College English* 68.2 (Nov. 2005): 168–85. Print.

Kennedy, X. J., Dorothy M. Kennedy, and Jane E. Aaron, eds. *The Bedford Reader.* 10th ed. Boston: Bedford/St. Martin's, 2010. Print.

Klein, Rebecca. "Texas Textbook Battle Heats Up with Claims of Conservative Bias." *Huffington Post.* TheHuffingtonPost.com, Inc., 11 Sept. 2014. Web. 20 Sept. 2014.

Kleine, Michael W. "Teaching from a Single Textbook 'Rhetoric': The Potential Heaviness of the Book." Olsen et al., 137–61. Print.

Liu, Yameng. "Self, Other, In-Between: Cross-Cultural Composition Readers and the Reconstruction of Cultural Identities." Olsen et al. 69–91. Print.

Olsen, Gary, Xin Liu Gale, and Fred Gale, eds. *(Re)visioning Composition Textbooks: Conflicts of Culture, Ideology, and Pedagogy.* Albany: SUNY P, 2000. Print.

Schultz, Marc. "Upcoming NewSouth 'Huck Finn' Eliminates the 'N' Word." *PublishersWeekly.com.* Publishers Weekly, 3 Jan. 2011. Web. 1 Sept. 2014.

Shrodes, Caroline F., Michael F. Shugrue, Marc F. DiPaolo, and Christian Matuschek, eds. *The Conscious Reader.* 11th ed. New York: Pearson, 2009.

THE TRIUMPH OF WHITENESS: DUAL CREDIT COURSES AND HIERARCHICAL RACISM IN TEXAS

Casie Moreland and Keith D. Miller

EDUARDO BONILLA-SILVA, George Lipsitz, Zeus Leonardo, and other whiteness theorists often emphasize the continuity of the American rhetoric and culture of whiteness, a continuity that, different theorists argue, extends from centuries of slavery throughout the twentieth century. In his well-known *Racism without Racists*, Bonilla-Silva emphasizes this view of the continuity and endurance of whiteness and white privilege by subtitling his book *Color-Blind Racism and the Persistence of Racial Inequality of America*. Leonardo makes a similar claim for the persistence of whiteness: "[White domination] does not form out of random acts of hatred, although these are condemnable, but rather out of a patterned and *enduring* treatment of social groups" (139, emphasis ours). Making a parallel argument, Lipsitz declares, "The highest levels of judicial, legislative, and executive power have worked together to *preserve* white privileges" in the present (38, emphasis ours). Some whiteness theorists emphasize the decades-spanning extension of whiteness so much that it seems fair to call this emphasis one of their major themes.

Other whiteness theorists, such as Thomas Nakayama and Robert Krizek, contend that while the culture and rhetoric of whiteness is "pervasive" in American life, culture and rhetoric usually operate in a fashion that is relatively "invisible" (298). But, by claiming that whiteness is now more diffuse and less visible, theorists risk giving some readers the impression that whiteness is becoming less powerful and less damaging. Of course, threads of continuity certainly link the culture of white domination that has prevailed in every era of American history, at least since slaves were introduced in the Jamestown colony in 1619. Yet, we contend, deplorable racial attitudes, practices, denials, and hierarchies do not simply persist and endure but instead sometimes fluctuate and evolve, and not merely in the direction of becoming more sophisticated and less visible.

In the case of Texas, a resurgence of an inward-looking white culture has *increasingly* blinded many elected officials and educational administrators alike and led them to *fortify* white privilege and *enlarge* existing racial hierarchies in a fashion that is decidedly overt and quite visible. These officials and educational administrators in Texas did so when, in a discriminatory fashion, they engineered and proliferated dual credit programs in high schools, which are programs offering courses that count simultaneously for high school and college graduation credits. This phenomenon indicates that, far from simply continuing or simply evolving into instantiations that prove more diffuse and less visible, the culture and rhetoric of whiteness sometimes emerge into forms that are *more explicit, more visible,* and *more damaging.*

In the case of public schools in Texas, the culture and rhetoric of whiteness has now evolved into a more engulfing and more harmful form than what ordinarily prevailed during the 1970s, 1980s, and early 1990s, before these courses spread. Such a development should spur theorists to reconceptualize whiteness as a culture and a rhetoric *capable of expanding and buttressing white advantage and white control.*

We forward this argument in four steps. First, despite our disagreement with Lipsitz's apparent assumption about the stability of whiteness, we embrace and outline his theory and analysis to explain how structural racism and white domination continue to plague American life. We choose Lipsitz in part because he focuses squarely not simply on attitudes and assumptions but on material and economic advantages that accrue to whites, especially to affluent whites. Second, we sketch the history and current status of what are often dubbed dual enrollment (DE) or credit (DC) courses in the United States and the response of composition scholars and the Conference on College Composition and Communication. Third, we analyze the unfolding of DC courses in Texas in ways that perpetuate, strengthen, and enlarge white domination. Fourth, we explore implications of our work for a reconfiguration of whiteness theory in order to account for instantiations of a culture of whiteness that is enlarged and strengthened.

Lipsitz's Theory and Analysis of White Domination

In *The Possessive Investment in Whiteness*, Lipsitz identifies ways that people who are categorized as white benefit from structural racism. He describes in detail how whites enjoy economic advantages, such as lower interest rates and higher approval rates for home loans; greater access to educational and job opportunities; and the ability to transfer wealth. According to Lipsitz, these advantages emerge in many domains of American life, including the economy, war, politics, music, movies, and art.

Lipsitz describes specifically how the arenas of housing, employment, and education interlink, functioning with each other to perpetuate structural racism. According to his analysis, unequal access to education leads to unequal opportunities for jobs, which leads to fewer opportunities to own homes. As he explains, "owner-occupied homes constitutes the single greatest sources of wealth for white Americans" (33). More specifically, whites are structurally at an advantage because of the ways that whiteness often leads to wealth through a continuing process that, in his words, "enable[s] white parents to give their children financial advantages over children of other groups" (33). He continues, "Unequal opportunities for education play a crucial role in racializing life chances in the United States" (33). And he notes, "White resistance and refusal in housing and education work to deprive minority children of both intergenerational transfers of wealth and the tools to better their own conditions" (38).

The Rise of DC Courses and the Response of Composition Scholars and CCCC

Many American high school students take specially designated upper-level courses for which they receive credit toward both high school graduation and college graduation. Dual enrollment (DE) options appear in varied configurations and go by such names as current enrollment (CE), advanced placement (AP), international baccalaureate (IB), early college (EC), and dual credit (DC). In this work we focus specifically on dual credit (DC) courses, the name by which the state of Texas identifies college courses offered to high school students that allow them to gain high school and college credits simultaneously. Many scholars date DC programs back to at least the 1970s. As Kristine Hansen explains, DC classes that were developed in the 1970s did so as a means to "challenge high school students who would be bored with the regular high school curriculum and are ready to begin college work" (25). At Syracuse University, a DC program known as "Project Advance" announces on its website that it began in 1972 "as an attempt to address 'senioritis,'" a form of academic ennui that besets certain advanced high school students, especially after they have already been accepted for college. Hansen notes,

> AP, IB, and [DC] programs are aimed squarely at those who want to get ahead because they offer students the promise of starting and therefore finishing college early, distinguishing themselves from the common herd, and enhancing their chances of being admitted to a good university, where they will get even further ahead. (3)

Not only do many students in DC courses both begin and finish their college careers sooner, but they also accrue large financial advantages inasmuch as their high schools often pay their tuition fees to the colleges that supply course credits. Such payments save those students and their parents many thousands of dollars. Further, even when DC students pay the same college tuition fees that they would otherwise pay after high school, many of them still save hundreds or thousands of dollars because they still live with their parents, thus eliminating the need to pay for room and board at a college or university while taking college-level courses.

These huge advantages have spurred the development of DC programs across the nation. According to a study conducted by the U.S. Department of Education, in 2010–11 an astonishing 1.277 million students participated in programs that allow students to earn high school and college credits simultaneously (Marken et al. 3). As Chris Anson observes, DC courses in composition are among those that have spread widely (247); yet, despite their rising popularity, DC programs have received surprisingly little attention from composition scholars. Those who write about DC courses in composition, including those who contributed essays for a scholarly anthology about them (Hansen and Farris), provide informative and helpful essays. But this scholarship largely fails to address racialized dimensions of DC courses and their tendency to enshrine white domination. So does a recent, otherwise useful official CCCC statement about DC courses (Farris et al). But, lamentably, the culture and politics of white domination impacted many DC courses almost from their beginning. These classes often (not always) tended to flourish in relatively affluent high schools that regularly dispatched their graduates to colleges and universities, not in inner-city high schools characterized by large dropout rates and graduates who failed to attend college. The racially and economically disparate implementation of DC programs is especially well documented in Texas, and the numbers are worth considering in some detail.

The Unfolding of DC Courses in Texas

In 2007 public school boards throughout Texas implemented legislation that requires each of their systems to make at least twelve hours of college credit available to high school students. The passage of this requirement prompted a massive increase in the number of students enrolled in DC courses throughout the state. According to the Texas Education Administration (TEA), an official state agency, a staggering 94,232 students enrolled in such Texas programs during the 2009–10 academic year (Friedman et al. iii). Today the TEA uses the FAQ portion of its website to tout DC courses as a means for students of every economic level to receive "advanced academic instruction beyond, or in greater depth than" the knowledge measured by the statewide standardized exam known as the Texas Essential Knowledge and Skills test. According to the TEA, "rigorous and meaningful [DC] coursework in high school prepares students for success in college . . . [,] which benefits both the students and the economy." This assertion reinforces the claim of the National Alliance of Concurrent Enrollment Partnerships (NACEP) that DC courses offer a "low-cost scalable model for bringing accelerated courses to urban, suburban, and rural high schools" ("What is Concurrent Enrollment?").

Designed, implemented, and written by Lawrence B. Friedman, Lisa Hoogstra, Andrew Swanlund, Shazia Miller, Manyee Wong, Daniel O'Brien, and Natalie Tucker, a TEA study of 2011 analyzes DC courses in Texas from 2007 to 2010. These TEA researchers investigated the state context for DC programs and courses, analyzed funding for the DC courses, and made policy recommendations to the state legislature based on the data results. Friedman and his coauthors chose a sample of fifteen institutions of higher education (IHEs), which included twelve community college districts (CCDs), three universities that are major DC providers within the state, forty-eight high schools, and their corresponding local education agencies (LEAs).

The institutions were chosen, in part, based on their geographic location, with the goal of incorporating a wide range of different students in geographically and demographically different areas in Texas. Among the studied CCDs, seven served many counties, five served small areas, and three were adjacent to the Texas-Mexico border. According to the TEA report, "CCDs were selected that had high, low, moderate, and high

populations of Hispanic students (ranging from 18% to 97%) and economically disadvantaged students (ranging from 22% to 85%) as determined
by the percentage of students enrolled in schools served by the CCD"
(Friedman et al. 9).

Information from these institutions was gathered through telephone surveys and the analysis of supplemental as well as financial data.[1] Twelve of
the fifteen IHEs completed telephone surveys regarding the state context
(curriculum, courses, quality, responsibilities of costs, faculty, curriculum,
subject areas) of the DC programs. These telephone surveys provided investigators with qualitative as well as quantitative data that may have been
unavailable otherwise. The purpose of the telephone surveys was to gain
a better understanding of the administration of the DC programs as well
as to contextualize the programs in regard to the requirements, incentives,
guidelines, and outcomes as they align with or deviate from the guidelines
of the high schools and colleges that participate in the programs. Of the
telephone surveys, three were created for the study. One was for DC administrators at community colleges and universities, one for the LEA administrators, and one for high school staff (Friedman et al. 10). Administrators
from all fifteen IHEs, thirty-six administrators from sampled LEAs, and
thirty-four administrators or staff from high schools completed surveys (ii).
Fourteen IHEs, twenty-two LEAs, and twenty-four high schools provided
usable data. The number of survey questions varied: twenty-two for IHE
administrators, fourteen for LEA administrators, and thirty-four for high
school administrators or staff. Some questions prompted specific answers,
such as, "Which of the following factors—financial need, merit, or high
school attended—affect high school students' tuition rate or awarding of
scholarships?" (A 6). Other questions were open-ended, for example, "In
your opinion, what were some of the factors that supported the effective
implementation and delivery of dual credit courses offered by your college/
university?" (A 6).

Fourteen of the fifteen IHEs provided supplementary financial data,
enrollment data, and demographic information. TEA researchers gathered
financial data in order to, in their words, "determine, at a course level,
varying costs associated with [DC] programs as well as various sources of
funding and revenues used to support these programs during the 2009–10
academic year" (Friedman et al. 11). This financial data is important because
a large consideration is how students pay for courses and what percentage of
students are economically disadvantaged. According to the TEA researchers, students qualify as economically advantaged or disadvantaged based

on whether they qualify for free or reduced-price lunches according to the National School Lunch and Child Nutrition Program—a qualification that is determined by their economic status according to the U.S. Department of Health and Human Services.

Using the surveys and supplementary data, the TEA authors elaborate the highly racialized implementation of DC classes:

> The majority of students enrolled in courses for [DC] were either white or Hispanic. On average, 46% of students enrolled in courses for dual credit were white, 40% were Hispanic, and 10% were African American. Less than 5% were Asian/Pacific Islander. . . . In 2009–10, 35% of all high school students in Texas were white, 46% were Hispanic, 14% were African American, and 5% were Asian/Pacific Islander. Less than 1% of students were categorized as "other." White students thus were overrepresented in courses for dual credit in 2009–2010, and other racial/ethnic groups were underrepresented; this was particularly the case for African-American students. (Friedman et al. 16–17)

Of these DC students, the majority were white females who speak English as a first language and are "not [from] economically disadvantaged backgrounds" (17).

According to the TEA tract, "white students were overrepresented, and other racial/ethnic groups, particularly African-American students, were underrepresented . . . within the high school population as a whole" (Friedman et al. iii). Also, the number of Texans enrolled in public schools who are classified or who identify as Hispanic exceeds the number of students who identify or are classified as white. However, white students significantly outnumber Hispanic students in DC programs. During 2007–11, 50 percent of all high school students in Texas were considered economically disadvantaged, but only 37 percent of students enrolled in DC courses came from economically disadvantaged backgrounds (Friedman et al. 17). As these findings show, the schools whose students were more economically advantaged were able to enlist a higher number of students in the DC programs; the majority of those students were white.

The TEA authors note that economically disadvantaged students enroll in more vocational courses than do economically advantaged students. Likewise, students who were not white took more vocational classes than did whites. In the words of the TEA writers,

> African American students took greater concentrations of coursework for [DC] in career or technical education and computer science and lower concentrations

in core academic subjects such as social studies/history and English language arts compared with white and Asian students. Economically disadvantaged students also took greater concentrations of coursework in career or technical education and computer science than students who were not economically disadvantaged. Such difference may reflect long-standing achievement gaps among students in these subgroups. The student eligibility requirements for career or technical education courses are lower than those for core academic courses. (Friedman et al. iii)

These vocational classes in career or technical education and computer science range from culinary arts and hospitality to automotive repair, and computer drafting.

Lipsitz helps explain how this entire process occurs: "Inadequate funding for inner-city schools means that minority youths frequently encounter larger classes, fewer counselors, more inexperienced teachers, and more poorly equipped laboratories and libraries than their white counterparts" (38). The presence of fewer counselors not only impacts DC programs in inner-city schools, but those in other low-income areas as well. The TEA report declares that—per the telephone survey administered—counselors play a key role in explaining the availability and positive aspects of DC courses. An inadequate number of counselors in a high school can mean that information about DC programs may not be available to lower-income students. Clearly, those who lack knowledge of the programs do not understand how, where, or why to enroll in the programs. By contrast, students enrolled in more economically advantaged school districts gain more awareness of the programs, enlist in large numbers, and receive credit.

Taken as a whole, this TEA report, though expressing no sense of outrage, amounts to a damning indictment of the DC system in Texas because it clearly explains that the DC courses promote white advantage and white domination. Recall that one stated goal of DC programs in Texas is to benefit not only students who are excelling academically but also those qualified as "at-risk"—a goal also emphasized in the CCCC Statement. Unfortunately, the data shows that Texas has largely—and badly—failed to benefit many such students. According to the TEA, students' racial identities and the financial capacities of their families and schools clearly impact enrollment in DC courses.

Some schools simply pay for their students' DC courses (Texas Education Agency). Of course, the schools that pay for the courses are schools that have more money. And the finances of a school system stem from the available tax base in a particular geographical area: the richer the tax base, the more tax money can be extracted to fund the school system. As the TEA researchers assert, "school funding based on property tax assessments in most localities gives better opportunities to white children than to children from minority communities" (Friedman et al. 33). The TEA investigators add: "Requiring students and families to pay part of the cost of courses can create problems for participation in dual credit programs. For example, students from low-income families, perhaps the very at-risk students the LEA is targeting, may be precluded from participating if the cost is too high" (Friedman et al. 4). Obviously, some students' inability to pay for such programs works mightily against the goal of providing greater opportunities to all students.

Not only do students who enroll in DC courses get a "head start" on college, but they also enjoy a better chance of graduating from both high school and college. Composition scholars Joanna Castner Post, Vicki Beard Simmons, and Stephanie Vanderslice comment, "Significant data supports the assertion that participation in concurrent enrollment programs *does* ultimately lead to college success" (169). Post and her colleagues continue: "According to [Education Commission of the States], 25 percent of students who earn nine or more concurrent enrollment credits not only complete college but also continue on to graduate school" (169).[2] If this is the case, and if the educational goal is to advance "all students" or "students from every economic level," then the DC courses and programs conspicuously fail to meet their own guidelines. Instead they are, in Lipsitz's poignant phrase, "racializing life chances" of students as they reinvent, strengthen, and enlarge the entrenched socioeconomic hierarchy and structural racism of American society.

In a small number of states, some people have attempted to eliminate economic barriers for students by requiring that the schools pay all students' tuition. However, these activists have yet to succeed in certain states, including Texas, where funding for the courses continues to rely on the value of the homes in respective areas. Lipsitz observes that "whiteness never works in isolation; it functions as part of a broader dynamic grid created through intersections of race, gender, class, and sexuality" (73).

Like many other whiteness theorists, Lipsitz omits what is often another important point of intersection for whiteness—the ability or inability to speak English as a first language. In Texas and across much of the nation, white students enrolled in DC courses often speak English as a first language. Numerous Latino/a students and their parents do not—a phenomenon that, we suspect, contributes to uneven awareness of the benefits of DC courses in Texas and thus to the lopsidedly white enrollment in those courses. To Lipsitz's dynamic grid of race, gender, class, and sexuality, we add the use of English as a first language as an additional variable that intersects with whiteness.

While this essay addresses conditions in Texas, some evidence suggests that our argument about Texas may, unfortunately, fit other parts of the United States as well. A 2005 research report released by the U.S. Department of Education documents that schools with higher numbers of nonwhite students offer fewer DC courses than schools with larger numbers of white students (Marken et al. 5).

Racial segregation has often plagued American education. In the *Brown vs. Board of Education* case of 1954, the Supreme Court officially outlawed segregation in public schools. However, almost immediately after *Brown*, many public-school officials, faced with the prospect of racially mixed schools, reconfigured segregation by grouping student cohorts through a process often known as "tracking." Educated in different decades, both of us—Moreland in a small town in East Texas, Miller in a small town in South Texas—attended public schools that "tracked" students in a segregated fashion.

Tracking still occurs. Reporting in 2004 about a tracked high school in Portland, Oregon, Jessica Singer found that by simply looking at the zip codes of the "regular" and "honors" students, she could determine that, in her words, "90% of honors students came from the affluent neighborhoods that fed into our school" (212). As Jeannie Oakes explains, while alleging that they base these "tracks" on ability levels, school officials often instead base them partly or mainly on students' racial identities and on parents' socioeconomic status. Directly reflecting larger social patterns of marginalization and structural racism, DC courses in Texas currently amount to a reconceived version of "tracking" based, as in the past, partly or mainly on racial identity and socioeconomic status.

There is a difference, however—an important difference: the DC programs in Texas are proving *worse* than "tracking." Before anyone created DC courses, young, affluent white Texans at least had to complete four years of high school and four years at a college or university before they could graduate and start their careers. Now many of them don't have to. Instead, DC courses grant them opportunities to graduate *earlier* than their parents did and thus to begin climbing their professional career ladders *sooner* than their parents did. But many less affluent students, including large numbers of nonwhites, still *do* have to complete four years of high school and another four years at a college or university. Thus, because the selective availability of DC courses discriminates against less affluent students, many of these students, upon graduation, start climbing their professional ladders *later* than many of their affluent white counterparts, who graduated from college either a semester or an entire year earlier. For that reason, these less affluent students are *more* disadvantaged than their previously "tracked" parents were. In short, by shutting out many lower-income students—including large numbers of nonwhites—from DC courses while affording already privileged, affluent white students with faster access to college graduation, the system of DC courses in Texas significantly intensifies and worsens the system of white domination that plagued that state before it ever implemented DC courses.

Implications for Reconsidering Whiteness Theory

Eduardo Bonilla-Silva argues that the neoliberals wield the language of abstract liberalism (including such phrases as "equal opportunity") to justify practices that are, in effect, resolutely racist—a process that he labels "color-blind racism" (Bonilla-Silva; Behm and Miller; Martinez). Early proponents of DC courses certainly brandished the language of abstract liberalism when they argued that DC courses would enhance opportunity for all. These predictions proved woefully mistaken when officials and educators implemented DC courses in Texas. In that case, the language of abstract liberalism, in effect, obscures and masks huge socioeconomic and racial disparities that DC courses not only perpetuate but also worsen.

Certainly educators and state officials in Texas need to dramatically change the way that DC courses are funded and implemented in their state. Further, Lipsitz, Bonilla-Silva, and other whiteness theorists need to recognize *more than* the possibility of the partly masked continuation and preservation of whiteness, decade after decade. Two other whiteness theorists, Brianne Hastie and David Rimmington, appear to move beyond that position when they declare, "Invocation of (neo)liberal values often *further entrenches* systemic disadvantage, but behind the veneer of individual differences" (195, emphasis ours). Moving further, we contend that affluent whites can do more than merely continue and preserve—or even further entrench—their privileges. We claim that whites sometimes can significantly enlarge those privileges. Unfortunately, with respect to DC courses in Texas, that possibility is already here.

Notes

1. The telephone surveys allowed room for more qualitative research; the supplementary financial data was collected from these institutions in the form of workbooks, which resulted in quantitative data. The purpose of gathering this information was "to determine, at a course level, varying costs associated with dual credit programs as well as various sources of funding and revenues used to support these programs during the 2009–10 academic year" (11). The types of data requested include the course information, expenditures, and revenue.

2. See also Swanson.

Works Cited

"About Us." *Syracuse University Project Advance (SUPA).* Syracuse U, n.p., 2013. Web. 14 Aug. 2013.

Ansen, Chris M. "Absentee Landlords or Owner-Tenants? Formulating Standards for Dual-Credit Composition Programs." Hansen and Farris 245–71. Print.

Behm, Nicholas, and Keith D. Miller. "Challenging the Frameworks of Color-Blind Racism: Why We Need a Fourth Wave of Writing Assessment Scholarship." *Race and Writing Assessment.* Ed. Asao Inoue and Mya Poe. New York: Lang, 2012. 127–38. Print.

Bonilla-Silva, Eduardo. *Racism without Racists: Color-Blind Racism and the Persistence of Racial Inequality in the United States.* 2nd ed. Lanham, MD: Rowman and Littlefield, 2006. Print.

Farris, Christine, Linda Ferreira-Buckley, Randall McClure, Miles McCrimmon, and Barbara Schneider. "Statement: Dual Credit-Concurrent Enrollment Composition-Policy and Best Practices." *Conference on College Composition and Communication.* NCTE, 19 Nov. 2012. Web. 8 Aug. 2013.

Friedman, Lawrence B., Lisa Hoogstra, Andrew Swanlund, Shazia Miller, Manyee Wong, Daniel O'Brien, and Natalie Tucker. "Research Study of Texas Dual Credit Programs and Courses." *Texas Education Agency.* TEA, Mar. 2011. PDF file. 8 Mar. 2013.

Hansen, Christine, and Christine Farris, eds. *College Credit for Writing in High School: The "Taking Care of" Business.* Urbana, IL: NCTE, 2010. Print.

———. "The Composition Marketplace: Shopping for Credit versus Learning to Write." Hansen and Farris 1–39. Print.

Hastie, Brianne, and David Rimmington. "'200 Years of White Affirmative Action': White Privilege Discourse in Discussions of Racial Inequality." *Discourse and Society* 25.2 (2014): 186–204. Print.

Leonardo, Zeus. "The Color of Supremacy: Beyond the Discourse of 'White Privilege.'" *Educational Philosophy and Theory* 36.2 (2004): 137–53. Print.

Lipsitz, George. *The Possessive Investment in Whiteness: How White People Profit from Identity Politics*. Philadelphia: Temple UP, 2006. Print.

Marken, Stephanie, Lucinda Gray, and Laurie Lewis. "Dual Enrollment Programs and Courses for High School Students at Postsecondary Institutions: 2010–11." *National Center for Education Statistics*. U.S. Department of Education, Feb. 2013. Web. 9 March 2013.

Martinez, Aja. "'The American Way': Resisting the Empire of Force and Color-Blind Racism." *College English* 71.6 (2009): 584–95. Print.

Nakayama, Thomas, and Robert Krizek. "Whiteness: A Strategic Rhetoric." *Quarterly Journal of Speech* 81.3 (1995): 291–309. Print.

Oakes, Jeannie. *Keeping Track: How Schools Structure Inequality*. New Haven, CT: Yale UP, 1985. Print.

Post, Joanna Castner, Vicki Beard Simmons, and Stephanie Vanderslice. "Round Up the Horses—The Carts Are Racing Downhill! Programmatic Catch-Up to a Quickly Growing Concurrent Credit Program." Hansen and Farris 165–88. Print.

Schneider, Barbara. "Early College High Schools: Double-Time." Hansen and Farris 141–64. Print.

Singer, Jessie. "Getting Students Off the Track." *The New Teacher Book: Finding Purpose, Balance, and Hope during Your First Years in the Classroom*. Ed. Kelley Dawson Salas, Rita Tenorio, Stephanie Walters, and Dale Weiss. Milwaukee: Rethinking Schools, 2004. 210–16. Print.

Swanson, Joni L. *An Analysis of the Impact of High School Dual Enrollment Course Participation on Post-Secondary Academic Success, Persistence, and Degree Completion*. Thesis. The University of Iowa. 2008. Print.

Texas Education Agency (TEA). "Dual Credit: Frequently Asked Questions." *Texas Education Agency*. TEA, n.d. Aug. 2011. PDF file. 8 Aug. 2013.

Waits, Tiffany, J. Carl Setzer, and Laurie Lewis. "Dual Credit and Exam-Based Courses in U.S. Public High Schools: 2002–03 (NCES 2005–009)." *U.S. Department of Education*. Washington, DC: National Center for Education Statistics, April 2005. PDF file.

"What Is Concurrent Enrollment?" *The National Alliance of Concurrent Partnerships*. NACEP, n.d. Web. 13 Oct. 2012.

PART FOUR

HAUNTINGS IN PEDAGOGIES

BLACK, WHITE, AND COLORS IN BETWEEN—
WHITENESS HAUNTING FEMINIST STUDIES

Hui Wu

IN THE TWENTY-FIRST century, what should or should not whiteness studies be doing? This question leads to more questions than answers. First, is the twenty-first century postracial or is it still a time of racial discrimination and white dominance? Second, before talking about what whiteness studies should or should not be doing, how do we define whiteness studies? Is whiteness an indicator of hegemony, or is it a composition of sociopolitical stratifications? Next, do the theoretical and methodological frameworks of whiteness studies differ from those of cultural studies, women's studies, and diversity studies? Are whiteness studies a subfield within studies of race and ethnicity? If so, how do whiteness studies differ from studies of other ethnicities? Finally, what constitutes the focus and priority of whiteness studies?

Pondering these questions, I am drawn by the phrase "haunting whiteness" in the book, which provides a useful angle upon which I can reflect, especially as a nonwhite, immigrant, academic woman, who joined other feminist rhetorical critics—such as Gesa Kirsch and Jacqueline Jones Royster, and Joyce Irene Middleton—who address methodological problems caused by privileged white feminist frameworks, just like the ones that stunt my readings of post-Mao Chinese women writers ("Alternative," "Historical Studies," "Paradigm"). I join these feminist scholars who argue that theoretically and pedagogically the dominant framework does not allow us to explain the lot of women of other cultures, ethnicities, and classes. White feminist literary theory focusing on individualism, self-identity, and women's sexuality hardly provides a valid critical lens for the understanding of non-white, non-middle-class women's lives and writing. Nor does it respond to post-Mao Chinese women's rhetoric or explain their lived experiences. First, the concept of individualism is inherited from the Eurocentric white male tradition for the independent pursuit of the self, so it is still patriarchal. Second, sexuality as an analytical concept is developed from white women's gender perspectives against white men and for their sexual emancipation from white men. The "body talk" about desire, language use, and meaning continues to put the female under the male gaze as a sexual object, instead of liberating it from sexual oppression, as I have argued elsewhere ("Post-Mao" 414–17). To African American women, the fight for women's sexuality is a family quarrel between white women and white men (Morrison 21). Other women want "something real: women talking about human rights rather than sexual rights" (Morrison 30). For these reasons,

> privileged feminists have largely been unable to speak to, with, and for diverse groups of women because they either do not understand fully the interrelatedness of sex, race, and class oppression or refuse to take this interrelatedness seriously. Feminist analyses of women's lot tend to focus exclusively on gender and do not provide a solid foundation on which to construct feminist theory. (hooks 15)

In fact, "white women have taken up the position of gatekeepers of the racial status quo (i.e., the culture of whiteness) of the academy" (Douglas 61).

To delve further into how whiteness haunts feminist studies, I am using my course in feminist critical theory as a case in point. Usually, courses in feminist theory study European and American white feminist theorists like Judith Butler, Alison Jaggar, Sandra Gilbert and Susan Gubar, Helene Cixous, Jane Gallop, Toril Moi, and Annette Kolodny. Literally, they teach white feminist theory about white women. My course, instead, parallels feminist theories by white, black, and Chinese women in comparison to enable students to understand how whiteness haunts more critically. Students were disturbed by leading white feminist theories obsessed with sex and body talks—"libido," "genitals" (Cixous "Laugh"), "metaphorical penis," "genital drive" (Gilbert and Gubar "Infection"), "the womb," "the daughter's desire for her father," and "intercourse" (Gallop "Father's Seduction"), just to name a few. They then understand that established white feminist canons have inherited male-dominated European psychoanalytical terms, consequently reducing literary creation and power to the search for women's sexuality and sexed body. Students also noticed that nearly a decade prior to white feminist canons coming of age, African American women writer Alice Walker already called attention to Southern women writers' "underprivileged" background and their sense of solidarity, while criticizing white male writers' supremacy and sharing her concern about feminists' responsibility for community development (231–37). Reading Virginia Woolf, who wanted a room of her own and enough money to support her writing life, Walker asks, "What then are we to make of Phillis Wheatley, a slave, who owned not even herself?" (235). Contrary to white feminists' search for the individual self like their white male counterparts, she sees "the mountain of work" African American women writers must do collectively to show the "significance of the past" so that "future generations" would not stumble (276). In 1971 Morrison articulated the "role of black women" "to continue the struggle in concert with black men for liberation and self-determination of blacks" (21). She reminds us that black, or "colored," women were once segregated from "white ladies" (22). Reading Walker and Morrison, my students have realized that the Eurocentric white feminist theories originated from "a female mind controlled completely by male-type thinking" (Morrison 21). Guided by African American and post-Mao Chinese women writers, my students have learned that real feminists advocate women's human rights rather than sexual rights and that other women's feminist theories, to a large degree, embrace relational and collective thinking to educate men and liberate women (Wu "Post-Mao").

While students developed personal and academic connections to African American and post-Mao Chinese women's feminist theories, the interrelatedness among sex, race, class, human rights, and human equality became evident. Working on a chronology of feminist theory based on the reading list, students came to realize that African American feminist theory took shape nearly a decade earlier than that of white academic feminists but has been omitted from mainstream anthologies of feminist theory. They have learned other feminist theories in juxtaposition to white academic feminist theories, dispelling haunting whiteness. More important, students understand the complex roles that race, culture, and class play in theory building and recognize the inability of dominant white feminist canons to speak to nonwhite, non-middle-class women.

In short, my teaching scenario may not have provided answers to the beginning questions but testifies that whiteness studies should start with a critical perspective on the taken-for-granted white dominance in order to understand how the white ghost quietly and consistently haunts feminist studies. Embracing the perspectives from non-Western, nonwhite, non-middle-class feminist standpoints is what whiteness studies need. In other words, whiteness studies may encounter setbacks unless they are conducted with a historical awareness of the privileged versus the underprivileged, the oppressor versus the oppressed, and the dominant versus the dominated, as well as rights versus wrongs.

Works Cited

Cixous, Helene. "The Laugh of the Medusa." Warhol and Herndl 334–49.

Douglas, Delia D. "Black/Out: The White Face of Multiculturalism and the Violence of the Canadian Academic Imperial Project." *Presumed Incompetent: The Intersections of Race and Class for Women in Academic.* Ed. Gabriella Gutiérrez y Muhs et al. Boulder: UP of Colorado, 2012. 50–64.

Gallop, Jane. "The Father's Seduction." Warhol and Herndl 413–31.

Gilbert, Sandra M, and Susan Gubar. "Infection in the Sentence: The Woman Writer and the Anxiety of Authorship." Warhol and Herndl, 289–300.

hooks, bell. *Feminist Theory: From Margin to Center.* London: Pluto P, 2000.

Kirsch, Gisa, and Jacqueline Jones Royster. "Feminist Rhetorical Practices: In Search of Excellence." *College Composition and Communication* 61.4 (2010): 640–72.

Middleton, Joyce Irene. "Post-Civil-Rights Whiteness and Diversity: When Are We Going to Stop Talking about Race?" *CCCC Conversation on Diversity Blog.* cccc-blog.blogspot.com 21 May 2009. Web. 21. Dec. 2014.

Morrison, Toni. *What Moves at the Margin.* Jackson: U of Mississippi P, 2008.

Walker, Alice. *In Search of Our Mother's Gardens.* Orlando, FL: Harcourt Brace, 1983.

Warhol, Robin R., and Diane Price Herndl, eds. *Feminisms: An Anthology of Literary Theory and Criticism.* New Brunswick, NJ: Rutgers UP, 1996.

Wu, Hui. "The Alternative Feminist Rhetoric of Post-Mao Chinese Women Writers." *Alternative Rhetorics.* Ed. L. Gray-Rosendale and S. Gruber. Albany: SUNY P, 2001. 219–34.

——. "Historical Studies of Women Here and There: Methodological Challenges to Dominant Interpretive Frameworks." *Rhetoric Society Quarterly* 32.1 (2002): 81–98.

——. *Once Iron Girls: Essays on Gender by Post-Mao Chinese Literary Women.* Lanham, MD: Lexington Books, 2010.

——. "The Paradigm of Margaret Cavendish: Reading Women's Rhetorics in a Global Context." Ed. Jacqueline Jones Royster and Annemarie Mann Simpkins. *Calling Cards: Theory and Practice in Studies of Race, Gender, and Culture.* Albany: SUNY Press, 2005. 171–85.

——. "Post-Mao Chinese Literary Women's Rhetoric Revisited: A Case for an *Enlightened* Feminist Rhetorical Theory." *College English.* 72.4 (2010): 406–23.

ON THE COVER OF THE *ROLLING STONE*: DECONSTRUCTING MONSTERS AND TERRORISM IN AN ERA OF POSTRACIAL WHITENESS

Leda Cooks

ON JULY 17, 2013, approximately three months after the bombs went off at the Boston Marathon, killing three people and wounding approximately 264 others, *Rolling Stone* magazine released their cover and feature story on Dzhokhar Tsarnaev (now known as the Boston Marathon bomber) amid great controversy. ABC News, the *Boston Globe*, the *Guardian*, *The Week*, among many other media outlets, immediately expressed concern, sarcasm, and outrage over the sultry and seemingly sympathetic photo of the young man (Castellano and Dolak). Mo Rocca, among many other pundits, celebrities, and politicians, tweeted his displeasure at the cover: "Who knew *Rolling Stone (RS)* was the magazine for dreamboat terrorist cover boys? Should rename it *Tamil Tiger Beat*." The outrage over the picture was based largely in the perception that it celebrated (and arguably humanized) a terrorist and monster, as epitomized by the response by Harold Maass (Maass). Walmart, CVS, Walgreens, and Tedeschi Food Stores, among others, had even banned the magazine from their shelves. Nonetheless, by December 2013 that issue of the magazine made it to the top of *Adweek*'s "hot list," which noted that the Tsarnaev cover was the "most memorable cover of the year" and doubled *Rolling Stone*'s newsstand sales from a normal 60,000 to 120,000 (Kelly).

The *Rolling Stone* cover and accompanying narrative told the story of "how a popular, promising student was failed by his family, fell into radical Islam, and became a monster" (Rietman). The similarities to the 1999 *Time* magazine cover story of the Columbine High School killers (titled "The Monsters Next Door") were intentional, down to the familiar story of the bright, seemingly normal young white man who is not what he seems to be (Peralta; Voorhes). However, although Tsarnaev was, geographically speaking, the ultimate white male (hailing from the Caucasus Mountains), he was rarely, if ever, reported as white in the coverage of his capture, arrest, and subsequent investigation of his family and friends. That he was a Chechen immigrant and a radical(ized) Islamic terrorist appeared in contradiction to his appearance as a handsome, smart, and well-liked student. And it was the deliberate attention to this contradiction and its comparison to the profile of the high school killers that seemed to draw so much anger at the *Rolling Stone* cover and article.

The story of Dzhokhar Tsarnaev, the bomber, the terrorist, the assimilated college student from Cambridge, Massachusetts, both mirrors and deviates from that of the Columbine killers in ways that point to the insidious workings of whiteness and the interior or exterior motivations for deviance and monstrosity. Although school shooters and serial killers officially carry out their crimes through differing methods, their profiles have increasingly melded together in popular imagination and news reports. Their stories have provoked fascination and been the basis of cinematic portrayals and genre television shows. Often told as mysteries, these tales portray the unraveling of twisted individuals and perversions brought on by circumstance. The differentiation from the profile of bombers in racial/ethnic and religious identity and ideology is important and essentially blurred in the *Rolling Stone* image of Dzhokhar Tsarnaev. As I will argue in this chapter, these profiles of monsters are not antithetical to, but rather are constitutive of, white identities.

The discursive and symbolic means by which monsters and people "become" or cannot become white are important to identify, for they tell us a good deal about the operations of power in the dominant culture. Also, discussing the ways that representations of terror, whether fictional or real, secure or disrupt the boundaries around social group identities speaks to the perceived threats to these boundaries and the socially constructed nature of all identities.

Whiteness, as many scholars and commentators have argued, is constituted through a set of practices that organize the structural hierarchy of racial categories. And yet whiteness is also more than a racial category; it is the standard against which other intersecting identifications are measured (race, class, nationality, gender, ability, etc.). Whereas monsters in early

U.S. media and early twentieth-century cinema have been viewed by critical scholars as the projection of white fears of Others (Braidotti; Rony), the Gothic turn in cinema (e.g., *Frankenstein* and *Dracula*) was toward monsters that were *abnormally* (too pale or too malformed) white (Daileader) and thus outside the realm of identification by the "average white" viewer. In a turn from the Gothic monster of fantasy to the "ripped from the headlines" monster of detective dramas and serial killer horror movies, the more terrifying portrayals in recent U.S. news and popular culture have been the monsters *within* white culture: often the very embodiment of the *ideal white*, the middle-class, heterosexual, able-bodied, and physically attractive male we thought we knew.

So, how and why was Tsarnaev depicted by Reitman both as the Monster radicalized through Islam and as the "Monster Next Door"? The *Rolling Stone* cover and story about the new "killers next door" evoked, perversely, the discourse and embodiment of the white serial/mass killer through the color-blind story of a popular boy who grew up in the suburbs of Boston, played sports, had diverse friends, and liked to party. The postracial[1] framing of the typical high school mass murderer story displaced terror of unknown (and in this case, foreign) danger onto the familiar and comfortable story of the typical family, only now the neighborhood white folks were substituted for immigrants from a conflict-ridden outpost of the former Soviet Union. The story and its aftermath served to unmask the *racialization* of the Other by pointing both toward and away from white identity, white (suburban) spaces, and U.S. citizenship.

The stories of these killers' "next-door" monstrosity are central to the themes discussed in this chapter: of the construction of monsters as the embodiment both of our exterior differences as well as our unexamined interiorities, of a deconstruction of whiteness in an era of postracial color blindness, and of beginning to address these seemingly disparate ideas in the university classroom. However, to understand how high school serial killers, the surviving Boston bomber, and monsters might be surrogates for and signifiers of whiteness, I first must briefly discuss some of the ways "white" signifies the basis for humanity: normal, neutral, and banal. In short, whiteness is unremarkable, and, in a postracial environment of color blindness, this normativity is often seen by my students as a good thing—one color among many others equally placed in a rainbow of identities. Therefore, to discuss and point attention to the performance of the racial dynamics of whiteness and the inequities it produces can mark one as immoral and, ironically, as a racist.

Throughout this chapter I try to separate white cultural practices from white bodies; thus at times I may refer to "white culture" or "whiteness" as a set of behaviors that any "body" might perform (Keating). I use the term "white-identified" to discuss those bodies-in-practice. Although at times I conflate white bodies with whiteness, I do not see them as always already tightly linked. In other words, white bodies can perform in ways that resist white identification, just as people of color may perform in white-identified ways. I look at how tracking the specificity, plurality, and materiality of performances of whiteness in cultural representations and embodiments of monsters might be an opening for a pedagogy of whiteness in postracial times, specifically the im/possibility of enacting and embodying whiteness as a form of antiracist activism (Carillo-Rowe and Malhotra). I then offer a brief glimpse at some of the ways monsters, serial killers, and school shooters have been represented and racialized in dominant U.S. culture. I do so in order to show the ways that the rhetoric about Tsarnaev (as a monster, as a mass killer, and a terrorist) has already been primed by popular and filmic culture for particular readings and to explore the reasons the *Rolling Stone* cover, in attempting to resituate the accused bomber "next door" in the frame of the (white, seemingly normal) Columbine killers, provoked such controversy.

I return to the *Rolling Stone* profile and its intertextual referencing of the 1999 *Time* magazine cover to discuss how these perspectives by incongruity work to deflect white racial identification (the magazine's majority white readers refuse the "next-door" familiarity of community assumed in the Tsarnaev story). In the last section of the chapter, I use my class's reactions to and subsequent discussion of the profiling of the bombers as illustrative of the potential for a critical understanding of whiteness. I then discuss my attempts in a different course to develop a pedagogical approach to addressing the racial dynamics of whiteness through monsters, serial killers, terrorists, and dis/embodiment.

Whiteness as Humanity

Whiteness studies throughout the last decade have emphasized its *normalcy*. Indeed, in the United States, where postracialism pervades mainstream culture as code for an individualist approach to success or failure, and where merit is determined economically through hard work or business savvy, whiteness is pervasive as the norm against which others are measured. White people's cultural standards, government policies, laws, and education are naturalized as common cultural sense and, as such, structure our educational, medical, economic, political and legal institutions. Whiteness scholars have also linked *normalcy* with the premise of white power as invisibility, as everywhere but also nowhere because it is not identified with the power of a cultural group or its practices, except in cases of individual or collective excess (white supremacy and movements). Whiteness is the practice of a dominant culture, through which what is known is named and defined as knowable and, as such, becomes the political, cultural, and material means through which social hierarchy is enacted. The dis/identification of white people with race is reflected in the increasing discomfort with which even the word "race" is often met in what has been often deemed as postracial culture. For white-identified people, to elect to see or discuss race in such a cultural milieu, seemingly, is to mark one as racist, to make one's racism visible.

Another attribute that would seemingly characterize this invisibility is whiteness's ability (as the exercise of power) to shift and mutate, to haunt all bodies by never being fully evidenced in white skin nor fully absent from bodies of color. Yet for those not located as white, those variously dis-placed by race, class, gender, or ability, whiteness is quite visible in institutional spaces that privilege certain cultural practices (museums, schools, universities, legal systems, etc.); in the behaviors, affect, and attire seen as "proper"; and in the access and authority exercised by those who possess "it." Notably, these intersections of identities and various locations relative to an ideal/unreal whiteness present opportunities for all people to see the operations of cultural power and their various accountability to intervene in a shifting and often amorphous set of relations toward a more equitable society.

In various works, bell hooks describes whiteness historically and today as a kind of terrorism and portrays whites as oblivious to their own visibility as monsters: "They do not imagine that the way whiteness makes its presence felt in black life, most often as terrorizing imposition, a power that wounds, hurts, tortures, is a reality that disrupts the fantasy of whiteness as representing goodness" ("Representing Whiteness" 341). Whiteness can terrorize through its all-knowing certainty, its facts, and its "objective" superiority. In what follows I briefly discuss several attributes of whiteness that parallel my later discussion on monstrosity: *(1)* its (seeming) neutrality, banality, and unremarkability; *(2)* its hegemony; *(3)* its plurality and the labor of white embodiment. These dimensions reflect and refract the dynamics of racialization in a postracial society. At a time when much of the mainstream discourse indicates that race is no longer an issue, the headlines in my "progressive" community, even as I write this chapter, repeatedly tell stories of racist bullying—racist graffiti painted on the doors of the dorms of students of color on my campus and on bulletin boards; a high school teacher who resigned due to repeated racist graffiti threatening her in her classroom, in school bathrooms, and at her home. Simultaneously, the day's news headlines speak of two "Columbine copycat" threats at local high schools, white boys on social media, and the schools' often unsuccessful attempts to track down the perpetrators, who often are victims of perceived bullying or alienation themselves.

Whiteness as neutral, banal, and unremarkable. In a postracial era marked by individualism, meritocracy, and colorblindness (Herakova et al. 273), whiteness studies scholars such as Richard Dyer, Ruth Frankenburg, Michelle Fine et al., and many others have focused on white racial identity as the basis from which ideas of race and raciality have been constructed and through which white people have constituted and maintained hierarchies of identities. White racial identity and culture include norms and laws for appropriate behavior: ways of speaking, dressing, and eating as well as manners, appearance, domestic location, and emotion, among others. These norms are obscured when they are embedded in the educational, legal, and governmental structures of society and circulated through institutional and popular cultural forms.

Whiteness is the foundation for entrenched cultural, political, and legal values regarding equality based on the perceived value of merit, hard work, and cultural imperialism. This entrenchment of values results in the belief among many white-identified people that the recognition of difference, and especially racial difference, leads to inequalities in society. In fact, this belief is at the core of the normativity and neutralization of power, an enactment of power on the part of white-identified people that asks for conformity to the norm *before* the recognition of equality. The message is, "If you act in accordance to my social rules and make me feel comfortable, I will recognize you as an equal." For example, in a postracial society, the diverse bodies on display as a sign of equality of cultures, or "multiculturalism" in the media (advertising and programming), must be attractive but with Caucasian facial structure, must display a narrow range of white identified behaviors, and must (at least on the surface) have adapted to or adopted white culture.

Connected to neutrality is the perception of the everydayness or banality of whiteness. That is, for many white-identified people, white culture is not distinguishable and therefore is unremarkable or mundane (Cooks). This leads to the perception among some white people that whites lack "culture" or ethnicity, and so they may choose to consume other cultural subjectivities and objects to enhance their status as "unique" and "cool," as Joel Dinerstein has noted. In her essay "Eating the Other," bell hooks discusses the currency of adopted marginality, to be picked up and discarded at will by those privileged enough to perceive themselves as invisible, without racial or ethnic identity. If whiteness, much like *Man* in Kenneth Burke's definition, exists only in its negation of other cultural categories (not black, not Arabic etc.), then it is an empty category. As Burke might describe it, whiteness is always already (and paradoxically) *positive* through conditioning its existence as a cultural category based on the negative, on what it is not (Burke).

Whiteness as hegemonic. Whiteness thus involves a centering of power that relies on marginalization and displacement to be recognized, and the center is always under negotiation, in tension precisely because it cannot be fully embodied by anyone, whether identified as the "right" or optic white (Moon 182) or as a deviation from the norm. In other words, white identity is hegemonic and relies on the consent of the boundary to maintain a superior position. In the United States immigrant groups of Irish, Jewish, and Italian descent (among other European groups) have alternately been refused and incorporated as "white" (Ignatiev; King; Roediger). Mexican landowners, living in what is now the U.S. Southwest after the Mexican-American War, were given U.S. citizenship and were granted white status under the 1848 Treaty of Guadalupe Hildalgo, although this status held no legal force and was denied. Likewise, lawsuits in the U.S. South throughout history have used the "one drop rule" to determine "legal" whiteness as access to status and/in space: property ownership, placement in schools, transportation, marriage, among other things. (Bynum). In this manner, race in the United States was never merely a matter of phenotype but also of property and status. The construction of racial categories in the United States has demonstrated a "Possessive investment [in] Whiteness" (Lipsitz)—in short, a pervasive investment in sustaining the power of the dominant group, although that group has varied ethnically over the course of U.S. history. Throughout history, from the institutionalization of slavery to the Chinese Exclusion Act, to the economic crisis brought on by subprime mortgage loans, to the concerns over illegal immigrants and the drain on social services, to the portrayal of these and other issues in the media and popular culture, the discursive struggle has also been one of securing status and control (over resources, narratives, institutions, and, finally, bodies). In the postracial era, perhaps the largest hegemonic force is that of neoliberalism, which proclaims economic status as the ultimate equalizer and renders (most) all social and cultural group identities irrelevant to the acquisition of capital.

Whiteness as plurality and intersectionality. While authentic whiteness could never be performed nor conclusively demonstrated, the "right" embodiment of whiteness was inferred through, among other things, correct class, sexuality, gender, ability, education, and body size (Ellsworth; Moon). Importantly, none of these identity categories are stable, but they are identifiable through "competent" performance (Warren). This aspect of whiteness, its *plurality*, means that not all bodies achieve the same status as white, though whiteness may serve as a referent for white- and nonwhite-identified bodies (Keating; Carillo-Rowe and Malhotra). Indeed, whiteness as a set of practices is not the same as having a white body or identifying as white. One may fall in status as white if marginalized in any other identity category, and thus all categories are interdependent and racial competence registered only in terms of their sum (Yep 100–105). For nominally white people, then, one's membership as dominant or marginalized in any category determines whether more or less labor may be involved in be(com)ing white. In viewing whiteness as a dynamic of intersectional identity categories, I am deliberately *not* embedding whiteness in the bodies of white people. Instead I am hoping to position it particularly as discourse and performance, enacted, embodied, and sedimented in cultural forms and structures with material, social, and political consequences. Like a monster, whiteness shape-shifts and mutates in the context of its deployment. In her essay "Representing Whiteness in the Black Imagination," hooks describes whiteness as a terrifying monster that is constantly reinventing itself: "To name that whiteness in the black imagination is often a representation of terror: one must face a palimpsest of written histories that erase and deny, that reinvent the past to make present the vision of racial harmony and pluralism more plausible" (342). Although many scholars of race and racial whiteness have focused on the ways monstrosity has signaled marginal identities, the emphasis in the remainder of this essay is on the ways whiteness, as humanity, gets defined through and against monstrosity.

Monsters, Thresholds, and White Dis/embodiment

In Western thought, dating back to Aristotle, monsters have been a source of fascination and fear, boundary creatures whose embodiment (much like the characterization of whiteness throughout this paper) signified elements that refused binary categorization or comprehension. For the ancients, the monster was a negation of the natural form and could also signal the wishes of the gods (Goss). In the Middle Ages monsters began to be understood as omens, signs from either a benevolent or a vindictive God. As science became more widely accepted however, monsters were also seen as mutations and aberrations of a valid and acceptable nature/natural form (Uebel 265). In the modern era, monsters came to signify the limits of how technologies are incorporated into the human form. Braidotti notes, too, the changes in monstrous forms that reflect the fears of an era. As concerns over the impact on humans of nuclear technologies increased, for instance, the ir-radiated mutant or the monster-machine-gone-wrong became cinematic horror genres. These creatures thrived on their ability to terrorize through their visible grotesqueness and heinous actions (294–300).

In the last century, the representation and containment of evil in the grotesque, the mutant, the racially or ethnically different monster, became tenuous in light of evidence that evil on a massive scale was perpetrated by the diminutive, normal-looking Nazi: Eichmann. Hannah Arendt, frus-trated by attempts to portray Eichmann as grotesque or a mutant, argued in "The Banality of Evil" that it was actually his ordinariness, his role of being a "good worker" that helped to create the monstrosity of the Holocaust. By (controversially) locating evil outside of Eichmann's body and in the social systems in which he operated, Arendt was attempting to show the ways the systemization of ideology was productive of monstrosity. In performing well at his job, Eichmann became a monster. The accusation that her argument actually vindicated Eichmann shows the difficulty of theorizing evil as social and culturally created, as values, beliefs and actions in which normal people may participate and be implicated (Butler). Despite Arendt's attempts to point to dominant cultural and systemic monstrosities, the shift in the figure of the monster from the grotesque to the banal or everyday (white) man did not indicate a corresponding concern with the evils of hegemonic power.

Feminist and critical scholars have invoked the normalizing, hegemonic, and patriarchal when discussing the ways monsters have been signified in society. In a reverse symbolic move, the violence done to bodies con-sidered abject or impure, rather than being located externally in forces of hegemony, is often located internally, in traits considered inherent to marginalized peoples. Several feminist and postcolonial scholars have taken up the partial, ephemeral, and in-between characteristics of monsters as important to a rethinking and reperformance of marginalized identities. It is the very inability of monsters to be categorized, represented, and named that can be empowering to those bodies that have always been objectified (Grosz; Haraway). In *Borderlands*, Gloria Anzaldúa refuses the move to locate evil in the monster and instead cites the in-betweenness, the very indistinguishability of the indefinable bodies of the borderlands as the basis for a powerful subjectivity. She takes up the monster as a boundary creature, as an opening to alternative forms of identification. The shape-shifter is feared for its resistance to containment; the marginal woman, forever unclassifiable, is powerful in her ability not to be known. The power to give name and order to society is the power to give form and corporeality to the normal and the abnormal, the virtuous and the abject. Monsters enact the breakdown of the order: the chaos inherent in the boundaries created between the other and the self.

As boundary dwellers, monsters implicate the fragility of the construction of the binaries: their performance, often created to solidify cultural values, also works toward their disappearance. Because monsters are unpredictable, their purpose has shifted and changed over time. Their embeddedness in stories and myths, as well as their rearticulation and animation in performance, serves cultural/social stability as well as the signaling of cultural change (Cohen).

Monstrosity and Evil: Serial Killers, Mass Murderers, and the Banal

The (white-appearing) banal monster took on iconic form in the United States in the mid to late twentieth century in the form of the serial killer. Serial killers were storied on screen and in true-crime reportage as cult heroes who transgressed the boundaries of society. As white, male, primarily middle-class, intelligent, and reasonably attractive, many of these killers represented the ideal intersections of whiteness. Importantly, those that did not were singled out for other aspects of their social identities that signaled marginalization (white trash, gay, etc.). That their actions provoke fascination rather than disgust speaks to the ways whiteness defines and defends the boundaries around racial identities. The widespread attention paid to real-life serial killers such as Jack the Ripper and Son of Sam was evident in the nicknames assigned to them as well as the lack of attention to their victims. Later in the century, serial killers such as Ted Bundy and Jeffrey Dahmer were well known precisely for their ability to pass as normal, intelligent, and even likeable men (Morton).

Although the definition remains somewhat ambiguous, the FBI has described the serial killer as someone who commits three or more murders with a cooling-off period between each murder ("Serial Killers" FBI.gov). Serial killers are thus differentiated from mass murderers by this cooling-off period and by the differing organization of and motivations for the murders.

The importance placed on the actions of serial killers versus mass murderers also deflects attention from the ways (white) identities are defined and maintained through these definitions. That is, while (mainly) white serial killers are profiled through their individual actions, mass killers who are not defined as white are notable through their racial, religious, or ethnic identities. As serial killers and school shooters have become more potent dominant cultural monsters, we might ask, "How does the race of the monster add to or undermine their status as monster?" "How is it that the actions of these white monsters never seems to put their racial status in jeopardy?" Indeed, these are questions that underlie the representations of crime and criminal activity in the United States and often lead to misconceptions about which groups commit crimes and which groups suffer disproportionate consequences for those crimes (Simon).

While there are overlaps in the profiles of serial killers and school shooters, psychologically school shooters that are mass murderers commit multiple murders in one (not repeated) act, generally with a plan. My interest here is in the different ways these crimes are signified and reported, as these differences are important to the ways each profile signifies whiteness. Similar to serial killers, school shooters have been primarily white, and when they have been otherwise, their ethnic identity has been highlighted along with their psychological profile in reports of the shootings (e.g., Jeffrey Weise and Seung-Hui Cho). The portrayal of school shootings deviates from that of serial killers where white identity figures prominently in the reporting. Schools, and particularly schools in middle-class white communities, are considered especially safe spaces because they contain the most vulnerable in our society. Although there had been several school shootings prior to Columbine High School, the location of those shootings, in Littleton, Colorado, a well-off suburb outside of Denver, seemed to mark a special case and space of violation.

Monsters Next Door?

As plurality, whiteness exists at the intersections of class, gender, sexuality, education, nationality, and more to mark one as (almost) white. Responses from many major news outlets online to the Tsarnaev *Rolling Stone* story posed the *Time* cover adjacent to a picture of the *Rolling Stone* cover. This "perspective by incongruity"[2] used both phrasing and photos to juxtapose incompatible realities. The familiarity of the boys pictured in the *Time* cover after the 1999 Columbine High School shooting—a cover that read "The

Monsters Next Door" and showed the yearbook photographs of innocent-looking white boys, Klebold and Harris, who happened to be mass murderers—was a familiarity based on the "right" or "optic" whiteness (Moon 182). The other side of that familiarity was the horror of their crimes and the terror that we (white people) could not predict their goodness or actions on their skin color. Although the cover caused a good deal of controversy at the time, the majority of the concern was that the story contributed to making the killers into celebrities and glorifying a culture of violence. It seems ironic, then, that when serial killers and school shooters are profiled and their crimes reported, the expected and predicted demographic is white and male, and yet these social categories are never analyzed for their contributions to the deviance. "Their" (the killers') very normality and how that was/is defined predicts and bounds "our" humanity. This phenomenon becomes all too evident when the killer is identified based on one or more marginalized social categories, since their deviance (and motivation) from whiteness is already assumed in that very identification. The normalization of whiteness produces, among several errors in epistemology, its own mystification, which escapes interrogation of its Truth (Minnich).

In "Representing Whiteness in the Black Imagination," hooks describes the ways "whiteness exists without knowledge of blackness even as it collectively asserts control . . . link[ing] issues of recognition to the practice of imperialist racial domination" (339). For hooks, whiteness works as terrorism and as a kind of monster for those defined as marginal or invisible within its histories, literatures, institutions and in its daily practices. Whiteness is a terrorism of inhumane acts, sometimes overtly heinous, but often employed in the name of what is best for people of color or what will help them become better people (i.e., more like white people). In hooks's reversal of the dominant portrayal of terrorism and monstrosity, she serves to dis-place white people in the position of the object, their cultural practices seen as dangerous by those who do not identify as white. Although hooks does not connect all white people to the white monsters of her youth, there is an important relationship here to the symbolic function of monsters more generally to mark boundaries, and specifically to the operations of whiteness in dominant cultural portrayals of monsters. Monsters, like terrorists, threaten the stability of society, and throughout the history of race in the United States white culture has represented people of color as threats to society and to humanity. Alternatively, when white people are portrayed as monsters in dominant culture, their own inhumanity never represents the traits or practices of the dominant (white) social group.

Just as all monsters have served a liminal function throughout history, reporting on, profiling, narrating, and mythologizing serial killers and school shooters helps us understand the ways their racial identities are deflected, allowing them a monstrosity that cannot and must not reflect back on white culture. As is often the case with serial killers, the emphasis on figuring out their motivations, the (external) circumstances that drove them to their heinous actions, outweighs the focus on the impact and consequences of those actions and renders the victims invisible. The closer the perpetrators are to dominant positions of race, class, gender, and nationality, the more "interesting" the incongruity of their actions becomes to the public. Tsarnaev, despite the *Rolling Stone* cover story, appeared to be an "average" (immigrant, Islamic) white boy with a loving family, who spoke "American" English and was fully immersed in "American" culture. However, repeated allusions in follow-up stories to the *Time* Columbine cover implied that he could never be "the Monster next door." He could be a monster, however, as the backlash to the *Rolling Stone* cover amply illustrated, just not the incongruous variety. Over time, any interest in the similarities to other (white, male) domestic terrorism/mass murderers dwindled and the media focus on interior motivations that may have driven the brothers, and Dzhokhar in particular, disappeared to be replaced with discussions of his foreign ties to terrorism, manifested in self-radicalization via the internet.

The *Rolling Stone* cover and accompanying article pointed toward and away from whiteness. By first implicitly comparing the Tsarnaevs to the Columbine killers, both monsters next door, Reitman was demonstrating their similarity via their perceived familiarity and innocence despite obvious ethnic and class differences. She did this through offering a personal profile of Dhzokhar Tsarnaev, one that explored "his world," looking for external clues to his motivations, much as is the path of portraying the psychological histories of white school shooters. However, the story moved away from the implicit comparison by then finding the bomber's motivation both in his Chechen heritage and his adoption of Islamic fundamentalism. With this turn, the Monster Next Door was made known but not familiar: a stranger next door whose hatred of Americans was necessarily linked to his ethnicity and religion. The story dropped any interrogation of the assumptions that lay behind the "monster next door" and relied on the subsequent pinning of radical Islam as the source for and channel of the monster's fury. The qualities of "next-doorness" and of whiteness are connected precisely through the characteristics mentioned above: normalcy, banality, and the mundane. These qualities worked (and still work) to position the Columbine killers in the 1999 *Time* article as particularly scary due to their seemingly unremarkable qualities. The *Rolling Stone* story's move to a new kind of neighborhood (Cambridge via Chechnya) with new kinds of (immigrant) neighbors, rather than pointing to the dangers of white culture and alienation, merely shored up the boundaries of us against the radicalism and fundamentalism associated with Islam ("Boston Strong").

Moving toward a Pedagogy of Monstrous Whiteness

April 15, 2013, was a state holiday in Massachusetts, and so when the bombs exploded at the Boston marathon, the students in my "Self, Selfishness, and Society" large lecture class had the day off. Many had gone to their homes in the Boston area, and although none were at the race, several knew people who were there. A day and a half later when we met for class, the majority of the students had sifted through mountains of information on social media about who the bombers were (Arab terrorists), their motivation for the attacks (hatred of Americans), and their current location (according to pervasive rumors, our campus).

In a few days, their theories seemed to be realized: the hunt was on for two Arab-appearing men. Then we found out the suspects were identified as brothers from Chechnya: the older was now dead and the younger was on the run. On April 20, as I was watching live coverage of the manhunt for Dzhokhar Tsarnaev at a local bar, the conversations around me reflected my own astonishment at the photo of the attractive young man pasted to the bottom of the screen. "Really? He's the other bomber?" I wondered what we had expected to see.[3]

In the days following the marathon bombings in Boston, when I asked my students, as sophisticated consumers of media, about their own theories, all but one student in the class said that they thought the bombers were likely not from the United States, and most said that the bombers were likely of Middle Eastern origin. No one mentioned gender explicitly, although all referred to the bombers as male. One student, a socially awkward self-identified white male whose class status and body size marked him as not quite the "optic" white (Moon), said that the bomber was likely a white college student. Some students laughed, but many just rolled their eyes. I then asked the students to consider who committed the majority of mass murders in the United States? What might they look like? Where did they come from and what language did they speak? Did they look like the majority of the class? Did they talk like us?

In teams of six or seven students, the class began to construct a profile. The response from most of these students was that people who committed mass murders in the United States came from the United States, and were white and male. Similar to school shooters, who were, according to them, also mainly from the United States and white, serial killers (although they noted a female exception) were also primarily male. I asked them,

> Is this a stereotype of white males in the United States? When you see a white male student on campus, do you think, "That dude is a serial killer"? Why do some associations (e.g., more African American males are in prison, therefore more African Americans commit crime) lead to stereotypes of groups, and others do not?

The class was silent, and I began to question whether I had asked too much of them. Then a student said, "This [the attacks] is not about white people or black people. It's about people who hate us. It just feels like an attack on us, on Boston . . . on the United States."

Throughout the semester we had been discussing whiteness, and students responded in ways familiar to me, as I had been discussing these issues for twenty plus years in a community and university that considered itself progressive. Still, the discourse had shifted in the past decade or so from one careful to acknowledge race, as something nonwhite people cared about, to the strong feeling on the part of mostly white-identified students that "race is no longer an issue," that to speak of race makes one racist, and the fact that President Obama was elected and then reelected signified the achievement of equality among all races in the United States.

As mentioned above, these *postracial* discourses limit the ability to discuss whiteness as an organizing system for race talk by constructing language itself as the problem. Indeed, the discursive construction of race is a problem, but to not name the processes through which inequities among groups have been solidified (and embodied) psychologically, socially, culturally, economically, and politically is to ignore, and thus, to exacerbate the problem. By identifying the ways power works, not only through representation (a multiracial but black president) but also through the ways we take up and make real the performances of race, we can begin to understand its complexity as the centering of social, cultural, economic, political, and other forms of power.

Postracial discourses on race and whiteness do not exist in a vacuum but in a climate of increased surveillance, where privatization of everything has led to the downgrading of anything "public" to that of low economic status ("public" housing, transportation, schools, etc.) and where the individual is held in higher esteem than the collective or the community. As Henry Giroux observes,

> Since the Reagan/Thatcher revolution of the 1980's, we have been told that there is no such thing as society and, indeed, . . . institutions committed to public welfare have been disappearing . . . Rather than being cherished as a symbol of the future, youth are now seen as a threat and a problem to be contained. A seismic change has taken place in which youth are now being framed as both a generation of suspects and a danger to public life. (109)

On college campuses, it seems obvious that our students are feeling more economic insecurity and have accumulated greater debt than in the past. It is a time of increased access to higher education but less retention of students marginalized by race and class identities and less financial gain from the credential upon graduation. In short, few white-identified students seem to feel the responsibility to look at their accountability to the benefits they might gain from their participation in white culture.

Pedagogical Reflections on Whiteness and Monstrosity

That semester was over when the *Rolling Stone* cover came out, and, in the time since, I have used the covers as an opening to discuss whiteness in the "postracial" classroom. In the spring semester of 2014, I began my performance studies class with an essay assignment and the question, "Who were your monsters as a child, and who are they now?" Students responded by naming scary clowns, the Wicked Witch of the West, supernatural beings, and videogame monsters. I asked, "Did you ever identify with monsters or were you ever labeled a monster?" The class was quiet, and I wondered whether they felt it was a safe space to respond with honesty and vulnerability. And so, perhaps to stress my own vulnerability and by way of illustration, I mentioned that my father nicknamed me "Lurch" (of *The Addams Family* fame) as a child. The monster and I had much in common. Lurch, like me, was a threshold figure, both literally and figuratively. Both of us dwelled on the boundaries of family, ambiguously positioned with acceptance ever a tenuous proposition. Because my father intended the nickname as an insult, I decided that I was indeed Lurch-like and gladly took on that embodiment. However, the fact that I *chose* to be monstrous, while an aspect of my privilege and agency, did not and does not ensure the consequences of my intent, that

I would overturn the pejorative meanings of monsterhood or of acting in monstrous ways.

Identification with monsters may happen for a variety of reasons, from abjection to celebration, and although none of my students indicated such an affiliation, asking the question shows how we are marked by our dis/embodiments. After I told my story, I discussed the various ways monsters have been embodied, as fantastical, as grotesque, and as mundane (as mentioned throughout this essay). For Anzaldúa, taking on the monster's body opens the possibility of taking up its special powers, of celebrating the in-betweenness of boundary dwellers. For hooks, the importance lies in dis-embodiment, in untangling the symbolism that has connected people of color to the monstrous, and placing the power of terrorism in and on the white body. For me, neither approach leaves us (nonwhite identified or white identified) with easy or uncomplicated ways of ethically acting in relation to the monster. We discussed in class Arendt's portrayal of Eichmann as a mundane monster, and then we talked about the ways monsters are represented in the dominant U.S. culture as the embodiment of evil. After noting the evolution to more realistic cultural monsters, I showed the students the *Rolling Stone* cover and asked how the rhetoric of monstrosity works and what it produces: boundaries (of good and evil) may be identified in the figure and actions of the monster, and these boundaries simultaneously produce the monster itself. In the *Rolling Stone* cover students saw the boundaries of nationalism—they did not view the Tsarnaev bombers as American, and so it was harder for them to make the comparison to the *Time* cover of the Columbine killers. Another opening for discussion . . .

It has been my goal in this chapter to (re)introduce white visibility through rhetorics of monstrosity and to briefly illustrate its use in the classroom. "The Monster Next Door" can be a metonym for whiteness and as such should be profiled not in terms of individual motivations and characteristics but in terms of how the rhetoric of identification and profiling is *productive* and creative (Halberstam; Foucault) of white cultural identities. There is power in invisibility and protection from vulnerability (Simpson 145). The invocation of the boy or girl next door brings to mind a specific kind of neighborhood, where people live in houses with lawns and driveways, and neighbors are known to each other. The boy or girl next door is white, middle class, heterosexual, from the United States, and speaks English as a native language. Most importantly, the boy or girl next door is normal and thus banal. For those who identify as white, the "monster next door" could serve as a mirror rather than a deflection.

Notes

1. I use the term *postracial* here to signify a way of framing race that suggests that it is no longer a relevant category in U.S. society. Enid Logan describes the key features of a postracial landscape as persistent inequality, increase of immigrants of color, emergence of plural black identities, crisis in white identity, the globalizing of racial anxieties, color-blind ideologies, and universalism.

2. Perspective by incongruity (Burke *Permanence and Change, Attitudes toward History*) is generally described as making the familiar strange through language, art, picture, or metaphor.

3. As a white, middle-class, middle-aged female in a sports bar with many younger white males and females of similar class and race demographics, I felt both comfort and unease at the gathering together around the capture of "the terrorist," as he was being called. The proximity of the danger had united the community around Boston, with chants and merchandising of "Boston Strong" already ubiquitous. The sense of relief at the containment of a threat was offset by my unease with the anticipation built in the broadcasted live "manhunt" and the bar crowd's need for retaliation (many shouting, "Kill him!"). The *uncanniness* (Freud) of the live-action shots, the repeated news' stories of Tsarnaev as "terrorist" and "mass murderer," and the photo of an attractive boy looking shyly into the camera consistently posted at the bottom of the screen lay in something deeper explored in this chapter.

Works Cited

Anzaldúa, Gloria. *Borderlands: The New Mestiza/LaFrontera*. 2nd ed. 1987. San Francisco: Aunt Lute Books, 1999. Print.

Arendt, Hannah. "Banality of Evil." *Eichmann in Jerusalem: A Report on the Banality of Evil*. London: Faber and Faber, 1963. Print.

Braidotti, Rosi. "Signs of Wonder and Traces of Doubt: On Teratology and Embodied Differences." *Between Monsters, Goddesses, and Cyborgs: Feminist Confrontations with Science, Medicine, and Cyberspace*. Ed. Nina Lykke and Rosi Braidotti. London: Zed Books, 1996. Print.

Brock, Bernard L., Kenneth Burke, Parke G. Burgess, and Herbert W. Simons. "Dramatism as Ontology or Epistemology: A Symposium." *Communication Quarterly* 33.1 (1985): 17–33.

Burke, Kenneth. *Attitudes towards History*. 3rd ed. 1937. U of California P, 1984. Print.

———. *Permanence and Change*. 3rd ed. 1935. U of California P, 1984. Print.

Butler, Judith. "Hannah Arendt's Challenge to Adolf Eichmann." *Guardian.* 29 Aug. 2011. Web. 14 Dec. 2015.

Bynum, Victoria. *The Long Shadow of the Civil War.* Chapel Hill: U of North Carolina P, 2010. Print.

Carrillo Rowe, Aimee, and Sheena Malhotra. "(Un)hinging Whiteness." *Whiteness, Pedagogy, Performance: Dis/placing Race.* Ed. Leda Cooks and Jennifer Simpson. Lanham, MD: Lexington Books, 2007. 271–98. Print.

Castellano, Anthony, and Kevin Dolak. "*Rolling Stone* responds to Dzhokhar Tsarnaev Cover Backlash." ABC News. 17 July 2013. Web. 1 March 2014.

Cohen, Jeffrey Jerome, ed. "Preface: In a Time of Monsters." *Monster Theory: Reading Culture.* Minneapolis: U of Minnesota P, 1996. Print.

Cooks, Leda, and Jennifer Simpson, eds. *Whiteness, Pedagogy, Performance: Dis/placing Race.* Lanham, MD: Lexington Books, 2007. Print.

Daileader, Cynthia. *Racism, Misogyny, and the Othello Myth.* Cambridge: Cambridge UP, 2005. Print.

Dinerstein, Joel. "Lester Young and the Birth of Cool," *Signifyin(g), Sanctifyin', and Slam Dunking.* Ed. Gina Caponi. Amherst: U of Massachusetts P, 1999. Print.

Dyer, Richard. *White.* New York: Routledge, 1997. Print.

Goss, Theodora. "A Brief History of Monsters." *Weird Fiction Review.* 3 Dec. 2012. Web. 4 Mar. 2014.

Fine, Michelle, et al. *Off White Readings on Race, Power, and Society.* New York: Routledge, 1997. Print.

Foucault, Michel. *Power/Knowledge: Selected Interviews and Other Writings 1972–1977.* Ed. Colin Gordon. New York: Pantheon Books, 1980. Print.

Frankenburg, Ruth. *White Women, Race Matters: Social Construction of Whiteness.* New York: Routledge, 1993. Print.

Giroux, Henry A. "Higher Education and the Politics and Pedagogy of Educated Hope." *On Critical Pedagogy.* New York: Continuum International, 2011. Print.

Grosz, Elizabeth. *Space, Time, and Perversion: The Politics of Bodies.* Sydney: Allen and Unwin, 1995. Print.

Halberstam, Judith. *Skin Shows: Gothic Horror and the Technology of Monsters.* Durham, NC: Duke UP, 1995. Print.

Haraway, Donna J. *Simians, Cyborgs, and Women: The Reinvention of Nature.* New York: Routledge, 1991. Print.

Herakova, Liliana, Dijana Jelaca, Razvan Sibii, and Leda Cooks. "Voicing Silence and Imagining Citizenship: Dialogues about Whiteness in a 'Postracial' Era." *Communication Studies* 62.4 (2011): 372–88. Web. 30 Oct. 2014.

Holmes, Ronald M., and Stephen T. Holmes. *Mass Murder in the United States*. New York: Prentice Hall, 2000. Print

———. *Serial Murder*. 3rd ed. Thousand Oaks, CA: Sage, 2010. Print.

hooks, bell. "Eating the Other" *Black Looks: Race and Representation*. Boston: South End Books, 1992. Print.

———. *Outlaw Culture: Resisting Representations*. New York: Routledge, 1994. Print.

———. "Representing Whiteness in the Black Imagination," *Displacing Race: Essays in Social and Cultural Criticism*. Ed. Ruth Frankenberg. Durham: Duke UP, 1999. Print.

Ignatiev, Noel. *How the Irish Became White*. New York: Routledge, 1995. Print.

Kaplan, H. Roy. *The Myth of Post-Racial America: Searching for Equality in the Age of Materialism*. Lanham, MD: Rowman and Littlefield Education, 2011. Print.

Keating, AnaLouise. *Teaching Transformation*. New York: Palgrave Macmillan, 2007. Print.

Kelly, Keith. "'Bomb' Cover a Hit for *Rolling Stone*." *New York Post*. 4 Dec. 2013. Web. 20 Oct. 2014.

King, Desmond. *Making Americans: Immigration, Race, and the Origins of the Diverse Democracy*. Boston: Harvard UP, 2002. Print.

Lipsitz, George. "The Possessive Investment in Whiteness: Racialized Social Democracy and the 'White' Problem in American Studies." *American Quarterly* 47.3 (1995): 369–87. Print.

Logan, Enid Lynette. *"At This Defining Moment": Barack Obama's Presidential Candidacy and the New Politics of Race*. New York: New York UP, 2011. Print.

Maass, Harold. "Does *Rolling Stone*'s Tsarnaev Cover Glamorize Terrorism?" *The Week*. 17 July 2013. Web. 4 Mar. 2014.

Minnich, Elizabeth Kamarck. *Transforming Knowledge*. Philadelphia: Temple UP, 1990. Print.

Moon, Dreama. "White Enculturation and Bourgeois Ideology." *Whiteness: The Communication of Social Identity*. Eds. Judith Martin and Thomas Nakayama. Thousand Oaks, CA: Sage Publications, 1998. Print.

Morton, Robert J., and Mark A. Hilts, eds. *Serial Murder: Multidisciplinary Perspectives for Investigators*. Federal Bureau of Investigation. 2005. Web. 2 Feb. 2014.

Peralta, Eyder. "*Rolling Stone*'s Tsarnaev Cover: What's Stirring Such Passions?" *The Two Way: NPR blog*. 17 July 2013. Web. 1 Mar. 2014.

Reitman, Janet. "Jahar's World." *Rolling Stone*. 17 July 2013. Web. 1 Mar. 2014.

Rocca, Mo (@MoRocca). "Who knew Rolling Stone [*sic*] was the magazine for dreamboat terrorist cover boys? Should rename it Tamil Tiger Beat." 16 July 2013, 10:57 P.M. Tweet.

Roediger, David. *The Wages of Whiteness: Race and the Making of the American Working Class*. Rev. ed. New York: Verso, 1999. Print.

Rony, Fatimah Tobing. *The Third Eye: Race, Cinema, and the Ethnographic Spectacle*. Durham, NC: Duke University Press. 1996. Print.

"Serial Killers—Definition." FBI.gov, n.p. *The Federal Bureau of Investigation*. Web.

Simon, David. "The End Game for American Civic Responsibility." *Audacity of Despair*. 14 Aug. 2014. Web. 15 Oct. 2014.

Simpson, Jennifer. "The Color-Blind Double Bind: Whiteness and the (Im) possibility of Dialogue." *Communication Theory* 18.1 (2008): 139–49. Print.

Uebel, Michael. "Unthinking the Monster: Twelfth-Century Response to Saracen Alterity." *Monster Theory: Reading Culture*. Ed. Jeffrey Jerome Cohen. Minneapolis: U of Minnesota P, 1996. Print.

Voorhes, Josh. "*Rolling Stone*'s Dzhokhar Cover." *Slate*. 17 July 2013. Web. 2 Mar. 2014.

Warren, John. *Performing Purity: Whiteness, Pedagogy, and the Reconstitution of Power*. New York: Peter Lang, 2003. Print.

Yep, Gust. "Pedagogy of the Opaque: The Subject of Whiteness in Communication and Diversity Courses." *Whiteness, Pedagogy, Performance: Dis/placing Race*. Ed. Leda Cooks and Jennifer Simpson. Lanham, MD: Lexington Books, 2007. 87–110. Print.

THE PEDAGOGICAL ROLE OF A WHITE INSTRUCTOR'S RACIAL AWARENESS NARRATIVE

Meagan Rodgers

White teachers/researchers should not rely on others to unsettle their own positions of privilege and power.

—Amy Goodburn, "Racing (Erasing) White Privilege
in Teacher/Research Writing about Race"

IN 1998 COMPOSITION scholar Amy Goodburn used the occasion of the then-recent verdict in the racially divisive O. J. Simpson criminal case to contextualize a reflection on her whiteness within her own work. She found a tendency in that work to discursively "erase" her race and therefore her race privilege. She used that finding to call for white researchers and educators to consider their own privilege and how it impacts their ongoing work. More recent topics—from the "not guilty" verdict in the trial of George Zimmerman to the #BlackLivesMatter movement—show that, despite the passage of twenty years since the Simpson verdict, we remain a society largely unable to productively discuss—much less resolve—racial tensions.

The Zimmerman case is merely one recent example of the tensions that attend racial discourse in the United States. Though issues of race are national—even international—in scope, they are also always personal and local. Though biologically irrelevant, race is individually embodied and socially experienced. Discrimination attends skin color; privilege attends skin color.

The culture of the United States—social, political, and economic—is built on a tacit acceptance of white supremacy. Scholars including bell hooks, George Lipsitz, and Charles W. Mills have all shed light on the prevalence and persistence of white privilege.

In this environment, I wonder what antiracist white educators can do to undermine white privilege? Though academic work in race and privilege studies is robust, protests like the one in Ferguson, Missouri, in August 2014 are evidence of a racial divide that is difficult for many whites in the United States to recognize or comprehend. White activists such as Noel Ignatiev and Tim Wise serve as instructive models of race traitors. Other activists, inspired by the observations and reflections of writers like Peggy McIntosh, have adopted similar first-person stances to interrogate their own race and privilege. Such practitioners argue that the personal narrative can add to the body of antiracist work by making evident to whites the often-invisible facets of white privilege.

Under the auspices of making whiteness visible (and thereby more destructible), one specific tactic has been for white scholars and instructors to share narratives of coming to awareness of their whiteness. As this practice has been embraced by some, it has also been critiqued for its potential to recenter the white subject as a victim—a mental shift that runs contrary to the broad antiracist goals of dismantling white privilege and highlighting suppressed minority voices and opportunities.

In this chapter, I reconceive the racial awareness narrative in light of recent scholarship on emotion, rhetoric, and critical emotional literacy, arguing for its considered use as a pedagogical tool for undermining the white subject. The white ethnographic narrative has been criticized for its de facto recentering of the white subject, leading Wendy Ryden to condemn the "tyranny of narrative" (38) and call instead for dialogic practices. Instead of dismissing the narrative, I argue we should restructure it to model for students a critical and emotionally literate antiracist stance that may function dialogically. To model this restructuring, I reflect on my own narrative practice and share one student's response to the practice.

White Writers, Awareness Narratives, and Critiques

I have adopted the term "awareness narrative" from Jill Swiencicki, who explains the term as a process by which whites "us[e] personal reflection as a springboard into an understanding of the production of difference, and a disaffiliation from whiteness that constitutes the self through dialogue" (338).

These narratives employ "rhetorics in which those who identify as white confront and explore their racial privilege" (339). In her discussion, Swiencicki invites readers to contemplate the narrative performances of Julie Landsman, *A White Teacher Talks about Race*, and Gary Howard, *We Can't Teach What We Don't Know: White Teachers, Multiracial Schools*. In both instances, Swiencicki is concerned with the ways that awareness narratives featuring rhetorics of shame and injury interrupt rather than facilitate antiracist goals (343). While not wholly dismissing the narrative practice, Swiencicki encourages forward movement in developing new antiracist practices that transcend traditional narrative performances.

White folks telling stories about race is fraught territory—as further evidenced by concerns voiced by Wendy Ryden. While the racial awareness narrative may be delivered with the intention of decentering privilege and moving whiteness from invisibility to visibility, Ryden points out that "relinquishing" the privacy of whiteness via a confessional narrative "does not necessarily result in disruption of the privilege but rather a claiming of existential status" (26). Even as a speaker is ostensibly claiming new ethical authority by acknowledging her whiteness, the ethical quality of that new authority can be undermined by the nature of the racial disclosure. Ryden illustrates this point in her critical rereading of a narrative written by Lynn Worsham for the afterword to the 1998 collection *Feminism and Composition Studies: In Other Words*. As Worsham brings the edited collection to a close, she reflects on the family story about Blue Betty, an African American domestic worker present during Worsham's early childhood. Worsham interrogates the family anecdote, mining it and its context in order to speculate about the function of narrative and the mechanisms of white privilege. Further, Ryden explains:

> [Worsham] says we must recognize Blue Betty "as a racist story, one that perpetuates as surely as it resists white supremacy" (342) in its silent erasure of Betty as a narrating subject. But what Worsham seems less able to recognize is that insight into this racism is an insufficient strategy to avoid its replication in this academic iteration of the story. Despite (or perhaps in some ways because of) the metatextual apparatus that is replete throughout the essay, in which Worsham authenticates her ethical authority by relentlessly questioning and theorizing motives and effects, the story of Blue Betty is not rescued from the pitfalls of the awareness narrative genre that reinvigorates the white subject as a focus of inquiry, in this case the narrating consciousness of Worsham. (35)

Though critical of this narrative, Ryden is not asking for a moratorium on the practice. Instead, she encourages white scholars to work though these narratives dialogically instead of "enshrin[ing]" (38) them in static narrative performances. Instead of highlighting white shame or trauma, this scholarship illustrates the importance of a narrative performance that can be used pedagogically to reveal and undermine white privilege.

Critical Emotional Literacy

Recent work at the intersection of emotion, rhetoric, and composition has given me the tools to reconceive the awareness narrative. A key text in this line of inquiry is Laura Micciche's 2007 *Doing Emotion*. Micciche asserts that although emotion is central to our acting and thinking—as teachers, researchers, and learners—it has not been central to the work of composition. Though the field has "neglect[ed] or underestimate[d]" (1) the role of emotion in epistemology, nonetheless "emotion is central to what make[s] something thinkable, which is to say that the act of conceptualizing inserts emotion into thought and so into experience, the social world, politics, the whole shebang" (47). Accordingly, we must analyze, theorize, and teach with an eye not only toward reason but also toward the role of affect in leading people to accept or reject reason. Micciche calls scholars to learn to "name the presence of emotion" (108) across academic contexts. How, then, might we alter our practices in order to prevent emotion from misguiding our focus toward white injury rather than white privilege?

Composition and rhetoric scholar Jennifer Trainor pursues this line of thinking when asking us to consider the ways in which white students' racial beliefs are made intractable by the connection between emotion and reason. Her 2008 study "The Emotioned Power of Racism: An Ethnographic Portrait of an All-White High School" is one example of an attempt to rethink the assumptions that underlie instruction. Specifically, Trainor looked at the affective assumptions underlying racial beliefs commonly asserted by students in a predominantly white high school. She found that students—even though they mean well—espouse racist beliefs because such beliefs are not based solely in reason; they are buttressed by affective attachment. Trainor explains,

> Racist discourses are best understood as psychosocial rhetorical phenomena—forms of persuasion that need to be understood not only for their political meanings and implications but also *for their persuasive subjective and affective coherence*—and that racist discourses structure feelings linked to *but surprisingly rarely reducible to*, the racial politics such discourses forward. (85, emphasis in original)

Because discourse is rooted in both reason and affect, an antiracist pedagogy must address both if it hopes to be effective. In considering the implications of this observation, Trainor asks: "Can we make our own performance of emotioned positions—our commitment to racial justice, for example, our enthusiasm for difference and complexity—more salient so that they might serve as alternative models for students?" (110). In Trainor's work, I read an encouragement to white antiracist instructors to model the negotiation of the emotionally weighted topics of white privilege, complicity, and action.

Becoming adept at recognizing and deploying emotion within narratives and other forms of discourse is what Amy E. Winans calls "critical emotional literacy" (150). In her 2012 study, Winans considered how emotion and reason are bound together in classes at her rural, predominantly white university. She advocates for a pedagogical approach that encompasses "critical emotional literacy." She explains that by "cultivat[ing] critical awareness of emotions both cognitively *and* experientially" (emphasis in original 156), we can model and guide students through the acknowledgment and processing of emotionally charged considerations of difference. As most teachers have likely seen, "classes that uncover and challenge deeply held assumptions regarding difference evoke strong emotions on the part of students, whether or not those emotions are expressed openly" (151). Further, Winans defines critical emotional literacy as "the ability to understand how emotions function, particularly in terms of the ways that they inform identity, impact our relationship to social norms, and guide our attention" (155). When narratives like the ones critiqued by Swiencicki and Ryden "guide our attention" to the suffering and trauma of the white subject, then it is questionable how effectively such work serves antiracist goals. However, as I am arguing, when edited with a critical eye toward the function of emotion, an awareness narrative can undermine the white subject and his white privilege.

A Pedagogy of Critical Emotional Literacy

I have shared an awareness narrative in two different classes offered at a small, predominantly white public liberal arts college in the south-central United States. Both were upper-level English classes that focused on race and white privilege and how those themes are manifested in text and culture. Here, my remarks refer specifically to a course titled "Reading Race in Literature and Culture."[1] The syllabus included Toni Morrison's "Recitatif" and *The Bluest Eye* and the films *Suture* (1993) and *Bamboozled* (2000), along with scholarly articles that discussed these texts. Ten students enrolled in the course: all traditional age, all female, and all white.

In coming to decide how to share a racial awareness narrative of my own, I was concerned about the possible effects of sharing my anecdote with students who do not identify as white. Specifically, African American students, whose pasts within white privilege are unknown to me, are likely to read white racial awareness narratives—particularly those that contain confessions of racist thinking as part of the project of undermining the white subject—very differently than white students would. Though a teacher's job is in part to anticipate the ways her students might receive and respond to the work of the course, such foresight is particularly compromised in cases where white instructors (who are blinded[2] to the ways in which whites benefit from white privilege) attempt to anticipate how nonwhite students may be affected by emotionally charged racial content. In particular, I am worried about the emotional violence a black student may experience as a result of hearing my narrative.

Specifically, I am influenced here by African American social justice commentator Jessie-Lane Metz, whose voice was salient in the aftermath of the verdict in the George Zimmerman case. She details conversations she's had many times with white feminist allies who, in their stated effort to be antiracist, confess their own racist thinking to her:

> The pain I felt reading [a white ally's confession of racism] is personal, similar to the pain I feel every time (more often than I care to think about) that a white friend or acquaintance, in a discussion about racism, admits to me, with some pride about their self-awareness, that they are particularly afraid of Black men. As though perhaps this acknowledgement is an effort in anti-racism, or as if exposing a Black person to one's anti-Black racism is somehow anti-racist work, rather than another act of racism. ("Ally-phobia")

In contemplating Metz's remarks, I can certainly imagine the well-meaning white folks who, as they educate themselves about racism and privilege, come to significant observations about the ways that systemic white privilege has shaped their own thinking. White folks *must* come to these realizations in order to begin to consciously resist them. However, Metz's words make it clear that whites have an obligation not to do this race work at the expense of black folks. Accordingly, the teacher must consider each classroom context individually.

Clearly, then, I am a white teacher talking to and about classrooms that are entirely white. I realize that by creating this caveat to my argument about the use of awareness narratives, I risk reinscribing whiteness as something *different* or *special*. However, I am also destabilizing my own authority in the classroom. By confessing my complicity with race privilege, and sharing my subsequent actions to fight racism, I am modeling a critical and reflective behavior that I hope students will adopt. Not only is this a practice of critical emotional literacy but it is also a response to a call made by bell hooks in her essay "Engaged Pedagogy" in *Teaching to Transgress*:

> Professors who expect students to share confessional narratives but who are themselves unwilling to share are exercising power in a manner that could be coercive. In my classrooms, I do not expect students to take any risks that I would not take, to share in any way that I would not share. When professors bring narratives of their experiences into classroom discussions it eliminates the possibility that we can function as all-knowing, silent interrogators. It is often productive if professors take the first risk, linking confessional narratives to academic discussions so as to show how experience can illuminate and enhance our understanding of academic material. (21)

After consulting hooks, Ryden, Metz, and others, I see a path forward. White teachers need to model critical emotional literacy by sharing their own ambivalent histories with white privilege. Narrative can be used this way only if the story models the narrator's problematic emotional stance toward the experience.

I have attempted this modeling by sharing a personal anecdote about a moment in which I was both unintentionally racist and consciously antiracist. Perhaps the most important step I took to share my thinking (and model critical emotional literacy) is by sharing this anecdote on the first day of class:

> A few years ago, I was walking down the street in downtown Akron with my brother. It was a midweek afternoon and we were walking from the car to a store. The street was not very busy. As we were walking, I noticed a black man walking toward us on the same side of the street. My immediate thought was to check and make sure my purse was secure. My second thought was, "Wow, that was racist." Aware of how irrational and racist my initial thought was, I made a point to not do anything about my purse. I didn't move it to the other side of my body; I didn't clutch it closer. Eventually, we passed in opposite directions incident free. At that time, I had been studying racism and privilege for a few years. I considered myself an educated and ethical antiracist

person. But in that instant, my first reaction was to think the worst of a man just because of the color of his skin.

At that time (and still today), I consider myself antiracist. My actions as an antiracist educator and scholar bear that out, I think. But at that time (and still today), I was (and still am) in part the product of being raised in a white racist society—one built, as philosopher Charles W. Mills explains, on "the differential privileging of the whites as a group with respect to the nonwhites as a group" (11). As a result of living in such a society, we learn (I have learned), at a knee-jerk-reaction level, to be wary of black men. Systemic racism serves to maintain the enduring societal suspicion of black men. One need only look to recent national news to see some of the most tragic consequences of unfounded white fear (Michael Brown, Eric Garner, Trayvon Martin, Tamir Rice). Though I am saddened that my brain first went to a racist stereotype, I was aware that my reaction was faulty, and I was able to choose to act in a nonracist way as a corrective.

When I have shared this story in a classroom, I've felt bodily discomfort. I hesitate and pause as I begin. I force myself to make eye contact with the students, to emphasize the human, experiential connection between us. I do this because I am convinced that in order to help other white students see and dismantle white privilege, white teachers must act as models (Trainor; Winans) by acknowledging complicity within their own experience. Perhaps by seeing my complicity with white privilege, paired with my deliberate choice not to act on it, each student might conceive of ways to locate and interrogate problematic instances in her own life.

In my racial awareness narrative, I recall a short moment of time in which I experienced a disconnect between my immediate unintentional reaction and my subsequent intentional one. This is not the only racial awareness narrative I could have shared—I can recall several moments in which I had epiphanies related to whiteness, race, and privilege—but it is the moment I find particularly instructive because of the shame it evokes in me. When I share this anecdote with a class, I name that shame. I state that I am uneasy with myself in this story but that I share it for specific reasons. Instead of stalling on that shame, instead of focusing on how I felt or whether or not I was a "bad" white person, I placed that shame alongside my conscious choice on how I acted. Though I don't use the terms "awareness narrative" or "critical emotional literacy" in class, I have built a narrative practice that shows several things:

- My initial complicity with white privilege. In the instant when I thought to move my purse, I was reacting to a lesson I have learned from our white supremacist society: that black men are dangerous.
- My choice not to act on that initial reaction. I show that we each have control over our actions, even if we cannot always choose our unintentional reactions.
- My fallibility. While a confession of a personal point of shame may initially feel like a way to undercut one's authority, I am convinced that in the context of working with white students, this move actually increases my ethical authority. I show that I am not speaking from a holier-than-thou perch; I am a person who has made racially troubling mistakes, but I am acting on a long-term commitment to antiracist action.

I believe there's value in this practice because it shows that we can work to improve ourselves even when we know our thinking is flawed. In that moment, I did not follow my initial embodied reaction. Instead I used intention and education to inform my choice.

One Student's Response

Katie[3] was one of the ten women enrolled in "Reading Race in Literature and Culture." At the time of the class, I had already known her from other English classes and as a tutor under my supervision in the writing center. She was a kind and lively student, well-liked by peers and professors. Though coming from a conservative background that is typical of students in this region of the United States, Katie was actively interested in understanding feminist theories and practices. After she graduated, I had the chance to reflect on the class with her. I was interested in the pedagogical effectiveness of my narrative. She shared this response with me.

On the first day of any class, even with teachers that I have had before, there is an underlying skepticism, or perhaps wariness, of what the upcoming class might pertain. Classes involving difficult subjects, such as race, are particularly sensitive and that shows in the atmosphere of the class, even on the first day. I knew most of the girls in the room, except for two, so I was fairly comfortable already with the discussing or sharing that we might have to do. . . . Class started how it usually does on the first day, with the passing out of syllabi and the occasional quiet comment to friends about their vacations from school. The two people I did not know were relatively quiet and sat off to the side. Once Dr. Rodgers began her discussion of the goals she had in teaching this class, I think we all became apprehensive at the amount of work she had hoped to achieve and accomplish with such a thick and touchy topic. But then she told her anecdote about actively noticing herself thinking racist thoughts and suddenly we all became connected in this one moment. I myself became more at ease. Here the teacher was admitting she too had faults and was not fully free of society's influence in the matters of racism. Just because of this one little example of her accidental racist thought allowed me to be comfortable in sharing and realizing my thoughts and actions that might have been/be racist. I no longer had to hide those thoughts in shame. I could accept them, examine them, and then change my way of thinking to be free of prejudice.

After her story, I noticed the air in the room was less restricted. This thirty-second retelling had changed the way we viewed the class's beginnings and most definitely the results of the course. I think we all now had a more open-minded hope in what we all wanted to get out of the class. Afterwards, the ladies I did not know before conversed with me and my friends easily. We now shared something in common; we were going to tackle this difficult subject together. I do not think we would have connected in the same way had Dr. Rodgers not made herself open to criticism and judgment, thus changing the class as a whole.

I am interested in Katie's response because of the ways it reflects the potential of pedagogically implementing an emotionally literate awareness narrative. Katie says that after the anecdote, she "became more at ease." Her use of this bodily metaphor shows the lived connection between emotion and thought to which Micciche, Trainor, Winans, and hooks all refer. Katie states that, by seeing my own embodied conflict, she was then more "comfortable" with the prospect of examining her own racial thinking.

Katie's response is just what I had hoped for. She saw that this wasn't going to be a class where the teacher was perfect and the students would learn about their own racist faults as white people. To borrow from hooks, I was taking the risks and sharing my experience in the same way I was asking of them. Specifically, the point I wanted to get across to students is that racism is so pervasive in our society that even when whites identify ourselves as earnestly and consciously antiracist, we still rely on scripts and reactions that are grounded in systemic white privilege. By modeling an imperfect but nonetheless present antiracist identity, I was able to set the tone for the course—one in which we could acknowledge our actions in the past so as to create new tactics for ethical antiracist action in the future.

This type of narrative performance is a practice of critical emotional literacy. Further, I see this as an example of the kinds of race work that white folks need to be doing in order to forward the broad antiracist project of dismantling privilege. Though Jessie-Lane Metz enjoins white allies to avoid doing their race work at the expense of black folks, she also creates the potential space for these interactions among whites: "Maybe it is useful for white people to have these conversations amongst themselves. I'm not white, so I don't know what white folks need to do to get there" (qtd. in Waldman). Katie's reaction to my awareness narrative shows that such conversations can be used to antiracist ends.

I have attempted to proceed with caution as I respond to calls for antiracist pedagogical practice. When, in 1999, Amy Goodburn reflected on her own earlier work in an effort to reveal the workings of her own racially problematic thinking, she found that although white privilege's general modes of operation are invisible to whites, such modes can be seen in hindsight. Whites can learn to identify the usually invisible privilege by seeing how other white folks have come to recognize white privilege. As Goodburn concludes, she advocates for whites to continue this type of work. "I feel it is imperative to acknowledge that constructions of whiteness are inherent in how we teach and do research and that, therefore, systems of white privilege do need to be interrogated with respect to how students and teachers are textually represented" (83). Though her call is not new, it remains urgent. As scholars (including the editors and contributors in this volume) are pushing forward our thinking on the conceptions of whiteness, antiracist instructors continue to need theoretically grounded pedagogical tools.

With awareness narratives like the one I share here, white antiracist educators can model for white students what it is like to productively exist both within and against white privilege. But simple awareness, without action, does not lead to social change. White guilt and shame are numbing if not paralytic. But an emotionally literate stance toward privilege can educate whites about invisible privilege and model forward-looking antiracist action.

Notes

1. In hindsight, a more accurate name for the course would be "Reading Race and Privilege in Literature and Culture."

2. Philosopher Charles W. Mills explains that white privilege has thrived in the West in part because of an "epistemology of ignorance" (93) in which "the only people who can find it psychologically possible to deny the centrality of race are those who are racially privileged, for whom race is invisible precisely because the world is structured around them" (76). Mills explains the implication of this

structure: "Whites will then act in racist ways *while* thinking of themselves as acting morally. In other words, they will experience genuine cognitive difficulties in recognizing certain behavior patterns *as* racist" (emphasis in original 93). Because whites experience these difficulties, it is possible that even as whites act intentionally to disrupt racism and white privilege, they may be unable to see or comprehend the ways they are reinscribing racism. Therefore, even as my teaching is informed by antiracist scholarship and practices, my whiteness may still be impeded by my ability to anticipate how nonwhite students react to my narrative.

3. I am very grateful to Katie for sharing her thoughts with me and for reading multiple drafts of this chapter to ensure that I represented her words clearly and fairly.

Works Cited

Goodburn, Amy. "Racing (Erasing) White Privilege in Teacher/Research Writing about Race." *Race, Rhetoric, and Composition.* Ed. Keith Gilyard. Portsmouth, NH: Boynton/Cook Publishers, Inc., 1999. Print.

hooks, bell. *Teaching to Transgress: Education as the Practice of Freedom.* New York: Routledge, 1994. Print.

Ignatiev, Noel. *How the Irish Became White.* New York: Routledge, 2008. Print.

Lipsitz, George. *The Possessive Investment in Whiteness: How White People Profit from Identity Politics.* Rev. ed. Philadelphia: Temple UP, 2006. Print.

McIntosh, Peggy. "White Privilege: Unpacking the Invisible Knapsack." *Peace and Freedom Magazine* (July/Aug. 1989): 10–12. National Seed Project Organization. n.d. Web. 30 Jan. 2016.

Metz, Jessie-Lane. "Ally-phobia: On the Trayvon Martin Ruling, White Feminism, and the Worst of Best Intentions." *The Toast.* 24 Jul. 2013. Web. 7 Oct. 2013.

Micciche, Laura R. *Doing Emotion: Rhetoric, Writing, Teaching.* Portsmouth, NH: Boynton/Cook Publishers, Inc., 2007. Print.

Mills, Charles W. *The Racial Contract.* Ithaca, NY: Cornell UP, 1997. Print.

Ryden, Wendy. "Confessing Whiteness." *Reading, Writing, and the Rhetorics of Whiteness.* Ed. Wendy Ryden and Ian Marshall. New York: Routledge, 2012. 11–38. Print.

Swiencicki, Jill. "The Rhetoric of Awareness Narratives." *College English* 68.4 (2006): 337–54. Print.

Trainor, Jennifer. "The Emotioned Power of Racism: An Enthnographic Portrait of an All-White High School." *College Composition and Communication* 60.1 (2008): 82–112. Print.

Waldman, Katy. "How White People Shouldn't Talk about Race: Part Two." *The XX Factor: What Women Really Think*. The Slate Group. 29 Jul. 2013. Web. 7 Oct. 2013.

Winans, Amy E. "Approaches to Engaging Difference." *College English* 75.2 (2012): 150–67. Print.

Wise, Tim. *Colorblind: The Rise of Post-Racial Politics and the Retreat from Racial Equity*. San Francisco: City Lights P, 2010. Print.

Worsham, Lynn. "After Words: A Choice of Words Remains." *Feminism and Composition Studies: In Other Words*. Ed. Susan C. Jarratt and Lynn Worsham. New York: MLA, 1998. 329–56. Print.

PRACTICING MINDFULNESS:
A PEDAGOGICAL TOOL FOR
SPOTLIGHTING WHITENESS

Alice McIntyre

OVER THE PAST fifteen years I have reviewed over twenty-five articles, books, and dissertations that have examined whiteness and its relationship to teacher preparation. Although scholarship exploring whiteness has increased dramatically over those years, there does not appear to be a significant shift in how the majority of white students respond to the examination of whiteness. For example, many scholars continue to suggest that white, college-aged students resist identifying themselves as members of a racial group, deny the reality of whiteness, ignore the historical events that have sustained whiteness in the United States, and engage in talk that serves to insulate them from examining their individual and collective roles in the perpetuation of racism. In addition, some of the strategies educators use to examine whiteness—for example, inviting guest speakers, creating "safe spaces" where students feel comfortable speaking about racial issues, and using nonthreatening terminology to lessen students' discomfort about race-related topics—do not appear to disrupt how many white students make meaning of whiteness. It is my experience that when the above strategies are employed *uncritically*, or as drive-by pedagogies, they fail to generate the type of constructive dialogue that is needed to chip away at white students' beliefs about whiteness so as to make them less fixed, less rigid, and less powerful.

The intent of this chapter is twofold. First, I briefly discuss what many educators of color (see for example King 133–46; Macedo 183–206; Nieto

180–87; and Tatum 462–76) and antiwhiteness educators who identify as white (Castagno 314–33; Cochran-Smith 541–70; and Sleeter 157–71) have argued for decades: that when the above strategies are used uncritically, they fail to generate the type of constructive dialogue that is needed in order to chip away at white students' erroneous and misleading beliefs about whiteness. Second, I believe that no strategy, no set of readings, no pedagogical exercise, and no type of assignment—no matter how dazzling it may be—will assist white students in making connections between whiteness and their own individual and collective lives if the instructors who execute them do not have a similar connection, which is the focus of the latter part of this chapter. There I argue that it is essential that white instructors make whiteness a "central, self-reflective topic of inquiry" (Scheurich 8) in their own lives. By whiteness I refer to a system and ideology of white dominance and superiority that marginalizes and oppresses people of color while maintaining and sustaining privileges, opportunities, and resources for white people (Fine, Weis, Powell, and Wong; Frankenberg; Harris; hooks; Lopez; McIntyre, *Making Meaning*; Roediger; and Sleeter, "Preparing Teachers"). For me, naming and doing something to eradicate the effects of whiteness *in myself* is *as* important as other topics that need to be examined with prospective teachers. Therefore, I describe how I use mindfulness practices to cultivate and strengthen a more informed perspective about whiteness in myself in order to effect positive change in my teaching practices.

Category One: "Safe" Spaces

There are various strategies that a number of educators have applied, and critiqued, over the years in their efforts to address whiteness with white educators. One of the strategies some white instructors use is creating "safe spaces" where mainly white students can discuss whiteness (Amos 31–37; Aveling 261–74; McCarthy 127–33; McIntyre, "Exploring" 31–50; and Sleeter 94–106.). Unfortunately, the use of "safe spaces" can have the effect of taking the sting out of the discourse of whiteness. Instead of unearthing the destructiveness of whiteness, what tends to be focused on is making sure that instructors and students are not hurting one another's feelings as they make their way through a difficult, challenging, and disorienting experience.

White people facing racism in themselves and others, and examining the constellation of privileges associated with whiteness, is not a safe conversation. Nor should it be. Creating a safe, tolerant space where people respect what everyone says, *no matter how misinformed*, undermines the work of uncovering personal and collective racism with white students. These "safe spaces" where dialogue is created so that it is palatable to white instructors and students obfuscates the work that white teachers need to do to become more knowledgeable about the multidimensionality of whiteness.

Category Two: Teflon Terminology

The verbal interchanges between instructors and students provide opportunities for all involved to voice their opinions and articulate their positions on a host of topics related to whiteness, ranging from privilege to poverty, meritocracy to affirmative action, and the meaning of multicultural education to the meaning of racial justice. I have engaged in discussions with hundreds of white students over the years, encouraging and supporting the back-and-forthness of thoughts, ideas, questions, and life experiences. My goal in those discussions is to use language that is clear and direct, something that often makes white students sit up a little straighter and take notice. For example, I inform students that the word "diversity" means "difference," and I am not teaching them how to "appreciate difference." I am teaching them to examine why differences in skin color result in, among other things, differences in the way economic, social, and educational resources are allocated. Being clear about the term "diversity," as well as other whiteness-related terminology, and questioning students when the terms they use are vague, misleading, or inexact can be unnerving. Yet students need to be unnerved. If they are anything like me, they need to experience some cognitive and emotional discomfort that makes them *think about how they think* about whiteness. If they can stay with that discomfort, as mindfulness can teach them, they can learn to use it to better understand the interrelationship between themselves and the system of whiteness.

Category Three: Guest Speakers

Some white instructors invite speakers into their classes to tackle issues related to whiteness and racism. Guest speakers can provide rich, thought-provoking, and valuable experiences for students. They can also provide facts, figures, narratives, life experiences, and challenging questions that leave students with less room to run. On occasion, I have been one of those speakers. It is my experience that the white instructors who invite me to speak to their classes genuinely want to engage in discussions related to whiteness, yet they feel unable to find ways to address the brunt of the students' discomfort with the notion of their whiteness providing them unearned privileges, not to mention their own ideological blind spots.

One of the ways I gain a sense of confidence in myself as I engage in whiteness-related discussions is familiarizing myself with the life experiences of white European Americans who have committed themselves to antiwhiteness work (see Dees; Frankenberg; King; Segrest; and Stalvey). In addition, I read and critique existing research on whiteness, which provides me with opportunities to rethink programs, curricula, and pedagogical practices. Similarly, I dialogue with others, which helps me to rethink my assumptions, feelings, and experiences about the multiple issues related to whiteness (McIntyre "Engaging" 279–82).

I suggest that white instructors who want to explore whiteness with students engage in similar strategies because if a guest speaker's visit is to be of value, the instructor has to accompany the invitee and build on the material presented to the students. If the discussions related to whiteness are not maintained and sustained over time, then does it matter who the speaker is or what she or he said? Does it matter that the instructor did *something* to address whiteness?

I believe it *does* matter who speaks, how they speak, and what they speak about. I believe it matters significantly who the instructor is and how she or he presents her or his understanding of whiteness. I believe it matters because if we want prospective white teachers to effectively grapple with how whiteness is experienced in themselves, and in the field of education, then we need to grapple with it ourselves in more productive ways. I discuss how I engage that "grappling" process in more detail below.

Whiteness as a Living Practice

Conventional teaching about whiteness presents material for students to *think about*. My experience is that what may have more of an impact on students' abilities to submit to the rigor of self-examination regarding whiteness is when they see instructors bring awareness of *their own whiteness* to the foreground. This kind of awareness models more than thinking *about*—it represents a way of knowing from *within* (Simmer-Brown and Grace xvi). It represents a way of participating in an examination of whiteness with students by consistently participating in that examination within myself in a way that is directly linked to the pedagogical practices I use in the classroom.

I have written elsewhere about the ways I make my whiteness public, as well as the experiences that propelled me to better understand how my racial identity, social class background, and other factors mediate the choices, opportunities, and directions of my life (McIntyre, "Engaging in Cross-racial Dialogue"; *Exploring Whiteness*; *Antiracist Pedagogy*; *Making Meaning of Whiteness*). In those writings, I describe how I grapple with interrogating whiteness with white students, faculty, and administrators. I do so because I believe that describing life experiences that have shaped my views and contributed to my commitment to antiracism allows space for students and my peers to do the same. My overt racist actions as a young adolescent, my ignorance as it related to the history of racism and whiteness in the United States, and my anger and confusion when confronted by others about my racist thoughts and behaviors are fertile ground for demonstrating that it is possible for white people to change how they think about and act in relation to race, racism, and whiteness.

Although I speak to students about my relationship to and experiences with whiteness, I have not always been skilled in maintaining and sustaining discussions with white students without displaying my frustrations at their inability to "see" the effects of whiteness in their own lives. For example, instead of focusing on the students who actually *want* to engage in self-reflection and who really *want* to better understand the history of racism and whiteness, I sometimes pay more attention to those students who resist the prospect of interrogating whiteness (and by "pay more attention" I mean "go to war with"). That dynamic reflects more about what is happening *within me* than what is being expressed by the students. More specifically, what happens is that I get triggered by what I perceive as a student's racist or misinformed comment. Once triggered, I fixate on *that* remark, *that* student, and feel a strong need to make *that* student rethink her or his perspective. By doing that, I limit the scope of the discussion, as well as the participation of other students. I attended a workshop once and heard Pema Chodron explain that when we get stuck like this, we need to "take a breath" and move on in our thinking to create a more productive space within which to engage. In addition, my fixation on changing a student's mind, on controlling the way she or he thinks, is not only impossible, but leaves little room for the kind of openness that is necessary to be an effective educator. In an effort to change this all-too-familiar dynamic, I employ mindfulness techniques to deepen my connection to the challenges of teaching about whiteness.

Practicing Mindfulness in Relation to Whiteness

During the last decade, mindfulness practices have, among other things, enhanced teachers' ability to handle job demands more effectively (Ancon and Mendelson 156–70), reduced the stress elementary teachers experience in the classroom (Sessa 57–62), and strengthened primary school teachers' ability to focus on the present moment (Gold et al. 184–89). Other scholars, such as Timothy Davis (31–46); Jenny Lee (1–6); Deborah Schoeberlein; and Kimberly Schonert-Reichl and Molly Lawlor (137–51) also have examined mindfulness practices in education. Overwhelmingly, these educators and researchers found that teachers who used mindfulness practices became more self-aware, gained a greater understanding of themselves, and increased their capacity for self-reflection.

Although I was raised in a religion that emphasized prayer, I was not introduced to meditation and mindfulness practices until much later in life. Since then I have sought to understand how those practices can benefit my personal and professional life. The practices I employ stem mostly from my still-developing understanding of Buddhism. They are practices that have been espoused by a wide range of spiritual teachers across various traditions. In many of these approaches, people are invited to try a host of exercises to assist them in connecting with intense feelings and fixed beliefs: repeating mantras; sitting in particular positions; keeping eyes open or closed; and making use of candles, music, chanting, or silence. In addition, there are meditation and mindfulness practices that focus on breathing, imagining other people's suffering, or focusing on the particular events and personal experiences that shape a person's life.

Practicing mindfulness is not an intellectual or academic exercise where I list the privileges I receive due to my skin color or review the historical legacies of racism and oppression of "the Other" perpetuated by whites. Rather, for me, practicing mindfulness is both a pedagogical and spiritual way of being. By that I mean that it provides me with the opportunity to look deeper into myself in order to gain clarity about how I think, feel, and experience whiteness. That means that, at various times, I must sift through irrational guilt for being white, prideful self-righteousness when I compare myself to "those other white people" who don't get it, irritability at myself when I argue with resistant students, anger at the ever-present effects of whiteness in the world, and the discouragement I feel when I think that nothing I say is going to have any long-term effect on students' understanding of racial whiteness.

Sitting with those emotions and beliefs is difficult, yet necessary, if I want to cultivate a more insightful perspective about how whiteness manifests itself in my life and in the lives of the students I teach. When I can stay with the discomfort that comes with guilt, anger, or frustration, to name a few, I can more readily tap into the exact nature of what is happening *within me*. Thus, I am less provoked by students' comments, more accepting of the *very* slow process that takes place when we are trying to rethink old (and false) ideas about whiteness, and better able to accompany students who *want* to reevaluate and change their assumptions and actions about race-related issues. Yet practicing meditation and mindfulness just so I can gain more insight into myself is not enough. I need to link my practice to the actions I take in the classroom.

Moving from Cushion to Classroom

Meditation and mindfulness teachers offer a range of strategies for people to experiment with in their practice. For instance, Richard Brown has written extensively about the advantages of contemplative teacher education. He states that "moving from mindfulness on the meditation cushion to mindfulness in the classroom takes a lot of practice" (77). Thus, he suggests using a particular object to serve as a reminder to link one's mindfulness practice to one's teaching. When I want to practice mindfulness, I shut my office door, close the blinds, and choose a tangible item in my office as a focal point. I have a host of objects in my office that I use to help me focus: a beautiful portrait of Rosa Parks on the wall; a framed photograph on my desk of a group of young adolescents of color I worked with in Bridgeport, Connecticut; and a screen saver that is a photograph of my fifteen-year-old biracial (African American/white) niece. When I focus on one of those items, I remind myself that my intention is to gain clarity about and insight into whiteness yet remain without judgment during the process. Once I make that intention, I attend to the position of my body. I plant my feet on the floor, place my hands in my lap, and sit in a relaxed position. I do what many spiritual teachers (and my primary care doctor) suggest I do whenever I need to synchronize my mind, heart, and body: I become cognizant of my breathing. It is not so much whether I take deep breaths or focus on the in-breath or the out-breath. What is important is that I am intentional about how I engage my breathing and open to whatever I experience.

Each time I practice, my intention is to release any resistance I have that manifests itself in racing thoughts and strong emotions. I make room for that intention by releasing any resistance to examining my own thoughts and feelings about racism and whiteness and renewing my commitment to antiwhiteness pedagogy. As I practice breathing in and out and repeating "release and renew," my mind may generate thoughts that are completely unrelated to my intention. Sometimes I realize that I am thinking about what I am going to have for dinner. Other times I am distracted by the sound of a car driving by my window or the voices of passersby. I used to become frustrated with such distractions, which only made trying to sit in a mindful state an exercise in futility. Today, I am less likely to let those distractions divert me from the practice. When I find myself out of rhythm, I return to my breathing and to the main thought: "release and renew," "release and renew."

Let me provide a classroom example of how meditation informs my work with whiteness pedagogies. One day I was bothered by a remark a student made the previous evening in a class where the topic was immigration. (The class consisted of forty undergraduate students at a private university: thirty white, four Latino/a, four Asian, one African American, and one Filipino.) At one point during the discussion about a host of laws related to immigration, a white student said, "They [immigrants] should stop complaining and be grateful for what they get." The student's remark elicited a variety of responses from other students. A few students agreed with the remark, a few students talked about how the remark did not take into account the complexities of immigrants' lives, or about the colorism experienced by raced bodies who are read by U.S. racial stereotypes. The rest of the students remained silent, either afraid to state their views or overwhelmed and confused by their own beliefs and where those originated.

I, too, spoke to the student's comment. I questioned the genesis of her reasoning as well as the level of understanding she had about the history of immigration in the United States. In response, the student stated that she "followed the news" and was "in the majority in this country" in terms of her thinking about immigration. I asked her if she had data to support that claim, a question she chose not to answer. I suggested that she might want to provide evidence to support her perspective, to which she suggested that she had "said enough" and that nothing that I said "would change the facts." We both had stalled, in many ways, focusing on the "logic" of what she was saying rather recognizing the emotional components at stake in both of our views that disguised themselves in a cloak of attempting to be rational and logical about the situation.

Again, mindfulness-based reflection is productive for instructors who often get engulfed by ego-based perceptions. During my mindfulness practice the next morning, I kept returning to the student's comment. I tried to focus on my breathing, yet I found myself mentally pointing my finger at the student and being less than diplomatic in my response to her remark. After a few moments, I caught myself and refocused my mind on my breath. Before long, I again imagined myself demanding that the student explain to the class how she came to believe the contents of her remark. I caught myself again and went back to my breathing. This back-and-forth between breathing with a mindful intent and reacting to the student's remark went on until I finally gave up and quit.

I would say I failed miserably in the above practice, except I know that judging my practice as good or bad, as a success or a failure, is counterproductive. Most times I trust that the more I sit, breathe, and pay attention to the moment at hand, the more opportunities I have to, as noted earlier, gain some insight into the root causes of my disturbance—an exercise that is not always easy to do. That is because I often recognize *in myself* the very things I critique in others.

The frustration I experienced in my meditation was not so much about the student's remark; rather, it was what the remark set off in me. A few minutes after my not-so-productive meditation, I realized that the exact nature of my irritability was my failure to change the student's mind. When she resisted, I tried even harder, which both increased my fixation with her and her fixation with her point of view. It was only after recognizing the root of my disturbance that I saw the futility of what I was doing. Once I saw the disturbance, I took responsibility for *my own* thinking and actions, and in my mind I let the student take responsibility for hers. It is my experience that when college-aged students take responsibility for their own thinking and actions as they relate to whiteness, they are more intentional about trying to undo it rather than trying to deflect, ignore, or deny its existence.

Practicing the Pause

A mini-version of my sitting practice is pausing, which is also important in the classroom. When I pause in the midst of an emotionally charged discussion, I give myself a chance to suspend judgment and sort out how to respond to a student with the kind of language I referred to at the beginning of this piece: clear, direct, concise, and factual. I once heard someone speak about the value of "putting the I over the E" in situations where reacting with strong emotions might make the situation worse. By that she meant putting the intellect over the emotion. That did not mean stuffing one's emotions, ignoring one's feelings, or denying one's reaction to something; rather, it meant *thinking through* one's feelings before acting on them. In an effort to do that, I link my meditation practice to what occurs in the classroom. It is my on-the-spot "I over E" practice. Pausing in the midst of class discussions is not easy. Class time is limited and there are conflicting goals and objectives that need to be addressed. There is also a sense of urgency that is present in many educational settings, a sense that things need to move fast, that instructors need to jump from topic to topic over the course of a semester. I can fall into that pattern myself—moving too fast, trying to cover too much, and not taking the time that is necessary to genuinely, and with care, explore whiteness-related issues. In the above example, the student in question said something, and automatically I reacted. I forgot to pause, to attend to what was going on *inside me* at that particular moment. When I fail to pause, I strengthen the above habitual behaviors, which are simply pedagogically ineffective. Yet when I pause, I have an opportunity to keep the focus where it belongs—on whiteness, not on how I, or students, might *feel* about whiteness. By that I mean that I, and the students I teach, do not have to become attached to anger, guilt, or other distracting emotions. What is more beneficial in terms of gaining clarity about ourselves in the moment is holding onto uncomfortable feelings while at the same time exploring strategies for addressing the topic at hand. That does not mean I silence students or try to quell the emotional intensity that arises in me or in the students. Rather, I try to ride it out with a degree of openness and curiosity rather than with a fixed determination to do the impossible—change anyone else's mind but my own.

This is particularly important when something happens in the country or the world that is related to whiteness and to the content I am teaching. Unfortunately, there are too many events in the country and in the world at large that fit that description: the short- and long-term consequences of various statewide immigration policies, the effects of high-stakes testing on racial groups in public schools, the overpopulation of people of color in U.S. prisons, the killings of unarmed black men, and the experience of having a two-term African American president. Those and other discussions generated highly emotional responses from some students and silence from others. In addition, they triggered a host of emotions in me. I tend to be an animated instructor no matter what the topic of discussion is. I become even more "lively" when the discussion is focused on the near- and far-reaching effects of racism and whiteness. Therefore, it is important for me to pause, practice self-restraint, and respond to students' comments in ways that contribute to an informed and productive discussion.

Integrating Mindfulness Practice into the Student-Teaching Experience

During the last academic year, I introduced mindfulness practices to three white undergraduate students in the teacher preparation program I direct at a small, private, liberal arts college in the northeast region of the United

States. Although the focus of my mindfulness practice is related to teaching about whiteness, for the three students, the integration of mindfulness practices was linked to their overall student-teaching experiences.

The three students, Suzanne, Michelle, and Christina (all pseudonyms), had addressed issues related to poverty, racism, classism, immigration, under-resourced communities, unequal distribution of funding for schools, and a range of other topics during their coursework in the teacher-preparation program. In addition, the students had engaged in three prepracticum experiences in local public classrooms prior to their full-time student-teaching placements, which also took place in a public school. Thus, they had a working knowledge of urban school-related issues, including whiteness, as well as a familiarity with pedagogical practices to insure effective teaching for *all* students.

The students were provided with blank sketchbooks where they recorded moments during their fifteen-week student-teaching experiences when they were triggered, caught off-guard, or felt unsure of how to respond to someone or something. During our weekly meetings we reviewed what the students recorded in their sketchbooks—either by writing, drawing, imaging, or using other tools for representing their experiences. We also explored various strategies the students used when they felt anxious, frustrated, and overwhelmed—three emotions the students described as being the most challenging to address.

Two of the strategies the students used most often during their student-teaching experience were mediation and taking time to pause. Together, we defined meditation as concentrating the mind on an object for a certain amount of time and doing so in ways that were personal and practical to and for each student. The students decided to practice meditation for five minutes each morning in a setting of their choice. For example, Suzanne drank her coffee sitting on the back porch or in the sunroom each morning and tried to simply be present to whatever she was concentrating on. Michelle stood at the window and looked out at her backyard. Yet she often said, "I am not so sure about this stuff. I have a short attention span, and I think I only do quality meditation for about forty-five seconds." Christina did her five minutes of meditation while lying in bed in the morning. She said it seemed to work for her but she wasn't sure if "breathing in bed" was really meditating.

We had ongoing discussions about Michelle's skepticism, about whether "breathing in bed" constitutes meditation, and whether practicing meditation contributed to the students' mindsets while they were teaching. Not surprisingly, we did not reach consensus on those issues. Yet over the course of the semester, the students learned some practical lessons about how they might integrate meditation into their daily practice.

What proved more helpful to the students was the second strategy they experimented with: pausing in the classroom when they got hooked into repetitive behaviors that were ineffective at that particular moment. For example, halfway through the semester, one of the students observed that she laughed nervously whenever she was caught off guard by one of the third graders' comments or behaviors. By laughing inappropriately she disrupted the moment, confused the student(s), and, as she put it, "made matters worse." Thus, one of her goals during the semester was to pause when she was triggered by a student's speech or action and simply be aware of how she felt. She did not always know how she would respond in the moment when she would normally laugh or giggle. She *did* know that she wanted to refrain from laughing and simply stay with the uncertainty that characterized those moments.

Carol, a native of Greece, also experienced an intense moment of self-doubt teaching a fifth-grade classroom one day. The class included twenty-one students, the majority of whom were Latina/o and African American. Christina stated,

> We were teaching about ecosystems. I was saying the word wrong. I pronounced it "echosystem." Two boys started laughing at me and making fun of me. I told them that English is my second language, just like many of the students in the class. When I said that, one of the boys called me a racist.

Christina was confused by that comment. "I felt so embarrassed because even though English is not my first language, I should know how to pronounce that word. But being a racist? I couldn't even say anything to him. I froze. I just stood there and said nothing."

During a follow-up discussion, I asked Christina if she had asked the boy why he thought what she said was racist. She explained that she could not think of anything to say. "The whole experience made me feel like a failure. I said nothing," she stated. Suzanne and Michelle readily identified with Christina, saying that they would have done the same thing that she did—said nothing and been frozen in place.

During follow-up discussions, we talked about how challenging it is for newly minted student teachers to know how to respond to unpredictable moments in the context of teaching. It is even more challenging when the moments are related to race. Therefore, the students recognized the importance of developing and practicing strategies that would help them negotiate the sudden and surprising moments they faced during their teaching experiences.

Over time, the students viewed pausing as a tool for moving forward rather than as a tool for shutting down. They learned that "saying nothing" and "being frozen" for too long in front of a classroom of young people was ineffective. On the other hand, they knew that pausing so they could speak to the students with confidence helped them to remain open to whatever was in front of them. Rather than being embarrassed, or feeling inadequate or discouraged, the students began to see that they could stay with moments of uncertainty and actually use them to their advantage.

The students' ability to better understand their thoughts and emotions were not seen as distractions but as resources for developing insight into themselves. When acted upon, that insight helped them to make clearer connections between their thoughts, feelings, and actions. Over the long term, self-insight gave the students a degree of confidence in themselves that helped sustain them during the ongoing combustible discussions about race-related issues. That confidence was also a catalyst for them as they developed more equitable and just strategies for teaching *all* the students in their classrooms. Similarly, the students developed a more expansive understanding of the relationship between teaching, whiteness, and their positionalities as soon-to-be white teachers.

As the number of whites writing and teaching about whiteness increases, so do the questions about representation, interpretation, and the extent to which white educators can engage in a critique of a system that we benefit from in a host of different ways. Although many antiwhiteness educators, some of whom I refer to in this chapter, address those challenges from differing perspectives, they agree that, among other things, there needs to be rewriting of the history of race and whiteness into textbooks; a long-term, sustained process to integrate a critical study of whiteness into teacher preparation programs; a concerted effort by white educators to make changes in our curricula so that whiteness is made visible and studied with a critical and questioning eye; and a commitment by white educators to understand our own construction of what it means to be white and how that understanding—or lack thereof—informs our pedagogical practices (McIntyre 147–48).

Christine Sleeter has been an antiwhiteness educator for decades and continues to investigate how whiteness manifests itself in her life. She recently used critical family history as a methodology to examine the relationship between her family background and her racial identity as a white woman and educator (421–33). Like her, I am committed to investigating new and different ways that will help me, and the white students I teach, to move toward a more comprehensive and critical perspective about ourselves as white and about the overall system of whiteness of which we are integral parts. The opportunity for students to participate in self-reflective courses where they are asked to critique whiteness, not just for a semester but for the duration of their time in the teacher education program, is a significant move in that direction.

Engaging in meditation and mindfulness practice is another one of those ways. Thus far, I have not experienced any "whiteness awakenings" nor reached enlightenment about how to extricate myself from the messiness of making whiteness a living practice in my life. Nonetheless, practicing various forms of mindfulness *does* help me to be more attentive to how, as Miller states, I link the "curriculum [of my] inner life" (178) to the curriculum of my outer life. From my perspective, strengthening that link is an excellent use of my time and well worth my effort.

Works Cited

Amos, Yukari T. "'They Don't Want to Get It!' Interaction between Minority and White Pre-Service Teachers in a Multicultural Education Class." *Multicultural Education* (Summer 2010): 31–37. Print.

Ancon, Matthew R., and Tamar Mendelson. "Feasibility and Preliminary Outcomes of a Yoga and Mindfulness Intervention for School Teachers." *Advances in School Mental Health Promotion* 7.3 (2014): 156–70. Print.

Aveling, Nado. "'Hacking at Our Very Roots': Rearticulating White Racial Identity within the Context of Teacher Education." *Race Ethnicity and Education* 9.3 (2006): 261–74. Print.

Brown, Richard, C. "The Mindful Teacher as the Foundation of Contemplative Pedagogy." *Meditation and the Classroom: Contemplative Pedagogy for Religious Studies*. Ed. Judith Simmer-Brown and Fran Grace. Albany: SUNY P, 2011. 75–84. Print.

Castagno, Angelina E. "'I Don't Want to Hear That!' Legitimating Whiteness through Silence in Schools." *Anthropology and Education Quarterly* 39.3 (2008): 314–33. Print.

Cochran-Smith, Marilyn. "Uncertain Allies: Understanding the Boundaries of Race and Teaching." *Harvard Educational Review* 65.4 (1995): 541–70. Print.

Davis, Timothy S. "Mindfulness-Based Approaches and their Potential for Educational Psychology Practice." *Educational Psychology in Practice* 28.1 (2012): 31–46. Print.

Dees, Morris, with Steve Fiffer. *A Season of Justice: The Life and Times of Civil Rights Lawyer Morris Dees*. New York: Charles Scribner's Sons, 1991. Print.

Fine, Michelle, Lois Weis, Linda C. Powell, and L. Mun Wong. *Off White: Readings on Race, Power, and Society*. New York: Routledge, 1997. Print.

Frankenberg, Ruth. *White Women, Race Matters: The Social Construction of Whiteness*. Minneapolis: U of Minnesota P, 1993. Print.

Gold, Eluned, Alistair Smith, Ieuan Hopper, David Herne, Glenis Tansey, and Christine Hulland. "Mindfulness-Based Stress Reduction (MBSR) for Primary School Teachers." *Journal of Child and Family Studies* 19 (2010): 184–89. Print.

Grace, Fran. "From Content to Context to Contemplation: One Professor's Journey." *Meditation and the Classroom: Contemplative Pedagogy for Religious Studies*. Ed. Judith Simmer-Brown and Fran Grace. Albany: SUNY P, 2011. 47–64. Print.

Harris, Cheryl. "Whiteness as Property." *Harvard Law Review* 106.8 (1993): 1709–91. Print.

hooks, bell. *Teaching to Transgress: Education as the Practice of Freedom*. New York: Routledge, 1994. Print.

King, Joyce E. "Dysconscious Racism: Ideology, Identity, and the Miseducation of Teachers." *Journal of Negro Education* 60.2 (1991): 133–46. Print.

King, Larry. *Confessions of a White Racist*. New York: Viking Press, 1972. Print.

Lee, Jenny J. "Teaching Mindfulness at a Public Research University." *Journal of College and Character* 13.2 (2012): 1–6.

Lopez, Ian Haney. *White by Law: The Legal Construction of Race*. New York: New York UP, 1996. Print.

Macedo, Donaldo. "Literacy for Stupidification: The Pedagogy of Big Lies." *Harvard Educational Review* 63.2 (1993): 183–206. Print.

Marx, Sherry. *Revealing the Invisible: Confronting Passive Racism in Teacher Education*. New York: Routledge, 2006. Print.

McCarthy, Cameron. "Contradictions of Power and Identity: Whiteness Studies and the Call of Teacher Education." *Qualitative Studies in Education* 19.1 (2003): 127–33. Print.

McIntyre, Alice. "Antiracist Pedagogy in the University: The Ethical Challenges of Making Whiteness Public." *Practicing Feminist Ethics in Psychology*. Ed. Mary Brabeck. Washington, DC: APA, 2000. 55–74. Print.

———. "Engaging Diverse Groups of Colleagues in Conversation." *Everyday Antiracism: Getting Real about Race in School*. Ed. Mica Pollock. Cambridge, MA: Harvard UP, 2008. 279–82. Print.

———. "Exploring Whiteness and Multicultural Education with Prospective Teachers." *Curriculum Inquiry* 32.1 (2002): 31–50. Print.

———. *Making Meaning of Whiteness: Exploring the Racial Identity of White Teachers*. Albany: SUNY P, 1997. Print.

Miller, John P. *The Holistic Curriculum*. Toronto: U of Toronto P, 2007. Print.

Nieto, Sonia. "Placing Equity Front and Center: Some Thoughts on Transforming Teacher Education for a New Century." *Journal of Teacher Education* 51.3 (2000): 180–87. Print.

Roediger, David. *Working towards Whiteness: How America's Immigrants Became White; The Strange Journey from Ellis Island to the Suburbs.* New York: Basic Books, 2005. Print.

Scheurich, James. "Toward a White Discourse on White Racism." *Educational Researcher* 22.8 (1993): 5–10. Print.

Schoeberlein, Deborah. *Mindful Teaching and Teaching Mindfulness: A Guide for Anyone Who Teaches Anything.* Somerville, MA: Wisdom Publications, 2009. Print.

Schonert-Reichl, Kimberly A., and Molly S. Lawlor. "The Effects of a Mindfulness-Based Program on Pre- and Early Adolescents' Well-Being and Social and Emotional Competence." *Mindfulness* 1 (2010): 137–51. Print.

Segrest, Mab. *Memoir of a Race Traitor.* Boston: South End, 1994. Print.

Seidel, Jackie. "Some Thoughts on Teaching as Contemplative Practice." *Teachers College Record* 108.9 (2006): 1901–14. Print.

Sessa, Sandra A. "Meditation, Breath Work, and Focus Training for Teachers and Students—The Five Minutes a Day That Can Really Make a Difference." *Journal of College Teaching and Learning* 4.10 (2007): 57–62. Print.

Simmer-Brown, Judith, and Fran Grace. "Introduction." *Meditation and the Classroom: Contemplative Pedagogy for Religious Studies.* Ed. Judith Simmer-Brown and Fran Grace. Albany: SUNY P, 2011. xi–xxv. Print.

Sleeter, Christine E. "Becoming White: Reinterpreting a Family Story by Putting Race Back into the Picture." *Race Ethnicity and Education* 14.4 (2011): 421–33. Print.

———."How White Teachers Construct Race." *Race Identity and Representation in Education.* Ed. Cameron McCarthy and Warren Crichlow. New York: Routledge, 1993. 157–71. Print.

———."Preparing Teachers for Culturally Diverse Schools: Research and the Overwhelming Presence of Whiteness." *Journal of Teacher Education* 52.2 (2001): 94–106. Print.

Stalvey, Lois M. *Education of a WASP.* New York: Morrow, 1970. Print.

Tatum, Beverly. "Teaching White Students about Racism: The Search for White Allies and the Restoration of Hope." *Teachers College Record* 95 (1994): 462–76. Print.

PART FIVE

PROBLEMS HAUNTING THEORIES OF WHITENESS

REFLECTIONS

CALLING A WHITE A WHITE

Victor Villanueva

LET'S SEE, THEN. Light-skinned folks of mixed African and European descent are white in Haiti, mulatto in most of Latin America, and black in the United States. Most of Latin America is a mix of indigenous, European, and African, mixes that show up in different children born of identical parents. I know. I look in the mirror beside my sister and I see a white man alongside a black woman or *mulata*. As we've aged, my body has taken on a distinctly Amerindian quality; hers, an African quality. Maybe. Others look at me and see someone not white (olive; though the Irish are the ones who claimed being green before they became white). My sister stands beside me, looks in the mirror, and she sees two white people staring back, so much so that she marries a man who unselfconsciously speaks of having to control the Nazi blood coursing through his veins, as he speaks—*in my home!*—of lazy Mexicans and thieving Russian immigrants (who are Caucasians, from the Caucuses). And I know, no doubt at all, that he loves her. *Mulatas* are not part of his racialized landscape. Smoke and mirrors.

My oldest daughter, a natural blonde, lived in Chile for a while. While at the beach, she was told not to go to "*that* end of the beach," where the Others sunbathed. She couldn't make the distinction. The whites looked just as Latina to her as the nonwhites. Meanwhile, folks would speak of the German woman—her—in her presence, not knowing she was raised by a Puerto Rican man, the most fluent Spanish speaker of his children. Smoke and mirrors.

Driving up to Cincinnati with in-laws from the airport, which is located in Kentucky, at five in the evening, step-mother-in-law (kind of—it's complicated) says "There go the hillbillies." And I remember then-president Jimmy Carter's brother, Billy Carter, a member of an affluent family but just a good ol' boy, a brand of beer named after him—Billy Beer. Good ol' boy, hillbilly, redneck, trailer trash—more than a class distinction, a racialization within whiteness.

Race might be smoke and mirrors but *racism* is real enough. Unless we continue to grapple with two very important things, the pains inflicted by racism will continue—large, structurally imposed and structurally maintained pains. The first thing to realize is that race and its racism are social constructs, changing, shifting over time, mutable, shifting with shifting ideas concerning class and gender as well as race (as in "good ol' *boy*"). Today's white person could be yesterday's brown (or green—the Irish were "the green race"). The melanin-deprived can still be nonwhite. The second is that we are all culpable in racism's maintenance, that the absence of ill will is insufficient, that unless one takes part in actively seeking to dismantle racism, one is in effect taking part in its maintenance.

This is hardly a postracial era. The United States has twice elected a black man president, a mulatto really, whose ancestry does not go back to the American slave trade. Yet he remains colored, subject to racialized outrageousness (like a *New York Post* political cartoon or a CBS News item—two years apart—that both depict Obama as a monkey; or the famous "You lie!" outburst from the congressional floor).

We have called a spade a spade; it's time to call a white a white. By removing the anonymity of whiteness, by coloring everyone, without exception, we confront the prevalence of racism, so easily denied. We cannot recognize the construct if we deny being a part of it. We cannot help to dismantle the structure if we refuse to see it. Whiteness is a means of confronting and including. The problem of the color line continues, remains as much the challenge of the twenty-first century as it was the challenge of the twentieth.

CALLING WHITENESS STUDIES . . .

Sharon Crowley

WE OUGHT TO change the name to "white supremacy studies." What else is whiteness, after all, than the ideology of white supremacy embedded in and expressed by white bodies?

WHITENESS AS RACIALIZED SPACE: OBAMA AND THE RHETORICAL CONSTRAINTS OF PHENOTYPICAL BLACKNESS

Ersula Ore

IN 1993 ARKANSAS native Bill Clinton became the forty-second president of the United States. Clinton's cultural cache—the fact that he was born poor, grew up in a single-parent household, played the saxophone, and reportedly felt "comfortable" in black communities—led some to agree with Toni Morrison that Clinton was America's "first black president" (1). As Morrison explained, Clinton's titular status had been granted long before her 1998 proclamation. Singer, songwriter, and Parliament Funkadelic leader George Clinton set the designation in motion with his 1993 release, "Paint the White House Black." The song in a sense was an anthem to Clinton's projected ethos as a funk-loving, saxophone playing, weed-smoking white boy from the South; an individual who, Morrison opined, displayed "almost every trope of blackness" ("Talk" 2). But Clinton's "blackness" was nominal, symbolic, and most importantly, complimentary. Regardless of the tribute, he remained meanfully southern, phenotypically white and, thus, an acceptable candidate for the White House.

In 2004, however, discussions of a "black" White House resurfaced when Barack Obama, a young black senate candidate from Illinois, delivered the keynote for the 2004 Democratic National Convention (DNC). Obama approached the stage to boisterous applause as The Impressions' 1964 song "Keep on Pushing" played in the background. He was casual but personable, engaging the crowd and giving shout-outs to his home states of Kansas,

Illinois, and Hawaii. The audience roared. "Tonight is a particular honor for me," Obama began, "because let's face it, my presence on this stage is pretty unlikely" (Obama, "2004 Keynote"). The audience's silence suggested that it likewise agreed.

Like the Oval Office, the DNC podium is a physical and historical space normed "white" through a network of rhetorically situated racial-spatial practices. Obama knew that the body his 2004 audience was expecting was not *his body*. He unapologetically said as much when he punctuated his opening with just how "unlikely [his] presence on this stage" was. His statement communicated what those at the convention and those of us watching at home already knew; namely, that the DNC podium was envisioned as a *certain kind of space intended for a certain kind of body* (Williams; Mills *Racial Contract* and *Blackness Visible*; Olson). Obama's black body was not *that body*. The Impressions' 1964 hit, then, was more than catchy background music announcing the second African American since Barbara Jordan (1976) to occupy the space of the DNC podium as keynote. For me, Obama's unremitting forward stride toward white space against the backdrop of a civil rights–era soundtrack signals his connection to a quintessentially black tradition to "keep on keeping on" in the face of adversity.

Obama's playful declaration of the space behind the podium as space *not intended for him* illustrates an acute awareness of the rhetorical burden of being a phenotypically black rhetor in white racialized space. This is to say that Obama's phenotypical blackness creates rhetorical constraints for him for which Clinton's troping of blackness would never have to account. Obama's familiar tone and use of the plural possessive phrase "let's face it" quickly moves us all—those at the convention and those watching at home—from celebrating "diversity" as signified by a black man behind the DNC podium to implicating us in the truth that racial prejudice and racial injustice remain a shared reality of our time.

Obama's 2004 performance juxtaposed with Clinton's 1993 performance signifies on the pervasiveness of the color line in an era of supposed color blindness. While Clinton's performance of blackness failed to impede his ascent to the Oval Office, Obama's phenotypical blackness adversely impacted his. As the 2008 presidential race moved into its final stages, a number of white Americans began to display anxiety over the rising potential of a phenotypically black president. Bogus accusations contesting Obama's candidacy ranged from everything to conspiracies asserting a black nationalist bent to protests against documented evidence of his native-born status; to accusations of Islamic sympathizing. I find these responses interesting for what they illustrate about whiteness as racialized space. For me, these reactions to the prospect of a black president demonstrate how appeals to whiteness that collapse tropes of the black threat with those of the foreign invader work enthymemically to demarcate the space of the White House as space for "Whites Only." The most disturbing expression of this practice appeared shortly after Obama became the democratic presidential candidate. At the time, decorations depicting effigies of Obama lynched emerged on residential lawns and university campuses. These incidents are disquieting. The lynched black body is a profoundly violent trope of American belonging. It signifies the ultimate price blacks pay when believed to have transgressed physical and discursive spaces raced white.

America's tradition of lynching evidences a nonwhite reality that white racialized space is not just conceptual space; white racialized space *is real space* that produces *real material effects upon real material bodies*. These effects are suffered by all; by the subjects assumed to belong to white racialized space as well as the subjects assumed not to belong. For nonwhites, however, white racialized space has historically been proven to be inhospitable. As such it demands an acute understanding of racial hierarchy, racialized codes of conduct, and creative methods of usurping these rhetorical constraints in an effort to both safely navigate as well as demonstrate that qualities conventionally associated with whiteness—in other words, the ability to occupy the white space of the DNC podium, White House, or Oval Office—are not innate or normal but rather made commonsense by design. I see little difference, then, between twenty-first-century discursive practices such as those listed above that enthymemically racialize space and mid-twentieth-century signs of legalized segregation that read "No Blacks Allowed." If we acknowledge, rather than ignore, America's legacy of racism, segregation, and racialized violence, then it becomes difficult to read Obama effigies (and the Obama Bucks and birther debate that would come later) as anything other than twenty-first-century iterations of a tradition of rhetorically racializing certain spaces as spaces for "Whites Only." The continued practice of physically and discursively policing space in the midst of growing postracial discourse outs the fallacy of a postracial America. If citizens truly believed that race were a fiction, and if "color" were not read as "character," then perhaps the pattern among incidents such as Jena 6 (2006), Chief Douglas Zeigler (2008), Robbie Tolan (2008), Henry Louis Gates Jr. (2009), Trayvon Martin (2012), and Michael Brown (2014) would not be so easily read as material examples of twenty-first-century practices of racially demarcating space. These incidents evidence that black bodies either vying for access to white racialized space or already residents of white space run the risk of being delegitimized, satirized, warned to stay in their place, and, finally, when the threat of transgressing the color line is at its greatest, lynched. As these examples of racialized violence against nonwhites illustrate, America was very much a country that saw race during and after the 2008 election.

Unlike his predecessor Bill Clinton, Obama's phenotypical blackness creates rhetorical constraints for him that no amount of troping blackness could create for Clinton. Considering how black rhetors such as Obama deploy tropes of whiteness to mitigate white anxiety in the twenty-first century aids my larger effort to better understand how contemporary citizens communicate their sense of place and belonging within a nation that still very much relies upon culturally and historically informed understandings of "black space" and "white space" to navigate civic life. Racial and racist epistemologies are the always already of rhetorical space. Oftentimes the most strategic option for rhetors that lack the privilege of being the somatic norm is to find creative ways of mitigating white imaginings of "the dangerous trespasser" while maintaining a personal sense of self-respect. In his essay "Just Walk on By," journalist Brent Staples illustrates that negotiating damaging stereotypes like the black threat or black mugger takes a dynamic understanding of the relationship between whiteness, race, and space as well as rhetorical skill. While walking in the physically and historically white space of north-side Chicago, Staples whistles selections from Antonio Vivaldi's *Four Seasons*. The assumption upon which his safety is secured (and Staples's understanding of white and racialized logics evidenced) is that a black man intending to do harm "wouldn't be warbling bright, sunny" selections of classical music while walking down the street (Staples). Staples's performance follows suit with those of Mariah Stewart, Frederick Douglass, Ida B. Wells, and others whose ability to navigate white space was predicated upon their capability to mitigate the white racist stereotypes associated with their bodies. For me, Staples's reference to "warbly bright sunny selections" reflects *(1)* the importance of racial-spatial awareness for black rhetors operating in spaces racialized white and *(2)* his connection to a devastating reality: that his safety as a black man walking in white space is determined by *his* ability to mediate the stereotypes associated with his body, stereotypes that his white counterparts may or may not consciously hold but the consequences of which he may indefinitely suffer.

"Whistling Vivaldi" is a trope of whiteness that Staples employs to rhetorically identify with residents of white space. In this chapter I use Staples's experience with "whistling Vivaldi" as an analogy for how Obama mediates racialized anxieties associated with his bid for the white space of the presidency. Racial-spatial awareness is a rhetorical necessity for non-white rhetors operating in white space. I argue that Obama's rendition of "whistling Vivaldi" demonstrates a racial-spatial awareness specific to the rhetorical situation of the U.S. presidency. I illustrate this point through an examination of Dick Durbin's 2008 DNC keynote address and the video documentary of Obama's life that aired shortly after Durbin's address. The 2008 DNC is a historical precedent in that it is the first convention to announce a black presidential candidate. I turn to this documented moment in history because I see it as an ironic instance that helped solidify claims of an America beyond race alongside Obama's performance to the contrary. Obama's rendition of "whistling Vivaldi" is intricately orchestrated in that it uses the rhetoric of Durbin's keynote address and the rhetoric of the video documentary to render Obama "recognizably white" (Mills, *Racial Contract* 53). As Staples demonstrates, I see Obama's rendition of whistling Vivaldi as a response to the rhetorical burden of being a nonwhite body in white racialized space. While this chapter does not permit an extended examination of this historical moment, I take time here to flesh out one instance in which twenty-first-century campaign rhetoric illustrates an awareness of racial hierarchies, strategically engages those hierarchies, and in doing so belies claims of postraciality.

Racing the Space of the White House

Space gains its racialized character through a mix of racial-spatial practices: legal, social, economic, and political practices that designate particular spaces as exclusively inhabitable by particular raced bodies. Critical philosopher Charles Mills explains that the construction of race in general and the racialization of space in particular points back to the Enlightenment and political philosophers such as Thomas Hobbes, John Locke, Immanuel Kant and Jean-Jacques Rousseau, whose contractarian theories regarding the natural rights and duties of man, grounded in the juxtaposition of (white) man/human and (nonwhite) savage/subhuman, designated space occupied by whites as morally superior and space occupied by nonwhites as spoiled by the taint of the subhuman (*Racial Contract* 11–20). Nonwhite bodies were, thus, symbols of lack while white bodies stood as the representative norm. The U.S. Constitution, federal and state laws, and landmark decisions like *Dred Scott v. Sandford* (1857) and *Plessy v. Ferguson* (1896) are just a few examples of philosophical concepts made material through legal doctrine.

These philosophical laws gave rise to intricate exclusionary mechanisms that inhibited the political agency of nonwhites and directly contributed to the racializing—in this case, "whitening"—of the White House. And while constitutional and legislative reforms during the latter half of the nineteenth and middle of the twentieth centuries afforded minorities greater access to white space (via greater participation in decision-making processes) and theoretically increased access to political avenues leading to the White House, America's long tradition of exclusion, circumscribed black enfranchisement, and policing of the highways and byways leading to the Executive Office ensured that the physical space of the White House and the inhabitants of its Oval Office remained phenotypically white.

As both a conceptual and physical space racialized white, the "White House" constitutes rhetorical constraints for nonwhite rhetors like Obama. Rhetorical scholar Roxanne Mountford contributes to studies in the racialization of discursive and physical space by illustrating how the social imaginary and material imperatives comprising physical spaces like the pulpit constitute the rhetorical constraints of rhetors for which the space was never intended. Mountford's study of women preachers considers how the history of male clerical authority and imagined female lack saturating the cultural space of the pulpit comprise the rhetorical constraints of women in the pulpit. The pulpit has historically been conceived as "the embodiment of clerical"—meaning male—"authority" in that it is a physical and cultural space that anticipates and reinforces the masculine tradition of American Protestantism (17, 3). As such, it invariably contributes to the complications women preachers—both black and white—experience.

The racialized power saturating the white space of the White House also constitutes racialized rhetorical constraints for nonwhite rhetors that must be mediated. Although she doesn't use the language of rhetorical space, Shirley Wilson Logon's work on the rhetoric of nineteenth-century black women illustrates how structures of power saturating spaces occupied by black-speaking bodies constitutes the rhetorical constraints of rhetors' public performances. In *We Are Coming* Logan demonstrates how black female rhetors reconfigured their preconstructed ethos (a consequence of prevailing stereotypes of black womanhood) via "figures of communion" that worked rhetorically to "increase audience identity through references to a common past, tradition, or culture" (24). Figures of communion are essentially what Kenneth Burke refers to as modes of rhetorical identification. Modes of identification seek to demonstrate a "likeness" or "commonality" despite the various incongruences the audience may recognize between itself and the rhetor. Following

Burke, "the simplest way to overcome division" or miscommunication is for the rhetor to identify his ways with those of his audience. The rhetor achieves this union with the audience most effectively by adapting his "language . . . speech, [or] gesture" to those of his audience, and by expressing an "attitude . . . [or] idea" that signals commonality with his audience (Burke 55). For Burke, signaling "communion" is signaling "identification."

Mountford's and Logan's work on the body illustrates that female and nonwhite bodies are commonly conceived by their white audiences as bodies absent of "authority, eloquence, power, substance" (Mountford 13). As their studies demonstrate, social norms determining who can speak, who must remain silent, and who can occupy public spaces grant ultimate authority to move in and out of all spaces, to speak in all spaces, and to occupy all spaces, to white men. Together, Mountford and Logan's work on race, gender, and rhetorical identification alongside Mills's work in race and continental philosophy provide a critical framework for reading how Obama navigates "inhospitable space." Like Staples, black rhetors like Obama who operate in white racialized spaces may enact tropes of whiteness to demonstrate a shared "likeness" or "commonality" with their white audiences because acts of communion make foreign bodies less *strange*. Some may argue that this is not so much a *racial problem* as a *rhetorical problem* that must account for whiteness as a dominating racial ideology that haunts the geography of all communicative events. For me, they are one and the same, as the pursuit of such rhetorical performances is to render one's-self more *familiar* than *strange*. The more *familiar* rhetors appear to their audience, the more likely they will achieve grounds upon which to be heard. In the case of Brent Staples, whistling classical music mitigates the "strangeness" of his black body as it operates in white space, primarily because classical music is symbolic of aesthetic sophistication, refinement, culture, and taste—qualities conventionally associated with whiteness. Within the communicative geography of Staples's rhetorical moment, classical music operates as a figure of communion—what we might also refer to in this case as a trope of whiteness—that he deploys to ensure safe passage through north-side Chicago. While Staples's account speaks to how his black male body operates within the white imaginary as a symbolic of lack, the reactions he receives from white passersby (looks of suspicion, efforts to avoid him) elucidate that his black body is always already perceived as problematic by virtue of its blackness. Staples's reports of the noticeable difference between the attitudes of white passersby for whom he whistles and those he does not testifies to how strategic deployment of tropes of whiteness may help to make bodies marked "foreign" familiar.

The presidency is a rhetorical situation that presents a particularly unique set of constraints for Obama, constraints that he cannot outright ignore. He is compelled by the exigency of the presidency to present himself as "fit for"—despite his blackness—the Oval Office. Thus his performance must cohere with the collective imagining "the people"—have of the president. Keith Erickson explains this best using Burke's notion of dramatism, noting that "the tactical need of the moment . . . cannot justify modifying performances to fit diverse audiences, because they are typically unconvincing" (366). Under these conditions it becomes clear that to paint the presidency as anything other than what it has always been (which is "white") would be to lose the presidency; to articulate a solid antiracist, overtly racially conscious, or "pro-black" stance would be to lose the presidency. To be perceived as favoring one group over another would be to lose the presidency. Hereafter, the ultimate aim for Obama—as for any presidential candidate—is to stay within the bounds of his audience's expectations while at the same time appearing authentically presidential. In other words, in order to cohere with his audience's imaginings of the president, Obama must mediate the signifying power of his blackness while *"affirm[ing] visually mastery of the mythic presidency"* (emphasis original 360). Visually mastering the presidency is difficult for a body not originally conceived to have the authority to occupy the presidency. As Erickson explains, "true performance constitutes a prudent adaptation" to citizens' expectations and understanding of the "standards and traditions of the mythic presidency." If the performance does not stamp the rhetor as authentically presidential in the eyes of the audience, then the speaker fails (360). Because Obama's ability to achieve true performance is hindered by signifiers of blackness, his ability to visually master the presidency, then, turns on his ability to, like Staples, whistle a tune familiar to "the people."

Mediating White Anxiety in Racialized Spaces

Minutes before Obama's acceptance of the democratic presidential nomination, and just seconds before the video documentary of his life, Dick Durbin delivered the 2008 DNC Convention keynote address. Durbin's address added veracity to the video documentary that aired and its depiction of Obama as a man *familiar* and "recognizably white" (Mills 53). Speaking as the representative stand-in for "we the people" (as Mills and many others, including Martin Luther King Jr., remind us, "we the white people"), Durbin declared: "So many of *us know* this man. *We know how he thinks.*

We know his values. We know Barack Obama's journey has never been far from the pain and struggles so many Americans experience today" ("2008 Democratic Convention," emphasis added). Repeating what Durbin suggests the audience already knows of Obama's character bolsters the documentary's later portrayal of Obama as a man familiar to "the people."

Obama's situation illustrates the rhetorical problem of whiteness as racialized space. Obama is centrally located within a preexisting rhetorical context of conceived lack. He is phenotypically black, and by nature of that blackness, always already sinister, vile, morally depraved, and intellectually inept. His ability to perform the mythic presidency, then, depends upon his ability to mitigate damaging stereotypes associated with his body while at the same time meeting "the people's" expectations of the presidency. Durbin's keynote and the video documentary help Obama achieve this aim by pulling on tropes of Americanness to establish an interpretive framework through which "the people" can read *Obama's body* as *the body* for the "White House." Durbin's keynote assists this effort by signifying on the memory of Illinois senator and eleventh president Abraham Lincoln. While delivering his 2008 DNC keynote address, Durbin refers to Obama as the "other son of Illinois." The reference pulls on national memory of Lincoln as a president of prophetic promise. Lincoln is colloquially referred to as the man who "freed the slaves" and the man who "saved the union." As a rhetorical shorthand, troping Lincoln permits the audience to make meaning of the past they share with Obama and the prophetic promise that his leadership is destined to bring.

Durbin's allusion to Lincoln followed suit with Obama's own efforts to rhetorically frame himself as "Lincolnesque" and, thus, as a man familiar to "the people." Obama did this during the 2004 DNC keynote when he used the memory of Lincoln to cast himself as a sagacious, even-tempered, civic-minded, ethical, and balanced politician. He did it again when he selected the front of the Illinois capital building (the same place where Lincoln spoke 150 years ago) to announce his candidacy for president (Berkowitz and Raaii 366), and he would do it again while giving his 2008 inaugural speech. Durbin's allusion continued Obama's strategy of troping Lincoln by framing Obama within a narrative of deliverance, and casting him as a man destined to bring salvation to a people tired of racial division. With Obama's election, Durbin asserted, comes the "dawning of a new day," for he "will lead us to a better nation" ("2008 DNC Convention"). Durbin's strategic use of collective memory and religious symbolism helps to mitigate the adverse effects of Obama's racialized body by strengthening the audience's focus on the ways in which Obama—despite his signifiers of blackness—embodies fundamental principles of Americanness. Through Durbin, Americans at the convention and watching at home are brought to see that Obama's story is a part of "the larger American story." Durbin's references to Lincoln alongside his proclamation of Obama's promise and exceptionalism help to rhetorically whiten Obama by signaling his status as a "permanent resident" of white racialized space. Taken together, these references served to testify to Obama's character as a man "in place," whether walking the streets of north-side Chicago or running the country from the Oval Office. By grafting "his story" onto "the larger American story," Durbin helps Obama "whistle Vivaldi" and achieve the myth of the presidency.

The documentary continues Durbin's efforts by first visually signifying on classic narratives of the American Dream. The documentary opens with a sense of journey and travel. Scenic shots of the American Midwest and expansive panoramas of wheat fields and cornfields pass by. The picturesque landscapes suggest something virgin and promising. The first representatives of "the people" depicted are farmers and blue-collar workers. We see Obama out among "the people." He shakes hands with "the people"; he appears to listen intently as "the people" speak to him; he laughs with "the people." The video quickly moves us through what appears to be Obama's journey from the Heartland of his upbringing, to the Midwest city of his political assent. Pictures of a young Obama as a grassroots organizer in Chicago are followed by testimonies to his character as an ethical and vivacious civic leader. Congressmen describe Obama as the archetypal public servant. He is a man "compelled to serve" to the benefit and improved welfare of all citizens. As Illinois state senator Miguel del Valle explains, Obama's Ivy League education doesn't detach him from understanding the "day-to-day" troubles of the average American: unemployment, "factory closings," low-wage pay, and "failing schools." Illinois senator Laurence M. Walsh confirms Obama's integrity: "Pieces of legislation that he carried he believed in," Walsh affirmed. "He was not carrying it for a group; he was not carrying it for a lobbyist" ("2008 DNC Convention").

These performance frames paint Obama as a man whose politics are grounded in fundamental American values and interests: economic freedom, educational equality, personal liberty, and equal employment. Such frames help Obama sign *familiar* and less *strange*. One of the strongest and most consistent methods the documentary uses to assist Obama's performance of the presidency is deploying tropes of black racial erasure. The documentary is a collection of performance frames absent of nonwhite bodies.

The performance frames that get the most time depict Obama surrounded by white constituents, speaking to predominately white audiences, or surrounded by members of his white family. The video documentary upholds "the people's" racialized expectations of the president as a man who moves comfortably in all spaces as it depicts Obama as a black man who moves comfortably in spaces historically inaccessible to blacks. The abundance of screenshots depicting Obama living and working comfortably alongside elderly whites, professional and suit-wearing whites, white grandparents, his white mother, whites in hardhats, and whites in long white smocks, impresses upon viewers that although often the only black body in the frame, Obama nonetheless seems to *belong* in the frame. In the video documentary we get few if any images of Obama shaking hands or interacting with large crowds of nonwhite constituents. Instead we are bombarded by performance frames that rhetorically whiten Obama, the repetition of which infer his relative closeness and comfort in spaces racialized white. Obama's later admission to having been "shaped more by [his African] father's absence than his presence" strengthens a sense of white inundation in two ways: first, via the allusion of distance from members of any nonwhite community, and second, by stressing Obama's "Americanness" through subtle denouncement of his "Africanness." As Toni Morrison reminds us, "American means white" (qtd. in Mills 58). The rhetoric of the video documentary played on this associative link and helped to couch Obama's governing values within a racialized framework that eclipsed signifiers of his blackness by stressing his associations to Americanness and, therefore, whiteness. This web of associations situates Obama as an inheritor of core American values while also rendering his black body racially legible and aligned with "the people's" expectations of the mythic presidency. Such performance frames impress upon viewers that although black, Obama may not necessarily be the proverbial "fly in the buttermilk." Rather than the fly, Obama might be the president.

The visual and verbal rhetoric of the documentary assists Obama's performance of the mythic presidency in other ways that build on the association between Americanness and whiteness. One way is by depicting his bloodline and family origins as devoutly "American." Although not a serviceman himself, Obama's roots are patriotic in that his grandparents and primary caretakers served in World War II; his grandfather as a serviceman and his grandmother as a worker on a bomber assembly line. In the documentary Obama describes his grandparents Stanley and Madelyn Dunham as "hardworking" people of America's "heartland." "They weren't complainers." "They took life as it came." While the documentary depicts Obama's grandparents as a self-reliant, patriotic couple unafraid of hard work, it casts his mother, Stanley Anne Dunham, as Obama's moral compass. She was the "beating heart" of a very small family, Obama explained in the documentary. It was his mother's lessons in fairness, empathy, and equality that guided Obama's desire to pursue a life of civil service. As he explained,

> The only time I saw my mother really angry was when she saw cruelty, when she saw somebody being bullied or somebody being treated differently because of who they were. And if she saw me doing that she would be furious. And she would say to me: "Imagine standing in that person's shoes; how would that make you feel." That simple idea I'm not always sure I understood as a kid, but it stayed with me. ("2008 DNC Convention")

It was through lessons like these that Obama's mother taught him humility and compassion and helped him see that being on the receiving end of cruelty never feels good. Such performance frames only help to mitigate the rhetorical constraints associated with Obama's black body.

America's president and majority party presidential candidate winners have always been white men until Obama's 2008 win. The rhetoric of Durbin's keynote and verbal and visual rhetoric of the video documentary bolsters Obama's rendition of "whistling Vivaldi" by playing on preexisting visual expectations of the mythic presidency. As I have illustrated here, Obama's performance during the 2008 DNC Convention is the product of rhetorical constraints for which the conventional white male rhetor vying for the presidency would not have to account. Obama uses the documentary to deploy tropes of whiteness via tropes of Americanness tactically because it is a rhetorical necessity that he responds to the ways in which histories of race saturate rhetorical space. Obama's rendition of "whistling Vivaldi," then, does not so much directly or intentionally "whiten" him as much as it illustrates an available means of mitigating anxiety over his black body as it strides toward the white racialized space of America's Oval Office. I sit with Mills's reasoning on this point. Obama is not subjectively white, for "to achieve Whiteness"—that is, to successfully "become a white person"—means to follow "a cognitive model that precludes self-transparency and genuine understanding of social realities" (18). As his memoirs *Dreams of My Father* and *The Audacity of Hope*, his "A More Perfect Union" speech, and candid comments on national tragedies such as the Trayvon Martin case indicate, Obama is not unaware of the racialized and social realities of our time.

Whiteness is an ideological code that haunts discursive spaces (Williams; Delaney; Omi and Winant; Mills *Racial Contract* and *Blackness Visible*; Mountford; Morrison *Playing*; Bonilla-Silva). Additionally, because rhetoric racializes all bodies, Obama's rhetorical whitening should be considered a burden of operating in space racialized white. To clarify, Obama's rendition of "whistling Vivaldi" does not so much "whiten" him through appeals to Americanness—in other words, whiteness—as much as they illustrate his political need to calibrate his rhetoric for the ways in which space carries the residue of race. This is not to say that the rhetoric of Durbin's address and the documentary rhetorically whiten Obama because they have to. Because Clinton has the privilege of being the somatic norm, his troping of blackness is not perceived as threateningly authentic but rather as a contemporary iteration of a long tradition of minstrelsy. If Bill Clinton's performances were perceived as "authentically Black," then my conversation of whiteness as racialized space would likely have to account for how his performance of blackness contributed to his loss of the 1992 presidential race. As controversy over the misnamed Barack and Michelle "fist bump" exemplifies, phenotypical blackness denies black bodies the comfort of performing tropes of blackness while black and in white space. Because performing tropes of blackness while black results in a different set of outcomes for black bodies, it makes sense how performing whiteness as a way of mitigating damaging stereotypes of blackness can be a rhetorical necessity for black bodies in white space.

The chief reality constituting Obama's central rhetorical constraint is one with which all nonwhite bodies must contend; namely, the reality that all space is raced space, and as such, is comprised of a set of orthodoxies—accepted views, expectations, attitudes, and practices—that have been, through invariable repetition—what we might call, *tradition*—calcified so flawlessly that they express as commonsense, as natural, and as the unquestioned norm. These racialized norms and racial hierarchies create racialized rhetorical constraints for bodies that do not fit the somatic norm. In Obama's case, his bid for presidency is further compounded by the orthodoxies constituting the raced space of the White House and its inner sanctum, the Oval Office. Presidential qualities are normatively applied to white male bodies because the position of commander in chief of the United States of America has been, for the last 232 years, the exclusive purview of white men. This is to say, then, that Obama's whistling is not a form of "passing for white." Rather, it reflects an available means of contending with the racialized rhetorical constraints of whiteness.

It is clear, then, that the rhetorical constraints mediating Obama's bid for presidency are both racial and spatial. The white, male, and normalized space of the presidency creates a rhetorical problem for Obama that demands he strike a balance between the reality of his subjectivity as a black man and the imaginings of the people for whom he wishes to represent. As the rhetoric of Durbin's address and the visual and verbal rhetoric of the video documentary illustrate, the burden of having to rhetorically whiten oneself—in other words, "whistle Vivaldi"—outs the fallacy of an America beyond race. As Obama slyly intimated in 2004 and enacted in 2008, race clearly still matters.

Works Cited

Bonilla-Silva, Eduardo. *Racism without Racists: Color-Blind Racism and the Persistence of Racial Inequality in America*. Lanham, MD: Rowman and Littlefield, 2010. Print.

Burke, Kenneth. *A Rhetoric of Motives*. Berkley: U of California P, 1969. Print.

Delaney, David. *Race, Space, and the Law, 1836–1948*. Austin: U of Texas P, 2010. Print.

Douglass, Frederick. *Narrative of the Life of Frederick Douglass*. New York: Dover Publications, Inc. 1995. Print.

Erickson, Keith "Presidential Rhetoric's Visual Turn: Performance Fragments and the Politics of Illusionism." *Visual Rhetoric: A Reader in Communication and American Culture*. Ed. Lester Olson et al. Los Angeles: SAGE, 2008. 357–75. Print.

Logan, Shirley Wilson. *"We Are Coming": The Persuasive Discourse of Nineteenth-Century Black Women*. Carbondale: Southern Illinois UP, 1999. Print.

Mills, Charles. *Blackness Visible: Essays on Philosophy and Race*. Ithaca: Cornell UP, 1998. Print.

———. *The Racial Contract*. Ithaca: Cornell UP, 1997. Print.

Morrison, Toni. *Playing in the Dark: Whiteness and the Literary Imagination*. New York: Vintage, 1993. Print.

———. "Talk of the Town: Comment." *New Yorker* 5 Oct. 1998. Web. 12 Jan. 2014.

Mountford, Roxanne. *The Gendered Pulpit: Preaching in American Protest Spaces*. Carbondale: Southern Illinois UP, 2003. Print.

Obama, Barack. *The Audacity of Hope: Thoughts on Reclaiming the American Dream*. New York: Three Rivers Press, 2006. Print.

———. *Dreams from My Father: A Story of Race and Inheritance*. New York: Three Rivers Press, 2004. Print.

———. "Keynote Address." 2004 Democratic National Convention 27 July 2004. *American Rhetoric Online Speech Bank*. Web. 12 Sept. 2013.

Olson, Joel. *The Abolition of White Democracy*. Minneapolis: U of Minnesota P, 2004. Print.

Omi, Michael, and Howard Winant. *Racial Formation in the United States: From the 1960s to 1990s*. New York: Routledge, 1994. Print.

Staples, Brent. "Just Walk on By: A Black Man Ponders His Power to Alter Public Space." *Feminist Frontiers II: Rethinking, Sex, Gender, and Society*. Ed. Laurel Richardson and Veta Taylor. New York: Random House, 1989. 155–65. Print.

"2008 Democratic Convention, Day 4." 28 Aug. 2008. Web. 12 Sept. 2013.

Williams, Patricia. *Alchemy of Race and Rights: Diary of a Law Professor*. Cambridge, MA: Harvard UP, 1992. Print.

COLOR DEAFNESS:
WHITE WRITING AS PALIMPSEST FOR AFRICAN AMERICAN ENGLISH IN *BREAKING BAD* SCREEN CAPTIONING AND VIDEO TECHNOLOGIES

Nicole Ashanti McFarlane and Nicole E. Snell

SCREEN CAPTIONS AS white writing are integral to the history of cinematic production. Films like *Birth of a Nation* and *The Jazz Singer* transcribed the spoken word to open up meaning for early moviegoing audiences. Laid out in typographical detail as dialogue lines, these films also closed off meaning in significant ways to reinscribe notions of race. Ideas like staying "pure" or "becoming American" are meant to draw clear delineations about the racial identity and ethnic neutrality of whiteness. In contrast to the transcription of spoken words in silent movies and talkies is the new media practice of transcribing nonspeech information (NSI), introduced with the advent of closed captions in the mid- to late twentieth-century media technology environment of 1970s broadcast television. Transcriptions for screen viewing of NSI content and spoken language both strive toward the clarity and neutrality of colorless writing—although it is rarely, if ever, achieved. Whether as an act or an object, writing itself is immanently material. In *Writing Degree Zero*, Roland Barthes observes as much and we agree, especially in the case of screen captions. When it comes to sounds (both language-based and nonspeech) transcribed into screen texts, there exists "an example of a mode of writing, whose function is no longer only communication or expression, but the imposition of something beyond language, which is both History and the stand we take in it" (1). This recognition locates whiteness as a series of scenes by which notions of the postracial manifest as textual overlay in the form of misrepresentations of captioned language and NSI content.

Color Deafness as Palimpsest

In this study we examine the composure and style of African American English (AAE) alongside the white writing of screen-captioning technologies. Whiteness and screen typography—whether closed captioned, subtitled, open, or standard—each imply their own kinds of boundaries and perspectives. While others have also considered the idea of white privilege in film and video, the focal point of this essay deals with the mechanical habits that racially index, mock, and tokenize the speech and musical expressions of black and nonwhite Latino language communities and stigmatizes and ignores the significance of alternative sensorial exchange. The "ordered space" of closed captions and subtitles, then, can be viewed as an intersectional environment where race and ability converge and reify whiteness as a form of audist hegemony—defined here as favoring the ability to hear language and express vocalized speech. To traverse such a space, we engage in the act of rhetorically listening with a "third ear" as described by Kochhar-Lindgren as a means "to enable cross-sensory listening across domains of sound, silence, and the moving body in performance" (2). This examination of color deafness makes discernable what counts as "clear meaning" and concentrates attention on closed captioners as hidden interlocutors, not easily heard or seen to the untrained ear or eye. In listening to this sound in-between, our argument about race and whiteness and screen captioning draws upon sociolinguistic techniques to engage with topics of performative and linguistic marginalization. This polyschematic analysis draws attention to the linguistic overlay produced by closed captions and video subtitles. The "third ear" allows caption users to hear across a pastiche of sonic and visual space while shifting attention from obvious content to more nuanced forms of expression. In listening to these nuanced forms of expression it becomes apparent that a type of "screen white-out" occurs, being the active displacement of AAE by dominant white language conventions.

In focusing on the cult television series *Breaking Bad*, our analysis demonstrates how screen captions operate as an overtly racialized phenomenon by which whiteness indexes racial sign systems and structures preferential relations in order to naturalize historical processes. It is our contention that all forms of sound transcripts, to varying extents, rhetorically reinforce white privilege and mechanistically hem in nonwhite, non-Anglo languages to uphold "the comforting area of an ordered space" (Barthes 9). To explore such ordered spaces, this chapter challenges "ability" as something that is "natural" and charts the "interconnections among the profusion of both muted and blatant discourses" that categorize bodies by way of social and structural barriers (Thomson 13). The products of screen captioning technology order and reinforce dominant and subordinate power relations in the spatial area of the screen to reveal a false hierarchy of racialized bodies. Much research on historical and cultural elements of race exists, yet sensorial norming remains the most ignored axis of race. And because language frequently operates as a stand-in for racial phenotype, hearing proves about as significant to seeing when it comes to racial and ethnic discrimination. Our consideration of such audist frameworks resists notions of pathology so often attached to raced discourses and shifts the emphasis away from individual impairment. We situate white privilege as a form of spoken language discrimination to interrogate racial attitudes about sensorial and behavioral norms, and we question what it means to be properly oriented to and within the world. We contribute to the epistemological stance of D/deaf studies scholarship,[1] at the nexus of disability and performance studies, to challenge the medicalization of audist paradigms. To further problematize audism as a form of racial norming, we forward a critique of audism that compels one to rethink the production and consumption of racist frameworks.

Among its multiple frameworks, audism is but one means to manage racial differences. And nowhere more is speaking and hearing transformed into spatial practices than within the confines of closed captioning. So race can be defined, at least in part, by the complex of attitudes derived from audism. Peeling back the layers of white privilege shows a form of spoken language discrimination that interrogates racial attitudes about sensorial and behavioral norms operating along three major axes: historical, cultural, and sensorial. Sensorial norming, as the most ignored axis, is defined, in part, as the complex of attitudes derived from audism. Audism is the system of prejudices and discrimination stemming from the belief that being able to hear and express vocalized speech is an inherently better way of being, which must necessarily lead to a higher quality of life. Sensorial norms are defined as the assumptions made about the appropriate baseline of proper sensory orientation. The Deaf aesthetic, as discussed by Kanta Kochhar-Lindgren in her work about D/deaf theatre, problematizes sensorial norms. This alternative aesthetic pulls apart societal notions of what it means to hear and reestablishes the body in terms that, at least historically speaking, have only been positioned unfavorably—let alone idealized. The sensorial experience of deafness, therefore, makes space for the visual and kinesthetic aspects of vernacular speech. Deafness, as aesthetic expression, rearticulates silence such that the presence of the body speaks itself into the creation of new spaces. Moving away from mainstream cultural and experiential frames, in sign and in voice, produces dual systems of meaning for the inclusion of different sensorial frames. This shift of perspective is necessary to dispel misapprehensions about what constitutes meaningful communication. An analysis about closed captions and open digital subtitles encourages greater discernment among producers and consumers of new media and helps develop operational practices for listening to dual systems or rather hear the "sound in-between" and, in effect, denote a cross-cultural argot from the temporary meeting place wherein sound and gesture converge (Kochhar-Lindgren). This performative traversing of expression addresses heteroglossic bodies and admits movement to reimagine and recast the voice as speaking and listening in spatial practice, a spectrum of resonance that unconceals spoken *habitus*.

To recast and contest normative perceptions of ordinary social arrangements, such as in the creation and consumption of captioned media, we forward a rhetorical theory of listening across cultures and assert the material role of black cultural performances in the development of technology. Beyond notions of phenotype, African American identity is in part constituted through the linguistic and stylistic features of AAE language. The tonal and rhythmic features of blackness attributed to vocalized speech act as a proxy for race or the auditory equivalent of racial profiling, based on ethnic phenotype. The unspoken *habitus* of whiteness reaches even into the subject-object relations of hearing black-sounding names. Still, African Americans continue giving and receiving linguistically and orthographically unique, all while risking the stigma of being yet further subject to racial discrimination—often with the conscious awareness of such. This form of racism routinely results in a range of discriminatory social practices that impact residential, educational, economic, and medical outcomes, as well as those goods and services made available through emerging online marketplaces such as Airbnb and Uber (Fryer *passim*, Edelman 2). This indexing of whiteness indexes is but another way that racial sign systems enforce social hierarchies and naturalize historical processes. It is a discourse in which black people must negotiate language within a dominant framework of cultural stigmatization.

In this way, AAE encompasses an information design methodology that furthers technical discourses and values the material role of technology in black cultural performances. Resisting assumed patterns of whiteness that inform how race is understood alongside the sonic field is necessary for deciphering racialized mediascapes and demonstrates anew the exigency of topics related to racial power and privilege. As Krista Ratcliffe reminds, "the question of power relations among people enters the conversation about understanding, the political also emerges as a necessary element of rhetorical listening" (31). What mediascapes demand of viewers as they traverse the closed system of whiteness is more than the writing one sees in the black box of closed captions. It dictates which signs matter in that box. This theory, developed through observations of deaf theater, coincides with what we explicitly name as *color deafness*: the routine omission *and insertion* of racially significant sound information (Zdenek). Color deafness is the sum total of habits of production employed by screenwriters, subtitle producers, and closed-caption transcriptionists through the racialized exchange that occurs in the production of video captions and their screen consumption. To break out of this box—to be heard and seen—white accountability is necessary in the making of meaning. The study of color deafness helps decipher what counts as a "clear meaning" and concentrates attention on closed captioners as hidden interlocutors, not easily heard or seen to the untrained ear or eye.

Looking at digital representations of AAE in captioning and subtitles helps us better understand how whiteness interferes with the development and products of assistive technologies, since assumed patterns of whiteness systematize captioning's mediascapes thus informing how race is understood in the first place. What mediascapes demand of viewers as they traverse the closed system of whiteness is more than visual reception of the writing one sees in the black box of closed captions—it requires the kind of rhetorical listening for which Ratcliffe advocates. As Roland Barthes reminds, "the image is not merely the totality of utterances emitted . . . it is also the totality of utterances received" (*I-M-T* 47).

This "screen white-out" is separate from, but not totally unrelated to, linguistic discrimination of black vernacular speech patterns that challenge America's monocultural linguistic framework. African American voice is a type of ethnic identifier and it remains subject to racial discrimination. Understanding how these captioning technologies play an active part in what constitutes the edges of these sonic and imagistic mediascapes actively acknowledges the invaginations of their historically shifting and culturally reciprocal roles and invites both identification with and examination of a type of "screen white-out." It is our contention that all forms of captioning, in one way or another, function as a means to dominate and displace localized linguistic varieties to produce what in effect becomes a typographical palimpsest. This, in our view, becomes most apparent through looking at captions through the lens of AAE. This textual overlay of standardizing and norming black discourses through the act of mooring them into dominant Anglo language resituates "postracial" claims of objectivity in nonhuman rhetorics.

The difficulty of bringing language into action occurs when captioners transcribe language for viewers, whose own language is treated as foreign. Similar to Jacqueline Royster and other scholars of race rhetoric, we question enterprises that "support the [senses and sensations] of rhetoric, composition, and literacy studies as a field of study that embraces the imperative to understand truths and consequences of language more fully" (Royster 29). This study, likewise, calls for a reconsideration of "the beliefs and values which inevitably permit our attitudes and actions in discourse communities . . . to be systematic, even systemic" (30).

Polyschematic Soundscape and Screenwriting Analysis

This case study of select scenes from six episodes of *Breaking Bad* investigates the racialized processes that produce open transcriptions in the form of English-language subtitles and closed captions in line 21 typographic data transmission. Language is one of the media, as Stuart Hall contends, through which thoughts, ideas, and feelings come to represent a particular cultural moment. Representation through captioned language is but one means to gain greater context—either against or in connection with racial meanings (232). Whether such interpretations of captions end up closing off meaning on one end and opening it on another, screen captions index color deafness as but one more regime of racial representation. Indeed, the veracity of his analysis of media fragmentation and incompleteness encompasses the range of digital storytelling formats. Nowhere is this idea more true than in the case of screen captioning. Captioning speaks to the order of arrangement. Form and meaning in language with their root in rhetoric and linguistics are not to be found in the image alone. Rhetoric and linguistics are purposely coupled in polyschematic soundscape analysis to hear and explicitly uncover multiple strata within the vertical and horizontal plane of unspoken, and therefore hinted-at, language. While rare in the fixed image, this relay text becomes very important in film, where dialogue functions not simply as elucidation but really does advance action by setting forth meaning in the sequence of messages.

To make the sound in-between both visible and tangible, we document digital videos as a space where one encounters marginalized and dominant linguistic varieties within multimedia contexts (figure 15.1). To understand the multimedia contexts relevant to this study, it is necessary first to understand the nexus of captioning. The act of visually hearing language points out an engagement with the underlying (second order) mask of the screen. It is fundamental to this work that we disaggregate the various sorts of assistive captions in order to eliminate vague or overly generalized terms as they circulate in lay discourse. There are six different types of assistive captions for which we have developed a taxonomy or schema to track our analysis of screen captions. They are: *(1)* closed captions; *(2)* open permanent; *(3)* open digital; *(4)* online streaming; *(5)* voice recognition; and *(6)* user embedded.

The first type, commonly referred to as closed captions, is alternately referred to as *line 21 data*. This type of captioning is broadcast on a signal set aside by the FCC in 1970 for conveying transcriptions of dialogue, sound effects, musical cues, and other audio information to make sounds accessible to deaf or hard-of-hearing viewers. Line 21 captions are typically used in public accommodations, such as noisy restaurants or sports bars. They make audio information available when the television is on mute or cannot be heard in loud environments. The second type of assistive captions, hereafter referred to as *open permanent*, is a form of screen subtitles used for language translation. They are always visible and written for audiences that are likely to encounter spoken content as a foreign language. They are different from the closed variety in that their sole use is to translate foreign language dialogue or otherwise potentially incomprehensible speech content for viewing audiences. The third type of screen captions in this schema is *open digital*. Similarly, they make foreign languages comprehensible, while also allowing for more than one language translation option. For example, they allow viewers to understand dialogue in Spanish, French, or English—regardless of the language of spoken content. The impermanence of open digital captions, unlike that of open permanent subtitles seen in foreign cinema, is available through DVD technology and can be activated by remote control interface.

The final two forms of screen captions are also innovations brought about by the prevalence of digital video. While the fifth type of captions can also be selected via viewer interface, *online streaming*, as the name implies, is accessed through the on-off switch that is provided in online streaming platforms such as Hulu, Netflix, and AMC.com. *Open digital* and *online streaming* are digital forms of captioning that can be used as substitutions for

Figure 15.1

Nonspeech information about ambient music, featuring a hip-hop song playing in the background during Bryan Cranston's performance, as viewed through digital open captions (DVR or DVD subtitles).

Online streaming captions as viewed on an iTunes app.

Line 21 data–transmitted closed captions.

HDTV-modified captions of *line 21 data*, which allows the viewer to change the style (color, size, and typeface) of transcribed speech.

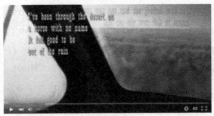

User-embedded captions of "Horse with No Name" lyrics uploaded as animated musical subtitles as created by YouTube subscriber channel account holder.

YouTube voice-recognition captions generating speech-to-text information to transcribe "Yeah, this is gonna help big time with that, BITCH!" into heavily garbled speech information for users in this fan subscriber's video montage.

closed captioning, although the quality of spoken dialogue and availability of narrative elements presented as NSI differs widely—depending upon the program, provider, or platform of delivery. The fifth type of screen captioning is paradoxically the most overlooked and yet ubiquitous within this schema. Readily accessed by most anyone with a smartphone, *voice-recognition* captions encode vocalized speech into text for visual reception. With widespread applications for mainstream use, voice recognition is an assistive technology that is especially popular in "speech-to-text" short messaging service text applications and for initiating smart device command functions because of how it enables hands-free language dictation. Additionally, voice-recognition captions are also seeing a steep uptick in usage by deaf and hard-of-hearing people utilizing mobile phone apps such as *Transcense* to decipher multi-voice contexts like meetings and conversations in restaurant settings. The sixth and final type of captioning is *user-embedded* captions or "prosumer" text annotations. *User-embedded* captions is the go-to captioning method for social media users who want to produce online video content. This type of captioning is most frequently added to videos uploaded by media users, especially in content developed for YouTube video blogging (or vlogging) channels. Open permanent, voice recognition, and user embedded are largely peripheral to this discussion. However, it should be noted that voice recognition may overlap with closed caption and is permitted for use as an alternative to the traditional technique of human transcribing of line 21 data captioning. This polyschematic rhetorical analysis compares *line 21 data* transmission of closed captions with *open and streaming* screen captions across new media. Our emphasis contrasts differences between the former technology and latter forms of digital screen captioning.

In the most basic sense, *line 21 data* captioning is a technology charged with the task of transcribing into text spoken dialogue and certain audible cues from media soundtracks. Each type of audio presents different amounts and types of visual information to audiences, as Zdenek points out ("More than Mere"). And, given the proliferation of computer-based media and the Twenty-First Century Communications and Video Accessibility Act of 2010, captioning is a technology that enables the viewing of the auditory dialogue in online streaming of media broadcasts. Charged with a similar task, *open-permanent* and *open-digital* subtitle captions provide textual interpretations of audible dialogue. Due to their original use, which is to translate foreign films into the target language of the audience, subtitles do not normally provide viewers with nonspeech content such as ringing telephones. Open-digital subtitle captions are also most often rendered in yellow or white text with no visible border, unlike the white text enclosed in a black box in ordinary line 21 data transmission.

Although it is usually assumed that closed, open, and streaming captions provide identical information to users, upon closer inspection we observe color deafness in action when we compare the video captions of *line 21 data* with that of *open digital* and *online streaming*. The presentation of the same sound information, within the same episodes of *Breaking Bad*—and almost all shows for that matter—will invariably be captioned differently across various media platforms, regardless of the broadcast technology or recording method. The linking of sound, image, and text has always been of primary concern regarding captioning and subtitles in their various forms. Both the production and broadcasting of them must contend with the constraints of time and space. Indeed, until recently screen captions had been held captive. However, due to changes in viewing behavior facilitated by DVR and DVD, viewers have gained unprecedented levels of control over the experience of viewing screen captions. Remote control is as much an idea as it is an object of technology that allows viewers to take in partial snippets (Tryon 25). Fragmentation and incompleteness inherent to viewers' interactions and experiences with new media are valuable to our discussion. Concepts of interactivity, consumer choice, and time-freedom are expanded in digital media. Among the host of preferences enabled through remote control technology is the activation of *line 21 data*, and *open-permanent* subtitles. The command over options for language, timing, and the speed by which one can stop and analyze captioned texts through discs and online streams can empower viewers to open up alternative readings. The fact that viewers may enable line 21 data for the reading of closed captions or, depending upon the platform, digitally activate or stream captions is an issue rarely thought of in terms of having a racial dimension.

With the advent of DVD and DVR—media platforms that enable the ability to turn on subtitles for films, whether foreign or domestic; and more importantly media that enables more control over time spent consuming video content—allows viewers control over the ability to pause, fast-forward, and rewind during any given episode. This new ability is in direct contrast to the more closed structures provided to viewers of older generations of subtitle and caption technology. Traditionally "the reader cannot stop and dwell on an interesting line; as the reader scans the text, the machine instantly obliterates it" (qtd. in Downey 50). Now viewers have the ability to replay and, more importantly, linger over certain scenes and the accompanying captions.

White Writing as Color Deafness

A crucial function of whiteness is its capacities for gatekeeping. Our contention about what information gets to be sent and the quality by which it is received must be approached with an ethos of cultural reciprocity. With this new capacity, the ability to capture what is said and frame the scene accurately becomes increasingly more important, especially since whiteness tends to operate at this behind-the-scenes level of invisibility. Indeed, the racialized implications forwarded by screen captioning become all the more apparent as blatant examples of mistranslation and deletion of pertinent information are more easily detected. Since the viewer of *open-digital* subtitles or *line 21 data* captions must depend on transcriptionists for the recognition of important racial signifiers, content ought to be culturally and linguistically accurate. Sean Zdenek, argues as much, since "captions must not be responsive to the objective qualities of sound but to the contexts in which sounds occur," and suggests the need for more rhetorically informed captioning practices ("Which Sounds," par. 8). This chapter reads the accumulation of meanings produced through captions in context with the repertoire of racial imagery expressed through spoken and NSI to inform this critique of audism as a form of racial hegemony. This is to say, all screen captions must be produced with better bi-dialectal proficiency, in whichever platform they appear. The result of such engagement is the discernment and identification of specific instances in which whiteness interferes with sincere, mutually respectful dialogues across cultural settings.

While the plausibility of *Breaking Bad* rests heavily on the narrative trajectory of whiteness as it is presented across the pilot episode all the way up to the series denouement, proof of whiteness's linguistic properties is typographically detailed through the creation and development of scripted dialogue all the way through to the production and transcriptioning screen captions. Other treatments of postracial politics in media and film, however, deal more generally with the positionalities of whiteness and African American ways of knowing and experiencing; our argument focuses the influence of whiteness as the eradication of meaning in the development and transmission of captions and subtitles. The racialized perspective of screenwriters and transcriptionists presents viewers with a narrative structure steeped in whiteness that "never has to speak its name" (Lipsitz 67). This discussion of whiteness recognizes how *line 21 data* transmission of closed captions and the digital activation of *open-digital* subtitles superimposed over narratives are illustrated in the following scene.

Walter White is presented with the opportunity to become the top king-pin in the methamphetamine drug trade of the Southwest. Walter meets with his competition and attempts to negotiate a deal between himself and the other party. This confrontation with Walter's antagonist occurs in the "Say My Name" episode, directed by Thomas Schnauz and takes place in the wake of Gus Fring's assassination:

> *(Opposite)* Who the hell are you?
>
> *(WW)* You know
>
> *(WW)* You all know exactly who I am
>
> *(WW)* Say my name
>
> *(Opposite)* Do what? I don't . . .
>
> *(Opposite)* I don't have a damn clue who the hell you are.
>
> *(WW)* Yeah, you do. I'm the cook.
>
> *(WW)* I'm the man who killed Gus Fring
>
> *(Opposite)* Bullsaaa.
>
> *(Opposite)* Cartel got Fring.
>
> *(WW)* Are you sure?
>
> *(WW)* That's right.
>
> *(WW)* Now, say my name.
>
> *(Opposite)* Heisenberg

What is first apparent is the misspelling of "bullshit" as *bullsaaa*, which occurs in the *open-digital* subtitles. This instance of lost meaning due to misspelling marks the major problem in screen captioning having to do with the differential quality of *open-digital* subtitles and *line 21 data* captions. Even though some lexical items such as double negatives, dropped "g" pronunciations, and the word "bullshit" are properly captioned in *line 21 data*, significant mistakes are made in *open digital*. Aside from this error not occurring in the *line 21 data* captioned scene, the above exchange demonstrates how so much of the plotline depends on Walter White's alias. With the name Heisenberg, Walt demonstrates the power of whiteness as it lies in the chirality of his identity and plays out through the acceptance of his opposite/sameness with Heisenberg. Walt's alter ego not only takes for granted the routine affordances of ordinary white privilege, but rather unleashes a blatant alignment with an organized crime syndicate of white supremacists. In contrast, Walt's identity up to this point also closely aligns with and ultimately encompasses, through strategic allusions, the persona of Walt Whitman: the influential poet of the twentieth century known for his epic poem, *Leaves of Grass*, about the Americanized everyman. Through these two alignments of the Walter White character's identity of Heisenberg and Walt Whitman, over the course of five seasons and across sixty-two episodes, the antihero is developed as a stand-in for the suburban everyman, a canonized stock figure that is representative of unspoken masculine white agency. Walter ironically acts as a postracial signifier that is predicated on the belief that race and racism no longer play a significant role in American life.

This is so because of the construction of the narratological whiteness of the Walter White character. Viewers (and, perhaps, the entire show's cast and crew for that matter) are led to believe that Walt's ethnic status as an Anglo Caucasian male living in Albuquerque, New Mexico, is merely incidental. The dramatic progression of the character's relentless grab for white masculine privilege is, at least on the surface, treated as though race is no more than a piffling sidebar. The implication is that the racial, cultural, and language background of Walter, and indeed all the characters, has no bearing on the subject whatsoever. Treating Walter White's whiteness as though it is completely ancillary to the show and utterly without consequence is what makes the show possible, since it positions Walter's race as a nonfactor. This underpinning logic runs throughout the entire series. That is, until the moment in which Walt's ethnic status and ideological bearings are made explicitly clear when he requests, in the final season, that an opposite character say his name: Heisenberg. Walt's demand that his competitor say his name reifies his whiteness, which, ordinarily, never has to be spoken. In demanding this, Walter White underscores, without shame or guilt, his whiteness.

It may be suggested that Walt's racial identity is a by-product of color-blind casting and that head writer and series creator Vince Gilligan only practiced due diligence in finding the best actors for the job. In support of this idea of racially neutral casting, one may simply point to the veritable racial spectrum of supporting characters as evidence, to say nothing of employing Giancarlo Esposito (known as character Gus Fring) in the role of a Chilean national and Walt White's chief antagonist.[2]

As Vorris Nunley makes clear, claims of color blindness are apt to yield any combination of social and political outcomes. As a postracial rhetoric, color-blind casting may denote racially progressive hiring practices aimed at diversifying the field of on-screen talent and promoting positive representations of primary characters in resistance to racial typecasting and defiance of negative stereotypes. On the other hand, color-blind casting may equally denote behind-the-scenes decisions that seek to depoliticize racially charged content through the erasure of nonwhite images, experiences, and opinions. This latter denotation of color blindness especially holds true whenever whiteness is allowed a "rhetorical escape by the de-voicing/silencing of African American rhetoric" (Nunley 341) through the faulty and inaccurate transmission of spoken and musical content by screen captioners that take for granted the white privilege of "standard" English speech production.

Authentic Hip-Hop and Token AAE

Jan T. Hill and Geneva Smitherman's appraisals of white youth who identify with hip-hop and rap are pertinent to our readings of transcribed sound information, since the plotline of *Breaking Bad* revolves around the illegal methamphetamine drug trade and features a number of primary characters that might be labeled "wiggers," most notably that of Jesse Pinkman as portrayed by actor Aaron Paul. Whereas Hill's concerns about linguistic marginalization are shared with Smitherman's warnings about white AAE crossover, the two differ on wiggers' sincerity of usage. Smitherman denotes the idea of wigger by offering little value judgment about its connotations with whiteness (*Black Talk* 237). Conversely Hill laments "wiggerisms" associated with "moth-eaten tokens of minstrelsy" and finds their use of AAE crossover akin to a covert racist discourse. Mary Bucholtz and Quiana Lopez build upon this idea of Hollywood wigger role performance as linguistic minstrelsy (685). Bucholtz and Lopez believe such manifestations of this whiteness archetype perform a complex form of neominstrelsy "whose race and class privilege renders him ludicrously inauthentic as a participant in hip hop" (682). Minstrel performances of black hipness by white actors, in the words of David Roediger, implicate the notion of the wigger when he reminds us that "race has been a source of drama, contestation, and tragedy not only for the minority of 'nonwhites' but also for the white majority" (664). As evidenced by the racial subplot of *Breaking Bad*, the tragic consequences of white privilege and racism are often lost when AAE is commodified as entertainment.

Crossover AAE is the stuff catchphrases are made of, especially when going viral. The Jesse Pinkman character popularized a style of outgoing voice message announcement recording where a white actor, playing a white drug dealer, imitates the affectations of a black hip-hopper, albeit superficially, with "*YO! YO! YO! ONE FOUR EIGHT THREE to the THREE to the SIX to the NINE!*

Representing the ABQ. What up BI-OTCH? Leave it at the tone [beep]" ("Cat's in the Bag . . .").[3] Imitating an inauthentic version of trendy hip-hop slang, Pinkman's voicemail announcement communicates what Kembrew McLeod terms the social-locational as a semantic dimension of hip-hop authenticity (139). This type of commercial mainstreaming of hip-hop language and AAE renders a superficially structured mocking of hip-hop's emphasis on claims of being from the "streets" that refers to a particularly conscious demonstration of "keeping it real" through the personal association and identification with certain regionally located communities as indicated by the international airport code for Albuquerque, New Mexico. Additionally, the character's voicemail message exhibits a number of other features common in token AAE and hip-hop AAE, including the metaplasmic insertions "to the" applied to space out the first few digits of the phone number, along with the repetitive use of the slang word "yo" as an exclamatory greeting and generalized linguistic filler, a copula deletion in the phrase, "what up," followed by the semantic morphology of bitch to *"bi-otch"* as a gender-neutral pronominal ironically connoting a relationship between equals. This fictionalized voicemail message constructs for the audience an understanding of Jesse Pinkman's identity as a wigger that is meant to highlight Walt's transgression from normative cultural codes. The superficiality of the character's AAE is easily captured in the *line 21 data* captions. However, transcriptions of African American language are far less accurate in scenes featuring dialogue with authentic AAE speakers.

The African American actor and stand-up comic Lavell Crawford represents this case in point in his performance in which he plays the role of recurring character Huell Babineaux in a scene from the third-to-last episode of the series (Gilligan "To'hajiilee"). Mistakes in captioning dialogue happen in *line 21 data* transmission of closed captions as well as in *open digital* and *online streaming*. Certain morphological elements in the misrepresentation of verbs superimpose incorrect corrections of Huell's spoken language,[4] such that "ain't" is captioned as "didn't" and "gone" is transcribed into "gonna." Oppositely, *line 21 data* captioning of the scene reveals the privileging of white speech as demonstrated by the perfectly rendered transcription of the scene's opposite character, Hank Schrader.

Much can also be made of the racially coded uses of Spanish in the series—based on everything from the title of several episodes to the *open-digital* subtitles captioning almost the entirety of one whole episode performed almost completely in Spanish. Jane H. Hill's discussion of whiteness and the usage of Mock Spanish in regards to the racialization of public space is most useful to this part of our discussion. Because the action of *Breaking Bad* is set in Albuquerque, New Mexico, Hill's concerns about AAE language crossover into the popular mainstream is shared by us. Through the semiotics of orthographically and grammatically incorrect mispronunciations, a parodic style of "hyperanglicized" stock phrases, authentic Spanish words are taken out of their original context in order to send indirect racial messages without having to explicitly refer to race itself as a particular discursive category (Hill 682). According to Hill, Mock Spanish is a covert racist discourse designed to index and stereotype the nonwhite ethnicity of historically Spanish-speaking populations for the "elevation of Whiteness" and denigration of people of color (683).

By extending the ideas of these interlocutors to our analysis of *open-digital* and *line 21 data* screen captions, we notice how whiteness obscures meaning for groups that are traditionally thought to be unaffected by white privilege. These issues certainly converge in our analysis as well. A clear example takes place in another episode of the show through which the screenplay narration is handled through a telephone voice message. Only this time, instead of the captions being a recording of an outgoing message, the transcribed scene is a spoken monologue of a character leaving a voicemail message. The captions display the protagonist's sister-in-law, Marie Schrader, inviting Walt and his wife out to a Chinese restaurant for dinner. The *line 21 data* and *open-digital* captions read, "Me and So, let me know if you guys wanna hang. Listen to me!: 'Hang,'—Walt Junior would be proud. I know the lingo. I'm still hip" ("Seven Thirty-Seven"). The character continues her one-sided voicemail message conversation and wonders if people in China ever crave little take-out boxes filled with mashed potatoes and meatloaf while trying to figure out how to use knives and forks.

Music as "White Noise"

The manner by which musical expressions are and *are not* communicated is vital to understanding the abilities and limits of captions for the conveyance of emotions. Aspects outside of dialog convey sentiment and mood, providing important context that, if missed, can disrupt the meaning and flow of the program because sound plays an important role in providing emotion in film. When the sound is not captioned, the meaning of the content being shown could be misinterpreted or misunderstood. The sonic overlay of musical content—whether to provide texture for a musical score, a soundtrack montage, or ambient background sounds—demonstrates a palimpsest of white writing that is more nuanced. Besides the captioned content—watched on DVR equipment or recorded from television—the scripted scene delivers a flagrant racial commentary about "ethnic" cuisine and white appropriations of slang terms. The scene's lack of NSI about a smooth jazz recording, transcribed onscreen as "[*soft instrumental music playing on car stereo*]," first in the kitchen and then in the car, also points to a common practice of how white captions close off cultural meanings. Although this particular instance of NSI is accurately included with *online-streaming* captions when watched on Netflix, viewers who rely on captions to view the show through cable broadcast and DVR playback will be unable to read a transcription about smooth jazz playing in the background. The notion that smooth jazz is so smooth as to represent no sound at all strips the social meaning of whiteness as being substantively neutral and without cultural resonance.

The significance of the musical note being omitted can say much about which sounds matter in the white writing of screen captions. *Breaking Bad* scenes that involve the ambient musical sound of rap recordings are described as "indecipherable rap music" with no attempt on interpreting repeated lyrics or chorus phrases—even when the song is fairly well known.[5] Frequently musical content is represented in the form of "♪" or musical notes. At best, the absence of this sign can imply that transcriptionists may not actually care enough about African American and black musical expressions to bother with accurate descriptions of it. Interpreted less charitably, one could make the argument that transcriptionists are engaged in the out-and-out refusal to acknowledge rap as a legitimate musical form. Returning to Sean Zdenek's argument about captioning style guides, our point about the individual agency of captioners' choices about representing musical content is made: "Even when they make or imply a distinction between significant and insignificant sounds, they do not provide criteria for distinguishing the former from the latter. Sometimes such a distinction is easy to make. At other times, the captioner must decide which sounds are significant and which are not" ("More than Mere" par. 37). What Zdenek seems to indicate about the decision-making process of transcriptionists is that the design of captions is a rhetorically informed undertaking that necessarily involves social and cultural value judgments, not to mention spatial considerations about what is practical given the constraints of cognitive load required for viewing the panorama of information provided by the image-word-sound ratio. In other words, some NSI captions displayed on the screen appear at the expense of other nonspeech sound information that may constitute potentially vital cultural details.

This is *not* to say that white captioners (or captioners of any other color, for that matter) actively engage in acts of racialized censorship; however, our suggestion does raise questions related to whiteness as an exercise in gatekeeping. Because whiteness impacts the rhetorical decisions concerning what information may be accessed by captions users, scenes with instrumental music not containing lyrics—especially in musical montage scenes in which the music is the message—strongly suggests that the writing process undertaken by captioners is racially informed, thereby producing a colorless writing.

Even though reggae music is not distinctly and exclusively coded to African American cultural expressions, the Jamaican genre of music is specifically associated with blackness. A reggae montage occurs in the second episode of the first season ("Cat's in the Bag . . ."). Walt attempts to obscure the source of his newfound involvement with the methamphetamine trade and deflect being questioned by his wife about his recent habit of socializing with wiggers. Therefore, he decides to smoke a marijuana joint, allowing the odor to linger for his wife's olfactory perception. This scene is represented as musical notes or "♪" in cable broadcast and DVR *line 21 data* captions, as well as in *open-digital* and *online-streaming* captions. Insofar as stereotypical references to this aspect of Afro-Caribbean culture are popularly linked to stereotypical images of ganja-smoking, dreadlocked Rastafarians, the reggae montage of Walter smoking marijuana exemplifies how whiteness operates as a technical conceit in caption production. This scene gives substance to our assertions about the need for captioners to take a bi-dialectal approach to the transmission of spoken and nonspoken transcriptions regardless of the speaking style assigned to racialized characters. This problem is complicated by the lack of policy regulations available to guide captioners in determining how to best frame word-image-sound information. In contrast, for ambient music featuring song recordings of classic rock, every lyric is transcribed, providing explicit detail replete with musical notes.[6] This phenomenon occurs in the depiction of *open-digital* subtitles, as well as *line 21 data* closed captions.

White Writing (Still a Closed Case?)

If color blindness is the dominant posture of the postracial era, then color deafness is the racialized affect of screen captioning. The verbal transcripts of captioning pronounce a desire to connect with the dominant utterances of the hearing world as much as they do the hegemonic vernaculars of white English. The design of captions often functions as a form of white gatekeeping when the conveyance of sonic information is regarded as universally ideal, straightforward communication that adheres to the linguistic conventions of white American Anglo culture. The model of *clear* and *direct* representation of speech in place of verbal performances of speech remains an assumptive default for caption design. This presumption about how captions are designed runs parallel to notions about the neutrality of whiteness. As noted in the introduction, it is important to recognize design of all kinds as social manifestations of material values laden with ideological and political content. This collective judgment about whiteness's tyranny of unacknowledged habits is to recognize its detrimental effects as diffuse, indirect, and frequently unintentional. The outcomes of interpersonal and symbolic racism in the cultural context of social institutions and public accommodations effectively translate into actual and substantive proof of the intention to discriminate.

This troubled process of "meaning," therefore, takes on static implications—even within this sentence, a rhetorical plate tectonics ultimately stems back to the shifting notion of ordered meaning as it interrogates our assumptions about the spoken and written word. If information is designed in a particular sequence, should it necessarily be read in an orderly fashion? How does the disorderly style of screen captions speak to racial formations as prearranged meaning? How might we rewrite or reread the words in the box, to speak them into a newly conscious, cinematic endeavor of style dispersion, one without end or complete sentences but perhaps only fragments of understanding? While there are literal fixed moments of text, as captions, in all their rigidity—the addition or omission of multiple characters or symbols—opens up choice, freedom and options for rhizomatic shifting (Deleuze and Guattari).

Notes

1. The D/deaf designation derives from a complex history that defines the D/deaf community. Deaf designated with a capital "D" refers to those individuals who identify with and believe that deafness signifies a culture defined not by a lack of ability to hear but by a unique disposition and cultural practices or rituals. Manual communication is often the primary language used by those who identify as Deaf. On the other hand, deaf as designated by a lowercase "d" is associated with the medical community's label applied to those who have a severe to profound hearing loss. Such a label signifies a lack or rather a disability and situates a deaf individual in negative contrast to those individuals

who have the ability to hear. Those who identify as deaf may or may not use manual communication and may or may not identify with and participate in Deaf culture.

2. Esposito is best known for playing iconic African American characters in the Spike Lee films *School Daze* and *Do the Right Thing*.

3. Since Jesse Pinkman's outgoing answering machine announcement technically constitutes NSI content that moves across scenes, captions are carried over and represented as italicized text within brackets.

4. HANK: Huell Babineaux. Know who I am? I'll take that as a yes. Uh, thanks for your patience. Un, as, un, agent Gomez said, you're not under arrest.

   HUELL: Why am I here?

   HANK: Well, you're here, un, for your own protection, sir.

   HUELL: How you figure that? *copula deletion

   HANK: Well, we both know how dangerous my brother-in-law can be. Nice poker face. Look, un, relax. There's not much new you can tell me about Walter White. Multiple murders, un, ties to a white power prison gang, ran the largest meth racket in the entire southwest. I'm not asking, you're not answering. Whoop-de-doo. Let's cut to the chase. You have a wire on Walt's phone. We intercepted a call between him and a certain Saul Goodman, Esquire. You know, your employer. Anyway, in the call, un, Walt said that he was going to, quote, "take care of one Jesse Pinkman," unquote. And that you were next on the hit list. That's why you're here.

   HUELL: Bullshit. That don't make no sense. *copula deletion

   HANK: We got the recording. I can—I can let you hear it. Your associate. Goodman's fixer. What's his name?

   GOMEZ: Some carrot top name Patrick Kuby. Boston PD ran him out of Beantown a few years back. Came out here for the sunshine.

   HANK: Yeah, Walt says he's gonna do that Kuby guy the same way he does you. In fact, Kuby's already missing. Sorry to say things aren't looking good for your redheaded buddy. Believe us, don't believe us. Suit yourself. Whatever you do I would not call Goodman. He sold you down the river big-time.

   HUELL: what you talkin' about?

GOMEZ: I wouldn't take it personally. Goodman's next on the chopping block if he doesn't do what Walt says. And to be fair, your, un, circus clown of a boss did try to spare you for all of, what, about 15 seconds [chuckles] before he decided to have Walt track you down. You see, Goodman's got a trace on your phone and as soon as you call him, Walt's gonna find out where you're hiding out, then it's just a matter of time before you end up like this. *show cell phone pic*

HUELL: [scoffs] oh, man. Oh, man. I swear to god, i didn't [ain't] know he was gonna [gone] kill the man . . . I didn't [ain't*] know he was gonna [gone] kill him. I didn't [ain't] know.

HANK: If we thought you did you'd be in lockup for conspiracy to commit murder instead of here, under our protection. So just tell us everything you know about White so we can get him before he gets you.

HUELL: why would he wanna kill me? I ain't do nothin' to him.

HANK: Who knows with this guy? From what he said to Goodman, it may have something to do with him trying to tie up loose ends regarding his poisoning and some kid named Brock. Or maybe it's 'cause you know where his money is.

HUELL: Well you ain't listening to people in the know. Me and Kuby rented a van for the dude. Loaded his cash up in a self-storage unit, handed over the keys to him at Goodman's and who knows where he took it from there.

HANK: a van, huh? How much money we talking?

HUELL: Seven barrels' worth.

HANK: When you—you say "barrels," you mean barrel barrels.

HUELL: Barrels, man. You know, plastic, black 55-gallon type. I got 'em at Home Depot. Filled up every last damn one of 'em too.

HANK: And, un, where did you rent the van?

HUELL: Lariat. The one on Candelaria and Monroe.

HANK: Lariat on Candelaria. Kuby rented the van.

HUELL: Mr. White dropped it off. He had us wash it before Kuby took it back.

HANK: Wash a rental. Why?

HUELL: It was filthy, man, like he had went off road with it. After we had hosed it down he grabbed a shovel out the back. Handed over the key and that was it. That's all I know.

HANK: Alright, un, Mr. Babineaux, Agent Gomez and I are going to, un, do everything we can to find this son of a bitch. Meantime, like I said, you're free to go. But if I were you, I wouldn't take one step out that door.

GOMEZ: Right and remember, no phone calls.

HANK: Oh, almost forgot. Un, I took the liberty of removing the battery so don't put that back in. Agent Van Oster will stay here with you. You're in good hands. He's our best man with a gun. Un, however, don't discuss the case with him because the less you distract him the better he can protect you.

HUELL: How long you gonna [gone*] be?

HANK: As long as it takes to keep you safe.

5. Although "Dirty South Hustla" by Carolina Slim chorus lyrics are not captioned, they can be heard clearly in the pilot episode of *Breaking Bad*:

I'm from da dirty dirty
We 'bout da money money
Betta watch yo game playa
Cuz we pimpin Cutty buddies
I'm a down souf hustla (an' I'm so fly)
Wid down south customers (they wanna buy!)

6. "Horse with No Name" by America plays on car radio with fully captioned lyrics.

Works Cited

Barthes, Roland. *Image-Music-Text*. Trans. Stephen Heath. 1977. New York: Hill and Wang, 1994. Print.

———. *Writing Degree Zero*. Trans. Annette Levers and Colin Smith. 1968. New York: Hill and Wang, 1985. Print.

Bucholtz, Mary, and Quiana Lopez. "Performing Blackness, Forming Whiteness: Linguistic Minstrelsy in Hollywood Film." *Journal of Sociolinguistics* 15.5 (2011): 680–706. *JSTOR*. Web. 15 Oct. 2011.

"Caballo Si Nombre." *Breaking Bad*. Writ. Peter Gould. Dir. Adam Bernstein. AMC. DirecTV, Charlotte, 2 Oct. 2013. Cable Broadcast.

"Cat's in the Bag . . ." *Breaking Bad*. Writ. Vince Gilligan. Dir. Adam Bernstein. AMC. DirecTV, Charlotte, 2 Oct. 2013. Cable Broadcast.

Deleuze, Gilles and Fèlix Guattari. *On the Line*. Trans. John Johnston. 1983. New York: Semiotext(e). Print.

Downey, Gregory J. *Closed Captioning: Subtitles, Stenography, and the Digital Conversion of Text with Television*. Baltimore: Johns Hopkins UP, 2008. Print.

Edelman, Benjamin, and Michael Luca. "Digital Discrimination: The Case of Airbnb.com." *Harvard Business School Working* Paper 14.54 (2014): *Social Science Research Network*. Web. 25 Nov. 2015.

Fryer, Roland G., Jr., and Steven D. Levitt. "The Causes and Consequences of Distinctively Black Names." *Quarterly Journal of Economics* (2004): 767–805. Web. 12. Mar. 2015.

Hall, Stuart. "The Spectacle of the Other." *Representation: Cultural Representations and Signifying Practices*. Ed. Stuart Hall. London: Sage, 1997. Print.

Hill, Jan H. "Language, Race, and White Public Space." *American Anthropologist* 100 (1998): 680–89. *JSTOR*. Web. 2 Sept. 2013.

Kochhar-Lindgren, Kanta. "Hearing Differences across Theatres: Experiments, Disability, and Performance." *Theatre Journal* 58.3 (2006): 417–36. Print.

Lipsitz, George. "The Possessive Investment in Whiteness." *White Privilege: Essential Readings on the Other Side of Racism*. 2nd ed. New York: Worth Publishers. 2005. Print.

McLeod, Kembrew. "Authenticity within Hip-Hop and Other Cultures Threatened with Assimilation." *Journal of Communication* 49 (1999): 134–50. Print.

Nunley, Vorris L. "*Crash*: Rhetorically Wrecking Discourses of Race, Tolerance, and White Privilege." *College English* 69 (2007): 335–46. *JSTOR*. Web. 12 Aug. 2013.

"Ozymandias." *Breaking Bad*. Writ. Rian Johnson. Dir. Moira Walley-Becket. AMC. DirecTV, Charlotte, 2 Oct. 2013. Cable Broadcast.

"Pilot." *Breaking Bad*. Writ. and dir. Vince Gilligan. AMC. DirecTV, Charlotte, 27 Sept. 2013. Cable Broadcast.

Ratcliffe, Krista. *Rhetorical Listening: Identification, Gender, Whiteness*. Carbondale: Southern Illinois UP, 2005. Print.

Roediger, David. "Guineas, Wiggers, and the Dramas of Racialized Character." *American Literary History* (1995): 654–68. *JSTOR*. 12 Feb. 2012.

Royster, Jacqueline Jones. "When the First Voice You Hear Is Not Your Own." *CCC* 47 (1996): 29–40. Print.

"Say My Name." *Breaking Bad*. Writ. and dir. Thomas Schnauz. AMC. DirecTV, Charlotte, 27 Sept. 2013. Cable Broadcast.

"Seven Thirty-Seven." *Breaking Bad*. Writ. J. Roberts. Dir. Bryan Cranston. AMC. DirecTV, Charlotte, 27 Sept. 2013. Cable Broadcast.

Smitherman, Geneva. *Black Talk: Words and Phrases from the Hood to the Amen Corner*. New York: Houghton Mifflin, 2000. Print.

———. *Talkin That Talk: African American Language and Culture*. New York: Routledge, 2000. Print.

Thomson, Rosemary Garland. "Introduction." *Freakery: Cultural Spectacles of the Extraordinary Body*. Ed. Rosemary Garland Thomson. New York: New York UP, 1996. Print

Tryon, Chuck. *Reinventing Cinema: Movies in the Age of Digital Convergence*. Piscataway, NJ: Rutgers UP, 2009. Print.

Zdenek, Sean. "More Than Mere Transcription: Closed Captioning as an Artful Practice User Experience Magazine." *User Experience Magazine*. 13 Mar. 2014. Web. 9 Jan. 2016.

———. "Which Sounds Are Significant? Toward a Rhetoric of Closed Captioning." *Disabilities Studies Quarterly* 31 (2011). Ohio State University Libraries Knowledge Bank. Web. 23 Feb. 2012.

16

WHITENESS AS ANTIDIALOGICAL

Ronald A. Kuykendall

AN IMPLICIT COMMITMENT of whiteness studies scholarship is antiracism and racial justice, but it is also the initiation of meaningful dialogue through the exploration of how whiteness as a racialized identity reinforces, perpetuates, and maintains white privilege and the effects of that privilege, such as white hegemony and white supremacy. However, whiteness studies' scholarship, although important for fighting racism, is insufficient to transform the normative practices of whiteness and the social structures that reproduce white privilege, white hegemony, and white supremacy, or, in other words, to get rid of whiteness. Part of the reason for this problem is because the inverted ethics of whiteness, which assumes rightness and hence normality, makes discussion difficult, if not impossible, since the logic of whiteness is antidialogical. Whiteness, because it is predicated on the power to grant recognition and legitimacy, exercises the right to impose meaning, objectives, and worldview on the racialized other and so makes the issue of race undiscussable. And this is part of the logic of whiteness; in the concrete situation of racism, antidialogue is not only necessary to the racist but is also indispensable to the preservation of whiteness. Therefore, to demonstrate whiteness as antidialogical, I will proceed to first reveal the logic of whiteness, then explain its inverted ethics, next define and discuss the effects of antidialogism, and finally argue the insufficiency of whiteness studies to eradicate whiteness. Throughout the chapter I will utilize the African

American experience as the primary example to exhibit the antidialogical nature of whiteness because this experience is more historically conspicuous.

The Logic of Whiteness

When you think about the logic of whiteness, that is, the reasoning upon which whiteness is predicated, what stands out is the justification on which whiteness rests: *innocence*. As described by Albert Memmi, the establishment of difference leads to the designation of inferior and superior and thus inequality and domination founded on the delegitimation of those categorized as inferior (40–41). Consequently, this mechanism is at work in racism, which Memmi describes as a behavior that is also a discourse that accuses, self-exonerates, and justifies aggressive hostility (52–53). In fact, Memmi asserts that racism is a predatory behavior that mythically reconstructs the other (the prey) and so serves as an alibi for the imposition of oppression (55). And that oppression, Memmi explains, erodes the personhood of the oppressed through torment, harassment, humiliation, and self-destruction and ultimately the *interiorization* of racist denigration that is nothing more than "the ingestion of a poison that eats away from the inside, and whose end is the victim's wholehearted adoption of the imposed image. How is one to defend oneself if one is driven into agreement with one's persecutor" (57)? Thus, as reasoned by Memmi, "racism is a form of charging the oppressed for the crimes, whether actual or potential, of the oppressor" (57), and as discourse racism is "a defense mechanism and an alibi, . . . a structure of aggression that claims, and is given, a presupposed rationality. This pretense is the sign of its cunning and its false assertion of its own humanity" (160).

The logic of racism, as explained by Memmi, is used by Steve Martinot to express the correlation between racism, whiteness, and white supremacy: "If it is white people who 'do' race, who have the power to racially categorize people, as the essential operation of racializing themselves as white, then there is no difference between whiteness and white supremacy" (28). Martinot is in agreement with Memmi when he asserts that "race is something that one group of people does to others" (10–11). It is a subordinating and dehumanizing process and so to "'racialize' and 'to humanize' stand opposite each other, in contradiction" (11). Hence, as explained by Martinot, race is

> a system of socio-political relations in which whites define themselves with respect to others they define as "non-white" for that purpose. Because whites are the definers, "race" is inseparable from white supremacy. That is, "race" as a

concept is inseparable from the white hierarchical domination that constructs it. Whiteness marks the primary symbology of race, in terms of which other symbols, and the divisions they name, become definable, again by whites. It is by exercising this power to define that whites render themselves the "transcendental norm" (as George Yancy puts it). In this matrix of that process, whites see themselves as virtuous, civilized, law-abiding, secure, and superior. (19)

Hence, there are material and cultural benefits to be gained from racialization. There is a dependency relation, and the dependency is that to continue the benefits the status quo must be maintained, that is, white supremacy and racism. In other words, whiteness needs an oppositional identity—the racialized other—to exist as whiteness, or specifically, in the words of Martinot, whiteness needs blackness to exist as whiteness. It must keep blacks in "place" (24). Because whiteness is predicated on racial difference it influences other identities and cultural spaces and therefore effects the cultural practices between and among nonwhites.

Consequently, as part of the logic of whiteness, there is the tendency to blame the victims, in the words of Memmi, for the crimes of their oppressors. For example, Eric Tranby and Douglas Hartmann use insights from whiteness studies and critical race theory to expand some of the arguments made by Michael Emerson and Christian Smith in their book *Divided by Faith* that analyzes racial attitudes and practices of evangelical Christians, which they assert approximated mainstream American racial discourse. Tranby and Hartmann report that evangelical interviewees responded to questions about African Americans and economic inequalities "in group-based negative stereotyping of African Americans" (345) that not only blamed African Americans as a group for their plight but used "clear, almost old-fashioned, racial stereotypes and prejudices" (345). This observation of a connection between individual racial attitudes and group-based antiblack attitudes was also made by Bobo, Kluegel, and Smith, who found that "there is a pronounced tendency of white Americans to view the 'race problem' as flowing from the freely chosen cultural behaviors of blacks themselves" (qtd. in Tranby and Hartman 345–46). In general, the contemporary status quo (i.e., white) view of issues and tensions associated with race focuses on African American attitudes and conduct that need to change. The waning of overt racial discrimination suggests that whatever difficulties African Americans face is a consequence of their own attitudes and behavior, a failure on their behalf to adapt to the demands of this nation. Special assistance or preferential treatment simply corrupts the character of African Americans. In support of this thesis, conservative African American intellectuals are cited by the mainstream as proof that African Americans have played the victim role too long and must take responsibility for themselves rather than blaming society; it also sustains rifts and divisions among African Americans that help to maintain white hegemony.

This blaming-the-victim argument is the old deficiency theory explanation popularized by Daniel Patrick Moynihan in the 1960s, which locates racial inequality and African American social pathologies within abnormal or deviant cultural traits such as weak family structure, language handicaps, lack of work discipline, present rather than future orientations, dependency, and lack of success orientation. This logic emphasizes cultural deficiencies as being responsible for the development of attitudes and values that limit opportunities or prevent escape from poverty. This "tangle of pathology" sets in motion a vicious circle resulting in drug addiction, crime, low educational achievement, and economic problems that reinforces the weak family structure and perpetuates abnormal and deviant cultural traits. Thus, it is not racism or genetics but African American cultural adaptations that are responsible for inequality and social pathologies (Kuykendall 2–3).

Thus, by focalizing racial issues, that is, isolating racial problems from their totality, this kind of manipulation increases alienation among African Americans and distorts their perception of reality, ultimately making it much easier for them to be divided. Racial problems are faced by individuals, but they are not individual problems but rather part of a totality. Isolating racial problems as individual problems separate from the problem of racial oppression weakens African American resistance and unification. It diverts attention from the real problem by focusing on its symptoms. This focalized view of racial problems opens the door to manipulation, and manipulation is another instrument by which whiteness maintains the status quo. The deceits and false promises of manipulation find fertile ground among divided and alienated people. This manipulation successfully blocks the emergence of critical consciousness by anesthetizing African Americans, keeping them from thinking, and distracting them from the true cause of their problem. It splinters African Americans into individual actors who only seek benefits as individuals, hence aiding in the strategy of division. Therefore, preventing unification of African Americans serves the interests of whiteness; white privilege requires that African Americans be divided.

As a result, this type of reasoning allows many white Americans to speak and think about the race problem in ways that remove them from complicity in the system of racial inequality. As described by William Ryan, whites "are, most crucially, rejecting the possibility of blaming, not the victims, but themselves. They are unconsciously passing judgments on themselves and bringing in a unanimous verdict of Not Guilty" (28). Consequently, as explained by David T. Wellman, white Americans can "be conscious of inequality and injustice without condemning themselves, to recognize a societal problem without implicating the society, and to defend their interests without referring to genes or race" (221). How is this possible? Because, asserts Wellman, "they recognize racial inequality either abstractly or as blocked access; they explain it in terms of the problems of its victims; and they 'solve' the problem with solutions that do not affect white people" (221). Instead, Wellman continues, "the solutions allow white people to recognize the need for change without having that change affect them in important ways," so "they get off the hook and defend their racial privilege as well" (221).

And the guilt referred to here is not necessarily indicative of a sense of personal responsibility, but rather defensiveness. This point was made by Andrew Hacker in his highly insightful and controversial book *Two Nations: Black and White, Separate, Hostile, Unequal*, in which he indicts white Americans for their responsibility in the persistence of black segregation and subordination. Hacker asserts that

> white Americans, regardless of their political persuasions, are well aware of how black people have suffered due to inequities imposed upon them by white Americans. . . . Yet white people who disavow responsibility deny an everyday reality: that to be black is to be consigned to the margins of American life. It is because of this that no white American, including those who insist that opportunities exist for persons of every race, would change places with even the most successful black American. All white Americans realize that their skin comprises an inestimable asset. (60)

Consequently, according to Hacker, whites may vehemently oppose programs that seem to benefit African Americans, because it is a way of denying "to themselves that the value imputed to being white has injured people who are black" (60).

Hacker was able to further demonstrate this denial and defensiveness when he presented this scenario to his white students:

> You will be visited tonight by an official you have never met. He begins by telling you that he is extremely embarrassed. The organization he represents has made a mistake, something that hardly ever happens. According to their

records, he goes on, you were to have been born black: to another set of parents, far from where you were raised. However, the rules being what they are, this error must be rectified, and as soon as possible. So at midnight tonight, you will become black. And this will mean not simply a darker skin, but the bodily and facial features associated with African ancestry. However, inside you will be the person you always were. Your knowledge and ideas will remain intact. But outwardly you will not be recognizable to anyone you now know.

Your visitor emphasizes that being born to the wrong parents was in no way your fault. Consequently, his organization is prepared to offer you some reasonable recompense. Would you, he asks, care to name a sum of money you might consider appropriate? He adds that his group is by no means poor. It can be quite generous when the circumstances warrant, as they seem to in your case. He finishes by saying that their records show you are scheduled to live another fifty years—as a black man or woman in America.

How much financial recompense would you request? (31–32)

According to Hacker, most white students respond by asking for 50 million dollars, a calculation that "conveys, as well as anything, the value that white people place on their own skins" (32). Obviously, this large sum of money buys protections, or at least softens the calamity of discrimination and hazards they expect to face as African Americans. This is clearly an acknowledgment of the low status of African Americans.

The Inverted Ethics of Whiteness

This kind of inverted thinking is characteristic of the inverted ethics of whiteness. The inverted ethics of whiteness is based on an assumption of rightness, and by definition ethics refers to rightness. However, whiteness acts in a manner contrary to rightness, fairness, and human dignity. In fact, whiteness is criminal according to Albert Memmi and Steve Martinot, that is, racialization is a *criminal activity* in which the "symbology of race has become the criminalization of the racialized, the socio-political function of that criminalization is precisely to decriminalize whites in their acts of racialization. It is the relation between criminalization of others and white self-decriminalization that makes the history of race and whiteness in the United States" (Martinot 20). Therefore, whiteness is a system of social practices "that holds itself together by rituals of unity and exclusion," and so when white people "do" race they are expressing practices, actions, and attitudes (Martinot 23). However, because these practices harm others, they are ethically criminal. But because whiteness inverts "justice, fairness, democratic procedure, and the ideals of human sanctity, which they [whites] rationalize on the basis of race" (Martinot 6), whites presume to be doing the right thing. There is an inherent assumption that this inverted ethics is right, and it is because of this that whites do not see their racism, or at least acknowledge it. Once again, as pointed out by Martinot, "when a person can injure others in a criminal manner and still feel him- or herself to be honest, or innocent, or civilized, it is society's cultural ethic that legitimizes that feeling" (7). In other words, the cultural ethics of whiteness makes this behavior normal, perhaps even natural.

But there is nothing natural about race or racism. Race as a cultural construct gives meaning to our experiences of the world and provides ready-made interpretations of what we experience; the more ingrained are beliefs and perceptions the more resistant to change. In fact, as pointed out by Agustin Fuentes, it is "not that we are naturally inclined to be racist, or even racial, but rather that race means something in our society and we have a whole suite of myths about what to expect and understand about people and races" (5). There is a strong tendency in our society to give more intrinsic value to what we deem as natural, but as Fuentes maintains, "assuming something is natural does not necessarily mean it is 'fit' or 'correct.' Nor does it necessarily mean that social and historical context did not have a hand in shaping it" (58–59). Hence, race "is the result of force, the force of imposition that then pretends to an inherency, something to be taken for granted" (Martinot 15). No one is born white or black, both are given their whiteness and blackness "by the white supremacist society into which they are born" and "made white or not white according to prior political criteria and prior political decisions" (Martinot 14).

Therefore, white self-decriminalization hampers discussion because it blames the victim and so preserves white domination and makes individual acts of racism possible and permissible. White self-decriminalization as an ethical inversion hides behind the assumption of individuality, where whites can "ignore their participation in what is done to other people socially" as if they are innocent because individual acts are not systemic (Martinot 22). Such an assumption "ignores the fact that the meanings individual acts obtain are social meanings, given by others, and that the acts of those of a hegemonic group are thereby given hegemonic meanings" (Martinot 22–23). Consequently, as a reflection of white self-decriminalization "a white person's acts represent only themselves while a black person's acts (for instance) represent 'their race'" (Martinot 23).

Antidialogism: Definitions and Effects

Now this overview brings us back to the originating premise of this essay, that is, whiteness is antidialogical. In using the term *antidialogical*, I invoke the meaning of that word as used by Paulo Freire, who asserts that antidialogue constitutes a relationship between self and other in which that relationship becomes, in the sense used by Martin Buber, an "I-It" relation. In other words, a self sees the other as an object to be dominated, and so that relation becomes oppressive (qtd. in Rule 928). Hence, to be antidialogical is not a simple matter of being nonconversant, but rather it is a way of exercising dominance and superiority; to be antidialogical is to express a vertical relationship between persons who assume dominant and subordinate positions and in which communication is a one-way expression. In fact, according to Freire, antidialogical activity impedes true communication and reduces the other to the status of a thing (123). Antidialogue has a predetermined agenda that assumes the ignorance of the other, and, as Freire explains, the one who is decreeing the ignorance of the other

> defines himself and the class to which he belongs as those who know or were born to know; he thereby defines others as alien entities. The words of his own class come to be "true" words which he imposes or attempts to impose on the others. . . . Under these circumstances, dialogue is impossible. (129)

Consequently, antidialogue is a means of dominance that dispossesses the other of their word and their expressiveness, and it is an indispensable tool in the preservation of dominance and oppression (134).

Freire distinguishes four characteristics of antidialogical action: conquest, divide and rule, manipulation, and cultural invasion. According to Freire, "[the] desire for conquest, (or rather the necessity of conquest), is at all times present in antidialogical action" (134). It involves the imposition of the conqueror's objectives on those to be conquered and includes among other methods *mythification*, which is indispensable to preserving the status quo and attempts to show the world as fixed, given, to which humans adapt. This kind of deceit is designed to increase the alienation and passivity of the oppressed and subjugated. The myths are designed to demonstrate that the status quo should be accepted and conformed to (135).

Another antidialogical characteristic is divisiveness, which not only isolates and deepens rifts among the oppressed but also blocks the unification of the oppressed, which would undoubtedly signify a serious threat to the hegemony of the oppressor (Freire 137–38). This kind of activity is a disciplinary device against the oppressed, who become threats to the power structure. But it also plays out in how the oppressor may grant recognition and social benefits to those oppressed who embrace the ways of the oppressor and so become sub-oppressors of their friends, associates, and companions. Consequently, explains Freire, "[dividing] in order to preserve the status quo, then, is necessarily a fundamental objective of the theory of antidialogical action" (142).

Manipulation, a third dimension of antidialogical action, is a means of making the oppressed conform to the oppressor's objectives (Freire 144). According to Freire, manipulation "attempts to anesthetize the people so they will not think," will not develop a critical or revolutionary consciousness (146). It attempts to persuade the oppressed to accept the oppressor as the model of success and so distracts the oppressed from the true cause of their problem and splinters them into self-seeking individuals (147). This is also described by Freire as being submerged in reality, that is, someone who is trapped in a concrete situation unaware of the cause of the condition; their perception is faulty; they are unable to achieve understanding or become aware of what reality is, or at least to interpret reality objectively, uninfluenced by emotion, conjecture, or personal prejudice. Alternatively, such a person submerged in reality becomes self-deprecating, detracting from self, seeing self as unworthy, incapable, sinful, wicked, shameful, blameworthy, immoral, and defiled.

Finally, cultural invasion as a fundamental characteristic of antidialogical action allows the invaders to penetrate the cultural context of the invaded and impose their views and objectives. Under cultural invasion the oppressor acts and the oppressed are objects acted upon; the oppressor molds and the oppressed are molded; the oppressor chooses and the oppressed follow that choice (Freire 150). Consequently, says Freire, cultural invasion "leads to the cultural inauthenticity of those invaded; they begin to respond to the values, the standards, and the goals of the invaders" (150); they "become convinced of their intrinsic inferiority" and so alienated from their own culture and from themselves that they "want to be like the invaders"—it is "the imposition of one world view upon another" (159). This situation of oppression produces an adhesion to, and identification with, the oppressor. The oppressed absorb the oppressors within themselves. This impairs the perceptions of the oppressed about themselves and their situation. At this point, the oppressed do not see themselves as the antithesis of the oppressors but rather see the oppressors as a model. In this way the oppressor lives within the oppressed. As hosts of the oppressor, the oppressed cannot perceive that without them, the oppressor could not exist. Oppression subjugates the oppressed, making them into beings-for-another.

Therefore, Freire's oppressor and oppressed model of inequality can account for the aforementioned discussion on the logic and inverted ethics of whiteness. To be antidialogical is to engage in a process of domination that objectifies the other, places the other in a subordinate position, and assumes the ignorance of the other, thereby making dialogue impossible. The whole point of antidialogical activity is to sustain the status quo through the exercise of behaviors that increase alienation and conformity; such behaviors are designed to defeat, divide, exploit, manipulate, and impose all for the purpose of maintaining hegemony. Hence, Freire's ideas about antidialogical action are the same actions we find perpetrated in the name of whiteness as have been demonstrated in the previous pages. The very logic of whiteness invokes all the same characteristics as antidialogical action, such as oppression, self-justification, accusation, dehumanization, criminalization, stereotyping, victim blaming, subjugation, division, manipulation, and invasion. To express whiteness is to be antidialogical, and antidialogue is the activity expressed by whiteness to maintain its hegemony. Therefore, antidialogue is indispensable to the preservation of whiteness.

Consequently, the white response to blacks' assertion of racism is never to actually discuss and dialogue about the issue because to dialogue would be to do the opposite of the antidialogical characteristics and activities. Thus, the white response is to ignore or punish those blacks making the assertion of racism if they can. But when these avenues are unavailable, either for political or tactical reasons, placation is offered in the form of concessions, cooptation, undermining, or repression. In the case of concessions a remedy is offered that addresses the symptoms rather than the cause but that, as previously pointed out by David Wellman, does not affect white people in significant ways, and so maintains white privilege. As for cooptation, the goal is to redirect the energy and anger of blacks into forms of behavior that are seen as more legitimate by the system and so therefore under the control of white hegemony. In the case of undermining, the goal is to shift public sympathy away from black demands by appearing to meet moral demands so as to appease the sympathizers. And finally, these placating maneuvers make it easier to repress those more radical and insistent elements as they are depicted as irrational and extremists (Piven and Cloward 29–31).

Insufficiency of Whiteness Studies

Now, if this perspective is what whiteness is about, then whiteness studies can do no more than provide an alternative perspective from which to engage white supremacy/racism. Whiteness studies can help to redirect the gaze from nonwhites to the white self, and, having established whiteness as the problem, it can "explore how whiteness as domination works to reinforce, perpetuate, and maintain white privilege, as well as bring about the effects of that privilege on those who are identified as white" (Pinder 101). Hence, whiteness studies can offer a critique of whiteness as a form of oppression and so unveil, expose, and shine a light on white privilege and the assumption that whiteness is normative and mainstream, which allows whiteness to be commingled with national interests and so taken for granted. However, whiteness studies can do nothing about eradicating whiteness.

Although there is an inherent assumption that whiteness studies promotes social justice and antiracism, it cannot get rid of whiteness. Only by getting rid of whiteness can we do away with white supremacy/racism, but to do so requires a revolutionary transformation of the power structure that is in place; short of this revolutionary transformation, "antiracist projects are not enough to decenter whiteness and free it of its normalization" (Pinder 136). In other words, the resolution of whiteness necessitates the disappearance of whiteness as a hegemonic force and so implies a revolutionary transformation that makes it impossible to be white; thus, a revolutionary strategy that works against whiteness/racism cannot act antidialogically. Because whiteness is a form of discourse, and antidialogism is a component of that discourse, antidialogism is responsible for creating a boundary that excludes and constrains communicative content, or, in other words, what can and cannot be said, and so imposes discipline through prohibition and the authorization of who can and cannot speak, who must be silent, and whose utterances are unworthy of attention.

But this is precisely the problem, because antiracist whiteness is impossible. As pointed out by Tamara Nopper, a white antiracist is an oxymoron because to claim whiteness is to be invested in white supremacy, so "anyone who claims to be white, even a white anti-racist, is identifying with a history of European imperialism and racism transported and further developed in the US" ("The White Anti-Racist is an Oxymoron"). Further, as pointed out by George Lipsitz, whites have a possessive investment in whiteness and profit from whiteness simply because they are white (7). And so "it is easy for antiracists to extricate themselves from racism because they are not the perpetrators of racist programs and policies" and so may claim "that racism has nothing to do with them because they are not racist," but what they cannot claim is "that whiteness has nothing to do with them" (Pinder 140).

Additionally, whiteness studies cannot transmit the felt experience of racism. As pointed out by George Yancy, "whites may approach race/whiteness as intellectually stimulating, something to master without personal risk" (26). But this is a hypocritical performance that disguises ways of being from ways of appearing. Thus, whites can engage race and racism at the conceptual level without challenging their own whiteness at the interpersonal level, and, as Yancy explains,

> their conceptual sophistication stands side by side with a form of wanton racism that goes unexamined because they refuse to do so. Indeed, they make a fetish, either in writing or at scholarly conferences, of displaying their self-consciousness regarding their whiteness. . . . Yet at the end of the day they remain covetous of positions of white power and continue to engage in acts of racism in their daily lives, failing to engage their own racist actions with the same enthusiasm that they bring to theory. (26)

This kind of activity makes antiracist whiteness disingenuous and so antidialogical and nonrevolutionary. Also, even if self-conscious and critical, antiracist whiteness does nothing to denormalize whiteness because privilege and entitlements continue to accumulate. White identity allows whites to be, as Alastair Bonnett explains it, "passive observers, of being altruistically motivated, of knowing that their 'racial' identity might be reviled and lambasted but never actually made slippery, torn open, or, indeed, abolished" (204).

Whiteness also trumps class consciousness. White identity is more important and valuable to white workers and poor whites because it is through whiteness that social, economic, political, and psychological benefits are accessible. Even among whites who have no real power, they can at least claim whiteness, since they "have nothing else to hold on to but their 'possessive investment in whiteness,' and this might be the reason why they wear their supremacy more pretentiously than other whites" (Pinder 145).

Also, the new abolitionists of whiteness, such as Noel Ignatiev, John Garvey, and David R. Roediger, who argue for race treason as a means of fighting racism, do in fact have as their goal eradicating whiteness and establishing a raceless society. However, their praxis is more rebellious than revolutionary. The general idea is to do away with whiteness as a social category. But the underlying assumption of this idea is that by eliminating the category you somehow transform the situation. This assumption ignores the fact that you must make it impossible to be white, and therefore social structures and institutions must change in such a way that it divests whiteness of its social and cultural capital. So, even well-intentioned whites who disavow their antidialogical actions face a difficult task: they recognize the need to renounce their whiteness, but, as Freire explains, "patterns of domination are so entrenched within them that this renunciation would become a threat to their own identities" (154). They will have to end their status as domina-tors; they will have to abandon the myths of race; they will have to cease being white, and this is a traumatic process, which almost naturally leads to rationalizations and evasions. Once again, as Freire points out, "divesting themselves of and renouncing their myths represents, at that moment, an act of self-violence. On the other hand, to reaffirm those myths is to reveal themselves. The only way out (which functions as a defense mechanism) is to project . . . their own usual practices," that is, antidialogical activities (155).

Therefore, the eradication of whiteness and, thus, antidialogism requires political class struggle, because whiteness and its effects of privilege, he-gemony, and supremacy are issues of power and therefore a political class conflict. Oliver C. Cox made this observation in his groundbreaking analysis of race in *Caste, Class, and Race*, where he asserted that the racial struggle has always been a political class struggle in which the purpose is control of the political system, and such control "will not come by way of an open interracial matching of power. As a matter of fact, the struggle has never been between all black and all white people—it is a political-class struggle" (573).

Finally, the effects of racism and the benefits of white privilege remain far too prevalent to assert that the United States has entered a "postracial" era, that is, an end to racism. Following the election of Barack Obama, commentaries emerged proclaiming the advent of a "postracial America." However, such an assertion is not only premature but fallacious and clearly ignores the persistence of discrimination and inequalities in employment, housing, and education, and the fact that black poverty, class location, and median income remain at the bottom. Therefore to suggest that race no longer matters is an antidialogical activity that, in the words of Linda Burnham, deceptively undermines "the efficacy of racial justice organizing and advocacy, and silences the anti-racist voice," (46) while preserving the racial hierarchy and protecting white privilege.

Therefore, the antidialogical nature of whiteness is a barrier to mean-ingful dialogue, that is, dialogue that is cooperative, liberatory, unifying, and transformative; dialogue that is revolutionary. For whiteness studies to become a revolutionary tool, it must perform what Paulo Freire described as "critical intervention" in which the reality of oppression must be confronted "critically, simultaneously objectifying and acting upon that reality" (37). It must unveil the world of whiteness and deal with the problem of racial consciousness. Thus, critical intervention leads to critical consciousness, which grasps true causality and submits it to analysis. But also, whiteness studies must constitute praxis, that is, reflection and action. As pointed out by Freire, "when a word is deprived of its dimension of action, reflection automatically suffers as well; and the word is changed into idle chatter, into *verbalism*, into an alienated and alienating 'blah'" (75–76). Freire continues, when "action is emphasized exclusively, to the detriment of reflection, the word is converted into *activism*. The latter—action for action's sake—negates true praxis" (76). Therefore, as Freire makes clear, "a revolution is achieved with neither verbalism nor activism, but rather with praxis, that is, with *reflection* and *action* directed at the structures to be transformed" (120). And unless whiteness studies become a revolutionary tool for the structural transformation of society, it will remain an academic program, a scholastic exercise that is intellectually thought provoking but useless as a project for fundamental change.

Works Cited

Bonnett, Alasdair. "Construction of Whiteness in European and American Anti-Racism." *Race, Identity, and Citizenship: A Reader.* Ed. Rudolfo D. Torres, Louis F. Miron, and Jonathan Xavier Ina. Malden, MA: Blackwell, 1999. Print.

Burnham, Linda. "Obama's Candidacy: The Advent of Post-Racial America and the End of Black Politics?" *Black Scholar* 38.4 (2008): 43–46. Print.

Cox, Oliver C. *Caste, Class, and Race: A Study in Social Dynamics.* New York: Modern Reader, 1970. Print.

Freire, Paulo. *Pedagogy of the Oppressed.* Trans. Myra Bergman Ramos. New York: Seabury P, 1970. Print.

Fuentes, Agustin. *Race, Monogamy, and Other Lies They Told You: Busting Myths about Human Nature.* Berkeley: U of California P, 2012. Print.

Hacker, Andrew. *Two Nations: Black and White, Separate, Hostile, Unequal.* New York: Charles Scribner's Sons, 1992. Print.

Ignatiev, Noel, and John Garvey. *Race Traitor.* New York: Routledge, 1996. Print.

Kuykendall, Ronald A. *Social Crisis and Social Demoralization: The Dynamics of Status in American Race Relations.* Portland, OR: Arissa Media Group, 2005. Print.

Lipsitz, George. *The Possessive Investment in Whiteness: How White People Profit from Identity Politics*. Philadelphia: Temple UP, 1998. Print.

Martinot, Steve. *The Machinery of Whiteness: Studies in the Structure of Racialization*. Philadelphia: Temple UP, 2010. Print.

Memmi, Albert. *Racism*. Trans. Steve Martinot. Minneapolis: U of Minnesota P, 2000. Print.

Nopper, Tamara K. "The White Anti-Racist Is an Oxymoron: An Open Letter to 'White Anti-Racist.'" *Race Traitor*. 2003. Web. 10 Oct. 2013.

Pinder, Sherrow O. *Whiteness and Racialized Ethnic Groups in the United States: The Politics of Remembering*. Lanham, MD: Lexington Books, 2012. Print.

Piven, Frances Fox, and Richard A Cloward. *Poor People's Movements: Why They Succeed, How They Fail*. New York: Vintage, 1977. Print.

Roediger, David R. *Towards the Abolition of Whiteness: Essays on Race, Politics, and Working Class History*. New York: Verso P, 1994. Print.

Rule, Peter. "Bakhtin and Freire: Dialogue, Dialectic, and Boundary Learning." *Educational Philosophy and Theory* 43.9 (2011): 924–42. Print.

Ryan, William. *Blaming the Victim*. New York: Vintage Books, 1971. Print.

Transby, Eric, and Douglas Hartmann. "'Race Problem': Extending Emerson and Smith's *Divided by Faith*." *Journal for the Scientific Study of Religion* 47.3 (2008): 341–59. Print.

Wellman, David T. *Portraits of White Racism*. New York: Cambridge UP, 1977. Print.

Yancy, George. *Look, a White! Philosophical Essays on Whiteness*. Philadelphia: Temple UP, 2012. Print.

EPILOGUE

Tammie M. Kennedy, Joyce Irene Middleton, and Krista Ratcliffe

We are neither colorblind nor post-racial.
> —Drew Gilpin Faust, "John Hope Franklin:
> Race and the Meaning of America"

Races are still only human inventions.
> —Ian Haney-López, *White by Law: The Legal Construction of Race*

Aristotle is still white. If we acknowledge it and historicize it, we can change it. —Kathleen Ethel Welch, "Who Made Aristotle White?"
> Symposium: "The Matter of Whiteness; Or, Why Whiteness
> Studies Is Important to Rhetoric and Composition Studies"

We three editors want to use this brief epilogue to invite new ways for thinking, writing, and rhetorically framing racial whiteness in twenty-first-century U.S. culture. Our introduction to this collection posits the research claim that if whiteness is, indeed, a trope with associated discourses and cultural scripts, then we need to examine how tropes of race both have changed over time and yet have not disappeared from our discourses nor from our actions. The chapters in this collection respond to this research claim. But because one collection alone cannot cover the breadth of this issue, silences about tropes of race remain. So we will use this epilogue to point out a few silences in whiteness studies in the twenty-first century, silences that could be investigated to generate new research about the racial concept of oxymoronic whiteness and, thus, provide us new ways for talking about race and whiteness in twenty-first-century U.S. culture.

While we believe this collection contains really great work, it is mostly silent about the changes in racial progress after the civil rights bills passed in the 1960s. The triumvirate of civil rights acts in the 1960s created new tropes for talking about race, American whiteness, and inequality, especially in sexuality studies, mixed-race studies, and immigration studies (too many Americans do not realize that immigration in the United States changed significantly in the 1960s). Some of these new tropes of racial progress are production; some, not so much.

One productive trope of racial progress is *intersectionality*. With Kimberlé Crenshaw's good work, we observe more with the concept of intersectionality now. Indeed, this methodology asks readers and writers to consider more than a single cultural identity for U.S. racial tropes. But questions of how whiteness functions as one intersectional element are ripe for research. For example, we might study the white Latinos/as in the United States (one of whom was running for the 2016 GOP nomination), white LGBTQIAs, and issues of colorism that are growing generally in the United States as well as their representation in television and film media. How must the United States observe and respond to these new racial tropes? That question should be explored and not ignored, much as President Obama's 2010 census did when it continued to use the same old tropes of race and racial whiteness.

But some newly emergent tropes about racial progress—such as *post-tracial*, *post-black*, and *post-white*—are decidedly unproductive because they invite a silence about continued problems within U.S. racial relations. Many U.S. citizens and the U.S. media, in particular, want to interpret and promote the twenty-first century as postracial. But scholars such as Drew Gilpin Faust, Ian Haney-López, and Kathleen Ethel Welch refute this impulse. So too does distinguished scholar Houston Baker, who challenges the more specific concept of post-blackness in his award-winning book *Betrayal: How Black Intellectuals Have Abandoned the Ideals of the Civil Rights Era* and in his more recent coedited work with K. Merinda Simmons, *The Trouble with Post-Blackness*. In the introduction to the latter book, Simmons ties the problem of the trope *post-blackness* to the uses of the term *whiteness*:

We should take pains to view whiteness (any mode of "dominance," for that matter) as itself a constructed and highly contingent space. This, put simply, is the trouble with post-blackness: in the attempt to analyze and describe—and thus bring awareness to and advocate for—particular modes of performing something called "black identity," the discourse on post-blackness keeps up and running an untroubled category of whiteness against which it demarcates itself. (3)

Not only is *post-blackness* a term that fosters a false mythology of current U.S. culture but it also encourages a one-size-fits-all, untroubled notion of whiteness. Our collection, we hope, begins to trouble the notion of whiteness as it is employed in the twenty-first century. But more work remains to be done.

We hope that scholars identify and analyze these and other cultural silences. Indeed, scholars might identify silences surrounding tropes of race and whiteness that were created after the new civil rights laws of the 1960s. Why, for example, isn't the trope *interracial marriage* more normalized in twenty-first-century U.S. discourses? What does it mean that President Obama has often referred to himself as an inheritor of civil rights, as a post–civil rights baby, and as a member of the "Joshua generation" (Remnick)? What are we to make of the myriad racial responses to the recent killings of Trayvon Martin, Michael Brown, Sandra Bland, Clementa Pinckney, Freddy Gray, and others? These killings happened just before and after the fifty-year celebration of the signing of the civil rights bills. Why has nothing interrupted the racializing and racial whiteness that continues in America? And more than simply identifying tropes, we might investigate what cultural scripts need to be articulated and how they should or should not be performed. For example, on the cusp of the twenty-first century, Amadou Diallo, a Guinese immigrant, was shot forty-one times when, instead of putting "his hands" up, his response to New York City police was to reach for his wallet to show an ID and prove his identity. What scripts should Diallo's children or certainly his grandchildren learn about racism, police actions, and American whiteness in order to avoid death?

Finally, in this epilogue, we return to the concept of oxymoronic whiteness, which suggests a cultural move forward for reconsidering racial formations in the United States in the twenty-first century. Michael Omi and Howard Winant did much of this work in their book on racial formation in the late 1990s. They inspired many to work on racial formation in the United States in the twenty-first century. One shift that has occurred is a move away from "either/or" thinking about racial formation toward a "both/ and" thinking about seemingly opposite racial tropes and rhetoric. But what silences surround an oxymoronic whiteness? These and the other racial silences haunting this anthology indicate the breadth of work remaining to be done, work that we invite and welcome.

Works Cited

Baker, Houston. *Betrayal: How Black Intellectuals Have Abandoned the Ideals of the Civil Rights Era*. New York: Columbia UP, 2009. Print.

Baker, Houston, and K. Merinda Simmons. "Introduction." *The Trouble with Post-Blackness*. Ed. Houston Baker and K. Merinda Simmons, 1–20. New York: Columbia UP, 2015. Print.

Crenshaw, Kimberlé. "Why Intersectionality Can't Wait." *Washington Post*. 24 Sept. 2015. Web. 27 Jan. 2016.

Faust, Drew Gilpin. "John Hope Franklin: Race and the Meaning of America." *New York Review of Books*. 17 Dec. 2015. Web. 27 Jan. 2016.

Haney-López, Ian. *White by Law: The Legal Construction of Race*. 10th anniv. ed. New York: New York UP, 2006. Print.

Remnick, David. "The Joshua Generation." *New Yorker*. 17 Nov. 2008. Web. 27 Jan. 2016.

Obama, Barack Hussein. "Remarks by the President at LBJ Presidential Library Civil Rights Summit." *whitehouse.gov*. 10 Apr. 2014. Web. 1 Feb. 2015.

Omi, Michael, and Howard Winant. *Racial Formation in the United States from the 1960s to the 1990s*. 2nd ed. New York: Routledge, 1994. Print.

Welch, Kathleen Ethel. "Who Made Aristotle White?" *Symposium: The Matter of Whiteness; Or, Why Whiteness Studies Is Important to Rhetoric and Composition Studies*. Ed. Tammie M. Kennedy, Joyce Irene Middleton, and Krista Ratcliffe. *Rhetoric Review* 24.4 (2005): 359–73. Print.

CONTRIBUTORS

INDEX

CONTRIBUTORS

Sarah E. Austin is an instructor of English at the U.S. Air Force Academy Preparatory School. She is a doctoral candidate in Texas Tech's technical communication and rhetoric program. Sarah is also the acting president for the Colorado Teachers of English to Speakers of Other Languages executive board, the book review editor for the *Journal of Veterans' Studies*, a member of the Center for the Study of Academic Labor's board of directors, and she serves on the 2017 CCCC Technical and Scientific Communication Awards Selection Committee. Her annotated bibliography regarding how to use media analyses to teach the rhetorical situation appears in *Feminist Teacher*.

Jennifer Beech is a professor of English at the University of Tennessee at Chattanooga, where she teaches a variety of rhetoric and writing courses. At the national level, she is a cochair of the Working-Class Culture and Pedagogy Special Interest Group of the Conference on College Composition and Communications. Her work has appeared in edited collections and in such journals as *College English*, *JAC*, *Pedagogy*, and *Open Words*.

Lee Bebout is an associate professor of English at Arizona State University, Tempe, where he is also affiliate faculty in the School of Transborder Studies and the Program in American Studies. He teaches courses on Chicana/o literature, whiteness, U.S. multiethnic literature, and critical race theory. He is the author of numerous articles and *Mythohistorical Interventions: The Chicano Movement and Its Legacies*. His second book, *Whiteness on the Border: Mapping the U.S. Racial Imagination in Brown and White*, will be published in November 2016.

Cedric Burrows is an assistant professor at Marquette University, where he teaches courses in rhetoric and composition. His article on Martin Luther King Jr. was recently published in the Oxford Online Bibliographies–American Literature. He has also published in the *Journal of Africana Religions*. His research interests include composition and rhetoric, African American rhetoric, cultural rhetoric, and social activism.

Leda Cooks is a professor in the Department of Communication at the University of Massachusetts Amherst, where she teaches courses in, among other subjects, dialogue, critical pedagogy, interracial communication, and food studies. She coedited *Whiteness, Pedagogy, Performance: Dis/Placing Race* and has published journal articles in the fields of communication and education on the topic. In 2014 she won the Thomas Ehrlich national award for her teaching and scholarship on civic engagement in higher education.

Sharon Crowley is a professor emeritus at Arizona State University. She received the 2015 Exemplar Award, a national lifetime-achievement honor from the Conference on College Composition and Communication. Her book *Toward a Civil Discourse* won the 2006 JAC Gary A. Olson Award, the 2007 NCTE David H. Russell Award, the 2008 Rhetoric Society of America Book Award, and the 2008 CCCC Outstanding Book Award.

Anita M. DeRouen is the director of writing and teaching and an assistant professor at Millsaps College in Jackson, Mississippi. Her main foci are composition and rhetoric, particularly issues related to the acquisition, practice, and retention of digital literacy skills. A secondary area of interest and study is the representation of racial identity in media culture. She is currently studying the use of group dialogic practices to foster healthy interracial communication in undergraduate student populations.

Tim Engles is a professor of English at Eastern Illinois University, where he specializes in critical whiteness studies, multicultural American literature, and contemporary American literature. His scholarship has appeared in numerous journals and collections, and he is coeditor of *Approaches to Teaching DeLillo's White Noise* (with John N. Duvall) and *Critical Essays on Don DeLillo* (with Hugh Ruppersburg).

Christine Farris is a professor of English at Indiana University. She is the author of *Subject to Change: New Composition Instructors' Theory and Practice*; a coeditor of *Under Construction: Working at the Intersections of Composition Theory, Research, and Practice*; and a coeditor of *Integrating Literature and Writing Instruction: First Year English, Humanities Core Courses, Seminars*. A book she coedited, *College Credit for Writing in High School: The "Taking*

Care of" Business won the Council of Writing Program Administrators Best Book Award in 2012.

Amy Goodburn is an associate vice chancellor for academic affairs and a professor of English at the University of Nebraska–Lincoln. Her interests include ethnographic and teacher research, the documenting of teaching and learning, and social justice pedagogies. Goodburn's publications include *Inquiry into the College Classroom, Making Teaching and Learning Visible,* and *Rewriting Success in Rhetoric and Composition Careers.*

M. Shane Grant is an independent scholar and theatre artist. His previous publication "'We're All Freaks Together': Whiteness and the Mitigation of Queer Community" can be found in the edited collection *Queer in the Choir Room: Essays on Gender and Sexuality in* Glee.

Gregory Jay is a professor of English at the University of Wisconsin–Milwaukee. He is the author of three books, including *American Literature and the Culture Wars,* as well as over forty articles, book chapters, and reviews. Among his essays on critical race studies are articles about D. W. Griffith and the American Indian, lynching in the work of Frederick Douglass and Herman Melville, Holocaust rhetoric and Anna Deavere Smith, and the teaching of whiteness in the literature classroom.

Tammie M. Kennedy is an associate professor of English at the University of Nebraska at Omaha. She has published in journals such as *Composition Studies, Feminist Formations, Rhetoric Review, JAC, English Journal,* and *Brevity: A Journal of Concise Literary NonFiction* as well as in edited collections. Much of her scholarly and creative work focuses on the rhetoric of remembering practices and how the embodied qualities of memory shape identity, writing, and knowledge production.

Ronald A. Kuykendall is an instructor of political science at Trident Technical College in Charleston, South Carolina. His previous publications include *Social Crisis and Social Demoralization: The Dynamics of Status in American Race Relations,* chapters in *This Country Must Change: Essays on the Necessity of Revolution in the USA* and in the *Greenwood Encyclopedia of the Great Black Migration* as well as articles in the *Journal of Black Studies* and the *Western Journal of Black Studies.*

Kristi McDuffie is the associate director of rhetoric at the University of Illinois at Urbana-Champaign. Her research and teaching interests center on digital writing, race rhetorics, and critical pedagogies. Her most recent project investigates the rhetorics of whiteness in online reader comments responding to immigration reform, and her other projects examine online activism and internet research methods.

Nicole Ashanti McFarlane researches how African Americans engage technologies to compose spaces of color and preside over blackness in the public sphere. She is an assistant professor of English Rhetoric and Composition at Fayetteville State University. She teaches courses in African American rhetorics, rhetorical theory, professional writing, and new media accessibility. She has published in *JAC, CCC, PRE/TEXT: A Journal of Rhetoric Theory,* and *Enculturation.*

Alice McIntyre is a professor and the chairperson of the Elementary Education Program at Hellenic College. Her previous publications include *Participatory Action Research; Women in Belfast: How Violence Shapes Identity; Inner-City Kids: Adolescents Confront Life and Violence in an Urban Community;* and *Making Meaning of Whiteness: Exploring the Racial Identity of White Teachers.*

Peter McLaren is the Distinguished Professor in Critical Studies in the College of Educational Studies at Chapman University, where he is a codirector of the Paulo Freire Democratic Project and an international ambassador for global ethics and social justice. He is also an honorary director of the Center for Critical Studies in Education at Northeast Normal University, Changchun, China. He has written or edited over forty-five books and hundreds of scholarly articles and chapters. His writings have been translated into more than twenty languages.

Joyce Irene Middleton is an associate chair of English and the former director of ethnic studies at East Carolina University in Greenville, North Carolina. Middleton has published not only essays on Nobel laureate Toni Morrison but also work on rhetoric, orality, and literacy; race, whiteness, and gender; ethnic studies; and film in a variety of major composition journals and anthologies. She also served as the chair of the diversity committee for the CCCC and as a coeditor of the biweekly blog CCCC Conversation for Diversity.

Keith D. Miller is an associate professor in English at Arizona State University. He is the author of *Martin Luther King's Biblical Epic: His Great, Final Speech* and *Voice of Deliverance: The Language of Martin Luther King, Jr. and Its Sources.* His work has also appeared in multiple journals including *College English, College Composition and Communication, Publication of the Modern Language Association, Rhetoric Society Quarterly, Journal of American History,* and *Rhetoric Review.*

Lilia D. Monzó is an assistant professor of education in the College of Educational Studies at Chapman University. She engages a Marxist humanist revolutionary critical pedagogy and decolonial approaches to confront capitalism and imperialism, racism, gender oppression, and the hyperexploitation of women of color. She has published in such journals as *Policy Futures* *in Education*, the *Journal of Critical Education Policy Studies*, *Anthropology and Education Quarterly*, *Postcolonial Directions in Education*, and the *Journal of Qualitative Studies in Education*.

Casie Moreland is a PhD candidate in writing, rhetorics, and literacies at Arizona State University, where she teaches multilingual composition, first-year composition, and writing for the professions. Her research interests include dual enrollment composition, indigenous rhetorics, Chican@ studies, feminist methodologies, and critical race theory.

Ersula Ore is an assistant professor of African and African American Studies and English at Arizona State University, where she teaches courses in rhetorical theory, critical theories of race, and the history and rhetoric of black women. Her forthcoming book *Lynching: A Rhetoric of Civic Belonging* examines lynching and later forms of antiblack violence such as police brutality as a performance of citizenship identity consonant with the racist ideology of classic contractarianism, governing laws, and America's national mythos.

Annette Harris Powell is an associate professor of English at Bellarmine University, where she directs first-year writing and teaches courses in writing and rhetoric, linguistics, and contemporary diaspora literature. Her work addresses the rhetoric of language, identity, and place, and how it shapes public discourse, as well as the relationship between language and literacy practices across material spaces and cultural borders. Her published work appears in *Computers and Composition* and various edited collections.

Catherine Prendergast is a professor of English at the University of Illinois at Urbana-Champaign and the author of *Literacy and Racial Justice* (2003) and *Buying into English* (2008). In 2014 she was awarded a Guggenheim fellowship to support her research for a work on the history of writers' colonies.

Krista Ratcliffe is a professor and the head of the English Department at Purdue University in West Lafayette, Indiana. Her publications include, among other works, *Anglo-American Feminist Challenges to the Rhetorical Tradition*; *Who's Having This Baby?* (with Helen Sterk, Carla Hay, Alice Kehoe, and Leona VandeVusse); and *Rhetorical Listening: Identification, Gender, Whiteness* (which won the 2006 *JAC* Gary Olson Award, the 2007 CCCC Outstanding Book Award, and the 2007 Rhetoric Society of America Book Award).

Meagan Rodgers is an associate professor of English at the University of Science and Arts of Oklahoma, where she also directs the Writing Center. Her research focuses on pedagogy, privilege, and whiteness studies. Her work has been published in *CEA Forum, Composition Forum, Computers and Composition Online*, and *ProfHacker* (at the *Chronicle of Higher Education*).

Nicole E. Snell is currently an assistant professor at Bentley University in the Department of Information Design and Corporate Communication. She teaches classes such as Crisis Communication Management, Digital Public Relations and Public Relations Writing. Her interdisciplinary research interest explores the intersection(s) of language, technology and culture through examination of both the rhetorical and phenomenological functions of existing and emerging new media and channels of mass communication that facilitate accessibility, such as captioning, for marginalized groups.

Jennifer Seibel Trainor is the author of several articles on race, whiteness, and literacy. Her book *Rethinking Racism: Emotion, Persuasion, and Literacy Education in an All-White Suburban High School* (2008) won the MLA's Mina Shaughnessy Prize for scholarship in composition. With Mary Soliday, she has recently published "Rethinking Regulation in the Age of the Literacy Machine" (*CCC*, Sept. 2016). She teaches undergraduate writing courses and graduate courses on literacy, critical pedagogy, and composition pedagogy at San Francisco State University.

Victor Villanueva is a Regents Professor and the Edward R. Meyer Distinguished Professor at Washington State University, where he directs the University Writing Program. Most prized among his awards and honors are the 1999 Rhetorician of the Year and the CCCC 2009 Exemplar. He has edited, coedited, or authored eight books and over fifty articles or chapters and has delivered more than one hundred talks. In all of it, his work has centered on the connections between language and racism.

Hui Wu is a professor of English at the University of Texas at Tyler. One of her articles, "Lost and Found in Translation: Modern Conceptualization of Chinese Rhetoric," won the 2010 Best Article Award from *Rhetoric Review*. Her books include *Once Iron Girls: Essays on Gender by Post-Mao Literary Women*; *Reading and Writing about the Disciplines: A Rhetorical Approach* (with Emily Standridge); and *"Guiguzi," China's First Treatise on Rhetoric: A Critical Translation and Commentary* (with Jan Swearingen).

INDEX

Page numbers in italics indicate illustrations.

diversity, as term, 237

diversity curriculum, 164

Divided by Faith (Tranby and Hartmann), 297

divisiveness, 302–3

Doing Emotion (Micciche), 225

domestics, black, 22, 26; intimacy,
discourse of, 29, 31–32; mammy
figure, 29, 30, 35–36; raising of
white children, 27

domination, white, 184, 185

Dos Vatos Films, 154

double consciousness, 31–32, 74–75;
white, 165

dramatism, 263

Dreams of My Father (Obama), 267

Du Bois, W. E. B., 49, 74–75

dual credit (DC) courses, 12,
182–94; affluent students benefit,
191–92; CCCC statement, 185,
189; funding for, 189–90; racializing life chances, 190; rise of and
response to, 184–86; in Texas,
186–92

Duggan, Lisa, 58, 59

Dunham, Madelyn, 266–67

Dunham, Stanley, 266–67

Dunham, Stanley Anne, 267

Durbin, Dick, 260, 263–65, 268

Dyer, Richard, 57–58, 113

Echeverría, Darius, 161

Eckford, Elizabeth, 42, 43, 51–52

economic discrimination, 184

education, 1, 11–12; Americanization
courses, 161; contemporary racial
dynamics and, 164–65; counselors, 189; curricular investment
in whiteness, 154–55, 160–63;

desegregation, 191; ethnic studies
as not "real," 157; hidden curriculum, 148–49; multicultural, 160;
tracking, 191; unequal opportunities, 184; vocational courses,
188–89. *See also* dual credit (DC)
courses; textbook industry

eHarmony, 11, 112–31; "29 Dimensions of Compatibility,"
114, 125–26, *126*; conservative
religious focus, 114–16; heteronormativity, 114–15; lawsuit, 116;
pages, 123–24; values and beliefs
section, *126*, 126–27; website appearance, 114–20, *116*; whiteness
as preferable, 114

Eichmann, Adolf, 209

"El Plan Espiritual de Aztlán," 156

Elementary (television drama), 54

*Elizabeth and Hazel: Two Women of
Little Rock* (Margolick), 51–52

Ellsworth, Elizabeth, 6

emotion, 82, 243–44

emotional literacy, critical, 225–30

"The Emotioned Power of Racism:
An Ethnographic Portrait of an
All-White High School," 225–26

employment opportunities, 184

English as a first language, 190–91

Enlightenment, 260

"The Enthymematic Hegemony of
Whiteness: The Enthymeme as
Antiracist Rhetorical Strategy"
(Jackson), 6

enthymemes, 6

equal opportunity, rhetoric of, 78,
79

equality, as conformity, 206

Erickson, Keith, 263